THE HISTORY OF EUROPEAN UNION LAW

This formative period of EU law witnessed an intense struggle over the emergence of a constitutional practice. While the supranational institutions, including the European Commission, the European Court of Justice and the European Parliament, as well as EU law academics helped to develop and promote the constitutional practice, member state governments and judiciaries were generally reluctant to embrace it. The struggle resulted in an uneasy stalemate in which the constitutional practice was allowed to influence the doctrines, shape and functioning of the European legal order that now underpins the EU, but a majority of member state governments rejected European constitutionalism as the legitimating principle of the new EU formed on basis of the Treaty of Maastricht (1992). The struggle and eventual stalemate over the constitutional practice traced in this book accounts for the fragile and partial system of rule of law that exists in the EU today.

BILL DAVIES is Associate Professor at the Department of Justice, Law & Criminology, American University and a leading expert on the legal history of European integration. He is the author of *Resisting the European Court of Justice* (2012), editor of *EU Law Stories* (2017) and has also published on American legal history: *Timothy B. Dyk: The Education of a Federal Judge* (2022).

MORTEN RASMUSSEN is Associate Professor at the SAXO Institute, University of Copenhagen and a leading expert on the legal histories of European integration and the League of Nations. He has published numerous articles and book chapters on these topics and is co-editor of *The Cambridge Handbook of the League of Nations and International law* (forthcoming 2026).

The History of European Union Law

CONSTITUTIONAL PRACTICE, 1950 TO 1993

Edited by

BILL DAVIES

American University

MORTEN RASMUSSEN

University of Copenhagen

CAMBRIDGE
UNIVERSITY PRESS

CAMBRIDGE
UNIVERSITY PRESS

Shaftesbury Road, Cambridge CB2 8EA, United Kingdom

One Liberty Plaza, 20th Floor, New York, NY 10006, USA

477 Williamstown Road, Port Melbourne, VIC 3207, Australia

314–321, 3rd Floor, Plot 3, Splendor Forum, Jasola District Centre, New Delhi – 110025, India

Cambridge University Press is part of Cambridge University Press & Assessment, a department of the University of Cambridge.

We share the University's mission to contribute to society through the pursuit of education, learning and research at the highest international levels of excellence.

www.cambridge.org
Information on this title: www.cambridge.org/9781009673921

DOI: 10.1017/9781009673891

When citing this work, please include a reference to the DOI 10.1017/9781009673891

First published 2026

Cover image: Title: A hearing before the Court / Court of Justice of the European Union

A catalogue record for this publication is available from the British Library

A Cataloging-in-Publication data record for this book is available from the Library of Congress

ISBN 978-1-009-67392-1 Hardback

For Louise, Anna, Jakob and Johanne.
For Liz and Bill, Sue and Jay.

Contents

Contributors

Philip Bajon writes on the constitutional history of the European Union, British and international public law, as well as the political history of western Europe. Bajon's recent work focuses on the law of EU institutions and the constitutional practice in European law. In his first monograph, he examined how French president Charles de Gaulle challenged the process of European unification in the 1960s, and how this consolidated the Community in the long run. In his forthcoming second book, Bajon analyses the rise of majority rule in the European federalising process, the resistance against this development and the political controversies over voting and vetoing. Bajon is also interested in biographical research and oral history. Together with Stefan Vogenauer, he is the editor of a forthcoming volume on *Key Biographies in the Legal History of the European Union, 1950–93*. Furthermore, he is the managing editor of the forthcoming volume in the series Methodica – Introductions to Research in Legal History, published by De Gruyter.

Alexandre Bernier is an expert on the French reception of European law from 1950 to 1993. He defended his doctoral dissertation at the University of Copenhagen (2017) on this topic and was part of the collective project 'Towards a New History of European Public Law – Battles over the Constitutional Practice, 1950 to 1993'. Bernier's dissertation contributed with a pathbreaking historical investigation of the interaction between France and European law based on an extensive use of national, European and private archives. It analyses the penetration of European law into French legal, judicial and academic circles, and it examines what role these circles and actors played in developing and deploying a new European legal order. Bernier has published his results in an article in *Contemporary European History* and a book chapter in a French anthology.

Rebekka Byberg is an expert on the transnational history of European law academia. She defended her doctoral dissertation at University of Copenhagen (2017) and was part of the collective project 'Towards a New History of European

Public Law – Battles over the Constitutional Practice, 1950 to 1993'. She has published her results in three pathbreaking articles in the *American Journal of Legal History* (2017), the *German Law Journal* (2017) and the *European Law Journal* (2017). She is also the co-editor of an anthology that explores the history of the enlargement process of the European Union that was published by Routledge in 2017.

Bill Davies is Associate Professor at the Department of Justice, Law & Criminology, American University and a leading expert on the legal history of European integration. He is the author of *Resisting the European Court of Justice* (2012), editor of *EU Law Stories* (2017) and has also published on American legal history: *Timothy B. Dyk: The Education of a Federal Judge* (2022).

Vera Fritz is an expert in the legal histories of European integration and the League of Nations. Her pathbreaking monograph *Juges et avocats généraux de la Cour de Justice de l'Union Européenne (1952–1972)* offers a biographical perspective on the judges and advocates general of the European Court of Justice during its formative years, shedding light on the professional and personal backgrounds that influenced the court's pioneering jurisprudence, as well as its relationship with the founding member states. She has published a number of articles in French and English on the history of the European Court of Justice, its judges and advocate generals. From 2021 to 2023, Vera Fritz was a Marie Skłodowska-Curie Fellow at the University of Copenhagen, working on a research project on the League of Nations and the codification of international law.

Karin van Leeuwen is a leading expert on law and politics in the Netherlands, exploring both its European and international dimensions. Her first book dealt with Dutch constitutional reforms (*Uit het spoor van Thorbecke*, Boom Amsterdam 2013). In the last more than a decade she has specialised in the Dutch role in the development of European Union law, publishing a string of articles on the topic. These include for example two pathbreaking articles: 'On Democratic Concerns and Legal Traditions: The Dutch 1953 and 1956 Constitutional Reforms "Towards" Europe' published in *Contemporary European History* in 2012 and 'Paving the Road to Legal Revolution: The Dutch Origins of the First Preliminary References in European Law (1957–1963)' published in the *European Law Journal* in 2018. Recently, van Leeuwen has worked on the League of Nations and international law and published on the Hague Academy and the establishment of the Permanent Court of International Justice, 1918 to 1922. She is currently co-editing a Cambridge University Press handbook of the League of Nations and international law.

Jan-Henrik Meyer's research combines the history, politics and law of European integration with environmental and energy history. Against the backdrop of debates on democracy, legitimacy and citizenship, his first book focused on the history of the European public sphere and enquired into how citizens and the media debated the emerging European Union. As part of his research on the emergence of the EU's environmental policy and law, he has examined the role of societal actors, international organisations and EU institutions, in particular the European Parliament. In the context of collaborative interdisciplinary EU and nationally funded research projects, he has studied the relations between nuclear energy and society in Europe, Denmark and West Germany. His current research traces the emergence of European environmental and energy law. Meyer has published extensively on the history of European integration, the history of the environment in international and European perspective, the history of nuclear energy and the history of European Union law.

Jonas Langeland Pedersen is an expert on the history of Denmark's reception of European law. He defended his dissertation at Aarhus University in 2016 and was part of the collective project 'Towards a New History of European Public Law – Battles over the Constitutional Practice, 1950 to 1993'. In his dissertation Pedersen focuses on how Danish civil servants and legal experts received, interpreted and interacted with European law.

Sigfrido M. Ramírez Pérez is an expert on the history of European integration, focusing on the economic and legal aspects of the process. He has published widely on the economic history of European integration, focusing on the role of the French and Italian car industries. More recently he has published several important contributions on the history of European law with a focus on the history of competition and social law. He has also participated in the second volume of the history of the European Commission (1973–1985) where he wrote the section on the legal service of the European Commission and contributed to those on external relations, enlargement and transportation policies. He has edited an anthology published by Routledge in 2024 together with Brian Shaev entitled *The Development of European Competition Policy: Social Democracy and Regulation.*

Morten Rasmussen is Associate Professor at the SAXO Institute, University of Copenhagen and a leading expert on the legal histories of European integration and the League of Nations. He has published numerous articles and book chapters on these topics and is co-editing a Cambridge Handbook of the League of Nations and international law.

Preface

The book before you is no ordinary anthology on the history of the European Union (EU), based on a simple collection of conference papers. It is much more than that. This is the final product of more than a decade of challenging work by a group of young, and by now increasingly middle-aged, historians who wanted to understand the history of EU law from its early beginnings in 1950 to the present day. The authors contributing to this volume (as well as Brigitte Leucht, Anne Boerger, Karen Gram-Skoldager and Ann-Christina Lauring Knudsen who do not contribute here) came together over a fifteen-year period from 2008 to 2023 in a group that proved unusual in several respects. All members had a strong desire to truly work together and learn from each other, a willingness to generously share key insights often acquired through endless hours of archival work and a spirit of intellectual curiosity and critical thinking, all without the strong competitive edge that much of academia is marred by. In that spirit, we hope that this book reflects not only the breadth of our research, but more importantly, the true nature of free and open intellectual exchange and the friendships made along the way.

This is also a book that offers a unique angle on EU law different from the standard scholarship, as suggested by the book cover. Here we see the judges of the Court of Justice of the European Coal and Steel Community, presiding at the first seat of the Court, Villa Vauban, but from a distant, oblique position, hovering above the bench. This is exactly what this book offers, an outside perspective on EU law, authored as it is by a group of historians, who were not originally trained in law. The position as outsiders to the field of EU law offered the advantage that it was easier to identify and cut through the mythologies and legitimation strategies that the Court of Justice of the European Union (CJEU) have propagated over the years than for most legal scholars, who through their education have been raised on those same myths.

How to study the history of EU law was far from obvious back in the late 2000s when we started out. No historians had yet attempted to delve into the jurisprudential dimension of European integration, a research field dominated by legal scholars and, more recently, social scientists. There were several factors that contributed to this neglect. Historiography on European integration had long been focused on the political and economic history, and there was a reluctance to address a seemingly technical field dominated by an institution, the CJEU, that had not yet opened its historical archive.[1] After all, historians typically work on the basis of primary sources drawn from historical archives, and how could any history of EU law be written without access to the records of its central institution?

Historians are nothing if not perseverant, and this did not deter the authors involved in writing this volume. In many respects, the lack of archival documentation from the CJEU turned out to be a blessing in disguise. Forced to look beyond the CJEU, we discovered a world of multiple other actors involved in the creation of EU law, ranging from the legal services of the supranational institutions, over the transnational networks of lawyers and academics, to national governments, administrative bodies, courts, lawyers, litigants and societal actors. In the process, we learned how important private archives, interviews and oral histories can (and should) be to the writing of twentieth-century European history. To systematically collect what turned out to be a vast pool of source material that casts a genuinely new light on the history of EU law required some serious footwork. Trying to identify the families of former judges and lawyers in more than ten countries to potentially find existing private papers required long travels, many phone calls, human diplomacy and the willing cooperation of the families contacted. Getting the European institutions to release their collections on the legal aspects of European integration often proved even harder; the biggest breakthrough happened when we finally managed to obtain access to the Commission's legal service archive that still resided in the dark basement of the famed Berlaymont building in Brussels. National archives always, it seems, work in entirely diverse ways, making the identification of relevant files on such a technical topic quite a challenge, particularly because national courts tend to be as reluctant to open their archives as the CJEU. Finally, we worked hard to search the archives of the International Federation of European Law as well as the national associations of EU law in the member states and the very first academic journals on EU law. This massive archival work not only constitutes the empirical backbone of the present volume, but it is also at the very heart of why the history presented in this volume differs from the state-of-the-art analyses of the field of law and politics. Simply put, it brings to light a wealth of new information, added depth and nuance and ultimately a new interpretation of the history of European law from 1950 to 1993.

Despite all the challenges in identifying and accessing the archives, we were met with generosity, understanding and patience from the many archivists as well as the former historical actors and eyewitnesses who facilitated our access to primary sources and helped us along the road. The list of thanks is long. We would like to

[1] The Historical Archive of the CJEU finally opened the judicial part (partly redacted) in 2016 and its administrative archive in 2021. It is located at the Historical Archives of the European Union (HAEU) in Florence, Italy.

thank the formidable Director of the Historical Archives of the European Union (HAEU) in Florence, Dieter Schlenker, who went to great lengths to generously support our research. The project has submitted its collective archive to the HAEU where it will eventually be opened to the international research community. We would also like to thank the former Head of the Historical Archives Service of the European Commission, Joceline Collonval, as well as Sylvia Perez and Elodie-Cécile Marrel of the European Commission. Huge thanks are also due to the former director of the library and archive of the legal service of the Commission, Marinus Christ, who helped guide us in that dark basement of the Berlaymont. The present and former staff members of the CJEU's information service, archive and library, including Henrik von Holstein, Bjarne Meyer, Rita Erhard and now judge William Valasidis, have additionally been crucial to our collection of critically necessary literature and sources. We would also like to thank Pascale Delbarre (Université Libre de Bruxelles), Francoise Nicod (Fondation Jean Monnet, Lausanne), Dominique Parcollet (Archives d'histoire contemporaine Sciences Po) and many other archivists that helped us along the way.

The eyewitnesses or families of former key actors who were willing to share their personal stories and family archives have played an immense role in our research. Thanks go to the family of Michel Gaudet, Matelda Cappelletti, the daughter of Mauro Cappelletti, Renée and Marie-Rose Delvaux – the daughters of former judge Louis Delvaux – as well as the families of Walter Much and Robert Krawielicki for their willingness to meet with us and to share information and archives with us. We have also benefited tremendously from the assistance of key personalities still going strong, such as Joseph H. H. Weiler, Claus Dieter Ehlermann, Michel Waelbroeck, David Edward, Jean-Victor Louis, Wilma Viscardini, Erica Ortmann, Paolo Gori, Jean-Jacques Beuve-Méry and Monica Seccombe. Finally, we would also like to express our gratitude to the great people we have sadly lost over the last years for their contributions such as Jean-Pierre Delahouse, Ole Lando, Pierre Mathijsen, Alfonso Mattera, Hjalte Rasmussen, Pierre Pescatore, Ernst Steindorff and Rolf Wägenbaur.

Many prominent legal scholars, social scientists and historians participated in our conferences and seminars and helped to develop our research. Their influence and assistance can hardly be overestimated. They include from the world of history Vincent Genin, Wolfram Kaiser, Johnny Laursen, N. Piers Ludlow, Kiran Klaus Patel, Federico Romero, Laurent Warlouzet, Jérôme Wilson and Tobias Witschke. Some wonderful versatile and intellectually sharp social scientists include Karen Alter, Julie Bailleux, Stefano Bartolini, Antonin Cohen, Michelle Egan, John Erik Fossum, Morten Kelstrup, Peter Lindseth, Nicola Lupo, Dorte Sindbjerg Martinsen, Mikael Rask Madsen, William Patterson, William Phelan, Mark Pollack, Kim Lane Scheppele, Antoine Vauchez and Marlene Wind. Last but not least, a large group of legal scholars that not only helped us understand the intricacies of EU law much better, but also often actively promoted our work in the legal community includes Matej Abejl, Alberto Alemanno, Amedeo Arena, Marina

Averani, Loïc Azoulai, Julio Baquero Cruz, Francesca Bignami, Leonard Besselink, Gráinne de Búrca, Graham Butler, Damian Chalmers, Monica Claes, Paul Craig, Marise Cremona, Peter Cullen, Hauke Delfs, Magnus Esmark, Dieter Grimm, Giuseppe Martinico, Laurence W. Gormley, Antonio Grilli, Peter Hay, Thomas Horsley, Francis Jacobs, Alexandra Kemmerer, Jan Komárek, Henning Koch, Dimitry Kochenov, Giuseppe Martinico, Agustín José Menéndez, Fernanda Nicola, Vincenzo Guizzi, Elaine Fahey, Miguel Maduro, Anna Katharina Mangold, Karen McAuliffe, Catherine McCauliff, Anne McNaughton, Ulla Neergaard, Daniel Sarmiento Ramirez-Escudero, Frank Schorkopf, Robert Schütze, Alexander Somek, Ditlev Tamm, Stefan Vogenauer and Giuliano Vosa.

Finally, we would like to thank the President of the CJEU, Koen Lenaerts, the numerous judges of the Court who have provided input and feedback on papers and presentations and the Court's Information Service, in particular Judge William Valasidis and Rita Erhard, for their new openness and the wonderful accessibility for our work in the last five years. We hope that this book will provide a reward for their dynamic work in opening up the institution both to its own past and to the present.

Our network benefited from numerous grants and support from academic and private institutions. Most importantly, a Danmarks Frie Forskningsfond (DFF) – Independence Research Fund Denmark grant meant that the project had a home at the University of Copenhagen from 2013–2016. Other grants include ones from the Carlsberg Foundation, Faculty of Humanities, University of Copenhagen, Centre of Modern European Studies, University of Copenhagen, the Luxembourg National Research Fund, Leverhulme Fellowships, the Bracton Centre for Legal History at the University of Exeter, the Scouloudi Historical Research awards, the European Union Center at the University of Illinois, the American Consortium for European Studies, the School of Public Affairs at American University, the Washington College of Law and Australian National University's Centre for European Studies. Finally, the group was adopted by the Max Planck Institute for Legal History and Legal Theory in 2016 and has now finally found a permanent and generous home in Frankfurt under the directorship of Stefan Vogenauer.

Our work in this book has been enhanced by the hard work and diligence of Robert Cardenasso, Noam Krainin and Jon Dipietro. Despite their best efforts, any errors in the text remain our own.

This is the first book on the legal history of European integration that is based on the systematic exploration of EU archives, the national archives of more than ten countries as well as more than fifty private archives from both Europe and the United States. We hope this is exactly the kind of book that all those archivists, eyewitnesses and academics that helped us produce it wanted to read. Finally, after so many years of arduous work, here it is.

Table of Cases

EUROPEAN COAL AND STEEL COMMUNITY/EUROPEAN COMMUNITY/EUROPEAN UNION

1/54, *French Republic v High Authority of the European Coal and Steel Community*, 1954, ECLI:EU:C:1954:7.

1/58, *Friedrich Stork & Cie v High Authority of the European Coal and Steel Community*, 1959, ECLI:EU:C:1959:4.

1/78, *International Atomic Energy Agency*, 1978, ECLI:EU:C:1978:202.

2/74, *Jean Reyners v Belgian State*, 1974, ECLI:EU:C:1974:68.

Joined Cases 3/76, 4/76, and 6/76, *Cornelis Kramer et al.*, 1976, ECLI:EU:C:1976:114.

6/54, *The Netherlands v ECSC High Authority*, 1955, ECLI:EU:C:1955:5.

6/64, *Costa v ENEL*, 1964, ECLI:EU:C:1964:66.

8/55, *Fédération Charbonnière de Belgique v High Authority of the European Coal and Steel Community*, 1956, ECLI:EU:C:1956:7.

8/70, *Commission of the European Communities v Italian Republic*, 1970, ECLI:EU:C:1970:9.

8/74, *Procureur du Roi v Benoît and Gustave Dassonville*, 1974, ECLI:EU:C:1974:82.

9/70, *Franz Grad v Finanzamt Traunstein*, 1970, EU:C:1970:78.

11/70, *Internationale Handelsgesellschaft mbH v Einfuhr- und Vorratsstelle für Getreide und Futtermittel*, 1970, EU:C:1970:114.

13/61, *Kledingverkoopbedrijf de Geus en Uitdenbogerd v Robert Bosch GmbH et al.*, 1962, ECLI:EU:C:1962:11.

13/68, *SpA Salgoil v Italian Ministry of Foreign Trade*, 1968, EU:C:1968:54.

20/64, *SARL Albatros v Société des pétroles et des combustibles liquides (Sopéco)*, 1964, ECLI:EU:C:1965:8.

22/70, *Commission of the European Communities v Council of the European Communities*, 1971, EU:C:1971:32.

26/62, *Van Gend en Loos v Nederlandse Administratie der Belastingen*, 1963, ECLI:EU:C:1963:1.

28–30/62, *Da Costa en Schaake NV and Others v Netherlands Inland Revenue Administration*. 1963, ECLI:EU:C:1963:6.

29/69, *Erich Stauder v City of Ulm – Sozialamt*, 1969, ECLI:EU:C:1969:57.

31/70, *Deutsche Getreide- und Futtermittel-Handelsgesellschaft mbH v Hauptzollamt Hamburg-Altona*, 1970, ECLI:EU:C:1970:108.

33/70, *SpA SACE v Finance Minister of the Italian Republic*, 1970, ECLI:EU: C:1970:118.

34/70, *Syndicat national du commerce extérieur des céréales et al. v Office national interprofessionnel des céréales et Ministère de l'Agriculture*, 1970, ECLI:EU: C:1970:119.

Joined Cases 36/59, 37/59, 38/59, and 40/59, *Präsident Ruhrkohlen-Verkaufsgesellschaft mbH et al. v High Authority of the European Coal and Steel Community*, 1960, ECLI:EU:C:1960:36.

36/74, *Walrave and Koch v Association Union Cycliste Internationale and Others*, 1974, ECLI:EU:C:1974:140.

36/75, *Roland Rutili v Ministre de l'Intérieur*, 1975, ECLI:EU:C:1975:137.

41/74, *Yvonne van Duyn v Home Office*, 1974, EU:C:1974:133.

43/75, *Gabrielle Defrenne v Société anonyme belge de navigation aérienne Sabena*, 1976, EU:C:1976:56.

44/73, *J. Nold Kohlen- und Baustoffgroßhandlung v Commission of the European Communities*, 1974, ECLI:EU:C:1974:51.

44/79, *Liselotte Hauer v Land Rheinland-Pfalz*, 1979, ECLI:EU:C:1979:290.

48/74, *Charmasson v Minister for Economic Affairs and Finance*, 1974, ECLI:EU: C:1974:137.

51/76, *Verbond van Nederlandse Ondernemingen v Inspecteur der Invoerrechten en Accijnzen*, 1977, ECLI:EU:C:1977:12.

57/65, *Alfons Lütticke GmbH v Hauptzollamt Saarlouis*, 1966, ECLI:EU: C:1966:34.

Joined Cases 73/63 and 74/63, *NV Internationale Crediet- en Handelsvereniging 'Rotterdam' et al. v Ministry of Agriculture and Fisheries*, 1964, ECLI:EU:C:1964:8.

106/77, *Amministrazione delle finanze dello Stato v Simmenthal*, 1978, ECLI:EU:C:1978:49.

120/78, *Rewe-Zentral AG v Bundesmonopolverwaltung für Branntwein*, 1979, ECLI:EU:C:1979:42.

142/77, *Statens Kontrol med ædle Metaller v Preben Larsen et al.*, 1978, ECLI:EU:C:1978:144.

143/83, *Commission of the European Communities v Kingdom of Denmark*, 1985, ECLI:EU:C:1985:34.

148/78, *Criminal proceedings against Tullio Ratti*, 1979, ECLI:EU:C:1979:110.

152/84, *M. H. Marshall v Southampton and South-West Hampshire Area Health Authority (Teaching)*, 1986, ECLI:EU:C:1986:84.

171/78, *Commission of the European Communities v Kingdom of Denmark*, 1980, ECLI:EU:C:1980:54.

194/94, *CIA Security International SA v Signalson SA and Securitel SPRL*, 1996, ECLI:EU:C:1996:172.

200/90, *Dansk Denkavit ApS and P. Poulsen Trading ApS v Skatteministeriet*, 1992, ECLI:EU:C:1992:152.

230/81, *Grand Duchy of Luxembourg v European Parliament*, 1983, ECLI:EU:C:1983:32.

231/78, *Commission of the European Communities v United Kingdom of Great Britain and Northern Ireland*, 1979, ECLI:EU:C:1979:101.

232/78, *Commission of the European Communities v French Republic*, 1979, ECLI:EU:C:1979:215.

243/89, *Commission of the European Communities v Kingdom of Denmark*, 1993, ECLI:EU:C:1993:257.

262/88, *Douglas Harvey Barber v Guardian Royal Exchange Assurance Group*, 1990, ECLI:EU:C:1990:209.

288/89, *Stichting Collectieve Antennevoorziening Gouda et al. v Commissariaat voor de Media*, 1991, ECLI:EU:C:1991:323.

294/83, *Parti écologiste 'Les Verts' v European Parliament*, 1986, ECLI:EU:C:1986:166.

352/85, *Bond van Adverteerders et al. v The Netherlands State*, 1988, ECLI:EU:C:1988:12.

730/79, *Philip Morris Holland BV v Commission of the European Communities*, 1980, ECLI:EU:C:1980:209.

BELGIUM

Cour de cassation, 27 May 1971, *État belge, Ministre des Affaires économiques v Société anonyme Fromagerie franco-suisse (Le Ski)*, 1672484252.

epublic v High Authority of *Højesteret*, 6 April 1998, Treaty of Maastricht, Case 361/1997.

DENMARK

Højesteret, 10 September 2012, *Sawo Holding A/S mod Skatteministeriet*, Case 33/ 2012.

Højesteret, 6 December 2016, *Dansk Industri (DI) acting on behalf of Ajos A/S v Estate of A*, Case 15/2014.

FRANCE

Cour de cassation (Chambre civile), 22 December 1931, *Sanchez*, *Dalloz* 1932. I.131.

Conseil d'État (Sections administratives), 6 November 1936, *Arrighi*, n° 41221, published in *Recueil Lebon* 966, 1936.

Cour de cassation (Chambre criminelle), 3 June 1950, *Hauck*, *Dalloz* 1950.I.521.

Cour d'Appel de Paris, 26 January 1963, *UNEF v Consten*, *Dalloz* 1963.189.

Conseil d'État (Section), 19 June 1964, *Société des pétroles Shell-Berre et autres (Shell Berre)*, n° 235345, published in *Recueil Lebon* 344, 1964.

Tribunal de commerce de Marseille, 13 May 1964, *Telefunken v Aubin et Pucci*, *Gaz. Pal.* 1965.3.

Cour d'Appel de Paris, 7 July 1965, SA *La Technique Minière LTM v Maschinenbau Ulm*, *Gaz. Pal.* 1965.2.90.

Cour d'Appel de Colmar, 1 June 1965, *La Hessische Knappschaft v La Maison Singer et fils*, *Gaz. Pal.* 1965.2.102.

Cour d'appel d'Orléans, 9 November 1967, *Stanislas Ciechelski v CRSS Centre d'Orléans*.

Conseil d'État (Section), 10 February 1967, *S.A. des Établissements Petitjean et autres (Petitjean)*, n° 59125, 59126, 59329, published in *Recueil Lebon* 63, 1967.

Cour de cassation (Chambre sociale), 24 October 1968, *Torrekens*, n° 568, *Dalloz* 1965.II.956, p. 677.

Conseil d'État (Section), 1 March 1968, *Syndicat Général de Fabricants de Semoules de France* (*Semoules*), n° 62814, published in *Recueil Lebon* 149, 1970.

Cour de cassation (Chambre criminelle), 22 October 1970, *Ramel*, n° 2776, *Dalloz* 1970.276, p. 657.

Conseil constitutionel, 16 July 1971, *Liberté d'association*, n° 71–44 DC.

Cour d'Appel de Paris, 7 July 1973, *Jacques Vabre*, n° 4164.

Conseil constitutionel, 15 January 1975, *Case IVG*, n° 74–54 DC.

Cour de cassation (Chambre mixte), 24 May 1975, *Jacques Vabre*, n° 73–13.556.

Conseil d'État (Assemblée), 22 December 1978, *Cohn-Bendit*, n° 11604, published in *Recueil Lebon* 524, 1980.

Conseil constitutionel, 3 September 1986, *Loi relative aux conditions d'entrée et de séjour des étrangers en France*, n° 82–216 DC.

Conseil constitutionel, 23 January 1987, *Loi transférant à la juridiction judiciaire le contentieux des décisions du Conseil de la concurrence*, n° 86–224 DC.

Conseil d'État (Assemblée), 20 October 1989, *Nicolo*, n° 108243, published in *Recueil Lebon* 190, 1990.

GERMANY

BVerfGE 6, 32, 16.01.1957, *Elfes*, 1 BvR 253/56.

BVerfGE 7, 198, 15.01.1958, *Lüth*, 1 BvR 400/51.

BVerfGE 22, 134, 05.07.1967, *EWG-Recht*, 2 BVL 29/63.

BVerfGE 22, 293, 18.10.1967, *EWG-Verordnung*, 1 BvR 248/63, 1 BvR 216/67.

BVerfGE 37, 271, 29.05.1974, *Solange I*, 2 BvL 52/71.

BVerfGE 52, 187, 25.07.1979, *Vielleicht*, 2 BvL 6/77.

BVerfGE 73, 339, 22.10.1986, *Solange II*, 2 BvR 197/83.

BVerfGE 75, 223, 08.04.1987, *Kloppenberg*, 2 BvR 687/85.

BVerfGE 89, 155, 12.10.1993, *Maastricht*, 2 BvR 2134, 2159/92.

BVerfGE 123, 267, 30.06.2009, *Lisbon*, 2 BvE 2/08, 2 BvE 5/08, 2 BvR 1010/08, 2 BvR 1022/08, 2 BvR 1259/08, 2 BvR 182/09.

BVerfGE 129, 300, 09.11.2011, *5% Threshold decision*, 2 BvC 4/10, 2 BvC 6/10, 2 BvC 8/10.

BVerfGE 132, 195, 12.09.2012, *ESM Decision*, 2 BvR 1390/12, 2 BvR 1421/12, 2 BvR 1438/12, 2 BvR 1439/12, 2 BvR 1440/12 und 2 BvR 6/12.

BVerfGE 135, 259, 26.02.2014, *3% Threshold decision*, 2 BvE 2/13, 2 BvE 5/13, 2 BvE 6/13, 2 BvE 7/13, 2 BvE 8/13, 2 BvE 9/13, 2 BvE 10/13, 2 BvE 12/13, 2 BvR 2220/13, 2 BvR 2221/13, 2 BvR 2238/13.

BVerfGE 142, 123, 21.06.2016, *Gauweiler Decision*, 2 BvR 2728/13, 2 BvR 2728/13, 2 BvR 2729/13, 2 BvR 2730/13, 2 BvR 2731/13, 2 BvE 13/13.

BVerfGE 154.17, 05.05.2020, *PSPP Decision*, 2 BvR 859/15, 2 BvR 1651/15, 2 BvR 2006/15, 2 BvR 980/16.

BVerfGE 157, 332, 15.04.2021, *NGEU Decision*, 2 BvR 547/21.

ITALY

Corte Costituzionale, *Costa v ENEL*, judgment no. 14 of 24 February 1964.

Corte Costituzionale, *Acciaierie S. Michele v CECA*, judgment no. 98 of 16 December 1965.

Corte Costituzionale, *Frontini e a.*, judgment no. 183 of 18 December 1973.

Corte Costituzionale, *Granital v Amministrazione delle Finanze*, judgment no. 170 of 5 June 1984.

Corte Costituzionale, *Fragd v Amministrazione delle Finanze*, judgment no. 232 of 13 April 1989.

NETHERLANDS

Hoge Raad. 17 December 1934. *Rhine Navigation Treaty. Nederlandse Jurisprudentie* 1935, nos. 5 and 11.

Hoge Raad. 25 January 1952. *New Reclaimed Land. Nederlandse Jurisprudentie* 1952, no. 125.

Hoge Raad. 6 March 1959. Nyugat II ruling. *Nederlandse Jurisprudentie* 1962, no. 2.

Zutphen District Court, 11 July 1958, *Tuberies Louis Julien S.A. v N.V. Van Katwijk's Papier en Cartonverwerkende Industrieën, Nederlandse Jurisprudentie* 426.

Hoge Raad, 6 March 1959, *Nyugat II ruling, Nederlandse Jurisprudentie* 1962, 2.

Amsterdam Court of Appeal 3 March 1960, *K.I.M. Rijwielfabriek N. V. v Sieverding*, SEW Europa. 80.

Rotterdam District Court, 9 July 1960, *Linde's Eismaschinen Aktiengesellschaft and Heybroeck Zelander N.V. v v.o.f. Kledingverkoopbedrijf De Geus en Uitdenbogerd, Sociaal-Economische Wetgeving*, 1961, 180.

Rotterdam District Court, 26 October 1960, *Robert Bosch GmbH and W. van Rijn N.V. v v.o.f. Kledingverkoopbedrijf De Geus en Uitdenbogerd, Nederlandse Jurisprudentie*, 1961, 159.

The Hague District Court, 14 December 1960, *Aarts v Vereniging van Fabrikanten van Plakband en Parafinepapier, Sociaal-Economische Wetgeving* 265.

Hoge Raad, 13 January 1961, *K.I.M. Rijwielfabriek N.V. v Sieverding, Nederlandse Jurisprudentie*, 1962, 245.

Amsterdam District Court, 21 March 1961, *Bosch & Van Rijn v KIM & Slootmans*. Unpublished; retrieved from Noord-Hollands Archief, Haarlem (NHA), Arrondissementsrechtbank Amsterdam 1960–1969 (593) inv. no. 938.

Arnhem Court of Appeal, 28 June 1961, *Tuberies, Sociaal-Economische Wetgeving* 125.

The Hague District Court, 24 November 1961, *Graetz N.V. Haarlem v J. Kadee, Voorburg, Nederlandse Jurisprudentie* (1962) 57.

Amsterdam Court of Appeal, 3 March 1960, *K.I.M. Rijwielfabriek N.V. v Sieverding, SEW Europa* 80.

Rotterdam District Court, 26 October 1960, *Robert Bosch GmbH and W. van Rijn N.V. v v.o.f. Kledingverkoopbedrijf De Geus en Uitdenbogerd, Nederlandse Jurisprudentie* 159.

Hague Court of Appeal, 30 June 1961, *Bosch & Van Rijn v De Geus en Uitdenbogerd, Nederlandse Jurisprudentie* 375.

Hoge Raad, 18 May 1962, *Bosch & Van Rijn v De Geus en Uitdenbogerd, Nederlandse Jurisprudentie* (1965) 115.

College van Beroep voor het Bedrijfsleven, 10 January 1962, NV *Maatschappij voor Vee- en Vleeshandel Meattrading, Rotterdam v Produktschap voor Vee en Vlees, 's-Gravenhage, Sociaal-Economische Wetgeving* 65.

Hoge Raad, 9 June 1976, *BNB: Beslissingen in belastingzaken* 1976/168.

Abbreviations

AG	Advocate General
AIGE	Associazione Italiana dei Giuristi Europei
AJE	Association des juristes européens
BVerfG	German Constitutional Court (Bundesverfassungsgericht)
CAP	Common Agricultural Policy
CDU	Christian Democratic Union (West German)
CISC	International Confederation of Christian Trade Unions
CIUF	Comité pour l'Indépendance et l'Unité de la France
CJEU	Court of Justice of the European Union
CML REV.	Common Market Law Review
COREPER	Committee of Permanent Representatives
CUI	Committee for the uniform interpretation of the treaty
DACS	Direction des affaires civiles et du sceau (of the French Ministry of Justice)
DG	Directorates-General
DIE	Directoraat Europese Integratie
DSE	Danish Society for European Law (Dansk selskab for europaret)
EC	European Community/European Communities
ECJ	European Court of Justice/Court of Justice
ECSC	European Coal and Steel Community
ECHR	European Convention on Human Rights
ECHR	European Commission of Human Rights (ECHR) (until the entry into force of Protocol 11 in 1998)
ECtHR	European Court of Human Rights
EDC	European Defence Community
EEC	European Economic Community
ELJ	European Law Journal
EP	European Parliament
EPC	European Political Community

ERTA	European Road Transport Agreement (the full name of the agreement is the European Agreement Concerning the Work of Crews of Vehicles Engaged in International Road Transport)
ESG	European Storebælt Group
EU	European Union
EUI	European University Institute
EURATOM	European Atomic Energy Community
FAC	Frankfurt Administrative Court
FIDE	Féderation International de Droit Europeénne
FTA	Free Trade Agreement
GATT	General Agreement on Tariffs and Trade
HAEU	Historical Archives of the European Union
ITL	Integration Through Law (project)
KVP	Katholieke Volkspartij
MEP	Member of the European Parliament
MP	Member of Parliament
MRP	Mouvement républicain Populaire
NATO	North Atlantic Treaty Organization
NJV	Nederlandse Juristenvereniging
NVER	Nederlandse Vereniging voor Europees Recht
PdvA	Partej van de Arbeid
RPF	Rassemblement du peuple Français
RPR	Rassemblement pour la République
SEA	Single European Act
SPD	Social Democratic Party (West German)
TEC	Treaty on European Community
TEU	The Treaty on European Union (also cited as TFEU; see below)
TFEU	Treaty on the Functioning of the European Union
UPR	Union pour la nouvelle République
UK	United Kingdom
US	United States
VAT	Value Added Tax
WGE	Wissenschaftliche Gesellschaft für Europarecht
WTO	World Trade Organization

History and Theory: Towards a New History of European Law

Morten Rasmussen

It was a turning point in the history of European integration and a unique moment for the first President of the European Commission, Walter Hallstein. On 16 June 1965 in the afternoon, Hallstein appeared before the European Parliament (EP) to express his strong support for the constitutional interpretation of European law[1] launched by the European Court of Justice (ECJ)[2] in the new *Van Gend en Loos* (1963) and *Costa v ENEL* (1964) judgments.[3] Here the ECJ had controversially assumed the competence to define the relationship between European law and national constitutional orders. By doing so the ECJ sidestepped the respective constitutional clauses of the member states on how to receive international (and European) law. Primary legal norms from the founding treaties, when clear and unambiguous, would have direct effect inside the legal order of the member states as well as primacy vis-à-vis national legislation, whether precedent or antecedent. This was a remarkable breakthrough for a constitutional interpretation of European law.[4] However, in the cautious terminology of the Court, it merely signified the emergence of a 'new legal order'.[5]

1 The term 'European law' covers the law of the European Coal and Steel Community (1952 to July 1967), the European Economic Community (1952 to July 1967) and EURATOM (1952 to July 1967), the merged European Community (from July 1967–1993) and the European Union (1993 onwards).

2 Throughout the book we use the name: European Court of Justice (ECJ) to describe the Court functioning in the European Coal and Steel Community, the European Economic Community, EURATOM and the European Community.

3 26/62 *Van Gend en Loos v Nederlandse Administratie der Belastingen*, 1963, ECLI:EU:C:1963:1 and 6/64 *Costa v ENEL*, 1964, ECLI:EU:C:1964:66.

4 In the two judgments, the ECJ had followed the recommendations of the Legal Service of the EEC Commission, and its director Michel Gaudet. While the terminology used by the court was the discrete and rather empty: 'new legal order', the vocabulary of the Legal Service to describe the doctrines recommended had originally been 'constitutional' in the Bosch case from 1961–13/61, *Kledingverkoopbedrijf de Geus en Uitdenbogerd v Robert Bosch GmbH et al.*, 1962, ECLI:EU:C:1962:11. (See the Mémoire, 25 October 1961, Historical Archive of the European Commission (HAEU), BAC. 371/1991, 577–578). The same view was made explicit by key actors, such as President of the ECJ, André Donner, and an important academic observer, Eric Stein, who both considered the two judgments a breakthrough for a constitutional and even a federal understanding of European law. Donner 1963; Stein 1965.

5 The terminology shifted from the *Van Gend en Loos* judgment ('a new order of international law') to the *Costa v ENEL* judgment ('a new legal order'). The first version much annoyed Michel Gaudet

Hallstein had long supported a constitutional basis for the European construction.[6] Already, when he led the West German delegations negotiating the Treaty of Paris (1950–1951) and the two Treaties of Rome (1955–1957), his ambition had been to create a federal Europe based on a genuine European constitution.[7] This was also a key part of his agenda as President of the European Commission of the European Economic Community (EEC)[8] from 1958, despite the limited results that had been achieved in this direction when negotiating the founding treaties.[9] To Hallstein, as he explained to an academic audience at the University of Padua in March 1962, it was crucial that the European Communities (EC) created a legal order that 'replaced violence and political pressure with the rule of law in the relations between the member states'.[10] Hallstein wanted a European version of the old mantra of international law: peace through law.

In his speech before the EP in June 1965, Hallstein concluded that the relationship between the legal order of the EC and national constitutional orders was of major political importance. It was in fact an existential question on which the establishment and implementation of the Common Market depended. A question, according to Hallstein, which required an answer based on legal methods. Not only had the ECJ now provided the right solution; the EP and the report produced on the matter by its legal committee also backed the new constitutional interpretation of European law.[11] A key objective of the Hallstein Commission had thus been achieved.

Until now Hallstein's speech has been overlooked by historians of European integration, who have instead understandably focused on the so-called 'Empty

because it still connected European law to international law. Archive of Michel Gaudet (AMG). Chronos 1963. Letter from Michel Gaudet to Pierre Pescatore, 16 May 1963.

6 Loth et al. 1995.

7 Whilst facing opposition to this from within his own team, Hallstein had used his considerable political leverage to ensure his views defined the West German negotiating position in 1951. On the sidelining of Herbert Kraus as the leader of the opposition, Davies 2015 and Chapter 6 below.

8 See for example the speech by Hallstein at the Congress of the International Law Association in 1960 where he emphasised that lawyers should embark on a federal understanding of the EC rather than one of international law. Only in this manner and on basis of a strong legal foundation could the dynamic nature of the Common Market project be properly pursued. Archives of Walter Hallstein (AWH), 337. Address by the President of the European Economic Community Professor Dr Walter Hallstein to the 49th Congress of the International Law Association (Hamburg, 8 August 1960).

9 Boerger 2012, 341.

10 Translated by the author from: 'in den Beziehungen zwischen den Mitgliedsstaaten werden Gewalt und politischer Druck durch die Herrschaft des Rechts ersetzt', taken from Die europäische Wirtschaftsgemeinschaft ist eine Rechtsgemeinschaft. AWH, vol. 1146. Rede des Präsidenten der Kommission der Europäischen Wirtschaftsgemeinschaft. Professor Dr. jur. Walter Hallstein vor der Universität in Padua am 12. März 1962.

11 Rapport fait au nom de la Commission Juridique sur la primauté du droit communautaire, Parlement européen, document de séance, 1965, 14. This report was developed by the legal committee of the EP led by the Belgian law socialist, federalist and law professor, Fernand Dehousse. The content and analysis of the report had been coordinated with Michel Gaudet and the Legal Service of the EEC Commission. Archive of Fernand Dehousse (AFD), 494. Commission juridique. Exposé de M. Gaudet, Directeur général du Service Juridique des Exécutifs européens (branche C.E.E.) devant la Commission Juridique en sa réunion du 18 février 1965. See also Chapter 4 for more details.

Chair Crisis' that broke out two weeks later.[12] During this crisis, French President Charles de Gaulle and his government boycotted the Council of Ministers until January 1966, and demanded a complete overhaul of the institutional system of the EC to reduce the independence of the supranational institutions and force the dismissal of the activist Hallstein Commission. The crisis was eventually resolved with the Luxembourg Compromise that introduced an informal veto right for the member states in the legislative process.[13] However, while the veto right gradually lost its original legitimacy in the 1980s with the introduction of the Single European Act, the constitutional interpretation of European law had come to stay and arguably remains one of the most lasting achievements of the Hallstein Commission. A legal revolution[14] had been born that would deeply shape the future of the EC. It was, however, far from complete. The breakthrough for a constitutional interpretation of European law may have been a crucial turning point in the early struggle over the institutional and political nature of European integration. But the political and legal battle over the development of a broader constitutional practice would continue until the establishment of the European Union (EU) in 1993.

This book explores the history of the battle over the constitutional practice of European law from 1950 to 1993. It offers the first archive-based history of what constitutes an important, yet still relatively unknown slice of European integration history. In the first half of the book, the role of the EC institutions as well as the transnational networks of European law scholarship will be explored. In the second half, the reception of the constitutional practice of European law in the member states will be analysed through the examples of West Germany, France, the Netherlands and Denmark. Altogether, the book offers a new revisionist historical interpretation of how European law evolved from 1950 to 1993. It argues that during this period European constitutionalism developed as a doctrinal and discursive practice of the ECJ, the Commission, the EP and European legal scholarship. This practice was, however, generally resisted and accepted only in a piecemeal fashion by national governments, administrations and courts until the mid-1980s. The Single European Act of 1986 forced the member states to participate more fully in the mechanisms of the legal order built by the ECJ because it underpinned the Single Market project coveted by the governments. However, during the negotiations on the Maastricht Treaty, a majority of member states, supported in parallel by a number of constitutional and high courts, nevertheless rejected to accept the constitutional practice as a key legitimating principle of the new EU.

12 Bajon 2012.

13 See Chapter 5.

14 For an in-depth discussion of why the constitutional breakthrough should be characterised a legal revolution consult Rasmussen 2014.

LAW AND POLITICS STUDIES IN CONTEXT

Although historians had overlooked the importance of law to the history of European integration until the last decade,[15] this was certainly not the case with the social sciences. Legal scholars have long researched and debated the nature of European law and its role in the integration process, and from the 1990s, first political science and then sociology also entered the fray. Which theories and interpretations of the development of European law from 1950 to 1993 did these disciplines produce? Interestingly, they tell essentially the same story, albeit with some variation. The essence is that European law was successfully constitutionalised by the ECJ. Through its case law the Court gradually transformed the Treaties of Rome into a proto-federal constitution. This development was eventually, it is furthermore argued, accepted by the member states. The EU, established in 1993, was consequently built on a European rule of law and European politics had been judicialised to the extent where European law would frame and at times even decide policy making.[16]

Before discussing the different variations of this core narrative of successful constitutionalisation, let us first explore where the notion came from originally. The claim that European law had been constitutionalised first entered academic discourse with the publication of a now famous article by an American legal scholar, Eric Stein, in 1981.[17] From the legal revolution in the early 1960s to 1980, legal scholarship on European law, to a large extent dominated by members of the ECJ or the Commission,[18] had employed the discreet and bland vocabulary of 'new legal order' invented by the court. This scholarship focused on functional analyses of European law and generally avoided debates on what constituted the nature of 'the new legal order'. If challenged, judges such as Pierre Pescatore from Luxembourg or Dutch André Donner chose a defensive stance, pointing out that the ECJ had simply drawn out the legal consequences of the Treaties of Rome and established a European rule of law (Article 164 of the European Economic Community Treaty (EEC Treaty)).[19] In this largely European debate, Stein, as a professor at the University of Michigan Law School at Ann Arbor, represented an outlier position. Stein did not shy away from a much more political interpretation of the nature of European law. Shaped by his experience as a Jewish refugee from Czechoslovakia before the war, he had witnessed most of his family perish in the Holocaust, and consequently developed a strong ideological belief in the importance of European unification.[20] Drawing by analogy on the American federal experience, by 1965, he already characterised the *Van Gend en Loos* and *Costa*

15 For the assessment of Ludlow 2010, 122.
16 Recent examples of this argument are Vauchez 2015; G. Davies 2016.
17 Stein 1981.
18 Schepel and Wesseling 1997.
19 Boerger and Rasmussen 2017; Byberg 2017b.
20 Boerger 2014.

v ENEL judgments as a constitutional breakthrough, where the ECJ had interpreted the treaties as if they were of a constitutional nature and rejected 'public international law as rationale for its power'.[21] Stein would defend this view with ideological zeal, and criticised other legal scholars behind the scenes, if they did not understand the political necessity of creating an autonomous European legal order. This was the case for example with the young Belgian scholar and lawyer Michel Waelbroeck, who considered the *Costa v ENEL* judgment to be quite a scandal because the ECJ had assumed the competence to replace the constitutional clauses of the member states on the reception of international law with its own system. In a forceful letter, Stein insisted that it was absolutely essential for the younger generation of scholars to support a progressive development of European law and not stay prisoners of 'their own national constitutional concepts grounded in German positivism'.[22] Despite his activism, Stein's views had little impact on the European legal debate before the 1980s.

His famous article from 1981 was first presented in a draft at a conference of the American Society of International Law in April 1978. Here he admitted that the paper title, 'The Emerging European Constitution', was 'unrealistic and Pollyannaish, if not outright propagandistic'.[23] However, this time his interpretation was finally picked up in Europe. At the Department of Law at the new European University Institute (EUI), Italian Professor Mauro Cappelletti was about to embark on a grand new research project entitled 'Integration through Law' that compared the American federal experience with the process of European integration, repeating an exercise already done by Stein in a conference in Bellagio at Lake Como in 1979.[24] The project, coordinated by an unknown, young, but very talented Israeli doctoral student, Joseph H. H. Weiler, who would quickly be promoted to professor, was of an entirely different scale, however. It involved a host of academics and practitioners and was closely coordinated with both the ECJ and the Legal Service of the Commission. Although published in a now classical multi-volume series in green cloth, it was arguably Weiler's own ambitious scholarship that laid the groundwork for the breakthrough of the thesis of considering the development of European law as one of successful constitutionalisation.[25]

Building on Stein, Weiler argued that the ECJ had constitutionalised the Treaties of Rome by creating a binding legal order with directly effective legal norms

21 Stein 1965, 491, citation from 513. Stein was also present in the Legal Service during the debates on how to develop a position on the *Van Gend en Loos* case. So, he had inside knowledge about the way it had been debated there.

22 Archive of Eric Stein (AES). 15 Waelbroeck. Letter from Michel Waelbroeck to Eric Stein, 16 December 1965 and Letter from Eric Stein to Michel Waelbroeck, 8 February 1966.

23 Stein 1978, 166.

24 Stein and Sandelow 1982.

25 Joseph H. H. Weiler was the de facto manager of the project. For the first historical analysis of the project based on unique primary sources drawn from the private archive of Mauro Cappelletti, see Byberg 2017c. See also Chapter 4.

supported by strong enforcement mechanisms such as the preliminary reference mechanism (Article 177 of the EEC Treaty), whereby private litigants and their lawyers could call on the national courts to ask the ECJ for advice with regard to the implementation of European law in member states. National governments accepted this development because the Luxembourg Compromise had granted the member states a veto right in the legislative process that counterbalanced the progressive tightening of the legal obligations of the EC. This nexus – Weiler did not necessarily believe there was a direct causal link between the two developments – was, however, broken by the Single European Act of 1986 that finally reintroduced majority voting in the legislative process to establish the new Single Market. He therefore predicted that national governments in response might curb the powers of the ECJ and limit judicial influence in the integration process.[26] Weiler's scholarship coincided with the revival of the EC in the second half of the 1980s and the strong institutional and political dynamics that appeared around the creation of the Single European Market. In this context, Weiler was propelled to academic stardom and his interpretation that European law had experienced a successful constitutionalisation entered the mainstream of the new broader field of European studies, which evolved from the late 1980s to explain the new dynamics of European integration at the end of the Cold War.

With Weiler as the most influential legal scholar in the broader field of European studies in the early 1990s, and the apparent successful role of European law as a remarkable feature of the new dynamics of European integration, it was perhaps predictable that the new generation of young American political scientists adopted the constitutionalisation thesis as the foundation for their own work on European law.[27] This new political science literature on European law first repeated the theoretical debates within their own field.[28] However, soon a group of young political scientists began to explore empirically how the constitutionalisation of European law had actually taken place, using new innovative theoretical and empirical approaches. Competing explanations emerged. By means of quantitative research on litigation, Alec Stone Sweet and Thomas L. Brunell argued that a self-sustaining dynamic had driven constitutionalisation and constituted a veritable motor of integration. European firms started a virtuous circle of trade liberalisation and legal integration through litigation before national courts, which then sent questions to the ECJ in Luxembourg by way of the preliminary reference mechanism. The case law of the ECJ that generally favoured trade liberalisation was then subsequently codified by Council legislation which in turn, facilitated more litigation.[29] To Stone Sweet and

26 Weiler 1991; Weiler 1994.

27 For an example of how Joseph H. H. Weiler and the 'Integration through Law' project inspired the new, young generation of American political scientists, see the recollections by Karen Alter in Alter 2010.

28 Burley and Mattli 1993; Garret 1995.

29 Sweet and Brunell 1998; Sweet 2000; Sweet and Brunell 2004.

R. Daniel Kelemen, 'integration through law' provided a dynamic strong enough to overcome the backlash from the member states predicted by Weiler. Consequently, 'constitutionalisation' led to a comprehensive judicialisation of the European Union.[30]

The question was now whether the self-sustaining mechanism theorised by Stone Sweet and Brunell on the basis of quantitative studies could be identified by qualitative empirical research.[31] This turned out not to be the case, when Karen Alter worked her way through the West German and French cases from 1950 to 1993. Based on interviews and publicly available sources, her understanding of the dynamics of the process of constitutionalisation turned out very differently. She concluded that the constitutionalisation of European law had rather been driven by lower national courts working in tandem with the ECJ. She also demonstrated how complex and conflictual the process actually was due to the widespread resistance in the member states, in particular from national courts of last resort and parts of the administrative and political elite. Her overall conclusion was nevertheless in line with the mainstream view that by the early 1990s constitutionalisation had been successful and a European rule of law established.[32] However, for all the great qualities of Karen Alter's account of the West German and French battles over the constitutional practice, its empirical foundations was limited to interviews and public sources. It was Alter's book that provided the direct inspiration for the doctoral research of one of the editors of this book.[33] This book will consequently move significantly beyond the state of the art due to its use of systematic archival research.

With Stone Sweet, Brunel and Alter confirming, although with alternative explanations, that European law had indeed been successfully constitutionalised, law and politics studies from the 2000s onwards began to focus on the contemporary role of the Court of Justice of the European Union (CJEU) and European law in the EU. New research attempted to refine what role the CJEU played in the policy-making process of the EU and focused on the extent the Court had been subject of critique.[34] Other strands of research led to an improved understanding of the reception of national administrations both of European legislation and CJEU case law.[35] While the field of law and politics studies have thus increased in sophistication over the last decades, researchers of the field did not return to re-examine the original understanding of how European law had been constitutionalised between 1950 and 1993.

Only very recently have two political scientists turned their attention to the period from 1950 to 1993. Tomasso Pavone has explored the role of the so-called Euro-lawyers from the 1960s to the 1980s, who out of ideological zeal and

30 Kelemen and Sweet 2017; Schmidt 2018.

31 The theory has received a most serious methodological critique for its quantitative analysis. Wind et al. 2009.

32 Alter studied the French and West German cases: Alter 1998a; Alter 2001.

33 Along with Piers Ludlow, another leading historian of the EU, Karen Alter was the examiner for Bill Davies's doctoral thesis at King's College London in 2007.

34 Recent and sophisticated examples of this trend are Vauchez 2015; G. Davies 2016.

35 Conant 2002; Martinsen 2015.

professional self-interest were crucial in producing a significant number of the cases that came through the ECJ's preliminary reference system during this period. Pavone's pathbreaking empirical results, which are based on interviews, as well as research in the archive of the CJEU, align very well with the results of the historical research in this volume. Another interesting contribution has come from William Phelan, who has explored the contribution of French politician and ECJ judge, Robert Lecourt, by analysing his legal writings since the interwar period and key judgments around the legal revolution in the first half of the 1960s.[36] From the perspective of the discipline of history, Phelan's work is perhaps somewhat limited by the lack of archival research, which might have produced a richer understanding of the personality of Lecourt and the historical context in which he worked.[37] However, Phelan manages nevertheless to re-interpret and nuance the doctrinal development around the legal revolution. The historical interest and pioneering contributions of Pavone and Phelan is a most promising new development that this book hopes to encourage further.

In the last two decades, a school of sociological research inspired by Pierre Bourdieu on the role of jurists and legal techniques in the European construction has also made an important contribution to the understanding of the history of European law from 1950 to 1993.[38] The sociological research has offered important new theoretical and empirical nuance in the analysis of the role of jurists, the legal profession, and the supranational institutions. The extent to which jurists had multiple roles in and outside European institutions, the mixture between politics and law and the blurring of the boundaries between European law academia and the supranational institutions are important insights that has inspired the work of this book. Most of the empirical studies conducted by sociologists have also included a historical dimension, which have contributed to our historical understanding of how European law has developed.[39] Nevertheless, seen from the approach developed in this book, the sociological literature is limited in two ways. Just as in political science, the alleged successful constitutionalisation of European law has not been questioned. Instead, sociological research has considered constitutionalisation the key process through which jurists in and outside the European construction have empowered both the supranational institutions and their own profession. Second, the strict Bourdieusian approach, the relatively narrow focus on the role of jurists and the supranational institutions and the lack of systematic archival research have tended to skew the empirical results produced.[40] As a result, the overall

36 Pavone 2022; Phelan 2017; Phelan 2019.

37 Robert Lecourt did unfortunately not leave behind a private archive.

38 A group of Bourdieu inspired scholars including Lola Avril, Julie Bailleux, Antonin Cohen, Mikael Rask Madsen, Guillaume Sacriste, Antoine Vauchez have worked in parallel with the historians producing this book since 2006.

39 Great examples are Cohen 2007; Vauchez 2008a; Bailleux 2014; Vauchez 2015.

40 The best and most nuanced empirical work is Bailleux 2014 which is based on a comprehensive effort of archival research.

understanding of the development of European law ends up lopsided with an overwhelming focus on the supranational institutions, their autonomy and power. What is missing in the account is the role of the European Council/Council of Ministers, as well as in-depth analyses of the responses by national governments, administrations and courts in the battle over European law.[41]

We must turn to recent legal scholarship to identify the first critical voices that question the mainstream interpretation.The new history of the legal dimension of the EU written by the German legal scholar Frank Schorkopf certainly offers a more balanced account of the broad developments from 1948 to 2007.[42] Schorkopf employs a multidimensional approach to the history of European law, which argues that the overall institutional frame of the European construction was decided by competing and complementary ideational positions: constitutionalism, intergovernmentalism and pragmatism. In this way he goes significantly beyond the mainstream interpretation's narrow focus on constitutionalisation and contextualises and nuances our understanding of the history of European law. His monograph thus stands as an excellent synthesis of existing research, including also the archive-based legal histories produced over the last decade by the contributors to this book. At the same time the approach of Schorkopf's book produces certain unfortunate limitations. First, while the ideational positions outlined capture most of the various institutional and political debates, the approach arguably tend to delude and even sidestep the core political conflict over the institutional and legal shape of the European construction between national governments unwilling to furnish the European construction with autonomous power and European federalists and constitutionalists that aimed exactly to do that.[43] Second, by employing a constitutional framework informed by the century long history of western constitutions, Schorkopf inadvertently ends up writing the legal history of the EU with the vocabulary of those political forces who strove for a European federal constitution. The great advantage of the approach is that it allows Schorkopf to author a book that directly contributes to the democratic debate of the contemporary EU using the constitutional approach as a yardstick for clarifying the status of the Union. The disadvantage is that his constitutional approach seriously skews our conceptual lenses and thus our understanding of how the battle over the legal dimension of the European construction has played out. This book instead introduces an open-ended approach that does not predefine the nature of the historical process explored.

In comparison to Schorkopf, the decade-old book of American legal scholar Peter Lindseth, *Power and Legitimacy*, had more critical bite regarding the dominant

41 This is the main weakness of the most impressive analysis of the development of European law from 1950 to the 2000s produced by the sociological school: Vauchez 2015.

42 Schorkopf 2023. See also the two important archive based legal histories of two of his doctoral students: Delfs 2015; Thiele, 2019.

43 This is a conflict that has been brought out much more clearly in the first attempt to offer an overall interpretation of the legal and institutional history of the EU from 1950 to the present day by Dorte S. Martinsen and Morten Rasmussen in a recent article. Rasmussen and Martinsen 2019.

constitutional paradigm of European law.[44] In his attack against the paradigm, Lindseth argued that European law had deep roots in the post-war administrative state of the member states. In fact, since 1958, European law had converged around the legitimating structures and normative principles of the post-war constitutional settlement of the administrative state. These include the delegation of responsibilities to independent agencies such as the Commission or the ECJ, combined with the collective oversight by the Council of Ministers. Although Lindseth's work illuminated the parallels between the rise of the administrative state and the way the EC has developed, his focus on the administrative roots of European law meant that he largely ignored how central the battle over the constitutional practice was to the broader development of European law from 1950 to 1993. The result amounts to an unbalanced account of the history of European law that may question the success of European constitutionalism but does so without exploring how precisely the latter failed.[45]

Conceptual contributions of legal scholars debating the nature of constitutionalism have also proved useful in the context of this book. The core question is what does it take for a political entity – a state or an international entity such as the EU – to obtain constitutional status? Here disagreement exists between legal scholars. One position promoted by the prominent scholar of German constitutional law, Dieter Grimm, argues that the EU is not fully constitutional because it has not experienced a constitutional moment, wherein it obtains popular endorsement. After all, the Constitutional Treaty was rejected by both the electorates of France and the Netherlands in two referenda in 2005. According to Grimm, it is thus fairly simple to ascertain whether a political entity has constitutional legitimacy or not. However, what if constitutional legitimacy could be constructed and obtained over time in a historical process, as argued by Finnish scholar Klaus Tuori?[46] What would it take for the EC to pass the threshold and obtain full constitutional legitimacy in the absence of popular assent? Would it be enough if the CJEU has developed a proto-federal legal order based on a constitutional interpretation combined with a constitutional discourse backed by key institutions and important social actors? Lindseth believes that no, this is not sufficient to replace a constitutional moment with explicit popular endorsement. In his view, for the EU to obtain genuine constitutional legitimacy, it would also need genuine political autonomy. This is clearly not (yet) the case with the EU today, which despite its independent supranational institutions remains dominated by the member state governments collectively in the European Council. Nor is the EU currently able systematically 'to mobilise fiscal and human resources for collective ends in a compulsory and legitimate fashion'. Even if the first European lending in international markets during the pandemic offered a first example of how it can be done.[47] In a European context another serious obstacle may well exist to a smooth process of

[44] Lindseth 2010.
[45] See the following review of Lindseth's book for a more detailed argument: Rasmussen 2011b.
[46] Grimm 2015; Tuori 2015.
[47] Lindseth 2016.

constitutionalisation. The member states of the EU have well-established, and sometimes centuries-old, political and legal cultures that situate constitutional legitimacy firmly in a national context, closely intertwined with national identity.[48] Compared to the American states around and in the decades following the American revolution, the national constitutions of EU member states are thus much more entrenched. In this context, it is difficult to see how a constitutional breakthrough for the EU can happen without a formal constitutional moment that includes popular endorsement.[49]

This book argues that although a constitutional practice evolved in European law from the early 1960s to 1993, including the gradual establishment of a proto-federal European legal order and an accompanying constitutional discourse supported by the supranational institutions and European law academia, European constitutionalism ultimately did not become the key legitimating principle underlying the Maastricht Treaty nor was it accepted by national judiciaries. Not only did the new treaty not present a 'constitutional moment', but it also formalised a consolidation of the collective power of national governments to run the new EU through the European Council and for national judiciaries to place conditions on the future course of European policy. This book thus argues, in contrast to the mainstream interpretation of the development of European law discussed above, that European constitutionalism failed to obtain a major breakthrough in the early 1990s.

HISTORIOGRAPHY AND METHODOLOGY

As the first archive based history of European law from 1950 to 1993, this book draws on and contributes to a number of new trends in the historiography of European integration.[50] From the late 1970s to 2000, historiography was largely dominated by either a focus on the role of European federalism or European identities in the integration process[51] or analyses of how the European states pursued security, commercial and economic interests by the means of European integration.[52] However, in the last two decades we have seen the gradual

48 Following this argument is not enough that post war constitutional reform in a number of Western European states (France, West Germany, Italy, Denmark and Netherlands) opened for the transfer of powers to international peace organisations. This may have signalled a new openness of national legal orders to the necessities of regulating the international sphere. However, it did not necessarily imply that the new international organisation automatically obtained direct constitutional legitimacy. For the opposite viewpoint consult Fossum and Menéndez 2011.

49 The analysis of the legal and social science scholar above draws on Rasmussen and Martinsen 2019.

50 For an excellent if slightly dated overview of the historiography of European integration consult Kaiser and Varsori 2010.

51 See Lipgens 1985; Lipgens 1986; Lipgens and Loth 1988; Lipgens and Loth 1991; Girault 1994. For a historiographical analysis focusing to some extent on the federal historiography see Ramírez Pérez 2016.

52 Key publications on diplomatic history: Girault and Frank 1995; Di Nolfo 2012. Publications with a focus on the commercial and economic interests of the European nation states: Milward 1984; Milward 1992; Milward and Sørensen 1993.

establishment of several new approaches and a broadening of topics explored. This includes archive-based research on the history of the supranational institutions,[53] including their administrative history, which have demonstrated their independent role as agenda setters with the ability to influence European policy making.[54] In addition, historians have also now explored how transnational networks and societal actors have shaped and underpinned the integration process.[55] A broad range of policy fields have been explored in depth such as for example the Common Agricultural Policy,[56] the Common Market,[57] the Common Commercial Policy,[58] the external policy versus former colonies,[59] monetary policy,[60] social policy,[61] environmental policy[62] and cultural policy.[63] Finally, the historians behind this volume have produced a significant body of research on the history of European law focusing in particular on the 1950s and 1960s.[64] Historians today thus conceive of European integration as being developed in a complex political and institutional process involving not only the member states, but also the far from powerless supranational institutions, underpinned by transnational networks and interested societal actors.[65] The history of European law from 1950 to 1993 analysed in this book only reinforces this understanding by highlighting how the supranational institutions, supported by European law academia, attempted to develop the EC in a constitutional, and even federal direction. Even if this alliance was ultimately unsuccessful in the early 1990s, as our book argues, its actions greatly shaped the development of European law in the period analysed.

53 For an excellent history of the High Authority consult Spierenburg and Poidevin 1994. The official histories of the European Commission offer a rich account of the activities and internal administration of the European Commission from 1958 to 1996, based on both primary sources and enormous oral history (European Commission 2014, European Commission 2019, European Commission 2007). See also Ludlow 2016 on the Jenkins Commission. For a first synthetic historical analysis of the history of the European Parliament, see Kaiser 2018. Finally, on the European Council, consult Mourlon-Druol 2010; Mourlon-Druol 2012b; Mourlon-Druol 2016.

54 Carbonell 2014; Seidel 2010.

55 Kaiser 2007, Kaiser et al. 2010; Kaiser and Meyer 2013.

56 Knudsen 2009; Patel 2009.

57 Warlouzet 2018.

58 Coppolaro 2013.

59 Garavini 2012.

60 Mourlon-Druol 2012b.

61 Andry 2022.

62 Meyer and Kaiser 2016; Kaijser, Lehtonen, Meyer and Rubio-Varas 2021.

63 Patel 2013a.

64 Key contributions are Davies and Rasmussen 2012; van Leeuwen 2012; Rasmussen 2012; Bernier 2012; Borger 2012; Davies 2012a; Davies 2012b; Rasmussen 2013; Boerger 2014; Boerger and Rasmussen 2014; Davies and Rasmussen 2014; Boerger and Rasmussen 2017; Nicola and Davies 2017; Rasmussen 2017; Byberg 2017a; Byberg 2017b; Byberg 2017c; Fritz 2018; van Leeuwen 2018; Rasmussen and Martinsen 2019; Rasmussen 2021a.

65 An argument brought forwards already in 2008: Kaiser et al. 2008. See also the interesting synthesis that adopts a similar approach: Patel 2020.

The book also connects to another important trend in the historiography of European integration, although in a more indirect manner. In several publications, Kiran Patel and Wolfram Kaiser have attempted to 'provincialise' European integration. First, they have argued that the EC was but one example among others of international cooperation after 1945 and only gained a more central status in the 1980s. Second, they have pointed out that European integration did not constitute a clear break with the interwar period, as typically claimed both by the European institutions and historians of European integration.[66] With regard to the history of European law, Patel has argued along similar lines by emphasising that European law did not originally differ significantly from international law; it was instead the self-fashioned constitutional claim that over time would help differentiate the EC from other international organisations.[67] The attempts to de-essentialise the history of European integration and integrate it within the broader historiographies of twentieth-century Europe and international history raises an important and fruitful agenda.

To fulfil its promise, however, it requires a solid empirical understanding of the multiple dimensions of European integration that are connected to the broader international context as well as the interwar period. In a new and relatively unexplored part of European integration history such as European law, this book offers for a first, solid archive-based empirical analysis by prioritising an internal European perspective that allows for an in-depth focus on both the European institutions and transnational European law academia, as well as a handful of crucial national histories. Nevertheless, there are without doubt several interesting roads that future researchers can take when connecting the constitutional battle over European law explored in this book to a broader international and temporal perspective. These range from studies of federalisation in a comparative perspective, comparing European integration to the United States of the nineteenth century and the German Zollverein, the links between European law and international law and finally the comparison between the legal dimensions of the EC and other international organisations.[68] This book offers a solid empirical starting point for such future exercises.

The inspiration from the institutional and transnational trends in European integration historiography is also reflected in the way we have approached the history of European law. The methodology employed in this book comes from political history. The aim is to offer an empirically rich and well contextualised history of European law, a history that focuses on the actual social practice that shaped European law and how it connected to the broader political and institutional history of European integration. To do this, we have systematically worked our way through all the relevant archives we could find, ranging from the archives from the European institutions to

66 Patel 2013b; Patel 2020; Kaiser and Patel 2018.

67 Patel 2013b, 665.

68 See for example three excellent social science and legal contributions: Egan 2015; Larsen 2021; Larsen 2022. We still lack good comparative historical work unfortunately.

national archives in more than ten countries and more than fifty private archives, to identify primary sources. This archival methodology stands in sharp contrast with the political scientists and sociologists, cited above, who have used one or two archives in their research. Using only a few archives created a serious methodological problem because all archives have a bias created by the institutions or persons that collected and curated the collection. Archives thus reflect the production of knowledge within an institution at the time and arguably constitutes a discursive sediment of power.[69] However, by systematically exploring all archives deemed relevant to a particular historical problematique, it is possible to introduce different perspectives on the topic at hand which allow the researcher to rigorously check the validity and reliability of their empirical analysis. An effort to explore relevant archival documentation is particularly important to the writing of legal history. The production of European law typically takes place in a black box, in closed meetings of courts and other institutions, administrative processes or networks. This black box is not accessible through public sources because the authority of law is partly based on the claim that law and politics constitute separate spheres, a claim that necessitates an element of cover-up of the social roots of law.[70] Only by identifying the paper trail of such meetings, networks and processes, can we enter the black box where law is produced. What we lay bare in this book, consequently, is how the social practice that produced European law was not only shaped by legal doctrines and arguments, but also by personal motives, ideology, culture, institutional and political interests.

The methodology outlined here differs from most classical scholarship of the history of international law as well as the new intellectual history of international law that has been pursued by legal scholars over the last two decades. Classical histories of international law have typically focused relatively narrowly on doctrinal history and been based on public sources and written law.[71] Beginning in the 1990s, a new school of intellectual history of international law, inspired by Quinton Skinner's Cambridge School of intellectual history, emerged around the former Finnish diplomat and eminent legal scholar Martti Koskenniemi and the *Journal of the History of International Law*.[72] This new intellectual history has revolutionised our understanding of the doctrinal and intellectual development of international law from 1870 onwards. However, most of its contributions are generally not based on systematic archival research.[73] Instead, over the last decade, and in parallel with our

69 Schwartz and Cook 2002.

70 Rasmussen 2010b.

71 For example, Nussbaum 1947. See also the classical work by Wilhelm Grewe that connected the key doctrines to the wider geopolitical context: Grewe 2013.

72 Two key works among numerous pathbreaking contributions: Koskenniemi 2001; Anghie 2007. For a general overview of the field with a certain focus on the French language literature consult: Guieu and Kévonian 2012.

73 The difference between the methodology of legal scholars and historians have sparked a fierce debate. For an analysis of this debate from the perspective of the approach adopted in this book: Rasmussen 2022.

work on the history of European law, mainstream historians have begun to change the state of the art of the legal history of international law, placing it within its broader societal context and doing so on basis of systematic archival work.[74] In this way, accidentally, our approach to the history of European law over the last decade, borrowed from political history, now appears to be at the very cutting edge of the broader field of legal history of international law.

Finally, a word on the history of European law as a new field of legal history. It is no accident that the discipline of European law has not yet developed a proper legal history taught at European and international universities. First, European law is a relatively young academic discipline and only consolidated in most member states from the 1990s onwards. At the same time, many legal historians worked, as mentioned above, on much older legal history until the 1990s, and those who did work on the history of international law generally had little interest in the variant that developed as part of the process of European integration from the 1950s onwards. Second, and equally important, the academic field of European law has always been deeply politicised due to its origins and continued proximity to those political European institutions. As a result, there has perhaps been a certain reluctance among some legal scholars to dig deep into the history of European law to avoid exposing the role of the academic discipline in promoting the constitutional practice of European law.[75] Recently this trend has been reversed with a new interest of legal scholars in the history of European law and in collaborating with historians and social scientists in order to explore it. The successful *EU Law Stories* published in 2017 spearheaded this new trend, but other recent publications have further contributed to a what now looks like a new wave of new legal and social scholarship interested in history.[76] We hope this book can further stimulate the interest of lawyers and social scientists in the legal history of European law by offering a general historical synthesis of the development of European law from 1950 to 1993 and new in-depth archive-based case studies of key actors and member states.

TOWARDS A NEW HISTORICAL INTERPRETATION OF THE HISTORY OF EUROPEAN LAW, 1950 TO 1993

The historical interpretation offered by this book is revisionist and presents a genuinely new understanding of the history of European law from 1950 to 1993. Let us conclude this introduction by presenting this new interpretation while

74 See for example: Snyder 2011; Jensen 2016; Priemel 2016; Payk 2018; Abbenhuis 2019.

75 Rasmussen 2021b.

76 Nicola and Davies 2017. It is greatly encouraging to see new publications from Fernanda Nicola, Amedeo Arena, William Phelan and Tomasso Pavone and Robert Schütze who have taken an interest in the history of European law and explore it brilliantly with a mixture of legal, social science and historical methodologies. See for example: Schütze 2018; Phelan 2019; Arena 2019; Pavone 2022; Gallo et al. 2024.

placing the contribution of each chapter within its broader framework.[77] First, however, we must carefully consider the approach employed to interpret the history of European law. We contend that by interpreting the history of European law as a successful process of constitutionalisation, or as in the case of Schorkopf as a constitutional history, researchers inadvertently tend to prioritise the perspective of the political forces that promoted European constitutionalism. A constitutional approach and terminology thus impose conceptual limitations on our understanding of the battle over the institutional and legal nature of the EC/EU.[78] To avoid this, we approach the history of European law as a unique historical process that is best analysed as open-ended or *sui generis*. Here the first task of the historian is to empirically describe and analyse the political and legal institutions and actors involved in battling over the nature of European law and what kind of broader societal processes shaped the development of European law, without taking our starting point from a specific theoretical framework that predetermine the analysis.

What our empirical research demonstrates is that a 'constitutional practice' developed in the field of European law from the early 1960s onwards, first as a breakthrough for a constitutional interpretation of the Treaties of Rome and European law, and later as an accompanying legitimating constitutional discourse performed primarily by the supranational institutions and European law academia. Instead of conflating this phenomenon with the overall development of European law, we will throughout the book use the term 'constitutional practice' to describe the concrete efforts of the institutions and actors that promote European constitutionalism.[79]

The term 'constitutional' is chosen despite its ambiguous meaning in different national legal traditions because the historical phenomenon, we explore, was associated with the political ideology of European federalism, based on a constitutional foundation, which emerged in Europe from the 1940s onwards. As the prospect and popularity of European federalism began to fade in the mid-1950s, after the defeat of the European Defence Community and the European Political Community, the potential constitutionality of the European law produced by the European Coal and Steel Community (ECSC) was instead described by legal scholars and practitioners with a different terminology such as 'supranational' (early 1950s), 'autonomous' (from the last half of 1950s onwards) and finally in the context of the EC 'new legal order' (1963–1964 onwards).[80] We do not claim that these alternating terms were completely identical with the original term 'constitutional' in all legal implications, nor for that sake that lawyers using these terms were always die-hard federalists. However, the new

77 The following is based on and further develops the interpretation launched in several recent publications: Rasmussen and Martinsen 2019; Rasmussen 2019; Rasmussen 2021a.

78 This would also be the case if we approached the European construction from the perspective of a classical international organisation or, as Peter Lindseth did as a mutation of the administrative state of the member states. See Lindseth 2010.

79 The concept of constitutional practice was first launched as a key element in Davies and Rasmussen 2012 and was further developed in Rasmussen and Martinsen 2019.

80 Boerger and Rasmussen 2014.

terminology did reflect a continued wish of the actors using them to position European law closer to state law than international law and thus lay the foundation for a future reform of the EC that would increase its political autonomy from the member states. In the 1980s, the term 'constitutional' to describe the nature of European law was finally reintroduced by a strand of legal academia. This old term was readily adopted by the supranational institutions, including the ECJ and European law academia. To conclude, we use 'constitutional' to characterise the legal practice we have identified because it most precisely clarifies the ideological links to European federalism that the alternative terminology was meant to obscure.

The term practice is chosen to describe the policies and actions of institutional and individual actors. We argue that the constitutional practice had at least two major elements. The first was the constitutional interpretation introduced and promoted by the ECJ (and the two other supranational institutions) from 1963 onwards and which the court gradually used through its case law to develop a proto-federal European legal order. The second element consisted of a legitimating constitutional discourse from part of European law academia and among the supranational institutions. These two elements evolved over time but merged together in the last half of the 1980s into a genuine European constitutionalism that the member states during the Maastricht Treaty negotiations had the option to based the European Union on.

The historical interpretation comes in two intertwined parts that is reflected in the composition of the book. The first part of the book argues that a constitutional practice developed in European law from the early 1960s onwards promoted by an alliance of the three supranational institutions, the court, commission and parliament and the emerging field of European law academia. In the Chapters 1, 2 and 3, we trace how the supranational institutions produced a breakthrough for a constitutional interpretation of European law with the judgments of *Van Gend en Loos* and *Costa v ENEL* in 1963 and 1964 respectively.[81] The motives of the key actors involved in the three institutions were an ambition to promote European federalism while simultaneously empowering the supranational institutions vis-à-vis the member states. Although the Empty Chair Crisis and the Luxembourg Compromise fatally weakened the Hallstein Commission in 1965–1966, the constitutional interpretation of European law was not rolled back by national governments. In fact, it grew over time into a broader constitutional practice. With the consolidation of a majority inside the court favouring a constitutional interpretation from 1967 onwards, as shown in Chapter 1, the ECJ continued to build a proto-federal constitutional order through its case law in the 1970s and 1980s. The constitutional interpretation of European law was backed and legitimised both by the Commission and the EP, but also from part of European law academia, as

81 26/62 *Van Gend en Loos v Nederlandse Administratie der Belastingen*, 1963, ECLI:EU:C:1963:1 and 6/64 *Costa v ENEL*, 1964, ECLI:EU:C:1964:66. For the most in depth studies of the two judgments consult Rasmussen 2014 and Arena 2019.

demonstrated in detail in Chapters 2, 3 and 4. However, a full constitutional discourse to legitimise the actions of the supranational institutions only came into being from the late 1970s onwards, as demonstrated in Chapter 4, when European law academia abandoned its formalist approach to European law and adopted a constitutional understanding of the European legal order. By the late 1980s, a constitutional practice was thus fully developed by the supranational institutions and European law academia and potentially laid the constitutional foundation for a move towards a federal EU during the Maastricht Treaty negotiations.

However, in contrast to the mainstream thesis on how European law developed, the member states did not readily acquiesce to the constitutional practice because they held a legislative veto right from 1966 onwards, as argued by Weiler. As Chapter 5 demonstrates, the real reason the constitutional practice was allowed to develop relatively unchecked was that the member states split over the question. This split had two consequences. On the one hand, national governments could not agree to reign in the ECJ despite the strong opposition to the constitutional interpretation of European law in several member states. France was for example ready several times to clip the wings of the court to stop the further development of a constitutional practice, but the smaller states including the Netherlands, Luxembourg, Belgium and Denmark defended the court. On the other hand, there was no consensus among national governments to codify the constitutional doctrines of the ECJ. The constitutional practice thus did not obtain the formal acceptance from the member states.[82] Chapter 5 thus demonstrates that the scepticism of several member states towards the constitutional practice was a long-term phenomenon stretching from the legal revolution in 1963–1964 to the negotiations of the Maastricht Treaty.

This is further confirmed by Chapters 6, 7, 8 and 9 that give a solid impression of how the constitutional practice was received at member state level. The book includes studies of four member states: France, West Germany, the Netherlands and Denmark. The four case studies are to some extent representative of the broader circle of member states that went from six original states: France, West Germany, Italy, the Netherlands, Belgium and Luxembourg to nine with the first enlargement in 1973, adding Britain, Denmark and Ireland, and finally to twelve when Greece (1981) and Spain and Portugal (1987) also joined. We include the two most important large states, France and West Germany, the most important country from the Benelux group, the Netherlands, and one of the newcomers from the first enlargement,

82 The Commission did attempt to push the member states towards indirectly embracing the case law including the key revolutionary doctrines of the ECJ through the development of the concept of the *acquis communautaire* – which included all EC decisions, rules and ECJ case law – in enlargement negotiations of the EC as a precondition for membership. In the preliminary accession opinion of the Commission in 1972 (a mandatory legal text for the signature of the accession treaty), the primacy of European law was explicitly mentioned and eventually ratified not only by the three new member states Britain, Denmark and Ireland but also by new member states in subsequent enlargement rounds. Perillo 2024, 95.

Denmark. At the same time, this book only constitutes a first attempt to the write the general history of how member states received European law.[83] Member states such as Italy, Belgian, Britain and Spain all play major roles in how European law developed and we urgently need more historical research at member state level.[84]

As the battle over the constitutional practice of European law played out at the European level, the member state institutions, ranging from governments and administrations to national courts and societal actors, all reacted in diverse ways to the development of the European legal order in the 1960s and 1970s. This was partly because the impact of European law only began to be seriously felt in the member states from the late 1970s onwards. Whereas national governments split in the Council of Ministers over the virtues of the constitutional interpretation of the ECJ from the late 1960s onwards, the reactions of national administrations and courts in most member states were generally sceptical of what was considered an unwarranted encroachment on member state prerogatives. National administrations in the member states typically attempted, very often successfully, to contain the impact of ECJ judgments and doctrines in order to mediate the consequences of European legislation to avoid interference in domestic politics. This pattern also includes otherwise pro-European member states such as the Netherlands and West Germany. Courts of the member states reacted in more complex configurations.

A general trend was that most national courts ignored European law either because of a lack of basic knowledge or because they considered it just another kind of international law that was best handled by the executive or legislative power. Across the member states national courts thus remained sceptical vis-à-vis the constitutional practice of the ECJ. The most important exceptions to this trend came from Belgium and the Netherlands (Chapter 8) where national courts relatively quickly began to cooperate with the ECJ and generally supported its constitutional case law. In West Germany (Chapter 6) and Italy, courts were also quick to engage, however, here the respective Constitutional Courts played a major role in launching a highly critical dialogue with the ECJ over the status of basic rights in European law and did not fully accept the constitutional interpretation of the ECJ. With the general passive approach of national courts to engage with European law, the Euro-lawyers explored by Pavone[85] thus played a significant role in the 1960s and 1970s producing the cases on basis of which the ECJ could further develop and refine its constitutional doctrines, as also demonstrated by Chapter 7. The book finally demonstrates that the rapid development of the European legal order by the ECJ in the 1970s often caused controversy in the

83 The four cases included are the member states that have been studied in-depth by members of the team of historians working on the history of European law. Behind each case studies lie a major research efforts leading in three cases to doctoral theses: Bernier 2017; Davies 2012b; Pedersen 2016 and finally with regard to Karin van Leeuwen the publication of two archive-based articles: van Leeuwen 2012; van Leeuwen 2018.

84 A new study of Italy is an encouraging sign. Gallo et al 2024.

85 Pavone 2022.

member states and led to several important attacks by national courts on the ECJ, most famously the *Solange* judgment by the West German Constitutional Court (Bundesverfassungsgericht, BVerfG) in 1974 and the *Cohn Bendit* judgment by the French Council of State (Conseil d'État) in 1979. Here Chapters 6 and 7 provide new rich stories of these key rebellions against the constitutional practice in Germany and France. All in all, member state receptions were more reluctant and sceptical than hitherto understood by the state of the art. However, at the same time the process was co-constitutive. National courts through their interaction with the ECJ, even if at time negative, contributed indirectly to the building of the European legal order. The varied national responses to the constitutional practice meant that the European legal order eventually became a patchwork, whose parameters continue to be part of the European judicial dialogue to this very day.[86]

Finally, the book argues that a complex and awkward stalemate developed in European law in the 1980s and early 1990s. On the one hand, the member states had to come to terms with the necessity of cooperating more loyally with the ECJ in the existing European legal order because from 1986 onwards the latter would become the legal basis of the Single Market. The analysis of the member states in Chapters 5, 6, 7, 8 and 9 offer unmistakable evidence of this shift in the priorities of the member states. The political and economic dynamics of the Single Market Project meant that it quickly became a central part of the European policies of all the member states. Consequently, there was now no way that national courts and administrations could continue to ignore the key features of the European legal order, including participation in the system of preliminary references, the doctrine of primacy and accepting the judgments of the Luxembourg court. Denmark for example, as demonstrated in Chapter 9, had to give up its strategy of ignoring or containing European law administratively in the late 1980s when two spectacular cases on respectively the 'Buy Danish clause' in the building of the bridge over the Great Belt and the AMBI labour market contribution of Danish employees blew up in the faces of Danish policy makers. Denmark was by no means alone in realising that European law could now not easily be ignored. This acceptance by the member states to contribute loyally to the functioning in the legal order built by the ECJ was expressed in the reference to the *acquis communautaire* in the Maastricht Treaty.[87] The member states thus finally accepted to base the new European Union on the concept of the acquis developed by the Commission.

On the other hand, this shift in attitudes towards European law did not mean that the member states accepted the constitutional claim underlying the case law of the ECJ or European constitutionalism as the core legitimating principle underlying

86 For an example of this in the fields of human rights and the direct effect of European law consult respectively: Davies 2012a; Rasmussen 2017.

87 Treaty of Maastricht, Article B, 5th indent.

the new European Union.[88] It was true that new legal reality prompted important new decision by three Supreme or Constitutional Courts from the largest member states, the Italian Constitutional Court (Corte Costituzionale) (1989), the Conseil d'État (1989) and the BVerfG (1993) that underlined their de facto acceptance of the way the European legal order functioned, including the need to participate in the preliminary reference system and respect the doctrine of primacy. However, the same decisions also rejected the constitutional interpretation of European law promoted by the ECJ. Instead, the three supreme courts defined the nature of European law from their own national vantage point. The EC/EU only existed, they argued, because the member states had delegated precisely defined competences to common institutions at European level. This implied that European law did not have constitutional autonomy and legitimacy, as claimed by the ECJ.[89] The rejection of European constitutionalism by the supreme courts of three of the most important member states was mirrored in the negotiations of the Maastricht Treaty in 1990–1991. Here the majority of national governments decided to place the European Council as the central institution in the new Union. National governments had since the establishment of the European Council in 1974 used the institution to dominate the political agenda of the EC. Collectively, national executives had thus strengthened their grip over the development of the EC. The new EU further consolidated and formalised the dominance of the intergovernmental pillar in the process of European integration. A majority of national governments rejected the plans of the Jacques Delors Commission to base the new European Union on a single (constitutional) treaty as a first step towards a federal Europe.[90] Instead, the Maastricht Treaty was organised in three pillars, two of which were based on intergovernmental principles of cooperation. The pillars have since been dissolved since the Lisbon Treaty (2008), however, the tendency of the European Council to occasionally opt for intergovernmental solutions continues. European constitutionalism was thus not adopted as the legitimating principle of the new European Union and the constitutional practice that had developed in European law did not obtain the ultimate vindication from national governments.

The defeat of European constitutionalism in the early 1990s was a central event in the making of the new EU, which as a result not only became dominated by the intergovernmental pillar but also did not take the shape of a full rule of law Union. Despite this defeat the battle over the potential constitutional nature of the EU did

88 In contrast to Perillo 2024, 95–96, this book argues that politically but also legally there is a crucial difference between the acceptance of the *acquis communautaire* and a decision to base the European Union on European constitutionalism as key legitimating principle.

89 Corte Costituzionale, *Fragd v Amministrazione delle Finanze*, judgment no. 232 of 13 April 1989; Conseil d'État (Assemblée), 20 October 1989, *Nicolo*, n° 108243, published in *Recueil Lebon* 190, 1990 and BVerfGE 89, 155, 12.10.1993, *Maastricht*, 2 BvR 2134, 2159/92. For a general treatment of these judgments consult: de Witte 1998. The Danish Supreme Court (Højesteret) followed the other three courts on 6 April 1998 with a similar judgment. 361/1997 Højesteret, 6 April 1998, Treaty of Maastricht.

90 Ludlow 2013; Loth 2013.

not end in 1991. It has continued these last more than thirty years and remains a fundamental fault line in the present-day EU. Over the last three decades the CJEU, supported by the supranational institutions and European law academia, have continued to develop and promote the constitutional features of the European legal order, while the gravity of political power still remains in a European Council that is not fully bound by the European rule of law. This duality continues to create tensions and ambiguity in an ever more powerful and influential Union. This book has explained why this situation first came into being. It will now be up to a new team of historians to explore the period since 1993 and tell us why the stalemate that developed from 1986 to 1993 has still not been resolved.

We hope this book will be read not only by lawyers and historians, but also social scientists. Although the chapters are in many respects pieces of legal history, the interpretation they collectively offer of the development of European law in what we might call its formative period from 1950 to 1993, and the new empirical insights they present, are certainly an important contribution to the broader field of law and politics studies today. We finally have a new interpretation of the history of European law in this period, built on solid empirical work, which can replace the old mainstream interpretation that has informed so much legal and social science scholarship over the last forty years.

One last remark on the structure of the book is warranted. The chapters of the book occasionally deals with the same seminal court cases or major developments in the history of the European law although analysed from different angles. We have prioritised that it should be possible for a reader to fully understand the analysis of each chapter on its own without having to read the entire book from start to finish. This means, however, that repetitions cannot be avoided and that some events will figure across several of the chapters of the book.

PART I

Supranational Institutions and Transnational Actors and the Battle over the Constitutional Practice of European Law

1

Inside the European Court of Justice

A Biographical Approach

Vera Fritz

> [I]t is hard to persuade me that the Community's constitution exists wholly apart from the human beings that man its constitutional court. . . . We ought not spend years studying the constitutional law of the European Community before starting the study of its constitutional lawmakers.
>
> Shapiro, Martin, 1979. 'Comparative Law and Comparative Politics'. *Southern California Law Review* 53: 540.

The history of the constitutional practice in European law could not be told without analysing the role played by the European Court of Justice (ECJ).[1] The ECJ's contribution to the development of a constitutional European legal order has been examined in countless publications by legal scholars and social scientists, who have tried to grasp how it consistently pursued its pro-integration path without provoking a rebellion by the member states.[2] In the historiography of European integration, however, the ECJ was absent for many decades. The main reason for this was the Court's long-standing unwillingness to give researchers access to its archives. Despite the Commission's decision of 1983[3] to give the public access to documents produced by the European Coal and Steel Community's (ECSC) institutions beyond the expiry period of thirty years, it was only in 2017 that the Court finally opened the judicial archive (which remains seriously censored with no access to the deliberations of the Court), followed in 2021 by the opening of the administrative archive. Both are placed at the Historical Archives of the European Union in Florence.

When the research for this chapter was conducted, the archive of the Court had not yet opened. To this author the challenge was consequently how to study the ECJ

1 The research presented in this chapter was funded by Luxembourg's National Research Fund (FNR). I am also grateful to Stefan Vogenauer, Will Phelan, Anthony Blackwell and the members of the research group 'Towards a New History of European Law', for their helpful feedback on presentations of this chapter.

2 For overviews of this literature see Conant 2007; Pollack 2013; Rasmussen 2013.

3 Decision No. 359/83/ECSC of the Commission, 8 February 1983, regarding the opening to the public of the Historical Archives of the European Coal and Steel Community.

without access to its archive. Interestingly the solution adopted would provide a new rich way of analysing the Court which now constitutes the groundwork for future work on the ECJ using the information offered by the archive.[4] As the citation that began this chapter suggested, a first solution is to focus on the judges that constituted the Court. Quite surprisingly, given their importance in the European integration project, the judges had received little attention from scholars. The vast literature produced on the European jurisdiction has essentially approached the ECJ for what it is: a *court* – an institution that delivers judgments. Only rarely have authors focused on the judges, even in the cases where the Court pronounced its most ground-breaking judgments.[5] This lack of research can, to a certain extent, be explained. Unlike the judges of the International Court of Justice and those of the European Court of Human Rights, the members of the ECJ cannot publicly express 'dissenting opinions'. They speak with only one voice and take the oath to preserve the secrecy of their deliberations, even after they leave the Court. Studying the judges can hence be perceived as being of little help in trying to find out more about how the ECJ's case law was crafted.

This chapter demonstrates that despite the secrecy of the ECJ's decision-making process, grasping *who* its judges were actually tells us much more than we could have anticipated about the Court's role in the establishment of the constitutional practice of European law.[6] For example, knowing with what professional experience and ideological background the judges came to the ECJ allows for assessment of its internal dynamics and helps in gaining a better understanding of *why* they opted for constitutional interpretations of the European treaties. It also sheds light on their relationship with national decision makers, which in turn provides explanations on why they were selected for their positions by their respective governments, and what the latter expected from them.

Relying on the results of in-depth biographical research on the first three generations of judges (from the early 1950s until mid-1970s), this chapter argues that the composition of the Court played a key role in the establishment and development of a constitutional interpretation of European law in the 1960s and 1970s.[7] After offering a brief overview of the professional and legal profiles which were represented at the Court during this foundational period, it explains why they were selected by the member states, and demonstrates how the appointment process

4 See Fritz 2018 for the full analysis on which this chapter is based.

5 Before the year 2000, only three researchers had investigated the identity of the judges: Feld 1963; Condorelli-Braun 1972; Kenney 1998. In his seminal work of 1986, Hjalte Rasmussen also presents the backgrounds of the first judges. However, his book does not delve into the details of their professional trajectories. See Rasmussen 1986. For more recent work, see Cohen 2013b; Vauchez 2015, Gallo et al. 2024. For information on the President of the ECJ Robert Lecourt, see Phelan 2019. On Advocate General Maurice Lagrange see Mangenot 2023.

6 For further reflections on the interest of judicial biographies in the study of the ECJ, see Phelan 2024.

7 This biographical research was carried out in a wide range of private archives as well as state and European archives.

created a pro-federalist bench of judges. It then analyses the dynamics inside the ECJ, and lays bare how initial divisions among the judges regarding the constitutional practice gave way at the end of the 1960s to a large consensus on the need for teleological interpretations of the European treaties, which explains why the Court's case law started to become more aggressive in the early 1970s. Finally, it shows that the nature of the selection processes of judges in the member states provided the ECJ with a political network which was often crucial in its judicial activity and the pursuit of its institutional interests. In this manner, the chapter demonstrates that the composition of the Court had a direct impact on its case law and that the identity, backgrounds and networks of the judges played a key role in the battle over the constitutional practice.

PROFESSIONAL AND LEGAL PROFILES OF THE FIRST MEMBERS OF THE EUROPEAN COURT OF JUSTICE

The ECJ came into being in December 1952, with the formal name of the Court of Justice of the ECSC.[8] In 1958, after the entry into force of the Treaties of Rome, the institution changed name to the Court of Justice of the European Communities (ECJ). Until the first European enlargement in 1973, it was composed of seven judges.[9] Three different 'generations' of judges can be identified: the generation of the ECSC pioneers that composed the Court from 1952 to 1958; the one which pronounced the 'revolutionary' judgments of 1963 and 1964 as the first members of the ECJ, under the leadership of a new and substantially younger president (1958–1964) and, finally, the one which pushed the constitutional interpretation of European law further (1964/1967–mid-1970s).[10] Since at no point in its history has the ECJ faced a complete renewal of its members, such a periodisation can obviously be debated. However, as will be demonstrated hereafter, the division into three periods constitutes a useful tool for analysing the dynamics inside the Court.

Virtually no magistrate in the classical sense (i.e., having evolved professionally only in the judiciary) was appointed in 1952. While three of the first judges had reached the highest jurisdictions of their country – Massimo Pilotti was attorney general of the Italian Corte di Cassazione from 1944 to 1948, Otto Riese became President of Chamber at the German Bundesgerichtshof in 1951 and Charles-Léon Hammes was a member of Luxembourg's Cour supérieure de justice from 1945 to 1952 – they also had considerable experience as international legal experts. Pilotti had represented Italy at numerous international conferences after the First World War and had worked as Deputy Secretary-General at the General Secretariat of the

8 For evident reasons of space, it is impossible to provide in-depth biographical portraits in this short chapter. For detailed biographies on the first members of the ECJ consult Fritz 2018.

9 As members of the Court counted moreover two advocates general.

10 The fact that key changes took place in the composition of the ECJ in 1967 and that a pro-federalist generation of judges took over that year has already been stressed by Davies and Rasmussen 2014.

League of Nations from 1932 to 1937. Riese, who was a professor of international law before he joined the Bundesgerichtshof, could count on thirty years' experience as a legal expert in air, maritime and international sales law for the German Ministry of Justice. Hammes worked for many years as a legal counsel for the Ministry of Justice of Luxembourg.

The Dutch Adrianus Van Kleffens spent most of his career as a legal expert in the Dutch Ministry of Economics, even though he was qualified to work in the judiciary. Like many of his colleagues, he had diplomatic experience as a legal expert in international negotiations, including those of the Benelux Treaty (1949–1950). The three other pioneer judges had never worked in the judiciary. Belgian Louis Delvaux was a lawyer who spent most of his career in politics (including as the Minister of Agriculture in 1945). Jacques Rueff was an economist of international reputation who had worked as a high official for the French state. In 1945, he led French negotiations on reparations to be paid by Germany. He had subsequently taken on the role of President of the Interallied Agency of Reparations (1950–1952). Petrus Serrarens was a Dutch member of parliament and leader of the International Confederation of Christian Trade Unions (CISC) for more than thirty years (1920–1952). He had represented his country at numerous international conferences, including conferences organised by the International Labour Organization. He had also participated in the negotiations leading to the establishment of the Council of Europe. Neither Serrarens nor Rueff were trained in law. The presence of two non-jurists at the Court of Justice of the ECSC prompted the drafting committee of the Treaties of Rome to sharpen up the conditions of access to European judicial posts.[11] While the Treaty of Paris only required the judges to offer all guarantees of independence and competence, candidates now had to fulfil the conditions required for the holding of the highest judicial office in their respective countries or be jurists of recognised competence (Article 167 of the EEC Treaty, Article 139 of the Euratom Treaty).[12] Interestingly, the governments of the member states showed during the 1960s a clear preference for the latter condition, and mostly appointed legal experts who had worked in the ministries rather than professional judges.[13]

After Pilotti's departure from Luxembourg in 1958, and Riese's resignation in early 1963, the second generation of members of the ECJ included even fewer professional judges than the ECSC group. Most of the selected candidates of the 1960s were either senior civil servants from Ministries of Foreign Affairs and Justice in particular or academics who worked as legal experts for their respective

[11] According to the member of the drafting committee, and future judge at the ECJ, Pierre Pescatore, the decision to put an end to the ECSC appointment mechanism which allowed the recruitment of judges without a law degree represented one of the first points on which the committee agreed. Pescatore 1982, 157.

[12] Despite these stricter conditions, Jacques Rueff was reappointed as Judge by the French government of 1958. Only Petrus Serrarens left the Court.

[13] The question of whether there were reasons for this appointment strategy will be debated later in this chapter.

governments. The new, young, Dutch judge André Donner (who replaced Van Kleffens and became the first President of the Court of the European Communities in 1958) was a professor of public law who had worked as a member of different Dutch legal committees charged with proposing reforms of the constitution in the first part of the 1950s. Nicola Catalano, the Italian judge who entered the ECJ in 1958, was a lawyer and law professor who was first recruited by the Italian Ministry of Foreign Affairs in 1948. After he spent four years at the Legal Service of the High Authority of the ECSC, the Italian government sent him to the negotiations of the Treaties of Rome. Stricto sensu, Catalano was, despite his nomination in 1958, not a member of the 'revolutionary' Court since he was replaced in 1962 by Alberto Trabucchi, who spent his entire career in academia as a highly regarded professor of private law. The second Italian judge who was appointed in 1958, Rino Rossi, had known a career as a magistrate, reaching the position of President of Chamber at the Corte di Cassazione. However, for many years he also worked under the authority of the Ministry of Foreign Affairs as a magistrate on the island of Rhodes, the administrative centre of the Aegean islands, which were under Italian control from 1912 to 1943.

The two German judges who worked at the ECJ during the first half of the 1960s were both partially members of the revolutionary bench of judges. Riese left the Court in the immediate aftermath of the *Van Gend en Loos* judgment[14] and was replaced by Walter Strauss, an official from the German Ministry of Justice who spent his entire career as a legal expert in the German public administration. Riese was on the panel of *Van Gend en Loos* judges, Strauss participated in the decision-making process of the famous *Costa v ENEL* ruling.[15] Finally, the revolutionary generation counted among its judges the French Robert Lecourt. Appointed in 1962 to replace Rueff, Lecourt was a lawyer, but spent most of his career in politics as a member of the Christian-democratic Mouvement Républicain Populaire. He had been Minister of Justice in France on several occasions.

The years 1964 to 1967 constitute a period of transition between the second and the third generation of judges. In October 1964, Judge Rossi left Luxembourg. Since Riese had already resigned from his judge position a year before, only five of the seven men who delivered *Van Gend en Loos* were still on the bench: Trabucchi, Lecourt, Donner, Hammes and Delvaux. The latter two left the Court in 1967. Following their departure, the institution was composed of a majority of new judges who had not experienced the 1963 and 1964 judgments from the inside. We can here speak of a 'third generation'. Most of those who arrived in Luxembourg after the 'founding' judgments had career paths like their predecessors. The Italian judge Riccardo Monaco (appointed in 1964) and the Luxembourgish Pierre Pescatore (appointed in 1967) had long careers as officials in the Ministries of Foreign Affairs of

14 26/62 *Van Gend en Loos v Nederlandse Administratie der Belastingen*, 1963, ECLI:EU:C:1963:1

15 6/64 *Costa v ENEL*, 1964, ECLI:EU:C:1964:66.

their respective home states. They have represented their governments as legal experts in international conferences, and as lawyers in several international court cases.

The second judge who was appointed in 1967, the Belgian Josse Mertens de Wilmars, had a career path very much like that of his predecessor Delvaux and colleague Lecourt. He was a lawyer who spent more than twenty years in politics, as a member of the Christian-democratic party Christelijke Volkspartij. It was only with the appointment of Hans Kutscher, who replaced Walter Strauss in 1970, that the European bench again included a judge who conducted most of his career in the judiciary. Kutscher had spent fifteen years at the West German Constitutional Court (Bundesverfassungsgericht, BVerfG). Prior to his appointment, he worked as a legal expert in the West German government.

The fact that the governments of the member states appointed for the Court of the European Communities fewer candidates that came from higher judicial positions than they had for the Court of the ECSC is striking. Between 1967 and 1970, only one of the seven members of the European bench had occupied a senior magistrate position prior to being appointed on the European level.[16] This observation echoes questions which have surrounded the selection process of the European judges since the very beginning of the European integration process: did national governments have a strategy in composing the ECJ? Did they deliberately appoint candidates who were known for their proximity with national administrations rather than senior high magistrates who spent most of their careers working independently from the member states? Did they try to control the Court via the appointment mechanism?

THE SELECTION PROCESS FOR THE MEMBERS OF THE COURT

According to the Treaties of Paris and Rome, the members of the ECJ were appointed for a term of six years by the member states of the communities acting in common agreement. In practice, however, each government was free to select its own candidate. During the first decades of the ECJ's existence, appointments by mutual agreement consisted of systematic endorsements of the choices made by the member states. This only changed in 2009, when for the first time an independent advisory panel gave its opinion on the suitability of candidates before governments made their appointments.[17] The biographical research carried out on the first members of the ECJ combined with archival material on the member states' nomination processes provide a detailed account of the rationale for the selection of the early members of the ECJ. The following section will present the three main findings of this research. They show that the generally pro-European governments of

[16] Riccardo Monaco – who had also spent twenty years in leading positions in the Italian Ministry of Foreign Affairs.

[17] As foreseen by Article 255 of the Treaty on the Functioning of the European Union. On this committee see: Dumbrovsky et al. 2014; Bobek 2015.

the six member states indirectly contributed through their selection procedures to nurture pro-integration dynamics inside the Court.

The first and most important result of the study of the first appointments at the ECJ is a methodological one. To draw conclusions with regard to the 'intentions' of the member states from the professional and legal profiles of the candidates chosen can lead to hasty and incorrect conclusions. The composition of the Court of Justice of the ECSC, for example, with its striking presence of judges with an economic background (above all the economist Rueff, who was not trained in law), can lead to thinking that the member states tried to minimise the judicial weight of the first Court or that they tried to form a sort of economic tribunal.[18] Archival evidence, however, shows that the governments at first wanted to nominate highly qualified legal experts when the Court of Justice of the ECSC was established in 1952. Italy, for example, had on its list of candidates next to the elected Pilotti, Tomaso Perassi, a law professor of international reputation, who could count substantial diplomatic experience amongst his qualities.[19] Belgium brought up the name of the most prestigious candidate that it could possibly find at the time for a judge position at the Court: Charles de Visscher, a renowned professor of international public law who had been a judge at the Permanent Court of Arbitration in The Hague, at the Permanent Court of International Justice and then at its successor, the International Court of Justice.[20] France turned first towards Pierre-Henri Teitgen, a senior French politician, prominent member of the French Resistance during the Second World War and professor of public law, as well as Paul Reuter, a professor of international law who had been Jean Monnet's first legal advisor during the negotiations of the Treaty of Paris.[21] The candidacy of Rueff only came up after several other qualified jurists refused to accept the position, and therefore cannot be interpreted as a deliberate choice by the governments to have an economist sit on the bench. Candidates who are selected for European institutions are not necessarily the first choice of their respective governments. Thus, we should be careful when ascribing intentions into their appointment.

Rueff's case is also relevant for the second result of the analysis of the selection process: not only professional and legal profiles mattered in the recruitment of the judges. Personal connections and political affiliations were also important and very often decisive.[22] The available historical documents indeed confirm an assumption

18 For example, Vauchez 2013, 76–77.

19 Dutch National Archives (NA-NL). 2.05.177, 18614. Legazione d'Italia nei Paesi Bassi, 21 July 1952. Perassi was in 1944 appointed Secretary-General of the contentious diplomatic affairs department in the Italian Ministry of Foreign Affairs.

20 National Archives of Belgium (NAB). Conseil de cabinet du 17 juillet 1952.

21 Archives of the German Ministry of Foreign Affairs (PAAA). B20-200, Bd. 54. Diplomatische Vertretung der Bundesrepublik Deutschland, Paris, 205/Tgb. No 3127, an das Auswärtige Amt, 27 August 1952. According to this German source, the French government tried with this nomination to 'get rid' of Teitgen, who was critical towards the government.

22 None of the six founding member states advertised the position at the ECJ between 1952 and 1972.

expressed as early as 1964, namely that the selection process of the members of the CJEU in the first decades of its existence was highly political.[23] Decisive personal connections were most of the time not visible in the official curriculum vitae of the candidates. One must take a closer look at the trajectory of each individual judge to lay bare the connections and identify the reasons that landed judges in Luxembourg. Largely unknown about Jacques Rueff, for example, is that he not only worked as an economist, but also had a brief stint of political activity. Like Antoine Pinay, the French prime minister at the time of his appointment, he was the co-founder and member of the steering committee of the political party Comité national des Républicains indépendants.[24] This personal connection with Pinay played into the selection of Jacques Rueff who recruited, in return, no other but Pinay's son, Pierre Pinay, as legal assistant (attaché) once he was in Luxembourg.[25]

As demonstrated first by Morten Rasmussen, the appointment of Lecourt (judge from 1962 to 1967 and then President of the court until 1976) was highly political as well.[26] After Lecourt left the French government led by Michel Debré in August 1961, he wanted to be appointed as the head of a national insurance company. This was however impossible because French legislation did not allow for the nomination of a former member of government to a state company within five years after the carrying out of political functions.[27] Prime Minister Debré consequently came up with other solutions: the triple presidency of three public companies/institutions namely the Comptoir de vente des charbons sarrois, the Conseil supérieur des alcools and the Mines de Bor or a judge position at the ECJ.[28] Lecourt opted for the latter. We do not know exactly what made Debré, a champion of Gaullism and national sovereignty, nominate an ardent federalist like Lecourt to become a European judge, but one answer is that he may have believed at the time that the ECJ was of little importance.

The former French Minister of Justice was not the only professional politician who arrived in Luxembourg because of a stagnating political career. The circumstances in which the Belgian Mertens de Wilmars was appointed in 1967 were similar. Mertens de Wilmars was a co-founder and long-time member of the Belgian Christian Democratic Party. Contrary to many other members of the party, however, he had never managed to get a position in the government and was not placed near the top of the party's election lists. He entered the Belgian Parliament three times as a supplementary delegate after the death or the resignation of the actual candidate. In the early 1960s, he gave up his political ambitions. Along with his interest in European law and integration, this disappointment about his

23 Feld 1963, 45.
24 Dard 2004, 46.
25 I would like to thank Morten Rasmussen for this information.
26 Rasmussen 2010b.
27 Archive of Michel Debré (AMD). 2 DE 11. Draft Letter from Michel Debré to Henri Dorey, December 1961.
28 AMD. 2 DE 11. Letter from Michel Debré to Robert Lecourt, 1 March 1962.

political career was one of the key reasons for his application for a judge position in 1967. For his party, this appointment was similar to the case of Lecourt – an opportunity to reward a loyal member with a prestigious position in public service.[29]

Despite the many appointments to the ECJ from the Ministries of Justice and Foreign Affairs during the 1960s, one should not automatically assume that they represented attempts by the member states to control the Court. Biographical research shows that Monaco (Director of the Legal Service of the Italian Ministry of Foreign Affairs before his appointment), Strauss (State Secretary at the German Ministry of Justice) and Pescatore (Secretary-General of Luxembourg's Ministry of Foreign Affairs), had all volunteered for a judge position.[30] These spontaneous applications of long-serving and trusted jurists were without doubt convenient for governments, as they could hope that individuals who had delivered quality work for their state in the past would not completely forget about national interests once they had become European judges. However, that does not mean that they were actively seeking to appoint high officials from ministries to control the Court, or curb and derail its constitutional interpretation. In fact, Monaco and Pescatore could be expected to become strong promoters of integration through law, as their application for open positions at the ECJ came from their interest in the European integration process, which both displayed not only as diplomats since their participation in the negotiations of the Treaties of Rome, but also as law scholars. Monaco, for example, co-founded the Rivista di diritto europeo in 1961. In 1963, Pescatore created an Institute of European Law at the University of Liège with Professor Fernand Dehousse. The case of Strauss's appointment was a bit different. After a long and brilliant career in the German Ministry of Justice, Strauss became frustrated with his position and aimed at giving his career a different orientation.[31] It is noteworthy that these candidates also had substantial personal and political affiliations: Strauss was a long-time member of the German Christian Democratic Union (CDU) and Pescatore was the brother-in-law of Luxembourg's Prime Minister at the time of his appointment.

The link between political affiliations and the selection process led to a certain vulnerability of the judges' mandates. After their six-year terms expired, new political leaders could decide to appoint 'their own' candidate. In 1958, when the newly appointed President of the Court Donner asked his government for a written guarantee that he would be reappointed after his term expired, he received the answer that such a document even if produced would have no legal value. The next government would be able to decide itself whether it wanted to reappoint him or

[29] Interview with Ivan Verougstraete (2013), former attaché of Josse Mertens de Wilmars from 1969 to 1972.

[30] Strauss and Pescatore had encountered competition in the race for the judge position but were ultimately chosen.

[31] Among others, because his propositions for legal reforms in West Germany encountered resistance.

not.[32] The most striking example of the vulnerability of the positions of the members of the Court was probably the replacement of the Italian judge Catalano, who was reappointed *pro forma* in 1961, with the instruction to resign shortly afterwards to make room for the brother of the Italian Minister of Finances, Trabucchi. Catalano resigned in March 1962 citing 'personal and family reasons'.[33]

The vulnerability of their positions led some members of the ECJ to engage into 're-(s)election campaigns' when their terms expired. When the Dutch judge Van Kleffens found out in 1958 that his government planned not to reappoint him in the new Court of Justice of the European Communities, he requested a meeting with the Secretary-General of the Dutch Ministry of Foreign Affairs to express his indignation about those rumours. He argued that in all the other member states it went without saying that all the members of the Court of Justice of the ECSC would be reappointed in the new Court.[34] The Dutch government still replaced him with another candidate. Advocates General of the Court faced the same methods of appointment as the judges and thus had equally vulnerable mandates. Karl Roemer, for example, was in a situation like Van Kleffens's in 1967 when he found out that the German government was considering replacing him with a younger candidate:[35] Ernst Féaux de la Croix, a high official from the Ministry of Finances. He reacted with a long letter to the German Ministry of Justice arguing that his age was not an argument against his reappointment.[36] He even went as far as suggesting to the German government to appoint him as a judge to the ECJ instead, and provided advice on how this solution could be made acceptable by the other member states.[37]

The third conclusion that can be drawn from the analysis of the judges' trajectories and documents stemming from national selection processes is that, quite surprisingly, the procedure was strikingly apolitical when it came to controlling the ECJ's pro-integration judicial activity. In other words, the candidates' views on European integration do not seem to have mattered all too much in their selection process. Not even one of the numerous sources gathered in the founding member states regarding the selection process of the first generation of judges refers to the candidates' ideas on

32 NA-NL. 2.05.118, 20025. Memorandum of E. H. van der Beugel, 23 May 1958.

33 Historical Archives of the European Union (HAEU). CM2/1962, 1183. Letter of resignation from Judge Nicola Catalano to the President of the Court André Donner, 30 November 1961.

34 NA-NL. 2.05.118, 20025. Memorandum no: 1458, Mr S. J. Baron van Tuyll van Serooskerken aan M, 10 January 1958.

35 Roemer was 68.

36 German Federal Archives (BArch). B 136, 8529. Letter from Karl Römer to Dr Werner Knieper, 20 July 1967.

37 As Italy had been allowed to appoint two judges since 1958, Germany could offer to trade that second position against the one of an advocate general. In order for France to accept that Italian-German deal, he suggested Germany support the election of Robert Lecourt as President of the Court. See BArch. B 136, 8529. Abteilung I, Ergebnisniederschrift, 19 April 1967 (Report of an encounter between Karl Roemer and German Secretary of State Rolf Otto Lahr).

European integration or the ECJ's constitutional case law. This indifference allowed for the appointment of highly pro-federalist judges in the late 1960s and early 1970s.

Equally important is that none of the consulted sources indicate that the national governments aimed at reorienting the ECJ's audacious jurisprudence via the selection process. At no point between the 1950s and the late 1970s did the member states individually or collectively attempt to compose a weak ECJ. The candidates should ideally be confirmed jurists with a previous international experience, that is, judges whose legitimacy could not be questioned.[38] To conclude it seems certain that, despite the ECJ's controversial case law, the member states never tried to control the Court via the selection process of the judges.

Political scientists have argued that the member states did not manage to control the Court via the appointment mechanism because the judges' délibéré was secret, making it impossible for governments to find out whether 'their' judge was a promoter of the constitutional interpretation inside the ECJ.[39] The biographical research shows that the notion that the national governments did not know the ideological tendencies of their judges is not correct. Many of the judges (Pescatore, Lecourt, Touffait, Kutscher and Mertens de Wilmars for example) made no secret of their ambitious views for the Court's role in the EC, both *before* and *during* their years as European judges.[40] Their governments cannot have ignored that they were the motors behind the ECJ's so-called 'activist' judgments. Yet none of them were sanctioned; they all left the Court of their own free will. Lecourt, who was reappointed in 1970, did not want his term renewed in 1976; Monaco (appointed in 1964 and reappointed in 1970) retired from office shortly before the end of his term and was replaced by another pro-integrationist judge, Francesco Capotorti;[41] Kutscher (appointed in 1970 and reappointed in 1976) resigned from office in 1980, at the age of sixty-nine; Mertens de Wilmars resigned in 1984 after seventeen years at the ECJ (age seventy-two); and Pescatore stayed until 1985 (eighteen years).

These appointments or reappointments of federalist-inclined candidates played a key role in the ECJ's capacity to uphold its constitutional interpretation of European law in the decade that followed the breakthrough of 1963/1964. They can be explained by two underlying factors. First, even if the constitutional case law of the ECJ was not always popular in the member states, or even to the extent that it was contained or resisted by various national actors, there generally existed in all the

38 The fact that the appointment mechanism was rather apolitical with regard to the member states' desire to compose a weak Court or control its pro-integration views does not mean that they did not worry about its judgments. Archival documents show that governments did have financial and economic concerns when it came to Court decisions.

39 See for example Alter 1998, 139; Pollack 1997, 117.

40 They expressed these views through publications and conference communications, which has led Will Phelan to argue that it should become a requirement to check on available writings of ECJ judges when engaging with European law. See Phelan 2024. One can add here that these judges were not at all strangers to the national political leaders, as they had spent years in national politics or in high positions in the Ministries of Foreign Affairs and Justice.

41 See Capotorti 1960.

member states an overarching consensus about the value of EC-membership.[42] This meant that the governments appointing the judges and advocates generals typically consisted of parties supporting European integration, and since political affiliations were highly important, the nominees had a pro-European outlook. The only real mystery when it comes to nominations is the appointment of Lecourt by Gaullist France in 1962. However, as shown in Chapters 5 and 7, the various governments of Gaullist France did not always pay sufficient attention to the legal dimension of the integration process. It was, for example, never part of the French grievances discussed during the Empty Chair Crisis. When Debré came back to the Ministry of Foreign Affairs from May 1968 to June 1969 with the intention to curb the ECJ, it was too late.[43] The new French President, Georges Pompidou, then nominated two pro-European Ministers of Justice and Foreign Affairs, René Pleven and Maurice Schumann, who were only happy to renew what proved to be the final term of Lecourt in 1970.

A second factor which tended to create a bias in the nomination process towards pro-European nominees was the development of the academic field of European law. While the governments encountered difficulties in finding qualified international law specialists willing to move to Luxembourg in the 1950s, European law began, in the following decade, to grow into a genuinely new discipline of law with several well-known specialists with both practical and academic experience. Monaco and Pescatore were precisely the prototype of these new experts in European law. Both had prolific academic careers. At the same time, they both held the highest positions in their Ministries of Foreign Affairs and defended their states' interests in countless international conferences and negotiations. When governments looked for suitable candidates from the mid-1960s onward, the best qualified – not that it always mattered – were now participants in a new transnational field of law that identified itself with the constitutional case law developed by the ECJ, as demonstrated in Chapter 4. While a strong interest in European law arguably was the main reason these candidates aimed to get a position at the Court, their competent and loyal services in national diplomacies convinced governments of their suitability for the position. Governments were aware of candidates' views on European integration, but such questions seemed not to matter. Instead, politics and personal connections decided nominations. This allowed for the ECJ to be composed of a highly pro-federal bench of judges, at the end of 1960s and 1970s. Let us now look at those pro-integration dynamics that prevailed inside the Court.

42 The only partial exception to this is Gaullist France from 1958 to 1969. But even Charles de Gaulle, despite his very sceptical stance on a supranational Europe, never seriously contemplated to exit the EC. See Chapter 7 for further details.

43 On Debré's plans to curb the Court see Fritz 2015.

THE DYNAMICS INSIDE THE EUROPEAN COURT OF JUSTICE

Since the judges' délibéré remains secret even after the opening of the ECJ's judicial archive, it is difficult to analyse how individual rulings came into existence. However, the biographical research on the different generations of judges makes it possible to put forth some explanations regarding the Court's hesitancy to pronounce ground-breaking judgments in the 1950s, as well as its constitutional judgments of the 1960s and 1970s. This biographical research laid bare that among the first members of the Court few identified the institution as a sort of embryo of a federal Supreme Court. None of the three high magistrates who worked at the Court between 1952 and 1958 (President Pilotti, who was moreover often ill and absent, Riese and Hammes) approved of the idea that the Court of Justice of the ECSC was of a constitutional or federal nature. Rueff was very much in favour of the European integration process for economic reasons, but he was not particularly interested in contributing to the making of a federal Europe.[44] The only fervent promoters of a federal Europe were the two judges Delvaux and Serrarens, and they were both not very influential at the Court. According to German sources, Delvaux did not have the personality to impose his views in the deliberation room and Serrarens lacked influence because he was not trained in law.[45] The absence of federal-inclined leadership in the Court is probably the main reason why the Court of Justice of the ECSC only timidly followed the Legal Service of the High Authority when it pushed for a constitutional interpretation of the Treaty of Paris.[46]

It was the arrival of Lecourt and Trabucchi in 1962 that finally changed the dynamics inside the ECJ and played a crucial role in paving the way for *Van Gend en Loos* and *Costa v ENEL*.[47] However, as Morten Rasmussen argued, not all the members of the Court seemed to have approved of the constitutional interpretation in the first half of the 1960s. After all, the vote in favour of direct effect of Article 12 EEC in *Van Gend* was only approved by four out of seven judges.[48] The in-depth study of the judges confirmed this analysis and laid bare that the disagreements probably also existed one year later in the *Costa v ENEL* case. The President of the Court André Donner, for example, did not share the opinion that the ECJ should take on the role of a constitutional jurisdiction. In 1966, he stressed that he fully understood and sympathised with the aspirations of the national judiciaries to remain the masters of their own judicial orders. He also did not hide the fact that, in 1951, he expressed himself against the introduction of the clause of primacy of

44 Chivvis 2010, 142–143.

45 On Delvaux, see his biographical portrait in the PAAA. B20-200, Bd. 420. On Serrarens, see B20-200, Bd. 28, Aufzeichnung, Betr.: Neuwahl der Richter und des Präsidenten des Gerichtshofes, 18 March 1957.

46 See on the Legal Service's role Rasmussen 2012 and Chapter 2.

47 Rasmussen 2014.

48 Rasmussen 2008. While Alberto Trabucchi, Robert Lecourt, Louis Delvaux and Rino Rossi voted in favour of direct effect, judges Otto Riese, Charles-Léon Hammes and André Donner voted against it.

international law in the Dutch constitution.[49] Donner's successor at the presidency, judge Hammes, was equally critical of the idea that the ECJ was to be of a similar nature to domestic supreme courts. In 1966, he openly rejected the notion that the ECJ had a constitutional and federal nature.[50] These internal divisions inside the Court may explain why, except for the Lütticke judgment of 1966[51] (stipulating the direct effect of Article 95 of the EEC Treaty), the ECJ refrained from pronouncing new groundbreaking judgments in the immediate years following the *Van Gend en Loos* and *Costa v ENEL* judgments.

If the second generation prompted the breakthrough for a constitutional interpretation of European law, it was the third generation that finally advanced and consolidated it. The main explanation for this is obviously the changing of the composition of the bench. When one looks at the composition of the ECJ, the year 1967 appears as one in which key changes took place inside the Court. First, the President of the Court Hammes, one of the judges who was sceptical towards the constitutional interpretation, left. He was replaced at the presidency by the long-time militant pro-European judge Lecourt. Second, two other judges with a strongly pro-European background entered the Court of Justice, Pescatore and Mertens de Wilmars. Pescatore had at that point been a champion of European supranationalism for years. During the Fouchet Plan negotiations in the early 1960s, for which he presided Luxembourg's delegation, he defended a highly federal view of the political union that was to be created.[52] It is also noteworthy that four years before his appointment, he expressed his desire to see the ECJ evolve into a 'courageous and strong' institution, which should guarantee the legitimate interests of the states, but also impose the EC's authority on them because they could too easily be tempted to take back with the left hand what they conceded with the right hand when signing the treaties.[53] Pescatore became the Court's 'troupe d'assaut' in terms of supranationalist views, as the attaché of Judge Mertens de Wilmars put it in an interview.[54] In 1976, Jean Foyer, a French Gaullist Minister, refused an appointment to the ECJ because he disagreed with the Court's case law on integration. His argument was that Pescatore was the 'doctrinaire' of this jurisprudence.[55]

The Belgian Mertens de Wilmars's views on European integration were more moderate than those of Pescatore. However, he was also a long-time defender of the European integration project and spent more than a decade in the Belgian section of the European Movement. In 1970, another judge joined this pro-European group,

[49] Donner 1966, 12. For Donner's position in this Dutch debate see van Leeuwen 2012, 368–369.

[50] Hammes 1966.

[51] 57/65 *Alfons Lütticke GmbH v Hauptzollamt Sarrelouis*, 1966, ECLI:EU:C:1966:34.

[52] However, his ideas were rejected by the other delegations. The negotiations eventually failed because the member states could not agree. For a detailed account of Pescatore's role in these negotiations see Fritz 2020.

[53] Pescatore 1965, 544–545.

[54] Interview with Ivan Verougstraete (2013).

[55] Mangenot 2000, 468.

namely Kutscher. In 1976, Kutscher gave a speech that was highly revealing of his ideas on the role of the Court of the EC. Only days before he became Lecourt's successor at President of the Court, he wondered 'how else ... the Court of Justice [should] carry out [the] function which it has been assigned except by an interpretation of Community law geared to the aims of the treaty, that is to say, one which is dynamic and teleological?'[56]

The Italian judge Monaco was also a defender of a dynamic interpretation of the Treaty. In 1963, he wrote that even though they could not move away from the text and the norms of the treaties, the European judges had to enter into their spirit and perform a delicate systematic approach while interpreting the Treaties of Rome.[57] It was hence not only the ECJ's most 'legendary' judges, Lecourt and Pescatore, who were willing to push the interpretation of the treaties towards the objective of 'an ever closer union', but an entire group of judges that were happy to do so. These new insights on the 1970s question the narrative that the Court's audacious judgments, following the *Van Gend en Loos* case,[58] were simply a logical consequence of 1963.[59] The biographical analysis rather leads to the following question: what would have been the actual impact of *Van Gend en Loos* without a highly pro-European generation of judges working at the ECJ during the following decade(s)? Most courts may look for consistency and thus tend to follow the same jurisprudential line. However, this alone does not explain the fact that the Court issued a number of judgments that significantly developed the constitutional interpretation of European law and step by step built what ultimately resembled a proto-federal legal order between the late 1960s and the early 1980s.

In 1968, the judges ruled that Article 31 and 32.1 of the EEC Treaty (member states shall in their mutual trade refrain from introducing new quantitative restrictions and making more restrictive quotas) could be directly invoked by nationals in front of their national courts (*Salgoil*[60]). In 1970, they opened the possibility for community acts other than regulations (directives and decisions for example) to have direct effect (*Franz Grad*[61]). In 1974, they held that a directive which had not been transposed into national law could be cited in national jurisdictions (*Van Duyn*[62]). In 1976, they adjudicated that nationals of member states could invoke Article 119 EEC Treaty in front of national courts (men and women should receive equal pay for equal work, *Defrenne II*).[63]

56 Kutscher 1976.

57 Monaco 1963.

58 26/62 *Van Gend en Loos vcde Nederlandse Administratie der Belastingen* [1963] ECLI:EU:C:1963:1.

59 To make direct effect have an impact, primacy was needed – to have primacy accepted, it was necessary to introduce the protection of basic rights in the Communities etc.

60 13/68 *SpA Salgoil v Italian Ministry of Foreign Trade*, 1968, ECLI:EU:C:1968:54.

61 9/70 *Franz Grad v Finanzamt Traunstein*, 1970, ECLI:EU:C:1970:78. On the history of the ECJ's jurisprudence of direct effect of directives, as well as member state resistance towards that jurisprudence, Rasmussen 2017.

62 41/74 *Yvonne van Duyn v Home Office*, 1974, ECLI:EU:C:1974:133.

63 43/75 *Gabrielle Defrenne v Société anonyme belge de navigation aérienne Sabena*, 1976, ECLI:EU:C:1976:56.

The notion of primacy of European law was expanded in an even more blunt way: in 1970, the European judges stated 'the validity of a Community measure ... *cannot* be affected by allegations that it runs counter to either fundamental rights as formulated by the constitution of that State or the principles of a national constitutional structure'.[64] In other words, no national text, not even a constitutional provision relating to fundamental rights, could prevail over European law which itself did not have a genuine catalogue of fundamental rights.[65] The extraordinary audacity of the ruling did not fail to provoke the resistance of the BVerfG.[66] Last but not least, the third generation of judges considerably expanded the Commission's powers to conclude agreements with third countries by ruling that 'each time the Community, with a view to implementing a common policy envisaged by the Treaty, adopts provisions laying down common rules, whatever form they may take, the member states no longer have the right, acting individually or even collectively, to undertake obligations with third countries which affect those rules or alter their scope'.[67]

This 'activist' case law, as it was referred to by the ECJ's critics, cannot be seen as merely a logical consequence of the revolutionary breakthrough of the constitutional interpretation in 1963 and 1964. More than half of the revolutionary generation did not sit at the bench anymore in 1970. A new, deeply pro-integrationist group of judges had taken over, and was now pushing the European integration process forwards in a political context that was all but favourable to the construction of a constitutional legal order. During the negotiations of the Treaties of Rome, the governments decided to diminish the powers of the supranational institutions compared with the ECSC, and instead turned the Council into the main decision-making body.[68] The Empty Chair Crisis and the Luxembourg Compromise demonstrated that the time was not right for pro-integration measures which could result in a further loss of sovereignty for member states. After de Gaulle's resignation in 1969, the new French President George Pompidou aimed at relaunching the European integration process, but his views on the role that should be played by European institutions did not differ much from the ones of his predecessor.[69] From the end of the 1960s to the mid-1970s, the European judges developed their very own pro-federal dynamic, and attempted to take a leadership role in the integration process. This dynamic was, to a significant extent, the result of the composition of

64 Italics added. 11/70 *Internationale Handelsgesellschaft mbH v Einfuhr- und Vorratsstelle für Getreide und Futtermittel*, 1970, ECLI:EU:C:1970:114.

65 The ruling argued that the ECJ itself safeguarded fundamental rights by taking as a primary source the constitutional traditions common to the member states.

66 Davies 2012b.

67 22/70 *Commission of the European Communities v Council of the European Communities*, 1971, ECLI:EU:C:1971:32.

68 Boerger 2012.

69 On Pompidou's standpoint towards European integration see Vaisse 1995.

the bench of judges – of which most members had pro-integrationist personal convictions. The judges' biographies demonstrate that the composition of the Court *did* matter and, interestingly, that the great advances made by the ECJ in its case law in this period were an indirect consequence of the choices made by individual member states in the nomination process.

THE POLITICAL AFFILIATIONS BETWEEN THE MEMBERS OF THE COURT AND NATIONAL GOVERNMENTS

As seen previously, political affiliations played heavily in the appointments of the first European judges. To be selected for a position at the Court, one needed to have a well-developed political network. The judge biographies show that even though the ECJ was supposed to work in complete independence from the member states, these political ties were not necessarily cut off once a candidate arrived in Luxembourg. Rueff, for example, worked on several accounts as an economic expert for the French government while he was a European judge.[70] He was not the only one to do so. During his several mandates at the Court, Judge Hammes presided over Luxembourg's private international law committee and chaired his state's delegation at several international conferences on private international law at The Hague. The German judge Riese continued during his mandate to work as a legal expert for Germany's ministries in both matters of air law and private international law. While spending nineteen years without interruption in Luxembourg, the President of the Court, and later judge Donner, served as a member, and even co-president of different Dutch committees where he oversaw reforms of the Dutch Constitution. The Italian judge Monaco worked as a legal expert for the Italian Ministry of Foreign Affairs in the first years after his appointment.

Quite naturally, personal and family networks were kept up. Roemer, the German Advocate General from 1952 to 1972, was married to the niece of Konrad Adenauer. Donner was the son of the former Minister of Justice and President of the Dutch Supreme Court, Jan Donner. Pescatore was, as aforementioned, the brother-in-law of Pierre Werner, Luxembourg's Prime Minister between 1958–1974 and 1979–1984 (Pescatore was judge from 1967 to 1985). If one adds to that the fact that several members of the Court had personal affiliations which resulted from long careers in national politics (this was notably the case of Lecourt, but also the two Belgian judges Delvaux and Mertens de Wilmars, who had been long-time members of the steering committee of the Belgian Christian Democratic Party), then it appears that the ECJ possessed a vast and quite significant political network.

This network proved in various regards to be a crucial asset for the Court: primarily, the judges could use their personal affiliations to evaluate to what extent cases were sensitive in the eyes of the member states. As confirmed by the former

[70] Cohen 2013a.

attaché of judge Mertens de Wilmars, Ivan Verougstraete, the keeping up of political affiliations was strongly encouraged inside the ECJ. Since the judges were anxious not to offend the fundamental interests of the governments, the use of its political network was part of the 'game of the Court'. It allowed the members of the Court to assess what was acceptable, and to be strategic in their decision-making, to avoid a rebellion by the member states.[71]

Second, the political network helped the judges gain the governments' trust and explain how their decisions were not meant to go against the interests of the member states, even if they followed a pro-integration dynamic which impacted their sovereignty.[72] Almost all of the selected candidates either had a political career or worked in, or for, the administration of their home state, mainly as legal counsellors for Ministries of Justice and Foreign Affairs. Many of them defended their state's interests in various international negotiations. There was no reason they would now make decisions which could directly harm their country's national interests. Thus, their professional trajectories, as well as their personal affiliations with national decision-makers, strengthened the ECJ's legitimacy and capacity to have even ambitious case law accepted by national governments. In that sense, the Court operated very much like national constitutional courts, which were also characterised by a strong proximity and interconnectedness with political decision-makers. This proximity gave governments the impression that their political incentives were better taken into consideration than if the court were staffed with traditional judges. However, it also made it more difficult for them to criticise constitutional courts or the ECJ, because their decisions emanated from individuals whom they selected themselves and know personally and professionally. Moreover, the European judges had, via these political ties, direct contact lines to the governments to defend the Court's actions and interests in behind-the-scenes discussions.

An example of the judges using their political network in the interest of their institution was the negotiations on the interpretation of the 1968 Brussels Convention on Jurisdiction and the Enforcement of Judgments in Civil and Commercial Matters. The Brussels Convention was the first private international law convention signed between the six member states of the EC. It replaced a complex web of existing national rules and bilateral agreements regarding the international enforcement of judgments in civil and commercial matters and aimed to establish an autonomous system of international jurisdiction in relation to the EC. As the Convention was going to radically alter the manner in which national courts were determining their jurisdiction and enforce decisions of other member states' courts in civil and commercial matter cases, a centralised interpretative authority should ideally be designated or created to ensure that it would be applied consistently. In the eyes of the European judges, this authority should be the ECJ.

71 Interview with Ivan Verougstraete (2013).

72 On the importance of this relationship of trust to strengthen the judges' legitimacy in the eyes of the governments, see Fritz 2019.

Similarly to the preliminary reference mechanism, which allowed the ECJ to answer questions for interpretation of the treaties raised by national courts, the Court should be granted the power to give authoritative answers to questions of interpretation that national judges could have regarding the Brussels Convention. However, since the preliminary ruling mechanism had known an unexpected progressive development in the 1960s this was not uncontroversial.[73] As the Brussels Convention was not a Community Act, but a separate private international law agreement signed between the member states, not all of the governments shared the point of view that the preliminary reference mechanism should be extended to the Brussels convention – especially since its rather vaguely formulated provisions left substantial room for interpretations. Special negotiations between legal experts of the six states were consequently organised to evaluate to what extent the competence to adjudicate on the Brussels Convention should be conferred upon the ECJ.

During these negotiations, France and Belgium proposed restrictive solutions for the powers that the ECJ was supposed to have over the terms laid out in the Brussels convention. These positions caused profound concern among the judges – several of which resorted to their political network to repeatedly urge national decision-makers to give them larger powers than originally proposed.[74] Whereas Judge Mertens de Wilmars sent a memorandum explaining the legal situation to the Belgian government, Pescatore opted for direct communication with the Belgian Minister of Foreign Affairs, Pierre Harmel. In letters addressed to Harmel, which were written in a strikingly blunt tone typical for Pescatore, he bemoaned to the Minister the fact that the experts' discussions were in his eyes taking an increasingly political turn '*especially*' due to the negative and wholly unjustified position adopted by the Belgian delegation. He also accused the Belgian experts of putting forth inefficacious solutions which could encourage the French government to aim for the dismantling of the judicial guarantees established by the Treaties of Rome. Harmel should, in Pescatore's view, take a personal interest in his government's experts' standpoint.[75]

President Lecourt, on his end, organised several informal meetings with key members of the new French government nominated by Pompidou including the new Ministers of Foreign and Justice Affairs, Maurice Schumann and René Pleven, in order to influence the very restrictive French position in the negotiations.[76] He

[73] In 1967, twenty-three out of thirty-seven cases introduced at the ECJ had been preliminary references. Between 1958 and 1966, however, the ECJ had in total only known twenty-six questions for a preliminary ruling. See statistics in Davies and Rasmussen 2014.

[74] The competence to interpret this first 'European' private international law convention was vested in the ECJ with the so-called 'Luxembourg protocol' of 1971. For a detailed account of these negotiations and the ECJ's political activism to gain more power, see Fritz 2015; Fritz 2017.

[75] See all of the cited documents in the Archives of the Belgian Ministry of Foreign Affairs (ABMFA). File 6. 641/1 CEE.

[76] See correspondence between Lecourt and Pleven after the encounter in the French National Archives (FNA), 19950411, 211.

argued during those meetings that not giving the ECJ the prerogative to exercise power through the Brussels Convention in the same manner as in the framework of the preliminary ruling procedure of the EC would establish a precedent that could harm the European integration process.[77] Even the Court's Belgian clerk, Albert Van Houtte, participated in the lobbying by sending several notes to the Belgian Ministry of Foreign Affairs asking whether the Belgian position had been re-examined, and arguing that the German and even the French delegations were willing to accept solutions that were based on Article 177 of the EEC Treaty.[78]

The ECJ's pressure was only successful to a certain extent. While Lecourt finally managed to convince Pleven and Schumann to give the French experts in the negotiations less restrictive instructions, the European judges did not manage to obtain a simple extension of the preliminary ruling mechanism.[79] Nonetheless, the way in which they used their political network in this situation to potentially obtain a large extension of their powers is striking. One must stress here that the members of the Court were not completely wrong when they suspected that the governments were trying to attack the ECJ's powers. Archival evidence demonstrates that the former French government under President de Gaulle had indeed been trying to obtain a revision of Article 177 of the EEC Treaty and hoped to establish a precedent for a more restricted version during the negotiations of the Brussels convention.[80] What this episode hence shows is that through their political network, the judges were apparently well informed about these hidden intentions and were capable of countering them, at least to a certain extent, with their own diplomatic efforts towards national decision-makers. In fact, their main success in these negotiations was arguably that they managed to alert the five other member states about the French intentions and led them to clearly spell out that they were *not* willing to revise the original Article 177 of the EEC Treaty in the future. The ECJ thus appears to have been, since its early years, a strategic actor, involved in the institutional battles of the EC and ready to fight for its own institutional interests.

CONCLUSION

While this chapter could not address the entire period covered in this book for practical reasons,[81] it has argued that we should pay greater attention to the

77 FNA. 19950411/211. Letter from Lecourt to Pleven, 17 July 1969, and 'Note relative à l'extension des compétences de la Cour de Justice des Communautés européennes'.

78 ABMFA. file 6. 641/1 CEE.

79 The possibility to send questions for interpretation of the Brussels convention to the ECJ was limited to courts judging in appeal. Courts of last instance were only obliged to consult the ECJ if they estimated that it was necessary.

80 See Fritz 2015 and Chapter 7.

81 The in-depth biographical study carried out on the first members of the Court required months of research in each of the six founding member states of the European Communities. For material and linguistic reasons, it was not possible to broaden the panel of judges to more member states. Moreover, extending the studied period would have led to difficulties in accessing the relevant archival material.

personalities that compose the ECJ's bench of judges. Through careful examination of judge biographies, it has demonstrated that the composition of the bench of judges directly shaped the dynamics that reigned inside the ECJ in the foundational years and the Court's case law. Few of the seven members of the first ECSC generation of judges initially embraced a federal vision of the Court. Moreover, they suffered from a fragile legitimacy to pronounce ground-breaking constitutional interpretations of the Treaty of Paris. President Pilotti was often absent for reasons of health, and two of the seven judges were not even trained in law. Remarkably, the change in the composition of the ECJ with the addition of Lecourt and Trabucchi in 1962 led to the embracement of the constitutional interpretations of the new Treaties of Rome recommended by the Legal Service of the Commission with a narrow majority favouring the *Van Gend en Loos* judgment in 1963. However, despite this legal revolution, the Court remained divided on the question of whether it should further push its new constitutional interpretation. It was only after 1967, with the nomination of a third generation of judges that a broader consensus emerged on the need for a dynamic reading of the treaties, which allowed the Court to continue, in a much more forceful way than in the early 1960s, to push the integration process forward through its rulings. The analysis of the judges' backgrounds demonstrates that the personal pro-European convictions of the third generation played a decisive role in the jurisprudence that the ECJ developed from the end of the 1960s to the mid-1970s.

At the same time, biographical research has also stressed the member states' role in making the ECJ's ambitious case law possible through the choices of judges made by the governments in the selection procedure. Two factors allowed the ECJ to uphold and strengthen its constitutional reading of the Treaties of Rome after the revolutionary interpretations in 1963 and 1964. First, in the 1960s, the Court was composed of federalist-inclined European specialists whom the national governments trusted because they had spent decades in national diplomacy. Second, a pro-European consensus reigned in most of the member states during the period analysed here, which meant that national (coalition) governments did not tend to worry too much about the federalist views of the candidates that they selected for positions at the ECJ. This did not, however, mean that the judges were completely exempt from any political 'attack' by the governments. Their positions were vulnerable because they had to be renewed every six years. They were also not completely protected from a revision of their powers. France, under Gaullist leadership, considered asking for a renegotiation of the Court's powers by the end of the 1960s. The ECJ's political network helped the judges prevent such an attack. Not only did their political connections and network give them a sense of how far they could go in their constitutional interpretation of European law, but it also gave them the possibility to lobby for the renewal of their mandate, as well as the extension of their powers. The composition of the Court hence played a key role in the establishment and the development of the constitutional practice in the 1960s and 1970s, from both a legal and a political point of view.

2

At the Vanguard of European Constitutionalism: The Role of the Legal Service of the European Commission

Sigfrido M. Ramírez Pérez

Legal historians have considered the Legal Service of the European Commission the consistent spearhead of attempts to construct political unity through law. In a pioneering article, Morten Rasmussen documented the way in which the Legal Service was able to play a leading role in the initial breakthrough of the constitutional practice of European law. Building on an earlier hypothesis presented by Eric Stein in 1981, Rasmussen identified the Legal Service as the origin of the core legal argument used by the European Court of Justice (ECJ) to justify the direct effect and primacy of European law. He documented that such a legal argument was to be traced back to Jean Monnet and Walter Hallstein, as first presidents of respectively the High Authority (HA) of the European Coal and Steel Community (ECSC) and of the European Commission of the European Economic Community (EEC). However, the central driver of the legal practice was the Legal Service and in particular its long-serving general director, Michel Gaudet.[1] This was later corroborated by other authors studying the influence of the Legal Service on the ECJ in specific legal cases, but also in the creation of a broader constitutional doctrine of European law structured by a supranational network of legal practitioners and academics.[2]

For more than forty years, punctuated by political blockades and institutional conflicts, the Legal Service took a systematic approach to create, develop and expand the reach and impact of European law within the Commission, and across the other European institutions such as the ECJ, the Council of Ministers and the European Parliament (EP). The Legal Service consistently fought for creating a new legal order of a constitutional nature, prevailing upon the law of member states to create a European Community of law.

This chapter will explore the role that the Legal Service played in the creation of European law from its launch in 1952 until 1992. The aim is to answer the question raised by recent research: Was the Legal Service the most important administrative actor in the creation of a constitutional practice of European law? The chapter is split

1 Rasmussen 2012.

2 Bailleux 2013; Vauchez 2015; Boerger and Rasmussen 2017; Byberg 2017d.

into five sections covering the chronological stages in the contribution of the Legal Service to the creation of a constitutional practice in European law. The first section deals with the role of the Legal Service during the formative years of European law during the ECSC years from 1952–1958. A second section covers the period from 1958 to 1969. During this period, the Legal Service comprised three branches of the three European Communities (with a section in the HA in Luxembourg and two sections in Brussels at the EEC Commission and the Euratom Commission) and only merged into one service with the Merger Treaty of 1967. The key figure during this period was Michel Gaudet, a French state lawyer from the French Council of State (Conseil d'État), who entered the Legal Service in 1953 but from 1958 served first as head of the EEC branch in Brussels, before becoming the Director-General of the unified Legal Service from 1967 to 1969. The third section will cover the period from the resignation of Gaudet in 1969 until 1977. This was a period of some turbulence not only for the Commission in general but also with regard to the leadership of the Legal Service. The Legal Service was first led by the German lawyer Walter Much until his death, and then by his Italian deputy, Walter Olmi, who was in charge of the interim direction of the Service between 1975 and 1977. The fourth section will consequently deal with what is arguably the second golden decade of the Legal Service, when the German Claus-Dieter Ehlermann became the new Director-General. Ehlermann stayed in office until 1986, where his mandate culminated with the vital role that he and other members of the Legal Service played in the crafting of the Single European Act of 1985. A concluding section will finally analyse how the legal and intellectual contribution of the Legal Service survived all the way to the Maastricht Treaty of 1991, when the leadership of the Legal Service moved into the hands of the former Director-General of the Legal Service of the Council of Ministers, the Frenchman Jean-Louis Dewost. His action was complemented by the active contribution of a former French member of the Legal Service, François Lamoureaux, who acted as the legal adviser of the Commission President, Jacques Delors in the last half of the 1980s. As such, this chapter aims to expand the previous research on the role of the Legal Service by providing a panoramic picture of the various means possessed by the Service to influence the development of the constitutional practice of European law.

THE CRADLE OF THE EUROPEAN LEGAL ORDER: FROM THE ECSC TO THE EC (1950–1957)

The important role of Germany in promoting a constitutional approach to the ECSC already during the negotiations on the Treaty of Paris has been well documented. The main artisans of federal constitutionalism were the Secretary of State of the Ministry of Foreign Affairs, Walter Hallstein, and the group of lawyers around him, during the negotiations of the Treaty of Paris. This group included Carl-Friedrich Ophüls, director of the Department on European Affairs of the Ministry of Foreign Affairs during the 1950s, and other scholars, politicians and civil servants like Professors Karl Carstens, Ernst Steindorff and Ernst Wohlfarth.[3] It was during the negotiations of the Treaty of Paris in 1950–1951 that the German delegation advocated not just for a Parliamentary Assembly, but more importantly, for the creation of a European Court of Justice. This proposed constitutional court was supposed to have a monopoly on the legal interpretation of the treaty. Moreover, the German delegation insisted that the court was not only accessible for the member states, as traditional international courts or arbitration, but also to private litigants. In the end, the German wish for a constitutional court was not adopted, and the ECJ became a curious mixture of an international and administrative court with some unique features such as the access for private litigants, even if it was seriously circumscribed compared to the original German proposals.[4]

The position of the Legal Service in the HA would quickly become central. As first President of this new innovative supranational executive power, Monnet was concerned with the limited autonomy of the HA and wished to create a light, competent and coherent administration like the Planning Commissariat, which he had directed in France during the post-war years. He suggested therefore to establish a Legal Service directly attached to the President. In August 1952, he tried to convince Paul Reuter who had advised Monnet during the first part of the negotiations over the Treaty of Paris to become director of the new service. But he turned down the offer. Reuter was not convinced that the use of two lawyers of the President in the meetings of the College would be accepted by the other members of the HA. He recommended instead to appoint a lawyer among the members of the HA, supplemented by the occasional presence of legal advisers if needed, like it was practiced in the secretariat of other international organisations.[5]

In line with Monnet's ideas for all HA services, the Legal Service was to be directed by a joint leadership of French and German civil servants. If in the summer of 1952, Monnet was busy identifying a French lawyer after Reuter's refusal to join, the reason was that he had already hired two German legal advisers: Robert Krawielicki and Walter Much. Krawielicki came from the German Ministry of Justice and had also worked for the Ministry of Economics. He was one of the few people who were directly involved in the German–American negotiations for a future German antitrust law. After this, he had contributed to the drafting of the provisions on competition of the Treaty of Paris and published a book which became the go-to reference for these questions. Krawielicki remained in the Legal Service until his death in 1966. From 1958 he became the head of the ECSC Legal Service branch and was a central figure in the building of the common service.[6] Walter Much, who would later succeed Krawielicki in Luxembourg in 1966 as the director

3 Davies 2015.
4 Boerger 2012.
5 Bailleux 2014, 226.
6 Schorkopf 2019.

of the ECSC Legal Service, came from the Public Law section of the same Ministry of Justice in Bonn. Much had entered European affairs at the request of Carl Friedrich Ophüls, who appointed him as member of the German delegation for the negotiations of the Treaty of Paris. He remained in the Ministry until the summer of 1952 when he was recruited by the HA. He had just defended his doctoral dissertation on the liability of public officials of the ECSC at the University of Frankfurt, under the direction of Professors Herman Mosler and Hans-Jürgen Schlochauer.[7] Much clearly had unique competences since also the German vice-president of the HA, Franz Etzel, would have loved to make him his personal attaché. Instead, Much wrote to Monnet directly offering his availability for the new Legal Service, where he was hired in August 1952.[8]

With regard to the French representative, Maurice Lagrange from the Conseil D'État, who had also acted as legal advisor during the negotiations on the Treaty of Paris and would soon assume the role as Advocate General at the ECJ, suggested to Monnet that a young colleague from Paris, Michel Gaudet, could be the right man.[9] Gaudet did not have any previous European experience and Monnet's decision to partner him with the much more experienced Krawielicki was probably related to the fact that Gaudet was supposed to remain the informal interface with Lagrange, who remained Monnet's informal legal adviser. The personal proximity to Monnet as a decisive element in these first strategic recruitments for the Legal Service is confirmed if we look at the other French lawyer appointed in 1953, Jean Poincaré, who was already in Luxembourg as chief of staff of his uncle, Léon Daum, the other French member of the HA.[10] Another consequential appointment for the future of European law was the nomination of the Italian member of the Legal Service. Coming from the Avvocatura dello Stato and having a doctorate in law, Nicola Catalano was one of the most experienced of all the members of the service, considering that he had already functioned as representative of his government in international negotiations. The fifth member of the pioneers, Jean Blondeel, was a Belgian private lawyer who had worked for the important American law firm Cleary, Gottlieb, Friendly and Ball before entering the Legal Service. This company had been selected by Monnet to support the HA in its relations with the United States and Blondeel thus provided a link between the HA's Legal Service and its key law firm. Like Poincaré and Catalano, Blondeel stayed in Luxembourg for only two to three years in office. The small team of six legal advisers worked under heavy pressure due to the huge amount of work that they had to manage. Not only did they take part in the meetings of the College of the HA, providing a preliminary legal analysis for any new decision, but they also represented the HA at meetings in the

7 Krawielicki 1952.

8 Davies (forthcoming).

9 Mangenot 2023.

10 Mangenot 2000; Leucht 2008.

Council of Ministers and the Assembly. Finally, they represented the HA before the ECJ. The workload would soon necessitate the hiring of additional staff.[11]

Historical analysis of this initial period confirms that the Legal Service, particularly Gaudet, quickly converted to the idea of interpreting European law as a new European constitutional law, with the ECJ playing a federal role similar to the US Supreme Court. In this respect the approach taken by Gaudet for example contrasted with the alternative vision put forward by the most prominent Advocate General Lagrange. For Lagrange, the interpretative method to follow was based on comparative administrative law, comparing the systems of the member states, and thus linking the rulings of the ECJ to the national legal traditions. To Lagrange the ECJ was an internal administrative court of the ECSC, similar to the Conseil d'État in France, with a discrete and indirect constitutional dimension. What he and Gaudet agreed on was that the ECJ was not an international tribunal of a special kind, which was the dominant view among several of the most prominent judges in the ECJ including the President Massimo Pilotti and the German judge Otto Riese.[12] Not surprisingly the ECJ, in the first case (1/54) brought by the French government against the HA, followed a textual methodology in the line of the interpretative method of international law, in spite of the attempts of Advocate General Lagrange, to convince the judges to follow a more teleological interpretation of Article 60 on cartels.[13] Gaudet had prepared the HA position with a French lawyer, Jean Coutard, and pushed for a teleological interpretation, and was greatly disappointed by Court's decision.[14] At stake was nothing less than the capacity of the HA to regulate steel prices in accordance with the general objective of the Treaty of Paris promoting competition in the Common Market. The Court instead chose to base its judgment on Article 60 that in relatively precise words outlined the procedure for handling the published steel price list. The French government, supported by Italy, did not want to offer the HA this flexibility because it offered more leeway for reconstructed private steel cartels that might offer German industries competitive advantages.[15] From a political viewpoint though, it was a great success that the French government had brought a first case to the Court. That it did so on a question related to the HA powers to control steel cartels confirmed the significant role that competition clauses had played since the negotiations of the Treaty of Paris.[16]

The early step of the ECJ towards a less textual interpretation came about already in case 8/55 initiated by the Fédération Charbonnière de Belgique (Fédéchar)

11 Boerger and Rasmussen 2017.

12 Rasmussen 2012.

13 1/54 *French Republic v High Authority of the European Coal and Steel Community*, 1954, ECLI:EU:C:1954:7.

14 Bailleux 2014.

15 Spierenburg and Poidevin 1994, 131–147.

16 Warlouzet and Witschke 2012.

against the HA for exceeding its powers in its capacity to fix prices.[17] In its ruling the ECJ acknowledged the theory of *effet utile* as a fundamental guideline for the necessary implied powers of the HA to reach the objectives of integrating the Common Market on coal. Such a theory postulated that the treaties had a clear intentionality when they were signed by the member states, and the Court had to avoid any subsequent act that would bar a treaty from its intended effect. Such a technique of interpretation was already used by the International Court of Justice in interpreting treaties in international law, but in a very restrictive manner. In this case, the ECJ provided an extensive interpretation of the Treaty of Paris.[18] In this act of self-empowerment by the ECJ, it did not go as far as requested by Lagrange to explicitly state what he had already written in various academic articles in 1954, namely that the ECSC resembled a proto-federal organisation much more than an international organisation, and therefore the ECJ had a specific constitutional role to play as a supreme administrative court.[19] While Lagrange's effort to portray the ECJ as a constitutional court was supported by other ECJ employees like the attaché Pierre Mathijsen, the Belgian registrar of the Court, Albert van Houtte and the Belgian judge Louis Delvaux, this was very much a minority position in the broader academic fields of international and comparative law.[20] At the Stresa Congress of July 1957 organised by the Legal Service of the HA to promote the project, the constitutional interpretation of European law suffered a defeat in favour of an interpretation that considered it merely an unusual subset of international law.[21]

The historical context in which the judgment in case 8/55 took place was also quite different from the first court case of the ECJ, as the French National Assembly had rejected the European Defence Community (EDC) in the summer of 1954, and, therefore, created great uncertainty about the future of the ECSC. This political situation was aggravated by Jean Monnet's decision on 9 November 1954 to not seek a renewed term as President of the HA. From this moment until the Messina conference of June 1955, Monnet remained very ambiguous about his own real intentions. Gaudet, who had now become a close collaborator, recommended against standing down until a successor took office because this could threaten the very survival of the ECSC. We know why Monnet was ambiguous about his decision. At the same time, he proposed to the ECSC governments, through the Belgian Minister of Foreign Affairs, Paul Henri Spaak, to extend the ECSC to two new sectors, energy and transportation, and create a new community for civil nuclear power. If the governments did so, he would stay in office. Spaak's original suggestion did not include the creation of a European Common Market. This was

17 8/55 *Fédération Charbonnière de Belgique v High Authority of the European Coal and Steel Community*, 1956, ECLI:EU:C:1956:7.

18 Itzcovich 2006, 108–109.

19 Rasmussen 2012, 379–380.

20 Boerger and Rasmussen 2017.

21 Bailleux 2010.

instead proposed by the Dutch Minister of Foreign Affairs, Johan Willem Beyen. Both Benelux politicians agreed to make a package deal to be presented at the Messina conference. It seems clear that to Monnet and Gaudet the preferable solution was to let the ECSC institutional framework host the new policy fields proposed. This hope would quickly prove elusive.[22]

Instead, the Messina conference decided to create a study group, the Spaak committee, to formulate concrete proposals on how to create a Common Market and Euratom, including what kind of institutional solutions should be used. The Spaak report was presented in April 1956 at the Venice Conference of ECSC member states and proposed the creation of a European Economic Community and EURATOM without any predefined links to the ECSC. Endorsing the report the governments decided to open an intergovernmental conference on this basis to be held at Val Duchesse castle on the outskirts of Brussels starting from late June. Nothing was yet decided, and nobody could have anticipated a successful conclusion of such talks with France after the rejection of the EDC. It was precisely in this context of uncertainty on the future of the ECSC project that Spaak appointed Gaudet to assist the committee of legal experts (Groupe de rédaction) in charge of the drafting of the treaties and the creation of the legal system of the two new Communities. This was not surprising because during the work of the Spaak committee, the Belgian leader had appointed the chief economist of the HA, Pierre Uri, who was, like Gaudet, one of the people close to Jean Monnet. As the history of the negotiations of the legal clauses have already been analysed in detail, we shall only focus on the role of the legal service members at this crucial moment.[23]

The reason the ECSC directors of the legal and economic departments were associated with the intergovernmental conference was clearly with the aim to safeguard the future of the ECSC during the creation of the two new Communities. This was not a simple task. The Spaak report did roughly propose the same institutional structure as the ECSC for the new Communities but with a very different decision-making system in which the Council would be the main decision-making body with the Commission relegated to holding the right of initiative. To create links between the three Communities, the Assembly and the Court could be shared, however. This was fiercely opposed by the French delegation. With regard to the legal system, the senior French legal adviser, Professor Georges Vedel, suggested for example that the creation of a non-permanent Court of Arbitration made up of technical experts would be sufficient for the EEC. After the breakthrough of the negotiations at the summit between the French Prime Minister Guy Mollet and the German Chancellor Konrad Adenauer in early November 1956, the French government finally removed its opposition and accepted the sharing of the Court and the Assembly between the ECSC and the two new Communities.[24]

22 Dûchene 1994, 262–283.
23 Boerger 2012. For the definitive analysis of the work on the Groupe de rédaction see Rasmussen 2023.
24 Melchionni 2007.

It is in this context that Michel Gaudet influenced the negotiations of the legal clauses when he joined the Groupe de rédaction in January 1957. The secretariat of the negotiations was directed by the General Secretariat of the ECSC Special Council of Ministers, Christian Calmes. Council legal director, Hubert Ehring, was also requested in the Groupe de rédaction. The leading role, however, was arguably played by Nicola Catalano, who had returned from the Legal Service to Rome at the end of 1955 and was present as legal adviser of the Italian Ministry of Foreign Affairs. In his disappointment with the decisions of the committee with regard to a heavily politicised infringement procedure (Article 169–171 of the EEC Treaty) Catalano proposed the preliminary reference system inspired by system of judicial review of the Italian Constitution. In what became Article 177 of the EEC Treaty, he suggested an open and dynamic system in which the ECJ not only had the right to judge the validity of European law but also its interpretation in cases raised by national courts.[25] The Luxembourg representative in the committee, Pierre Pescatore, authored several other key dispositions that could be cited as justifications for a federal interpretation of the treaties: Article 189 of the EEC Treaty (decision-making system including the direct applicability of regulations) and Article 235 of the EEC Treaty (system to provide new explicit powers without a treaty reform). Another crucial point that he introduced was the safeguard clause for the autonomy of the ECSC and Euratom from the EEC which would guarantee the long-term survival of both organisations in case of failure of the latter. Gaudet was, decisively, in charge of elaborating the final complete draft of the two treaties, as the original was in French.[26]

The subtle attempts by members of the Groupe de rédaction to insert constitutional and federal elements into the Treaties of Rome cannot be reduced to a conspiracy of integrationist legal technocrats. Despite the overwhelming consensus of the governments negotiating the Treaties of Rome to create a community of international law the establishment of which would be based on the political will of the member state, there were a significant number of key politicians and negotiators who still believed in European federalism and attempted to gently push the Treaties of Rome in this direction in the last months of the negotiations. If the Franco-German leadership exercised by Mollet and Adenauer did not prioritise institutional innovation to make sure the French National Assembly would ratify the two new treaties, the State Secretary of the Ministry of Foreign Affairs, Walter Hallstein, and the German Head of delegation, Carl Fridrich Ophüls, were attentive that federalist conceptions were not completely forgotten. Two other political leaders, the Belgian Socialist Spaak and the Christian-Democrat Prime Minister of Italy, Antonio Segni, were openly federalist. A Professor of Procedural Civil Law and former Dean of the University of Sassari, Segni had for many years been Minister for European affairs in

[25] For an in-depth analysis of Catalano's contribution see Rasmussen 2023, 23–29.

[26] Melchionni 2007, 73–103. (Interview with Pierre Pescatore, Luxembourg 21 May 1984.)

the various Italian governments. He was also responsible for appointing Catalano as legal expert and as judge at the ECJ right after the negotiations, in order to have him developing the potentialities introduced in the treaties.[27] In 1957 Catalano had published a commentary to the Treaties of Rome explaining his interpretation of the new treaties as an embryonic federation though only including a limited part of the economy, a so-called 'partial federation'.[28]

THE COMMON LEGAL SERVICE OF THE EUROPEAN COMMUNITIES (1958–1969)

The establishment of the two new European Communities initially in 1958 provoked an existential crisis in the ECSC. In September 1958 Monnet's successor, René Mayer, and his vice-president Franz Etzel, resigned due to their conviction that the ECSC would now be subordinated to other Communities, which they believed lacked the sufficient supranational character. This fear was certainly not unfounded. Following a 'horse trade' deal between the national governments, the appointment of the new Presidents – the German Walter Hallstein for the EEC, the French Louis Armand for the Euratom and the Belgian trade unionist Paul Finet for the ECSC – the new Common Assembly took the initiative to address the fragmented nature of European integration by asking the three executives to create common services. This made sense particularly in the legal field. In January 1958, Gaudet justified the creation of a common organisation of the Legal Services of the three executives with the importance of avoiding divergent interpretations of the treaties confronted as the executives were by a single ECJ. In the end an attempt to create a common organisation was set in motion together with the establishment of a unified Statistical Office and Press and Information Service as well. More pragmatically Gaudet managed, coordinating here closely with Krawielicki, to decisively participate in the selection of the new personnel for the legal services of the other institutions on the basis that the new officials had to be able to work in any of the three institutions.[29]

The three Presidents of the supranational executives appointed in concert the legal directors. According to Jean-Jacques Beuve-Mery, who assisted Gaudet in the transfer from Luxembourg to Brussels, Gaudet hesitated between accepting to become the Director of the Legal Service branch of the EEC or of the Euratom, out of the conviction that the EEC was initially more vulnerable than the Euratom, which always had been the key project to Monnet and Spaak.[30] However, when he learned that Hallstein and Jean Rey would become President and Vice-President

[27] Mura 2017.
[28] Catalano 1957.
[29] Bailleux 2014, 252–254.
[30] Historical Archive of the European Union (HAEU). Conhist.com. Interview of Jean-Jacques Beuve-Mery (INT 703) by Yves Conrad and Myriam Rancon, 14 November 2004.

respectively of the EEC Commission, all possible doubts about the political importance of the EEC disappeared. At the end of the day, Krawielicki remained in Luxembourg to take charge of the new Legal Service of the HA, seconded by Gerard Olivier, a French official who have joined the Legal Service in 1955. Gaudet moved to Brussels to take the responsibility of Legal Service of the EEC Commission. Both men suggested to the new Vice-President of the Euratom Commission, Dutch Emmanuel Sassen, to select the Dutch lawyer, Theo Vogelaar, as new director of the Euratom Legal Service. Vogelaar, according to the common recommendation written by Gaudet and Krawielicki, had already collaborated with the Legal Service of the HA, and would be useful for Euratom in its cooperation with the US. Vogelaar had been working since 1943 as legal and financial adviser of the Dutch textile firm C&A Brenninkmeijer. His most relevant experience of public service took place in 1952 when he had been the legal expert at the Dutch Commission of the London Conference to settle the war debts of Germany. Beyond the support from Gaudet and Krawielicki, Vogelaar was also supported by the former Secretary-General of the HA, Max Kohnstamm, who was still influential even though he had left the position in 1956 to second Monnet at the Action Committee for the United States of Europe.[31]

The Directors of the three Legal Services reported directly to the vice-presidents of their respective institutions who were put in charge of legal affairs. In the case of the EEC, Gaudet reported directly to Jean Rey. The Belgian liberal politician had a background as a professional lawyer and was strongly in favour of a federalisation of the EEC. Rey also had a direct experience with the supranational model of the ECSC. In his capacity as Minister of Economic Affairs, he had represented Belgium monthly from 1954 to 1958 in the Special Council of Ministers of the ECSC. A staunch supporter of the new Common Market approach to integration, instead of a sectorial approach *à la* Monnet, he had not been completely convinced that the new EEC Commission would not ultimately be reduced to a consultative secretariat of the Council, as he had explained to the President of the French European Movement, René Courtin, in January 1958. Courtin, however, had pointed out that the new EEC Commission would have an independent political role due to Article 149 of the EEC Treaty, which required unanimity of the Council to modify a Commission proposal. Moreover, the Commission was allowed to modify its own proposal after consulting the Assembly, which Courtin believed would soon be directly elected and thus gain in popular legitimacy. Courtin also recommended that the civil servants appointed were not just capable administrators with technical knowledge, but also 'convinced Europeans'. He offered to suggest a list of possible candidates to join the EEC Commission.[32]

[31] HAEU. CEAB. 12–481. Letter from Gaudet and Krawielicki to Giachero (ECSC), Sassen and von der Groeben, 26 March 1958.

[32] Archives Jean Rey (ARJ). 126 APP-51. Letter from René Courtin to Jean Rey, 14 January 1958.

From all oral testimonies and the correspondence between Rey and Gaudet, it is obvious that the relationship between the two men was one of mutual trust. According to Gaudet's assistants, this was not the case with President Hallstein, who was more prone to mark his distance not only to Gaudet but to all the staff surrounding him.[33] Therefore, the primary political interlocutor of Gaudet within the EEC Commission became Jean Rey, rather than Hallstein. This would eventually turn out to be a real asset since Rey became the successor of Hallstein as President of the new unified Commission after the merging of the three executives from September 1967 to 1970. During this latter period Gaudet was appointed as sole Director-General of the new unified Legal Service, having as deputy, the former Director of the Legal Service of the ECSC Council, Hubert Ehring. According to Jean-Claude Séché, the German oversaw the strategic area of the Common Market, leaving to Gaudet the more institutional questions.[34]

Back in 1958, Gaudet and Krawielicki had the responsibility to recruit all the new lawyers for the Legal Service branches of the EEC Commission and the HA. According to the oral testimonies of Gaudet's personal assistants, Jean-Jacques Beuve-Mery, hired in 1957 in Luxembourg, and Marc Sohier, who was hired in Brussels and assisted him from 1958 to 1963, Gaudet brought several young lawyers from the ECJ in Luxembourg to Brussels: Pierre Mathijsen who had worked as attaché of the Dutch judge Adrianus Van Kleffens, Pierre Pinay, the attaché of the French judge Jaques Rueff, and Jean-Pierre Delahousse, the assistant of the Advocate General Maurice Lagrange. By early 1962, the EEC Legal Service became a horizontally structured administrative service Table 2.1.

With the establishment of two new supranational executives and their branches of Legal Service, the new common Legal Service constituted a very significant expansion of legal expertise compared to the Legal Service of the HA before 1958. According to existing research, Gaudet followed a double strategy: on the one hand, he pushed the common Legal Service to develop a single strategy to promote a constitutional interpretation of the treaties before the ECJ.[35] On the other hand, he encouraged the creation of a transnational association of European law, the Fédération internationale pour le Droit Européen (FIDE), created in October 1961 to lay the foundations of a veritable academic and professional field of European law. This would help strengthen European law as an independent legal field, and in turn help legitimise the future case law of the ECJ.

There is now agreement between most researchers in the decisive role the example of the US federal experience played in Gaudet's legal strategy. This has been traced back to December 1957 when Gaudet had a revealing exchange of letters with a prominent US business lawyer, Donald Swatland, partner at the law firm

33 Boerger and Rasmussen 2017.

34 HAEU. Conhist.com. Interview of Jean-Claude Séché (INT 720) by Yves Conrad and Myriam Rancon, 8 June 2004.

35 Boerger and Rasmussen 2017.

TABLE 2.1 *Structure of the Legal Service of the European executives 1962*
(In bold the original members of the ECSC legal service in 1956)

SENIORITY	ECSC	EEC	EURATOM	COMMON SERVICES
	Robert Krawielicki (D)	**Michel Gaudet (F)**	Theo Vogelaar	
	Henri Manzanares (F)		Utermann (N)	
I	**Mario Berri (I)**			
	Frans Van Houten (N)			
II	**Walter Much (G) Gerard Olivier (F)**	Hubert Ehring (G)	Jean-Pierre Delahousse (F)	Jean De la Fontaine (L) – Legal personality
		Giancarlo Olmi (I)		
	Émile Reuter (L)	Jochen Thiesing (G)		
III	**Raymond Baeyens (B)**	Jean Bruyas (F)	Pierre Mathijsen (N)	Gerhard Bebr (US) – Anglo-American Law
	Heinrich Matthies (G)	Paul Leleux (B)		
	Giulio Pasetti (I)	Pierre Pinay (F)	Hans-Joachim Glaesner (G)	
	Italo Telchini (I)	Leendert Van den Burg (N)	Félix Oboussier (G)	
	Klaus Peter Zimmer (G)		Majoli (I)	
		Alberto Sciola-Lagrange (I)		
IV	Erich Zimmerman (G)		Jan Gissjels (B)	Philippe Biays (F) – Institutional issues

TABLE 2.1 *(continued)*

V	**Pierre Lamoureux (F)**	Angelo Grisoli (I)	Giovanni Motzo (I)	Jürgen Utermann (G)
VI		Jean-Jacques Beuve-Mery (F) Claus-Dieter Ehlermann (G) Robert Fischer (N)		
VII	**Robert Knoepfle (G)**	Emile Mennens (B)		Antonino Abate (I) – comparative law (in ECSC)
Lawyer-linguists for ECSCE and EEC	Graumann (G) Bennink-Bolt (N)	Helène Bauer-Bernet (F) Cesare Maestripieri (I)		

Elaborated from HAEU.CEAB-12–481.
ORGANISATION OF TEAMS OF THE LEGAL SERVICE (BRANCH EEC-COMMISSION), 1962
Assistant to the Director General: Marc Sohier and Philippe Biays.
Freedom of Establishment and Free circulation: Paul Leleux.
Competition: Jochen Thiesing assisted by Jean-Jacques Beuve-Mery and Robert Fischer.
Transport: Pierre Pinay and Rolf Waegenbaur.
Agriculture: Giancarlo Olmi assisted by Claus-Dieter Ehlermann and Sergio Ventura.
Documentation and research: Gerhard Bebr.
Other legal advisers: Jean Bruyas, Louis de la Fontaine, Angelo Grisoli, Emile Mennens, Alberto Sciolla-Lagrange, Jürgen Utermann, Leendert Van der Burg.

Cravath, Swaine and Moore, which was counselling the HA. Swatland recommended that Gaudet pushed the ECJ to play a role like the US Supreme Court. Gaudet accepted such a parallelism and hoped that the ECJ would endeavour a role of polity-building vis-à-vis its founders, the member states. American constitutional influence in the theorisation of Gaudet was completed with the study trip that he carried out in 1959 to the USA in which he met, among others, Professor Eric Stein, a Czech refugee who had served in the US State department as legal advisor to the American UN delegation before entering into academia.[36] The most concrete example of such influence was the creation in the Legal Service of an Office for Information and Research, which was placed in charge of performing legal research, and in particular monitoring the application of European law within the member states. For that service Gaudet chose another Czech refugee specialising in European law, a young academic who was teaching at Yale, Gerhard Bebr.

What was at stake was not just getting the backing of national administrations and courts for implementing the treaties, but also convincing other European institutions (Council and Parliamentary Assembly), economic (companies) and social forces (lawyers and citizens) to contribute to the building of this incipient polity. Therefore, the search for a simple scientific justification of European law has to be seen in the context of the need of both Presidents of the Commission and their Legal Service Director to create a material basis for this new polity, which was emerging in the form of an integrated economy and society. This political design to empower the EEC Commission in the creation of its political role in deciding upon economic policies informed the legal strategy of the Legal Service.[37] It is crucial to bear this in mind to avoid the interpretative risk of staying out of touch with the political and economic realities of European integration, which cannot be reduced to a constructivist interaction between legal elites. Therefore, the constitutional reading of the treaties was always supposed to be legitimised also by social and economic actors, who were often directly represented through the participation of their legal advisers in different legal fora. Their presence was necessary for them to understand how the nascent EEC economic policies would be affecting the companies that they were working for, and what kind of margins of legal action they would gain on their behalf.[38]

Several researchers have underlined the crucial importance of competition policy in the early development of the EEC Commission to become a key regulator of European economic policies. During the negotiations on how to develop a Common competition policy, Gaudet had been trying to indirectly influence

[36] The letter between Michel Gaudet and Donald Swatland was first cited at length in Rasmussen 2010. For an alternative analysis see also Bailleux 2013. For the trip to the United States, see Boerger and Rasmussen 2017. For a brilliant biography of Eric Stein see Boeger 2014.

[37] Rasmussen 2014.

[38] Illustrative of this embeddedness of European law into social and economic actors are the lists of participants to conferences on European Law where members of the Legal Service met legal advisers from businesses and academics. College of Europe (1964) and College of Europe (1965).

the shape on Council Regulation 17/62 precisely on the grounds that it would be so fundamental, promoting a uniform and direct application of Article 85 on cartels.[39] The intensive struggle between ordo-liberal and Keynesian conceptions for competition demonstrated that what was at stake was the very nature of the new Common Market and the precise role of the EEC Commission in its regulation.[40] Consequently, both member state interests and business interests exerted huge pressure on the EEC Commission and the ECJ when developing the legal rules of the Common Market.[41]

The breakthrough for a constitutional interpretation of European law finally came in 1963–1964 in the two seminal judgments by the ECJ in respectively the *Van Gend en Loos* and the *Costa v ENEL* cases.[42] The new approach adopted by the Court was first developed by Gaudet and presented by the Legal Service in the *Van Gend en Loos* case.[43] In its memorandum of the Legal Service which Gaudet presented in October, a legal position which advocated a teleological vision about how the ECJ should interpret the treaties was favoured, instead of one based on international law. The major justification for this changed approach was to ensure a uniform application of European Law in a diversity of constitutional settings which would allow private litigants to invoke European law in national courts. The gamble was only partially won in the *Van Gend en Loos* case. Not just because the ECJ ambiguously defined the European legal order as a new legal order of *international law*, but also because the Court remained cautious about affirming the primacy of European law over national law, even if the affirmation of the possible direct effect of norms of primary law was a first step into this direction.[44]

The second step was taken by the Court in 1964 with the *Costa v ENEL* judgment. Here the Legal Service asked the ECJ to finally complete its constitutional interpretation of the treaties and endorse the primacy of European law confronted with a previous ruling of the Italian Constitutional Court (Corte costituzionale) which gave priority to national law. After the ECJ judgment vindicated the EEC Commission, Gaudet asked Hallstein, Rey and the Italian commissioner Lionello Levi-Sandri to put all possible pressure on the Italian government and the Corte costituzionale to change this original stance. They were able to count on the support of Segni who had now become the new President of the Italian Republic. In different scholarly debates on the nature of European law, that typically displayed the opposite positions of the Professors Riccardo Monaco and Rolando Quadri, such as the 1961 Congress of the Italian Union of Catholic Lawyers, Segni had delivered his own legal interpretation, which went against the standard dualist doctrine for the

39 Leucht and Marquis 2013.
40 Shaey and Ramírez Péres 2024.
41 Ramírez Pérez and van der Scheur 2013.
42 26/62 *Van Gend en Loos v Nederlandse Administratie der Belastingen*, 1963, ECLI:EU:C:1963:1 and 6/64 *Costa v ENEL*, 1964, ECLI:EU:C:1964:66.
43 For an analysis of these doctrines see Rasmussen 2014.
44 Rasmussen 2008; 2014.

reception of international law in the Italian legal order. According to the traditional dualist doctrine, the validity of any international norm was not directly applicable in national legal orders by national courts but needed to be transposed by a domestic legal act. To Segni the key reason for direct effect and primacy of European law was that the alternative, namely to allow the member states to define how they received European law, would lead to a lack of uniform application of the European law across the member states that would put in jeopardy the Common Market. He also cited the fact that Council regulations already had direct applicability, thus needing no transposition to enter the Italian legal order, and pointed out that Article 177 of the EEC Treaty obliged all Italian courts to send cases to Luxembourg.[45] It is telling that Gaudet had been in touch with Segni on these particular points.[46] As Gaudet aimed to consolidate the constitutional interpretation of European law, he also encouraged FIDE to promote it in European law academia and among the legal practitioners of each of the member states. Not surprisingly, they dedicated their two major conferences in 1963 and 1965 to explore respectively direct effect and primacy, after having dedicated their first conference in 1961 to competition law. (See also Chapter 4.)

This initial breakthrough for a constitutional practice of European law brokered by the Legal Service was seriously threatened by the Empty Chair crisis in 1965–1966, as it became clear that the federal thrust led by Hallstein and the EEC Commission was unacceptable to the French President Charles de Gaulle. During the crisis Gaudet also lost the trust of Hallstein. The cause was a direct clash between the two over the preparation of a legal note on the French boycott of the Council and the possibility pushed by Hallstein to take France to court for infringing the treaties.[47] The note opposed such a strategy, despite the fact that the EEC Commission was the guardian of the EEC Treaty. The French boycott was instead portrayed as a problem related to the Council and, consequently, it was up to the other member states to pursue a possible infringement case against France (using Article 170 of the EEC Treaty). Such a tactical position was not appreciated by Hallstein, who proceeded to ask the deputy of Gaudet, Hubert Ehring, to prepare an alternative legal analysis that would set out the legal basis for an infringement procedure. In the end, the Commission never implemented such a risky strategy, but the loss of influence of Gaudet with Hallstein undermined his position, even if the days of the German President of the Commission were numbered after the Luxembourg Compromise between the member states had ended the crisis in January 1966. In 1966–1967, the merger of the three executives also ended up weakening the Legal Service, even though the new President of the Commission,

45 Itzcovich 2006, 272–275. See also Segni 1961.

46 Bailleux 2014, 314.

47 HAEU.BAC 49 2013 18. Memo by Gaudet 'Absence d'un Etat membre . . . ', 12 July 1965 and HAEU. BAC 49 2013 18. Letter from Gaudet to Hallstein 'Annahme der Tagesordnung durch den unvollständig besetzten Rat', 26 July 1965.

Rey, had appointed Gaudet at the helm of a new unified Legal Service. The position of the Service was increasingly undercut by the other Director-Generals of the Commission, who aimed to develop their own legal expertise and emancipate themselves from the legal straitjacket constituted by the external advice of the Legal Service. By the end of 1969, Gaudet finally resigned for family reasons, leaving the Legal Service in the hands of one of the German lawyers that he had met at his arrival to Luxembourg in 1952: Walter Much.[48]

THE LEGAL SERVICE IN TRANSITION (1970–1977)

The period between the departure of Gaudet and the arrival of Claus-Dieter Ehlermann in 1977 might be defined as a period of transition, reflecting in a sense the general process of European integration of the period that was characterised by paralysis and crises. However, looking at the major cases decided by the ECJ during the 1970s and the legal consequences of the first enlargement of the EC in 1973, the 1970s were not a period of crisis for European law. The ECJ carried out a controversial introduction of direct effect for certain types of Council directives (*Franz Grad v Finanzamt Traunstein* in 1970 and *Van Duyn* in 1974),[49] human rights (*International Handelsgesellschaft* in 1970 and *Nold* in 1974)[50] and the external commercial character of the EC (*ERTA* in 1971),[51] before entering into the definition of the legal norms to underpin the Common Market (*Dassonville* in 1974; *Defrenne* in 1976; 1979, *Rewe-Zentral* in 1979).[52] Through these cases and others, the ECJ gradually built a legal order that underpinned the key policies of the EC as well as bolstering its institutional system. From the breakthrough of the constitutional interpretation of European law in 1963–1964, the ECJ moved towards the establishment of a full proto-federal legal order by the end of the 1970s. Part of the explanation for this dynamism had to be found on the composition of the ECJ bench that included a solid majority of judges with a pro-European and federalist outlook (see Chapter 1). However, it was first in 1986 that the ECJ finally openly acknowledged that its interpretation of the treaties was in fact constitutional in the crucial judgment of *Parti écologiste 'Les Verts'*.[53]

48 Boerger and Rasmussen 2017, 77–80.

49 9/70 *Franz Grad v Finanzamt Traunstein*, 1970, ECLI:EU:C:1970:78 and 41/74 *Yvonne van Duyn v Home Office*, 1974, ECLI:EU:C:1974:133.

50 11/70 *Internationale Handelsgesellschaft mbH v Einfuhr- und Vorratsstelle für Getreide und Futtermittel*, 1970, ECLI:EU:C:1970:114 and 44/73 *J. Nold Kohlen- und Baustoffgroßhandlung v Commission of the European Communities*, 1974, ECLI:EU:C:1974:51.

51 22/70 *Commission of the European Communities v Council of the European Communities*, 1971, EU:C:1971:32.

52 8/74 *Procureur du Roi v Benoît and Gustave Dassonville*, 1974, ECLI:EU:C:1974:82; 43/75 *Gabrielle Defrenne v Société anonyme belge de navigation aérienne Sabena*, 1976, ECLI:EU:C:1976:56 and 120/78 *Rewe-Zentral AG v Bundesmonopolverwaltung für Branntwein*, 1979, ECLI:EU:C:1979:42.

53 294/83 Parti *écologiste 'Les Verts' v European Parliament*, 1986, ECLI:EU:C:1986:166. See Boerger and Davies 2017.

Recently it has been argued that the leadership of promoting the constitutional practice of European law moved from the Legal Service to the dynamic ECJ in the 1970s.[54] The President of the ECJ Robert Lecourt even expressed his disappointment in 1975 to the Secretary-General of the Commission, Emile Noël, that the positions adopted by the Legal Service in the first half of the 1970s had become aligned with those of the member states.[55] This did not mean, however, that the Legal Service necessarily had completely dropped the ball. Several more technical developments in fact helped to solidify the proto-federal legal order. One development related to the so-called the 'acquis communautaire', a descriptive concept of all the decisions, including the case law of the ECJ, that the EC had taken since its inception. The concept was first introduced during the first enlargement negotiations in the early 1960s and became a key technical tool in the enlargement negotiations of the EC from 1970 to 1972, where the applicant states were forced to accept the acquis communautaire to join, leaving any special requirements to a regime of transitional measures.[56] The fact that the Commission included the ECJ case law in the acquis communautaire was controversial among the member states, because it represented an attempt to codify the constitutional interpretation of European law. It also meant that the new three member states of the EC, Britain, Denmark and Ireland, formally recognised the constitutional doctrines of the ECJ as part of the accession agreement when they entered, a recognition the old member states had not given. The other technical advance developed by the Legal Service was the launch of the CELEX system, a pioneering database that included all the valid legal acts of the EC. CELEX allowed in 1972 the publication for the first time of the whole acquis communautaire in one single document, just in time for the first enlargement. Thanks to CELEX, the Legal Service could thus increasingly begin to master its key role as the guardian of whether European law was implemented correctly by the member states. This technical improvement would be put to good use when Claus-Dieter Ehlermann was finally appointed in 1978.[57]

Taking a closer look at the visions of European law of the three Director-Generals of the 1970s gives us a better understanding of the role of the Legal Service during this period. With regard to the views of Much, several oral interviews claim that he had a challenging time taking the baton of Gaudet, considering that he had mostly worked in ECSC affairs until he moved to Brussels in 1967. He was not the natural successor of Gaudet, whose intellectual heritage was rather held by Much's deputy, Gerard Olivier, who had led the team on the general nature of the European legal order, external relations, and inter-institutional affairs under Gaudet. Olivier represented the Legal Service during the famous *ERTA* case,[58] which confirmed the

54 Fritz 2018.

55 Archive of Emile Noël (AEM). d.447. Memorandum, 12 May 1975.

56 Rasmussen 2007.

57 Vauchez 2015, 172–185.

58 22/70 *Commission of the European Communities v Council of the European Communities*, 1971, ECLI:EU:C:1971:32.

implicit powers of the European Communities in external relations, including in international organisations.[59] In 1973, he decided to quit the Service to go back to the Conseil d'État after having served in the so-called Vedel Committee in 1972 that worked on possible institutional reform of the enlarged EC.[60]

Much did not share the constitutional approach to European law pursued by Gaudet and supported by Olivier. Instead, he was a long-time proponent of the structural congruence argument, which had been elaborated by the German Professor, Herbert Kraus, and which diverged from the original approach of constitutional federalism pursued by Hallstein and Ophüls during the negotiations of the Treaty of Paris. The major tenet of this German doctrinal position was that for a transfer of sovereign power to be legitimate, the European legal order had to parallel to some degree the constitutional standards of the member states, particularly in the key areas of democratic norms and protection of individual rights. It was precisely this doctrine which the West German Constitutional Court (Bundesverfassungsgericht, BVerfG) used in its famous *Solange* judgment of 1974, inaugurating an ongoing controversy between BVerfG and the ECJ. It seems that after this decision, Much played a significant role to ensure that the crisis created by the decision of the BVerfG was not followed by the opening of an infringement proceeding against Germany by the Commission.[61] (See Chapter 7.)

The solution that Much proposed in various speeches was a larger involvement of the EP and an increase of its power vis-à-vis the Commission and the Council. Despite his misgivings about the constitutional approach developed by Gaudet and continued by Olivier, Much had to act in defence of European law but rationalised this with his own arguments. One of his most relevant speeches that summarises his thinking was delivered in May 1973 during the visit to the Legal Service of the Consiglio Superiore della Magistratura (High Council of the Judiciary).[62] Indeed, with regard to Much and the Legal Service's view on the relationship between European law and national law this was one of his most revealing and strategic speeches, considering the importance of his interlocutors and the precise moment at which it was delivered. The President of this Italian institution for the self-government of Italian judges was Professor of International Law and long-serving Christian-Democratic Minister, Giacinto Bosco, who a few years later would become a judge at the ECJ from 1976 until 1988. The moment was also in context

59 McNaughton 2017.

60 Vedel Report (1972), Report of the Working Group examining the problem of the extension of power of the European Parliament of 25 March 1972, Bulletin of the EEC, April 1972 (Luxembourg: OPOCE), 7–85.

61 Davies 2015.

62 A self-governing body of the Italian judiciary, responsible for overseeing the careers, appointments, and discipline of judges and public prosecutors. It operates independently of the executive and legislative branches and its task is to ensure the independence of the Italian judiciary, which comprises both judges and public prosecutors. I would like to thank Amedeo Arena for this information.

of the pending decision of the Italian Corte costituzionale in the famous *Frontini* case,[63] which also put counter-limits on the expansionist drive of European law, on the basis that the latter had to respect the fundamental principles of the Italian constitutional order and human rights.[64]

For Much, the most crucial principle which distinguished the new legal order from international law was the introduction of the citizens 'with their rights and interests in the community "game". It is in the last instance the idea of community integration at the social and community level the one which goes particularly beyond the international conceptions attached to the idea of inter-state relationships'.[65] In front of a selected audience, he strongly attacked, following some previous words of the Italian Commissioner Carlo Scarascia-Mugnozza, the attempt by the Italian Parliament to transpose community regulations into internal legal acts. This fiction of transposing Council regulations put into doubt what the Italian courts had already accepted, namely the direct applicability of regulations. Regulations had direct applicability and created rights for private parties and therefore could not be interposed between Community regulation and its application by a discretionary power. He also trusted the Corte costituzionale to finally confirm the direct application of the dispositions of the Treaties of Rome, as it had done in the case of *Acciaierie S. Michele* in 1965. What was at stake was nothing more than the 'unity of the common market and the uniform application of community law' as put forward by the ECJ. But the most complex exercise concerned the question of the primacy of community law. Quoting the dualist conceptions dominant in Italy and Germany of the classic works of Anzilotti and Triepel respectively, he was optimistic that this doctrine would ultimately also be accepted by national judiciaries.[66]

Whether this speech had any impact on the *Frontini* judgment by the Corte costituzionale is difficult to say, but what is sure is that Much's new deputy, Giancarlo Olmi, worked hard to lobby the Italian legal elite on behalf of the Commission. Olmi was in many respects at the top of the hierarchy of legal advisors in the Legal Service. During the Gaudet years, he had been in charge of dealing with one of the most important and dynamic fields of European law, the Common Agricultural Policy. A former avvocato dello stato (council for the state), Olmi was also the best person to draft the memorandum that the President of the Commission François-Xavier Ortoli sent on 1 January 1973 to the Italian President of the Republic, Giovanni Leone, criticising the position of the Italian avvocato dello (state attorney) representing the Italian state in the *Frontini* case.[67] Olmi even went to Rome to

63 Corte Costituzionale, *Frontini e a.*, judgment no. 183 of 18 December 1973.

64 Itzcovich 2006, 220–223.

65 Corte Costituzionale, *Acciaierie S. Michele v CECA*, judgment no. 98 of 16 December 1965.

66 The quotations and summary are taken from the speech held at the Archive of Walter Much (AWM). D.4.JUR 949/73, 14 May 1973.

67 Italian Presidential Archives (IPA), CD-b.359, Letter of the President of the European Commission to the President of the Italian Republic, 1 December 1973. The avvocato dello stato argued that the Corte costituzionale could not address the question of the direct applicability of Community regulations,

influence the Italian government before the *Frontini* judgment of the Corte costituzionale in the hope that the Court would now finally abandon the resistance initiated against the constitutional interpretation of the ECJ in the *Costa v ENEL* case in 1964[68] as well as address the continued Italian resistance towards accepting the direct applicability of Council regulations. According to a handwritten note drafted by the diplomatic adviser of the President of the Republic, the impression was that the Corte costituzionale finally was ready to give 'a favourable decision to the wishes of the European Commission'.[69] However, while the *Frontini* judgment finally acknowledged the direct applicability of regulations, it also made clear that the acceptance of the primacy of European law did not apply if European law conflicted with Italian civil and political rights, hinting discretely at the same logic that the *Solange* judgment by the German BVerfG would build on a year later.[70] Nevertheless, the judgment was considered a most positive step towards cooperating with the EC. The President of the Corte costituzionale, Paolo Bonifacio, thus declared that the judgment took away 'any doubt about the pro-European loyalty (lealtà europeistica)' of the country, confirming that the Treaty of Rome was not to be interpreted by the 'old schemes of international law'.[71]

No doubt, Olmi was closer to Gaudet in his conceptions of European law, and he was able to promote the constitutional practice at the helm of the Legal Service as he became for two years the unofficial interim Director-General, replacing Much after his death in 1975. His ideological and legal stands are clearly explained in his introductory essay to the volume edited under his supervision at the Legal Service to mark thirty years of European Law in commemoration of the Schuman Plan in 1983. Olmi analysed the whole history of European integration presented as a federalist vision with a continuity of purpose if not in structure and events. The ECJ had originally been modelled on the French Conseil d'État but had now, according to Olmi, evolved towards a Constitutional Court equivalent to those of Germany and Italy. To Olmi the existence of three separate Communities from 1958 to 1967 had been a legal fiction because the ECJ had quickly decided to develop a single European legal order. Even though the focus of the EC remained economic, the aim of European integration was political. The constitutional interpretation of the ECJ based on a teleological methodology had fortunately allowed the Court to 'fill the gaps left by the Community legislature' to serve the citizens through its introduction of the doctrines of direct effect and primacy. The cases considered most relevant by Olmi beyond the two pioneering cases of *Van Gend en Loos* and

because it only had the competence to evaluate the national legislation reproducing them. Laderchi 1998, 163.

68 Corte Costituzionale, *Costa v ENEL*, judgment no. 14 of 24 February 1964.

69 IPA, CD-b.359, Handwritten note of the diplomatic adviser reporting the positive reply of the Corte costituzionale to the President of the Republic on 9 December 1973. The decision was only published on 27 December 1973.

70 Corte Costituzionale, *Frontini e a.*, judgment no. 183 of 18 December 1973.

71 Itzcovich 2006, 221.

Costa v ENEL, were the *ERTA* case of 1971 and the *Kramer* case of 1975,[72] as both confirmed the doctrine of implied powers of the external relations of the EC. Last, but not least, Olmi highlighted the *Stauder* case of 1969,[73] which for the first time acknowledged the importance of human rights in the European legal order, since it held a core part of the shared legal traditions of the member states. To Olmi the overall political objective of the integration project was to preserve peace and liberty and extend it to other peoples of Europe. This was something in which the Legal Service was directly involved in the new enlargement negotiations with Spain and Portugal. Commenting upon the alleged loss of 'prophetic' spirit in the Commission, Olmi confirmed the need for a more cautious approach, which was more pragmatically guided to obtain concrete results, rather than the original attempt of the Hallstein's EEC Commission to move simultaneously in all the policy fields included in the EEC Treaty.[74]

THE LEGAL SERVICE IN THE PATH TOWARDS THE SINGLE EUROPEAN ACT: 1977–1986

The appointment of Much's formal successor, Claus-Dieter Ehlermann, in March 1977, took almost two years, which required Olmi to act as the head of the Legal Service for an extensive period. This was due to an initial opposition by the French government to have once again a German Director-General, considering that another German from the legal service, Hans-Joachim Glaesner, had been appointed in 1975 as Director-General of the Legal Service of the Council, after having served as chief of staff of commissioners Ralf Dahrendorf and Guido Brunner, both from the German Liberal Party.[75] The deadlock was finally broken with the arrival of the new President of the Commission, Roy Jenkins, and the resolution of a political conflict within the ruling government coalition in Germany, where the Social Democratic German Commissioner, Wilhelm Haferkamp, managed to secure Ehlermann the post.[76] Ehlermann's decade at the helm of the Legal Service can best be seen as a period of modernisation, which helped to increase the prestige of the Service at the vanguard of European integration. This was achieved, however, by retaining some of the traditions from earlier periods. Ehlermann was a pure product of the Legal Service, which he had joined as a young man back in 1961, after having worked for two years as legal clerk of Hans Kutscher, when he was

[72] 22/70 *Commission of the European Communities v Council of the European Communities*, 1971, ECLI:EU:C:1971:32 and 3, 4 and 6/76 *Cornelis Kramer and others*, 1976, ECLI:EU:C:1976:114.

[73] 29/69 *Erich Stauder v City of Ulm – Sozialamt*, 1969, ECLI:EU:C:1969:57.

[74] Olmi 1983.

[75] HAEU. Histcom 2. Interview of Claus-Dieter Ehlermann by Angel Viñas and Sigfrido Ramírez Péres, 8 October 2010.

[76] The German government had originally proposed Christoph Sasse, Professor at the new European University Institute in Florence, who was supported by the German Liberal Party Commissioners. Bieber and Nickel 1981.

judge at the BVerfG. Before going to Karlsruhe, he had written his doctorate in Heidelberg and spent one year at the Law School in Michigan. At the Legal Service he spent eight years working under the direction of Olmi on the legal aspects of the Common Agricultural Policy, before turning to institutional matters in 1969 under the supervision of Olivier. Together with another Italian Legal Service member, Sergio Ventura, they became the linchpin of the secretariat of the Vedel Committee, set up at the request of Commissioner Altiero Spinelli to reform the functioning of the European institutions. Ehlermann's career path at the Legal Service was interrupted in 1973, when the French Commissioner, Claude Cheysson, suggested that he became director at the administration in charge of financial control, where he was responsible for the first amendment to the Treaties of Rome with the adoption of the Budgetary Treaty before returning to the Legal Service in 1977 now as its Director-General.[77]

Ehlermann's conceptions of European law in the process of European integration were marked by a strong support to the constitutional interpretation and practice launched by Gaudet, but with a particular focus on the strengthening of European democracy. In his view, the European experience was a political system *sui generis* best comparable to a federal model. However, Ehlermann was very clear in that he did not believe the EC would ever fully turn into a federal state. The political process produced at best fragile political consensus that could easily be unsettled if not for the strength of European law. In such a 'strange creature' of an organisation, law thus played a greater role than it did in the member states or in traditional international organisations. The Community was, paraphrasing Walter Hallstein, a creation of law, a source of law and was limited by law. For Ehlermann, the role of the ECJ was to supervise the other institutions, using its extensive powers to balance an unstable system, which resulted from the asymmetry of powers between institutions and the need to find political compromises to legislate in the Council. European law might be incomplete and complex, but it was also uniquely dynamic in order to perform a political role, with European lawyers filling the gaps with the application of general principles of law or comparative legal methods.[78]

In the ten years that Ehlermann remained at its head, the Legal Service returned to a more activist promotion of the constitutional practice. The Legal Service contributed to the strengthening of the control over the introduction of European legislation in the member states. This took place through the monitoring of the transposition of directives in close cooperation with Ehlermann's former boss and new ECJ president, Hans Kutscher. The observance of the correct implementation of European legislation in the member states became one of the central elements of the contribution of the Service to the well-functioning of the European legal order. However, this step also indirectly acknowledged that the preliminary reference

77 Ramírez Pérez 2014.

78 Ehlermann 1983; Ehlermann 1984; Ehlermann 1992.

mechanism was not sufficient to gain national compliance with European law. Instead, the Commission would use its new monitoring system to increase the number of infringement cases brought against member states to implement European law.[79]

The modernisation of the Legal Service also followed when Ehlermann highlighted the horizontal and collective aspect of the service in 1977, by making the rotation of its lawyers obligatory. This was made easier by the fact that the Commission College had not determined the internal structure of the Legal Service. Rotation, at least for young lawyers, was an accepted principle but was applied only occasionally. It was Ehlermann who made it systematic across the board. It was necessary to prevent lawyers from being too influenced by the Directorate-Generals they were advising and becoming too restricted by the ways and routines of their own field of specialisation. Mobility would also give them an overview of European law, enabling them to draw up opinions that took account not only of the sector under their responsibility but also of other sectors, thereby promoting the consistency of European law. Moreover, when mobility later became a general policy in the entire Commission administration, the service could point out that it already operated such a policy. However, given the difficulty being promoted in such a horizontal service with little defined hierarchy, senior members of the legal service moved to other Directorate-Generals, like Ehlermann himself had done, to be promoted to higher responsibilities. They brought with them the basic concepts of European law defined by the Legal Service, to which they often remained in touch, thereby becoming interlocutors between their new Directorate-Generals and the Legal Service. This was the case of senior lawyers like Sergio Ventura in the Directorate-General for Agriculture, Antonio Marchini-Camia in the Secretariat-General of the Commission, John Temple-Lang in the Directorate-General of competition and Luigi Boselli or Jacques Bourgeois in the Directorate-General of external relations.

The modernisation brought about by Ehlermann within the Legal Service did not stop at rotation. It also included better dissemination of information within the Service and wider participation in administrative management. In other words, the members of the Service were consulted more often on administrative matters, including promotions. Lawyers could have a voice through a 'transparency group', while secretaries of the Service had a system of self-organisation and were consulted on changes in assignment. Female employees like Denise Sorasio and Helène Bernet were promoted and given higher responsibilities, following in the footsteps of the first female legal service lawyer, Wilma Viscardini Donà.[80] The Legal Service remained small in size during this period. In 1974, there were only sixty-six A grade,

79 Vauchez 2015, 188–190.

80 HAEU. Histcom 2. Entretien avec Denise Sorasio par Elisabeth Palmero, 24 September 2011; HAEU. Histcom 2. Entretien avec Helène Bernet and Jean-Claude Séché, 15 June 2011 par Michel Dumoulin et Sigfrido Ramírez Pérez.

seventeen B grade, forty-four C grade and thirteen LA officials. The latter were responsible for reviewing the legal and linguistic concordance of legal documents and for translating written pleadings. Beyond that, the attitude introduced by Ehlermann was to attach less importance to grade than to the value of legal opinions expressed within the Legal Service for example during the Monday meetings where drafting advice for ongoing court cases and other major questions were discussed.

Furthermore, the Legal Service was not cut off from the outside world. Ehlermann also expanded the policy of opening the world of Commission lawyers to universities by encouraging colleagues who were wondering whether to leave the service to teach at universities and possibly embark on an academic career. This opening up undoubtedly contributed to making the Legal Service a cornerstone of the broader legal community of European law, which, in his time, Gaudet had helped establish with the support of the activities of FIDE. Ehlermann maintained this support but did not prioritise the organisation since not all the national associations were equally active, and FIDE merely consisted of a biannual Congress. He gave instead preference to the development of other alternatives in the form of direct involvement in the boards of the main journal in English (*Common Market Law Review*), French (*Cahiers du Droit Européen*) and German (*Europa-Recht*). More decisively, he also supported close cooperation with the new European University Institute (EUI) created in 1976 by helping to finance the large-scale research project Integration through law directed by Professor Mauro Cappelletti and his doctoral researcher, and then professor, Joseph H. H. Weiler. The key result of the project was a legitimation of the Legal Service's strategy since the early 1960s, namely that the ECJ had constitutionalised the European legal order. The next step was to codify the constitutional doctrines of European law through treaty reform and further develop the constitutional interpretation. An attempt to move in this direction came from the directly elected EP after 1979, in which the Italian federalist Altiero Spinelli drafted a report on a Draft Treaty to create a European Union, including a Bill of Rights with the help by legal experts from the EUI (see Chapter 4).[81]

The need for a Bill of Rights for the EC derived from the clarification made by Kutscher as ECJ President, that it was impossible to accept the accession of the EC to the European Convention on Human Rights (ECHR) of the Council of Europe. This had been a hot issue when Ehlermann arrived at the Legal Service. Right after the *Solange* judgment of the BVerfG in 1974, Much had first suggested that the German government made a constitutional amendment. This was not a realistic option and consequently it was another proposal from Advocate General Reischl that was pursued, namely, to produce a joint declaration of European institutions to respect the ECHR to appease the BVerfG. This joint declaration, which came about in 1977, was necessary until a proper fundamental rights catalogue could be

[81] Byberg 2017c.

approved. The likelihood of such approval was, at the time, quite slim, with strong opposition coming from London and Paris. In the end, the joint declaration, coupled with the adjusted case law from the ECJ in the late 1970s that referred to the ECHR and national traditions for fundamental rights, proved enough to mollify the BVerfG (see Chapter 6).[82]

Britain and France were at the forefront in the critique of another major development in European law which also marked the first years of Ehlermann at the Legal Service: the attempt to give direct effect to directives.[83] This question had been originally put forward by Gaudet to expand direct effect from Council regulations and certain norms of primary law to all secondary legislation, including Council directives, to enhance the efficiency of European law. A breakthrough for this interpretation happened in a string of judgments in the first half of the 1970s, where the ECJ gradually began to expand the types of directives that could be given direct effect.[84] After the judgment of *Van Duyn* in 1974, the doctrine developed by the ECJ meant that Article 189 of the EEC Treaty could not anymore be interpreted in a narrow sense. Any Community legal instrument could produce direct effect under the new criteria promoting the efficiency of European law (*effet utile*) established by the ECJ. The implementation of directives that originally had been the domain of the member states were now subject to the doctrine of direct effect in an increasing number of cases. This led to a furious reaction by some member states. The British House of Lords contested the ECJ's case law on the basis that directives could not produce rights horizontally between citizens, but could only bind member states. The House of Lords therefore recommended that it was up to the Council to define when a directive could have or not have direct effect. Responding to a more general dissatisfaction of the member states with this audacious new case law, the Legal Service led in this field by the Belgian Paul Leleux now changed tactic. To the European Parliament's legal committee, he accepted the British criticism, albeit reducing it to a general misunderstanding of the ECJ's case law and confirmed that directives could only be directed to member states and this direct effect could only work in a vertical manner. Suddenly, the logic of directive effect of directives was not solely based on the efficiency argument but tempered by the fact that directives had a 'destinaire'. The ECJ would condone this theory in the *Ratti* judgment in October 1979.[85]

By then the damage had been done, however, and the ECJ's tactical withdrawal looked more like an outright defeat. In another judgment in the *Rutili* case from October 1975, the ECJ had seriously limited the discretion of member states to refuse access of citizens from other member states moving beyond the *Van Duyn*

82 Davies 2012b.

83 This story has been analysed in depth in Rasmussen 2017.

84 9/70 *Franz Grad v Finanzamt Traunstein*, 1970, ECLI:EU:C:1970:78; 8/70 *Commission of the European Communities v Italian Republic*, 1970, ECLI:EU:C:1970:9; 33/70 *SpA SACE v Finance Minister of the Italian Republic*, ECLO:EU:C:1970.118 and 41/74 *Yvonne van Duyn v Home Office*, 1974, ECLI:EU:C:1974:133.

85 148/78 *Criminal proceedings against Tullio Ratti*, 1979, ECLI:EU:C:1979:110.

judgment that had been more protective of the rights of member states on this question.[86] Combined with the case law on the direct effect of directives, the encroachment on member state competence became unbearable to the Conseil d'État. In another case on free movement of member state citizens, the German Daniel Cohn-Bendit who had been a leading figure in the 1968 rebellion in France, was barred access to France. The Conseil d'État used the case to mount a full rebellion against the ECJ, by directly interpreting Article 189 of the EEC Treaty declaring that directives could have no direct effect and rejecting the option to send a preliminary reference to the ECJ.[87] The rebellion of the Conseil d'État came at a sensitive period in France's relation to the EC, where the President Giscard d'Estaing were ready to reform the ECJ to limit its powers, as discussed in depth in Chapter 7.

The Legal Service were at the centre of developing a response to France on behalf of the Commission. The option to bring an infringement case against France was if not dropped at least not made explicit, as it had been during the crisis with Germany over the *Solange* judgment in 1974. Instead, the letter from Commission President Roy Jenkins to the French Minister of Foreign Affairs in March 1979 asked for a clarification of the consequences of the Conseil d'État judgment to French EC membership. With the French government not responding, Ehlermann and Olmi involved the legal committee of the newly elected European Parliament to develop a position on the matter and thus indirectly put France under pressure. (See Chapter 3 for details.) After a second letter from Jenkins, the French government finally responded in March 1980 by claiming that there was no case and that France supported the integrity of European law. It would take a new President in France and a new more positive approach to European integration from 1981 onwards to gradually solve the crisis of non-cooperation of the Conseil d'État.

The Legal Service also made a substantial contribution to the functioning of the European legal order through the development of a series of cases from 1983 to 1986, in the field of external relations. The common theme of this contribution was to defend interpretations of the Treaties of Rome that promoted the process of integration. Until the beginning of the 1970s, legal scholars took the almost unanimous view that the EC did not have the power to engage in international agreements outside the few cases expressly provided for in the Treaties. The Commission opened a case following the advice of the Legal Service, and in particular of Gerard Olivier, which ultimately became the well-known *ERTA* case. In the judgment the ECJ followed the Commission by affirming the view that there was a 'parallelism' between the Community's internal and external powers, which it later had the opportunity to develop further. The recognition of these implicit powers had opened the way to broad interpretations concerning the possibility of

86 36/75 *Roland Rutili v Ministre de l'intérieur*, 1975, ECLI:EU:C:1975:137.

87 Conseil d'État (Assemblée), 22 December 1978, *Cohn-Bendit*, n° 11604, published in *Recueil Lebon* 524, 1980.

the EC acting as an entity under international law. The question of the EC's power to negotiate agreements with international partners alone (exclusive competence) or with the member states (mixed competence) had been the subject of lively political and legal disputes, such as the case of the International Rubber Agreement in 1978 and the agreements concerning other commodities (wheat, sugar, cocoa, coffee, tin). After Olivier had resigned from the Legal Service, the leadership in this field came into the hands of a French member of the Conseil d'État, Jean Groux, who had joined the Legal Service during the 1970s with some misgivings about the principles of this interpretative line, but he was quickly converted to the dominant constitutional paradigm of the Service.

The Legal Service then focused its attention on the effects of the international agreements concluded by the EC with non-member countries or international organisations. There were two schools of thought among legal writers: a classical school, based on dualist theory, which rejected out of hand any direct effect of international agreements and in any event required transposition by national legislation, and another school closer to the Community system itself, based on the monist theory, and favoured by the Legal Service, which was in favour of recognising, under certain conditions, the direct effect and primacy of such agreements. The ECJ did not settle this question of principle, instead preferring to adopt in a series of cases a more flexible position based on the specific characteristics, terms and spirit of each category of agreement.[88]

The period from the early 1970s to the early 1980s also witnessed the development of the legal foundation of the Common Market that would later be important when the Single European Act was adopted in 1986. This was done by using a teleological interpretation of the objectives pursued by the EEC Treaty. We can restrict ourselves here to recall the advances in the free movement of goods that enabled the removal of many 'hidden' restrictions to the detriment of goods from other member states (starting with the *Dassonville* judgment)[89] and the confirmation, in the absence of harmonised Community rules, of the principle of mutual recognition of national legislation protecting essential interests that had primacy over the free movement of goods (starting with the *Cassis de Dijon* judgment).[90] These went much further than the arguments supported by the prevailing doctrine, which regarded the prohibition laid down by the treaty as concerning only national measures discriminating against products from other member states.[91]

[88] Groux and Manin 1984 and HAEU. Histcom 2. Interview with Jean Groux by Michel Mangenot, 25 June 2010.

[89] 8/74 *Procureur du Roi v Benoît and Gustave Dassonville*, 1974, ECLI:EU:C:1974:82.

[90] 120/78 *Rewe-Zentral AG v Bundesmonopolverwaltung für Branntwein*, 1979, ECLI:EU:C:1979:42.

[91] Leucht 2017; Albors-Llorens et al. 2021.

FROM THE SINGLE EUROPEAN ACT TO THE TREATY OF MAASTRICHT (1987–1993)

One of the most decisive contributions of the Legal Service in promoting the constitutional practice was found in the direct involvement of former members of the Legal Service of the EC at the other Directorates-Generals where they could pursue a constitutional interpretation of European law in specific policy fields. However, from 1986 the export of Legal Service members took a new dimension, when Jean-François Lamoureux became legal advisor of the new Commission President Jacques Delors. In this capacity, he would take a prominent role after the decision was made to replace Ehlermann by the Frenchman Jean-Louis Dewost, former Director-General of the Legal Service of the Council since 1973 and with a background in the Conseil d'État.[92] The reason for the replacement of Ehlermann was strictly political. Delors had promised the British government that in exchange for accepting him as President, the position of Secretary-General would be given to the Deputy Secretary of Margaret Thatcher's office, David Williamson, after the retirement of the French Emile Noël. The French government wanted a compensation for the loss of such a strategic position by assuming again the leadership position of the Legal Service. Ehlermann in turn became the spokesperson of the Commission and would cooperate with Delors on a daily basis, as well as maintaining a direct link with Lamoureux, who remained as legal adviser of the President until 1991. Ehlermann and Lamoureux prepared and designed the contribution of the European Commission to the Single European Act in liaison with the Secretary-General of the Commission Emile Noël.[93]

A Doctor of Law, Lamoureux had worked as assistant at the Sorbonne of Professor Georges Vedel, who had been the legal advisor of the French delegation during the negotiations on the Treaties of Rome. As part of his time in the Legal Service he had specialised in international law. He shared the strong European convictions of Jacques Delors and had contributed with an important interpretation to promote the constitutional legal order. He viewed the Single European Act in continuity with the proposal for reform by Spinelli and the EP, the Draft Treaty Establishing the European Union. To Lamoureux the key challenges was to ensure that the core methodology of integration, the so-called Community method based on the supranational institutions, continued. Given the acute fear of several national governments for spillover the danger was that any expansion of competences of the EC could be based on separate treaties.[94] Lamoureux's fear would prove correct. During the negotiations on the Treaty of Maastricht, Lamoureux ensured that the

92 Mangenot 2004.

93 HAEU. Histcom 1. INT.748, Interview to Claus-Dieter Ehlermann by Yves Conrad and Myriam Rançon, 29 January 2004 and HAEU. Histcom 2. INT.150, Interview to Claus-Dieter Ehlermann by Sigfrido Ramírez Pérez and Angel Viñas, 8 October 2010.

94 Archive of François Lamoureux (AFL), d.31, François Lamoureux, 'L'Europe sort du blocage institutionnel', *Projet*, n°200, 55–71.

Commission proposed a single treaty with a federal ambition to encompass the new policy areas planned, where the Community method was at the centre and the constitutional practice of European law codified. However, a majority of member states rejected the proposal.[95] Instead, the Council secretariat led by Danish diplomat Niels Ersbøll now took over and helped develop a new treaty based on three pillars, where the Home and Justice Affairs and Foreign and Security policy were kept strictly on an intergovernmental basis, limiting the Community method to the first pillar. The European Council would be given the key coordinating and agenda-setting role as the leading institution of the entire Union. This fundamental defeat of the political ambitions of the Commission also meant that the Legal Service of the Council led by Jean-Claude Piris, another French member of the Conseil d'État, who had substituted Dewost, would become more important than the Commission's Legal Service during the treaty reforms after 1993.[96]

In general terms, the Legal Service during the Dewost period grew rapidly to be able to deal with the increasing workload created by the Single European Act, but it did so under the shadow of the Delors' powerful cabinet. If the Legal Service became more hierarchical under Dewost, who limited the contacts of the service members with academia, the nearly one hundred members retained their autonomy. Looking at the fact that some of the new leaders like the deputies of Dewost, Christian Timmermans and Allan Rosas continued their careers in the ECJ, the ability of the Legal Service to foster legal advisors of high quality for the other institutions seems to have remained intact.[97]

An example of the indirect influence of the Legal Service of the Commission is the case of the Spanish Professor of International Law, Gregorio Garzón Clariana. A student of Professor Manuel Diez de Velasco and a co-disciple of Professor Gil Carlos Rodriguez Iglesias, the two first Spanish judges at the ECJ, he led the Legal Service section on external relations. In 1994, he moved on to become the long-serving jurisconsult of the EP dealing with all successive treaty reforms until the Treaty of Lisbon in 2009, during the time that Rodriguez Iglesias presided over the ECJ (1994–2003).[98] Garzón Clariana created the first proper Legal Service in the EP, importing many of the legal and organisational traditions from the Legal Service of the European Commission.[99]

CONCLUSION

In conclusion, the constitutional practice based on a federalist understanding of the Treaties of Rome first originated in the ECSC Legal Service and the EEC Legal

95 Rasmussen and Martinsen 2019.

96 Jacqué 2012.

97 Van Leeuwen 2019.

98 Liber Amicorum en l'honneur de Gregorio Garzón Clariana 2006.

99 Ramírez Pérez 2016a.

Service, the latter under the leadership of Michel Gaudet. This line was adopted by the ECJ in 1963–1964 in the seminal *Van Gend en Loos* and *Costa v ENEL* rulings. After Gaudet left the directorship in 1969, the German Director-General Much seemingly did not share the same fervent belief in the constitutional interpretation of European law as Gaudet and the Legal Service lost its position as the key driver behind the making of a constitutional practice in European law. Instead, the ECJ under the Presidencies of Lecourt and Kutscher took over in a decade of unusual activity in defining the doctrines of a constitutional and proto-federal European legal order. It was only when Claus-Dieter Ehlermann became Director-General that the Legal Service again regained some of its lost position. Ehlermann changed priorities from the time of Gaudet both in the way he cultivated the academic field focus on journals and the European University Institute (EUI) instead of the partly failed European law associations and FIDE. In particular, Ehlermann's involvement with the integration through law project at the EUI turned out to be successful because it helped create a constitutional discourse to legitimise the legal order that the ECJ had built since the early 1960s. Ehlermann also focused on the implementation of directives and systematic use of infringement cases to improve the lacklustre implementation record of European law of the member states. After Ehlermann left the Legal Service in 1986, the leadership of the Commission with regard to developing the constitutional practice and codifying it in treaty reform fell to the new legal advisor of Delors, Lamoureux. Despite high ambitions for an important step towards a more federal European Union during the Maastricht Treaty negotiations, which would have included the codification of the constitutional practice of European law, a majority of national governments chose to create a European Union based on three pillars, two of which were intergovernmental in nature. While the acquis communautaire was codified as part of the Maastricht Treaty[100] and thus also the case law of the ECJ, the member states did not base the new European Union on European constitutionalism as a legitimating principle.

Inside the Commission administration, the Legal Service at first quickly obtained a key role, but lost influence in the second half of the 1960s after Gaudet had fallen out with Hallstein during the Empty Chair crisis. The Service probably only gained an influence similar to the first half of the 1960s during Ehlermann's tenure. Nevertheless, the Legal Service continued to influence not only the Commission but also other European institutions due to the fact that it developed talented young legal experts, who after some formative years in the Service would move on to other parts of the Commission's administration, to the Council or European Parliament and even to the ECJ. Figures such as Lamoureux and Garzón Clariana were perhaps the most prominent examples of this, but certainly not the only ones.

[100] Treaty of Maastricht, Article B, 5th indent.

3

The European Parliament and the Constitutionalisation of European Law

Jan-Henrik Meyer

The European Parliament (EP)'s role in the history of European Community (EC) and European Union (EU) politics is routinely underplayed.[1] This is quite remarkable, given that the first students of European integration in the late 1950s, legal scholar Eric Stein[2] and political scientist Ernst Haas,[3] explored how the EP and its predecessor, the Assembly of the European Coal and Steel Community (ECSC), and its members (MEPs) contributed to European integration. Both scholars examined parliamentary practices and observed how MEPs went to great lengths to be recognised as representatives of Europe in a true Parliament. Haas underscored MEPs' ideological ambition to 'deliberately and self-consciously seek to create a federal Europe'.[4]

Despite this early scholarly interest, until recently, historical research has ignored the EP. The most comprehensive study explaining how the EP achieved direct elections in 1979 and gained influence through successive treaty reforms was written by political scientist Berthold Rittberger.[5] A number of recent studies have picked up the loose threads of the early research, and emphasised the pro-European self-understanding and the specific strategies the formally largely powerless assembly has pursued.[6] In his history of symbolic politics, Jacob Krumrey has analysed the early EP's practice of performing as a parliament, their insistence on being treated 'as if' they were a powerful institution and highlighted the EP's strategies to obtain recognition and visibility.[7] Ann-Christina Lauring Knudsen examined MEPs' collective characteristics, and found self-selection and much pro-European commitment. She called for a new understanding of the much-criticised dual mandate,[8]

1 For an overview of the historiography see Dinan 2018 and 2021.
2 Stein 1959.
3 Haas 1958.
4 Haas 1958, 90.
5 Rittberger 2007.
6 See e.g. the special issues Gfeller et al. 2011; Patel and Salm 2021.
7 Krumrey 2018.
8 Knudsen 2014.

which helped not only to synchronise national and European agendas,[9] but also to put new policy issues on the European agenda, by connecting to the public and collaborating with the Commission. Even if all these instruments were not of a legally binding nature, they mattered, and advanced European policy-making,[10] notably regarding the Environment and Social Policy.[11]

Against this backdrop, this chapter argues that the EP's contribution is an important missing part of the puzzle regarding the establishment and development of a constitutional practice of European law. Other institutions were surely more influential in terms of legislative power and ability to define European law. However, the EP's initial lack of political powers did not necessarily stop the Parliament from producing forms of legitimacy. As I will show subsequently, this was an aspect that contemporary actors were fully aware of and sought to make use of.

Furthermore, this chapter argues that the EP – and its Legal Committee in particular – contributed to both the political development and discursive construction of the legitimacy of the constitutional practice.[12] The EP seemed particularly well-placed, and quite likely to contribute to such legitimation, in three respects: first, as an actor that comprised a plethora of legal experts and committed federalists; second, as a forum for European debates and next best proxy to a European public, an expert public that was well-connected to wider national publics at a time when MEPs were still members of national parliaments. And third, as a provider of legitimacy – as the representative of the European peoples, it was to embody the democratic element of the European institutional setup. The Commission in particular, but also most governments, agreed that the involvement of the EP granted the EC action additional legitimacy, as evidenced by their practices.[13] Legitimacy is understood here in a constructivist manner, and the EP was clearly a powerful architect of discourses invoking and thus rhetorically creating the normative justifiability of the European political order.[14]

The analysis will examine the EP's contribution at four important stages of the construction of a constitutional practice of European law before the Parliament gained new substantive powers in the Single European Act. First, already in the mid-1950s, the Assembly of the ECSC laid the foundations of European parliamentary practice and positioned itself with a view to European law. Second, in the mid-1960s, the EP strongly supported the constitutional interpretation of European law in the seminal *Van Gend en Loos* and the *Costa v ENEL* judgments of 1963 and 1964.[15] On

9 Meyer 2011 and 2014.
10 Meyer 2017.
11 Roos 2020 and Meyer 2020.
12 On the concept see Chapter 1 and Rasmussen and Martinsen 2019.
13 Rittberger 2009.
14 Beetham and Lord 1998.
15 26/62, *Van Gend en Loos v Nederlandse Administratie der Belastingen*, 1963, ECLI:EU:C:1963:1 and 6/64, *Costa v ENEL*, 1964, ECLI:EU:C:1964:66.

its own initiative, the EP produced a report and resolution on the primacy of European law in 1965 and collaborated extensively with other supranational institutions in the process.

In the 1970s, the Commission's and the ECJ's constitutional interpretation of European law was challenged by the highest courts of the largest member states. The EP responded in much the same manner to both the *Solange* decision of 1974, in which the West German Constitutional Court (Bundesverfassungsgericht, BVerfG) had criticised the lack of human rights protection in the EC that made it problematic to accept the primacy of European law, and the French Council of State's (Conseil d'État) 1978 *Cohn-Bendit* ruling, which did not accept the supremacy of European Law and a European Court.[16] Again, the EP closely cooperated with the Commission's (and the Council's) Legal Service(s). With rhetorical references to the revolutionary judgments of the 1960s, the EP engaged in discursive action and tradition-building, reaffirming those judgments as unequivocally accepted doctrines.

The conclusions will seek to illuminate how these findings contribute to the history of European law, with a view to the links and entanglements between actors and institutions. The chapter also seeks to offer new insights into the history of the EP, as a special case of transnational parliamentary assemblies. However, before delving into the specific cases, it is important to discuss how the EP became an independent actor in the legal field of the ECSC/EC.

THE EP LEGAL COMMITTEE

The original Schuman Plan for supranational integration of the coal and steel sectors of May 1950 had not foreseen a representative assembly. Such a body was only inserted into the institutional framework during the negotiations of the Treaty of Paris to improve democratic accountability. The Assembly's primary function was to review the activities of the High Authority (HA) – the predecessor of the European Commission – every year.[17] The ECSC Assembly not only shared the assembly hall of the Council of Europe in Strasbourg, but also a substantial number of members served in both parliaments. In May 1955 it set up a Legal Committee, by adding legal affairs to the remit of the already existing Committee on internal proceedings, petitions and immunities.[18]

When the European Economic Community (EEC) and Euratom were founded by the Treaties of Rome of 1957 to complement the original ECSC, the new

[16] Conseil d'État (Assemblée), 22 December 1978, *Cohn-Bendit*, n° 11604, published in *Recueil Lebon* 524, 1980.

[17] Boerger 2012, 341.

[18] Historical Archives of the European Parliament (HAEP), 1955. PV!JURI.1955_JURI-19550512001oFR. ECSC, Assemblée Commune, Commission des questions juridiques, du règlement de l'Assemblée Commune, des pétitions et des immunités, Compte rendu de la Réunion du jeudi 12 mai 1955, AC 1496.

'common' European Parliamentary Assembly was to serve all three Communities. In 1962, in an act of self-assertion, it adopted a new name: the 'European Parliament'. Its Legal Committee continued to be responsible for procedural questions and immunities – but no longer for petitions. There was some continuity of membership before and after 1958.[19] Given the expertise necessary for the complex legal matters they dealt with, the Committee was almost entirely composed of MEPs with a background in the legal profession. Between 1960 and 1965 the share of lawyers grew from 70 per cent in 1960 to 88 per cent in 1965.[20] Some of the members were well-known law professors and judges with ample expertise in matters of international, constitutional and private law relevant to the Common Market.[21] Others had previously worked in law firms, in public administration and in government office, such as the former Bavarian Minister of Justice, the Christian Socialist Otto Weinkamm, who presided over the Legal Committee during the debates on *Costa v ENEL*.[22]

Among the members in the 1950s and 1960s, the Belgian law professor and socialist Fernand Dehousse stands out.[23] He was one of the central figures within the EP, with multiple ties across academia, legal practice, federalist advocacy, diplomacy and politics. In 1952–1953, Dehousse had served as rapporteur on the constitutional committee of the Ad Hoc Assembly preparing the Treaty of the European Political Community (EPC), which was never ratified. From 1954 until 1961, Dehousse was also a member of the Council of Europe's Parliamentary Assembly and in 1964–1965 he became EP's Legal Committee's rapporteur on the new doctrine of the ECJ on the primacy of European law. He only briefly interrupted his long-lasting membership of the EP (1952–1971), when he was Belgian Minister of Education from August 1965 until March 1966.[24]

The EP Legal Committee thus included a wide range of legal and political expertise regarding the different member states and a commitment to European integration, which translated into a generally supportive stance towards the project of constructing a constitutional practice in European law.

19 HAEP, 1958. PV!JURI.1958_JURI-19580625001oFR. E.g. Eugène Schaus (Luxembourg) and Walter Scheel (West Germany), Procès-verbal et compte rendu analytique de la réunion tenue le 25 juin 1958, APE 424, Assemblée parlementaire européenne, Commission des questions juridiques, du règlement et des immunités.

20 Sacriste 2012, 38.

21 Sacriste 2012, 47.

22 Grünsteudel 1998.

23 Dehousse, Fernand. Report Drawn Up on Behalf of the Legal Committee on the Paramountcy of Community Law over the Laws of Member States. *European Parliament Working Documents* 1965–66, no. 43 (1965): 1–28.

24 Fonds Description: Historical Archives of the European Union (HAEU) Archive of Fernand Dehousse, (European University Institute, 2006), 5–6, 95, https://archives.eui.eu/files/inventories/15245.pdf.

BEFORE 1958: THE PARLIAMENTARY ASSEMBLY OF THE ECSC

From the very beginning, the Assembly, its Legal Committee and various members attempted to assert the role of the EP within the new institutional system. This battle involved fighting over internal, but also inter-institutional procedural issues. By arguing that the Assembly was more like a national parliament in a federal state than that of an international organisation, the MEPs corroborated a constitutional interpretation of the ECSC Treaty. In 1957 for instance, the Committee discussed who should have the right to speak in the Assembly. Party politics fuelled debate on this interinstitutional question. The West German Social Democratic Party (SPD) member of the Committee, Gerhard Kreyssig, refused to deal with a Secretary of State (Staatssekretär), who was merely considered a low-ranking civil servant. Instead, he demanded to inquire directly with the Christian Democratic Union (CDU) West German Minister of Economics Ludwig Erhard. Even though he was not a lawyer, but an economist, Kreyssig was clearly thinking in terms of establishing institutional practice in the long term. What the Committee accepted now, he argued, would also set a precedent for the new Euratom and EEC.[25]

As part of their strategy of self-assertion, the Committee skilfully drew on parliamentary resources, and had the Assembly's Secretariat draw up a comparative study of the constitutional situations in the member states. The study supported the Committee members' views that the EP ought to be treated like the parliaments of sovereign nation states.[26] The Assembly also defended its self-defined privileges vis-à-vis the Commission: in Article 29 (4) of its Rules of Procedure of 1958 it insisted that only members of the 'executive', but not their staff, had a right to speak in the Assembly and its committees.[27] These examples are well in line with Krumrey's observations that the Assembly engaged in performing 'as if' they were a real parliament.[28]

After the demise of the European Defence Community (EDC) and the EPC project in 1954,[29] parliamentary activism intensified. In a resolution of December 1954, the Assembly demanded to expand its political role, conforming more fully to the parliamentary model. Rather than being limited to scrutinising ECSC action after the fact, MEPs demanded to critically accompany the work of the HA and the member governments. Just two months after the failure of the EDC,

25 HAEP, 1957. PV!JURI.1957_JURI-19570626001oFR, 13. ECSC, Assemblée Commune, Commission des questions juridiques, du règlement de l'Assemblée Commune, des pétitions et des immunités, Compte rendu de la Réunion du mercredi 26 juin 1957, AC 3450.

26 HAEP, 1957. PV!JURI.1957_JURI-19570626006oFR. ECSC, Assemblée Commune, Commission des questions juridiques, du règlement de l'Assemblée Commune, des pétitions et des immunités, Note du Secrétariat des Commissions sur la position du Secrétaire et du Sous-Secrétaire d'Etat en Allemagne, France et Italie dans la droit constitutionel, Luxembourg, le 21 juin 1957, AC 3352.

27 Stein 1959, 242.

28 Krumrey 2018, 109–153.

29 Griffiths 2020.

which would have introduced direct elections, the resolution called for setting up a special committee to study how direct elections could nevertheless be achieved.[30]

The Assembly also insisted on having a role in the making of the new treaties being negotiated for EURATOM and the EEC.[31] In 1956, for instance, Kreyssig demanded a right to be heard on the draft treaties, as well as the changes necessary to adjust the Treaty of Paris to the Saar region's reintegration into West Germany. In the latter case, the Political Committee of the Assembly, not the nascent Legal Committee, had already started to work on this issue.[32] As part of their efforts of self-assertion, Legal Committee members were also reaching out to the public to inform about the new Common Assembly planned for the new European Communities, as for instance Kreyssig did in 1957, via *Die Neue Gesellschaft*, a newly founded journal widely read among West German Social Democrats.[33]

After the EDC/EPC failure, the Assembly's Italian President Giuseppe Pella started lobbying for further European integration. Although a lawyer, he held chairs as Professor of Economics in both Rome and Turin. He was a prominent member of the Italian Centre for Legal Studies, a forum in which Italian legal and political elites met. Advocating a broader and more political role of the ECSC as a 'supranational community', Pella went on a veritable crusade to national capitals to convince legal and political circles and government representatives.[34] As part of this campaign, Pella initiated a major Congress to place European integration on the European political, economic and legal agenda. Supported by a grant from the ECSC, the Italian Centre for Legal Studies held an international conference at Stresa in early May 1957. Nicknamed the 'Pella Congress', the event brought together more than 450 invited participants, among them lawyers, politicians, business representatives and journalists to examine legal and economic aspects of European integration. Many of the issues they studied, notably the ECSC's relations to member states, to third countries or other international organisations, touched upon the very nature of European law.[35]

An important target group was the community of international lawyers. Pella intended to win them over to espouse the 'constitutional autonomy' of European law through a thorough examination of the legal nature and legal accomplishments of the ECSC. Pella's attempt failed, however. Despite the efforts of Michel Gaudet from the Legal Service of the HA to advise and influence the legal committee led by

30 ECSC, Assemblée Commune, Résolution 27 du 2 décembre 1954, Official Journal of the ECSC, 11 December 1954 and Bailleux 2014, 163–165.

31 Haas 1958, 390.

32 HAEP, 1956. PV!JURI.1956_JURI-19561110001oFR., 21 §6. ECSC, Assemblée Commune, Commission des questions juridiques, du règlement de l'Assemblée Commune, des pétitions et des immunités, Compte rendu de la Réunion du samedi 10 novembre 1956, AC 2763.

33 Kreyssig 1957.

34 Bailleux 2014, 163.

35 Centro italiano di studi giuridici, *Actes officiels du Congrès international d'études sur la Communauté européenne du charbon et de l'acier, Milan-Stresa 31 mai–9 juin 1957 (1–7)* (Milano: A. Giuffrè, 1957) and Bailleux 2014, 167–169.

Paul de Vischer that authored the conference report, the latter concluded that European law was merely a new form of international law and did not have autonomy. The report caused a heated debate about the potential autonomy of European law at the conference pitting international lawyers against comparativists (or federalists) as Gaudet would explain in his private correspondence.[36] Several hand-picked members of the Assembly, such as members of the ECSC Assembly's Legal Committee and the Stresa Congress's steering committee, Luxembourg lawyer Eugène Schaus, and the Belgian constitutional law professor Pierre Wigny, argued against the report. They rejected categorising European law as merely a subfield of international law. Instead, they argued, along with the French Advocate General Maurice Lagrange, in favour of a federalist understanding of European law as 'autonomous'. It was hardly surprising that well-established international lawyers were loath to grant a special status to the nascent European law at a time when supranational integration was still in its infancy and various international organisations in Europe competed among each other.[37] In any case, Pella duly published the Congress proceedings, thus situating the event as an important point of reference for the subsequent debate about European integration and European law.[38]

The three strategies – demanding respect for and involvement of the Assembly, by insisting on procedural rules; using the parliamentary resources, such as expert reports; and reaching out to broader audiences for alliances and support – pioneered during this initial period, were to become part of the EP's long-term toolbox for self-assertion and the defence of the constitutional practice.

AFTER *COSTA V ENEL*: ADVANCING THE PRIMACY OF EUROPEAN LAW (1964–1965)

In the 1960s, the EP and its Legal Committee became staunch defenders of the new doctrines of direct effect and supremacy, established by the ECJ in the *Van Gend en Loos* (1963) and *Costa v ENEL* (1964) judgments.[39] The EP fulfilled different functions in the process: first, it served as a forum, also for the EEC Commission, to discuss ideas and raise concerns; second, the Committee and its key members were important actors, using the tool of reporting to raise awareness and demand action; third, its debates were to lend legitimacy to the new doctrine, a function

36 This issue was discussed in the committee chaired by the Belgian international law professor Paul de Visscher. Bailleux and Jackson 2010, 67–90, 77, 80, 86–87; Rasmussen 2012, 281; Greaves 2007, 59–88, 59.

37 Kaiser and Patel 2017.

38 Centro Italiano di Studi Giuridici. *Actes Officiels du Congrès International d'Études sur la Communauté Européenne du Charbon et de l'Acier, Milan-Stresa 31 Mai–9 Juin 1957 (1–7)*. Milan: A. Giuffrè, 1957.

39 26/62, *Van Gend en Loos v Nederlandse Administratie der Belastingen*, 1963, ECLI:EU:C:1963:1and Case 6/64, *Costa v ENEL*, 1964, ECLI:EU:C:1964:66.

highlighted by EEC Commission. In all this, the EP emphasised and asserted the importance of supranational European integration and its own institutional interests and collaborated closely with the EEC Commission and its Legal Service.

On 24 February 1964, the Italian Constitutional Court (Corte Costituzionale) struck down a case that had challenged the nationalisation of Italian utilities to form the state-owned monopoly electricity provider ENEL. European law expert and participant of the Stresa conference, Gian Galeazzo Stendardi,[40] considered this in contradiction with European law and provoked a reference of his test case first to the Corte Costituzionale. In its decision, the Corte Costituzionale followed the prevalent dualist view of Italian legal tradition. The Court held that new national legislation could override European law, according to the time-honoured principle *lex posterior derogat priori*.[41] Not taking no for an answer, Stendardi now convinced another Italian lower court to refer the case to the ECJ by means of a preliminary reference. In the *Costa v ENEL* judgment of 15 July 1964, the ECJ asserted the 'autonomous' nature of European Law and introduced the doctrine of primacy – more precisely the 'internal primacy' of European legislation when conflicting with national legislation.[42] Thus, the ECJ followed the lines of a monist understanding of the relationship between European and member state law.[43] Combined with the *Van Gend en Loos* judgment from the year before, the ECJ took upon itself to define how the member states were supposed to receive European law.[44]

The story of the EP's response to *Costa v ENEL* unfolded in two steps: first, what could be described as an agenda-setting phase, in which primacy was increasingly considered a problem to be addressed. In a second phase, the Committee developed its stance in a report of which it took the initiative – closely debating and coordinating with the EEC Commission and reaching out to the wider public. First, on 18 June 1964, a month before the ECJ's *Costa v ENEL* ruling, the EP had provided EEC Commission President Walter Hallstein with a forum to promote his views on European law to the public.[45] The benefit was mutual because Hallstein's choice of venue acknowledged and reaffirmed the EP's self-understanding as the legitimate representative of all European citizens.[46] Hallstein highlighted that European law must be interpreted solely by Community institutions and had primacy vis-à-vis national law. Hallstein's words had an afterlife: their importance was underlined as they were quoted in the subsequent EP report.[47]

40 Davies 2015, 448.
41 Arena 2019.
42 Rasmussen 2010a, 72.
43 Arena 2018, 6, 12, 17.
44 Rasmussen 2014.
45 Vauchez 2010a, 108–128, 120–122.
46 Meyer 2020.
47 HAEP. PV!JURI.1958_JURI-19580625 0010FR: 2 § 8. Dehousse, Fernand. 'Report Drawn Up on Behalf of the Legal Committee on the Paramountcy of Community Law over the Law of the Member States, 25 May 1965'.

About one month later at the 13 July 1964 meeting, two days before the ECJ judgment on *Costa v ENEL*, this was followed up by the Legal Committee. Dehousse pointed to the 'fundamental problem of the pre-eminence of Community Law over national laws', which should be discussed 'in the light of recent court decisions', including that of the Italian Constitutional Court.[48] Other leading members of the committee like the French lawyer Alain Poher, a Christian Democrat (Mouvement républicain Populaire (MRP)), were clearly aware of these developments too and considered it necessary for the EP's Legal Committee to take a stance. Poher suggested gathering comparative information – along the model of what the ECSC Committee had pursued in 1957 on the rights of national parliaments. He proposed asking the Secretariat of the EP to assemble documentation on relevant court decisions in the member states.[49] The information note issued by the Secretariat in October 1964 included an overview of the problems arising from conflicting competencies in the application of European law and detailed the constitutional situation in the member states. In a third part, it discussed the *Costa v ENEL* case – 'as a practical example'.[50]

The second step of the EP's response began in December 1964, when the Committee appointed Dehousse as rapporteur. Two months later, on 18 February 1965, the professor from Liège presented to the Committee a preliminary outline version of his report.[51] Dehousse did not at all celebrate the ECJ's affirmation of the primacy of European law in the *Costa v ENEL* judgment. Instead, he underlined his concern about the Italian constitutional court's judgment, which had questioned the primacy of European law.[52] By rhetorically emphasising the fragility of the ECJ's claim, he made the case for EP intervention even more compelling. The EP needed to get involved because the primacy of the Treaties of Rome was hardly accepted in many courts in the member states. This threatened the uniform implementation of the Treaties across the member states. To Dehousse, the *effet utile* was central; thus, primacy was indispensable for a functioning Common Market.[53]

48 HAEP. PV!JURI.1961_JURI-19640713001oFR: 7European Parliament, Commission Juridique. 'Réunion du Lundi, 13 Juillet 1964. Procès-Verbal, 15.07.1964, PE 12.334' (my translation, JHM).

49 HAEP. PV!JURI.1961_JURI-19640713001oFR: 7European Parliament, Commission Juridique. 'Réunion du Lundi, 13 Juillet 1964. Procès-Verbal, 15.07.1964, PE 12.334' (my translation, JHM).

50 HAEP. PE0_AP_RP!JURI.1961_A0-0043!650140DE: 11. EP, Sekretariat des Rechtsausschusses. 'Aufzeichnung über den Vorrang des Gemeinschaftsrechts vor dem Recht der Mitgliedsstaaten, 5.10.1964, PE 12.596'.

51 HAEP. PE0_AP_RP!JURI.1961_A0-0043!650120DE. EP, Commission Juridique. 'Réunion du Jeudi 18 Février 1965. Procès-Verbal, 25.02.1965, PE 13.433'. HAEP. PV!JURI.1961_JURI-196502180010FR: 3; EP, Rechtsausschuss. 'Einführende Aufzeichnung im Namen des Rechtsausschusses über den Vorrang des Gemeinschaftsrechts vor dem Recht der Mitgliedstaaten, PE 13.472'.

52 HAEP. PV!JURI.1961_JURI-196502180010FR: 4. EP, Commission Juridique. 'Réunion du Jeudi 18 Février 1965. Procès-Verbal, 25.02.1965, PE 13.433'.

53 HAEP. PV!JURI.1961_JURI-196502180010FR: 3. EP, Commission Juridique. 'Réunion du Jeudi 18 Février 1965. Procès-Verbal, 25.02.1965, PE 13.433'.

Alliance building among the supranational institutions was part of the Legal Committee's strategy. For the presentation of Dehousse's preliminary report, the Committee had invited the presidents of the three executives. While Hallstein did not attend, the influential head of the European Commission's Legal Service, Michel Gaudet,[54] addressed the Committee.[55] Gaudet highlighted three points. First, he argued that the existence of judicial review in Italy and West Germany meant that their respective constitutional courts might declare the ratification of the Treaties of Rome and the Treaty of Paris unconstitutional.[56] Second, Gaudet highlighted the importance of the principle of primacy as crucial because it prevented national lawmakers from making subsequent legislation that undermined treaty obligations and European rules. Gaudet appealed to the MEPs to support two tenets regarding European law which distinguished it from international law, namely, its direct effect ('l'applicabilité directe du droit commautaire') and its special legal structure ('il y a dans nos Communautés toutes une structure juridique que n'apparait pas par la voie des Traitée ordinaires').[57] Third, Gaudet suggested two alternative solutions: first, an acceptance of a 'conception dite fédéraliste', a sharing of powers ('un partage des compétences'), or firm allocation 'une fois pour toutes', or second, 'la théorie de l'effet utile', namely an approach based on a doctrine of efficiency to achieve the aims of European integration. The new doctrine of primacy was a great example, because without it, Gaudet claimed, the EC political and legal system would not function.[58]

Gaudet's rhetorical strategy resembled that of Dehousse. Gaudet equally expressed his concern about recent conflicts between national and European law.[59] Gaudet's worries were not purely rhetorical. Within the Commission's Legal Service, three aspects of the Italian judgment were discussed as particularly threatening: first, the judgment threatened the reciprocity principle between countries, which was the constitutional basis for French membership, and thus had the potential to antagonise a French President, Charles de Gaulle, who was already

54 Boerger and Rasmussen 2017; Bailleux 2013.

55 HAEP, 1965, PV!JURI.1961_JURI-19650218006oFR. European Parliament, Commission juridique, Exposé de M. Gaudet, Directeur-général du Service juridique des Exécutifs européennes, devant la Commission juridique en sa Réunion du jeudi 18 février 1965. PE 13.434, 1.

56 HAEP, 1965, PV!JURI.1961_JURI-19650218006oFR. European Parliament, Commission juridique, Exposé de M. Gaudet, Directeur-général du Service juridique des Exécutifs européennes, devant la Commission juridique en sa Réunion du jeudi 18 février 1965. PE 13.434, 6–7.

57 HAEP, 1965, PV!JURI.1961_JURI-19650218006oFR. European Parliament, Commission juridique, Exposé de M. Gaudet, Directeur-général du Service juridique des Exécutifs européennes, devant la Commission juridique en sa Réunion du jeudi 18 février 1965. PE 13.434.

58 HAEP, 1965, PV!JURI.1961_JURI-19650218006oFR. European Parliament, Commission juridique, Exposé de M. Gaudet, Directeur-général du Service juridique des Exécutifs européennes, devant la Commission juridique en sa Réunion du jeudi 18 février 1965. PE 13.434, 9–10.

59 HAEP, 1965, PV!JURI.1961_JURI-19650218006oFR. European Parliament, Commission juridique, Exposé de M. Gaudet, Directeur-général du Service juridique des Exécutifs européennes, devant la Commission juridique en sa Réunion du jeudi 18 février 1965. PE 13.434, 2–4 (quote, my translation, JHM).

a great sceptic of the EC. Second, it created a lasting rift between member states which due to their monist constitution could more easily come to terms with the doctrine of primacy, and the two countries with dualist constitutions, namely Italy and West Germany, which could not. Third, based on this judgment, Italian courts were induced to effectively ignore European law.[60] Like Hallstein, Gaudet viewed the EP as a link to the broader public and national parliaments. He appealed to the EP to act, emphasising that the EP was particularly well-placed to communicate the issue to the public and influence public opinion.[61]

In his response to Gaudet, Dehousse found it important to note that among the two solutions Gaudet had flagged, he preferred the approach of the *effet utile* doctrine over changing the EC into a fully federalist system,[62] an argument he kept highlighting in subsequent meetings.[63] In any case, Dehousse concurred with Gaudet on the role of the EP to inform the public, a function that was part of the parliamentary mandate.[64]

This parliamentary function – and the specific instruments for informing the public – were central in the subsequent Committee debates, texts of amendments, and in the final resolution, but also in an informal exchange with the EEC Commission. Representatives of the Commission's Legal Service routinely attended the meetings. In March 1965, Gaudet wrote to Dehousse, explaining the ongoing activities of the EEC Commission in reaching out to legal academics and students, and thanked the rapporteur for his efforts in this regard.[65] Dehousse made sure to spread the word about the challenges faced by the new doctrine of primacy[66] – as promised – to the different party groups to raise attention in advance of the May plenary, for instance to his own Socialist Party.[67] The contemporaries were clearly

60 Rasmussen 2010a, 71–72; Pavone 2018.

61 HAEP, 1965. PV!JURI.1961_JURI-19650218006oFR. European Parliament. Exposé de M. Gaudet, Directeur-général du Service juridique des Exécutifs européennes, devant la Commission juridique en sa Réunion du jeudi 18 février 1965. PE 13.434, 2–4. (quote, my translation, JHM).

62 HAEP, 1965. PV!JURI.1961_JURI-19650218006oFR. European Parliament. Exposé de M. Gaudet, Directeur-général du Service juridique des Exécutifs européennes, devant la Commission juridique en sa Réunion du jeudi 18 février 1965. PE 13.434, 7–8.

63 HAEP, 1965. PV!JURI.1961_JURI-19650315001oFR. European Parliament, Commission juridique. Réunion du 15 mars 1965. Procès-verbal, 19.03.1965, PE 13.548, 9. At the meeting, Dehousse also asked for a careful editing of the minutes of the previous meeting of 18 February, in which Gaudet had participated, which is suggestive of how much importance he attributed to these undertakings.

64 HAEP, 1965. PV!JURI.1961_JURI-19650218006oFR. European Parliament. Exposé de M. Gaudet, Directeur-général du Service juridique des Exécutifs européennes, devant la Commission juridique en sa Réunion du jeudi 18 février 1965. PE 13.434, 7–8.

65 Archive of Fernand Dehousse (AFD), 494: 1–3. Gaudet, Michel. 'Note à l'attention de M. le professeur [Fernand] Dehousse, Sénateur, membre du Parlement européen: Activités des exécutifs déployées dans le domaine de l'information des juristes nationaux sur le droit communautaire, 5 mars 1965', 1–3.

66 HAEP, 1965. PV!JURI.1961_JURI-19650315001oFR, 10. European Parliament, Commission juridique. Réunion du 15 mars 1965. Procès-verbal, 19.03.1965, PE 13.548.

67 AFD. 494. Dehousse, Fernand. 'La primauté du droit communautaire'. Courrier socialiste européen, no. 2 (18 mai 1965). HAEU Fernand Dehousse, 1–3.

aware of the power of practising what constructivist political science today would describe as the 'discursive construction' of the legitimacy of the new order.[68]

In his response to Gaudet at the Committee meeting, Dehousse had mentioned the upcoming 'Colloque de Bruges' of 8–10 April 1965 on 'Community Law and National Law' constituted a first step and an example of how to reach out to the public and academics.[69] This was organised by the College of Europe, the European movement's postgraduate training ground.[70] The event included European law professionals from the ECJ such as Advocate General Maurice Lagrange, the European institutions as well as legal scholars. At the conference a consensus quickly emerged to support the principle of primacy.[71] A short report of the event was annexed to Dehousse's final report.[72] Former ECJ Judge Nicola Catalano edited and published the contributions.[73]

Indeed, in the plenary debate on 17 June 1965 on Dehousse's report[74] which the author had presented the previous day,[75] the long-serving Dutch socialist MEP and lawyer Marinus van der Goes van Naters referred back to the proceedings of the conference.[76] Van der Goes van Naters, a member of the Political Committee, had long been interested in the question of the primacy of European law. Already in May 1964, even before Dehousse brought this up in the Legal Committee, he had posed a parliamentary question to the EEC Commission on the Corte Costituzionale's *Costa v ENEL* decision.[77] Van der Goes van Naters' question was not without impact. Representatives from the Legal Service discussed it at length in the Legal Committee. The question had led the Service to consider ways the Council could intervene on the question and had eventually contacted the Council.[78]

68 E.g. Risse 2009.

69 HAEP, 1965. PV!JURI.1961_JURI-196502180060FR. European Parliament. Exposé de M. Gaudet, Directeur-général du Service juridique des Exécutifs européennes, devant la Commission juridique en sa Réunion du jeudi 18 février 1965. PE 13.434, 7.

70 Poehls 2009.

71 Vauchez 2010b, 123.

72 Dehousse, Fernand. *Report Drawn Up on Behalf of the Legal Committee on the Paramountcy of Community Law over the Law of the Member States, 25 May 1965.* 25 'Annexe'.

73 Catalano 1965.

74 Naters, Marinus van der Goes van. 'Contribution to Debate on "Primacy of Community Law," Sitting of Thursday 17 June 1965'. Official Journal of the European Communities, Annex: Proceedings of the European Parliament, June 1965: 227–229 (F), 228.

75 Dehousse, Fernand. 'Contribution to Debate on "Primacy of Community Law," Sitting of Wednesday 16 June 1965'. Official Journal of the European Communities, Annex: Proceedings of the European Parliament, June 1965: 193–200 (NL).

76 Archive of Marinus van der Goes van Naters (AMGN). 1964–1966, 334. 15. I would like to thank Karin van Leeuwen for sharing this information with me.

77 Vauchez 2010, 122; Naters, Marinus van der Goes van. 'Question écrite no. 27/64 au Conseil de la C.E.E. et de la C.E.E.A.: "Force de loi des Traités de Rome en Italie," 22 mai 1964, et réponse, 31 juillet 1964'. Journal Officiel des Communautés Européennes 129 (11.8.1964): 2161–2162 (FR). Vauchez mixes up the date of publication (August) with the date of the submitting of the question (May).

78 European Parliament. Réunion du 15 mars 1965. Procès-verbal, 19.03.1965, PE 13.548.

At Bruges, van der Goes van Naters was the only MEP participating, as he claimed in his plenary speech. He quoted Catalano's words from the conference – as evidence of apparent Italian support for primacy: 'Si un traité limitant la souveraineté de l'État a établi une limitation de compétence des organes législatifs normaux, le parlement est devenue, de ce fait, incompétent pour adopter d'autres lois ordinaires en utilisant une compétence qui désormais ne lui appartient plus.'[79]

Similar views – defending the necessity of primacy for the functioning of the EC – were shared across country and party lines.[80] The subsequent intervention by his Dutch liberal MEP and lawyer Cornelis Berkhouwer, also a member of the Legal Committee, reaffirmed the doctrine of primacy, but also underlined the autonomous, special nature of European law, and rejected the applicability of the '*lex posterior derogat priori*' principle.[81] Given the Dutch constitutional reform of 1953, as explained in Chapter 8, for Dutch MEPs, the primacy of EC law posed little concern.[82]

After the plenary in June, the Legal Committee continued to discuss the issue on 7 October 1965 and rejected some of the amendments proposed, such as establishing an academy for European Law, which was deemed impracticable. The Committee settled for a much clearer public appeal to accept the primacy of European law than Dehousse's original wording. A letter was written to the President of the EP to ensure the 'clear and methodological' publication of European Law in the Official Journal of the European Communities.[83] Replacing Dehousse, who had left the EP in August, Committee President Weinkamm produced a short additional complementary report on the amendments discussed, until a resolution on the issue was finally adopted in late October 1965.[84]

The eventual resolution thus flagged three main aspects to describe the problem. First, the need for the 'correct application of the Treaties' by the means of the principle of the *effet utile* to achieve the 'aims' and enable the 'gradual development of the Communities'. Second, a deep concern over recent judgments of national courts challenging the application of European law. Third, the EP found it important to underscore the need for an

79 Naters, Marinus van der Goes van. 'Contribution to Debate on "Primacy of Community Law", Sitting of Thursday 17 June 1965'. Official Journal of the European Communities, Annex: Proceedings of the European Parliament, June 1965: 227–229 (F), 228. English translation: 'If a treaty limiting the sovereignty of the state establishes limitations on the powers of national legislative bodies, the latter becomes due to this limitation incompetent to adopt ordinary laws within these fields.'

80 Schmutzer 1966, 105–109; Weinkamm, Otto. 'Supplementary Report Drawn Up on Behalf of the Legal Committee on the Paramountcy of Community Law over the Law of the Member States, 18 October 1965'. European Parliament Working Documents 1965–66, no. 95: 1–2.

81 'on ne peut pas intervenir des préscriptions nationales dans l'ordre juridique séparé et autonome Communautés'. Berkhouwer, Cornelis. 'Contribution to Debate on "Primacy of Community Law," Sitting of Thursday 17 June 1965'. Official Journal of the European Communities, Annex: Proceedings of the European Parliament, June 1965: 229–230 (F), 229.

82 Van Leeuwen 2012.

83 HAEP, 1965. PV!JURI.1961_JURI-19651007001oFR. European Parliament, Commission juridique. Réunion du jeudi, 7 octobre 1965. Procès-verbal, 07.10.1965, PE 14.641. 3–8, Annexe (8 – quote).

84 Schmutzer 1966, 108.

independent judiciary. Considering these concerns, the resolution explicitly endorsed the principle of primacy: 'The European Parliament ... affirms the principle and the need to recognize the paramountcy of Community Law over the laws of the member states.' As a remedy to the general lack of information on European Law in the member states, the EP appealed to the member states to publish new European legislation in their 'official gazettes', specifying when such legislation had direct applicability.[85]

When defending the primacy of European law, the Legal Committee also pursued its own institutional self-interest: Dehousse's final report linked the member state acceptance of the primacy of European law to the problem of the democratic deficit and the role its own institution to mitigate this. Already in the very first paragraph of the report, it demanded a greater role in legislation for itself.[86] Similarly, in the Annex reporting on the 'colloque de Bruges', the rapporteur singled out a quote from the conference's chair Alphonse De Vreese that aptly underlined this demand: 'when our national courts are somewhat non-plussed when asked to give pre-eminence over the national law to a Community regulation emanating from a Community executive, can this not be traced back in every case to the lack – within the Community order – of any real democratic control on the part of a legislative assembly?'[87] Clearly, the close connection between general (EC) and specific (EP) institutional self-assertion became even more important in the 1970s, as the issue of the quality of Community democracy stayed on the agenda.

REJECTING *SOLANGE* BY ASSERTING DEMOCRACY AND HUMAN RIGHTS PROTECTION

Today, as the EP website proudly proclaims, fundamental rights are a constituent part of the Lisbon Treaty of 2008, after having been codified by a Convention in the Charter of Fundamental Rights solemnly proclaimed at the Nice Summit in 2000.[88] Already in the 1950s, in the shadow of World War II, human rights protection had been high on the European agenda. In its Article 3, the Draft Treaty of the European Political Community (EPC) of 1953 referred to the Council of Europe's Human Rights Protection and declared that 'the provisions of Part 1 of the Convention for the Protection of Human

85 Weinkamm 1965, 2.

86 HAEP, 25. Dehousse, Fernand. 'Report Drawn Up on Behalf of the Legal Committee on the Paramountcy of Community Law over the Law of the Member States, 25 May 1965. Annexe', §1 and see also Vauchez 2015.

87 HAEP, 25. Dehousse, Fernand. 'Report Drawn Up on Behalf of the Legal Committee on the Paramountcy of Community Law over the Law of the Member States, 25 May 1965. Annexe', §1.

88 Marzocchi 2018.

Rights and Fundamental Freedoms signed in Rome on 4th November 1950' were an integral part of the statute.[89]

However, after the failure of EDC and EPC, the 'relance européenne' led to the Treaties of Rome. Just like the Treaty of Paris these new treaties deliberately avoided to integrate constitutional norms smacking of federalism since these would have endangered ratification.[90] As a consequence, until the late 1960s, European law did not include any document explicitly protecting human and fundamental rights.

During the 1970s, throughout the Western World, the issue of human rights gained political importance in Western publics. Human rights featured centrally in the politics of East-West détente, and new NGOs advocated and defended such norms, notably Amnesty International.[91] The EP's Legal Committee was part of this broader trend and organised an exchange on these issues with members of the US Congress in 1976.[92] In April 1973, the EP had already produced a report on its own initiative and produced a resolution asking the Commission to report on human rights protection in EC lawmaking.[93]

Hence, the Legal Committee was familiar with the issues at stake when the BVerfG, ruled on 29 May 1974 in its famous *Solange* decision that it reserved a right to check European legislation applied in West Germany with a view to the protection of fundamental rights: 'as long as' (*Solange*) the protection of fundamental and human rights in the EC remained insufficiently congruent with the elaborate West German standards, such a reservation and claim of competence of the BVerfG, would apply.[94]

Just as in Italy, fundamental rights constituted a core element of West Germany's post-war constitution, the Basic Law (Grundgesetz) of 1949. Its makers had put such rights front and centre in a deliberate attempt to 'learn' from the experience of the crimes against humanity committed during the National Socialist dictatorship from 1933 to 1945.[95] In addition, within the West German law community, a new concept had become prominent since the late 1950s. The idea of 'structural congruence' meant that the Federal Republic should only transfer sovereignty to international bodies that had comparable protection in human rights and democracy.[96] This led

89 Ad Hoc Assembly. Draft Treaty Embodying the Statute of the European Community, Adopted by the Ad Hoc Assembly in Strasbourg on 10 March 1953. Information and Official Documents of the Constitutional Committee, Document 10: 52–143, 60; Loth 2015, 36–62.

90 Loth 2015, 53–62.

91 Eckel 2017, 291–301. See notably: Snyder 2011; Moyn 2010.

92 HAEP. PE0_AP_DE!1976_DE19761012-069900EN: 60. European Parliament. 'Debates of the European Parliament, Tuesday, 12 October 1976, Intervention by Mr Cousté'.

93 European Parliament. 'Resolution Concerning the Protection of the Fundamental Rights of Member States' Citizens When Community Law Is Drafted, 4 April 1973'. Official Journal of the European Communities (OJEC) C26, 30.04.1973: 7–8.

94 HAEP. PE 38.055: 1. European Parliament. 'Rechtsausschuss, Mitteilung an die Mitglieder. Beiliegend erhalten die Mitglieder den vollständigen Text eines Beschlusses des Bundesverfassungsgerichts der Bundesrepublik Deutschland zum "Vorrang von deutschem Verfassungsrecht über das sekundäre Gemeinschaftsrecht", Anlagen I und II, Luxemburg, 23. September 1974 (2 BvL 52/71)'.

95 Davies 2012b, 85–86.

96 Davies 2015.

to an increasingly sceptical view among West German lawyers towards the transfers of sovereignty – and concomitant human rights protection – that the idea of primacy implied. In the early 1970s, the EC hardly appeared as a beacon of democratic norms and fundamental rights: the heads of state and government were blocking direct elections to the EP and human rights remained unprotected in European law.[97] When the ECJ's *Internationale Handelsgesellschaft*[98] judgment of 1970 took the claim of primacy one step further and rejected the idea that European law could be limited by national constitutions and consequently their human rights protection, this effectively threw down the gauntlet to the BVerfG.[99] In the same judgment the ECJ conceded that the spirit of national constitutions needed to be considered, and in the subsequent *Nold*[100] judgment, the ECJ softened its stance somewhat. Nevertheless, the BVerfG decided to defend human and democratic rights, and its own role in their protection, to avoid their potential erosion via European legislation and ECJ rulings.[101]

The EP Legal Committee clearly considered the *Solange* decision a direct and dangerous challenge to the constitutional concept of European law it had advocated since the 1960s, along with the Commission and the ECJ. Hence, the MEPs problematised and rejected the *Solange* decision by the BVerfG in two steps –in a report and resolution concerning the supremacy of European law (1975/1976), and in discussions on a report produced by the Commission that provided a long-term view on how to remedy the issue of fundamental rights protection (1976/1977). The 1976 resolution repeated the EP's earlier stance: it reaffirmed the 'primacy of Community law over the domestic law of the member states' as a 'condition for the uniform application of Community law'. In addition, the Committee presented the *effet utile* argument in a new guise, more in line with the debates of the 1970s: the primacy of European law implied 'a guarantee of the equality of citizens . . . before Community law'.[102] The resolution asserted the role of the ECJ as 'the sole arbiter of the legality of the Council's and the Commission's acts',[103] and rejected the BVerfG's reservations – with a view to human rights

97 Davies 2012a, 423; Davies 2012b, 78–88.

98 11/70, *Internationale Handelsgesellschaft mbH v Einfuhr- und Vorratsstelle für Getreide und Futtermittel*, 1970, ECLI:EU:C:1970:114.

99 Davies and Rasmussen 2014, 125.

100 11/70, *Internationale Handelsgesellschaft mbH v Einfuhr- und Vorratsstelle für Getreide und Futtermittel*, 1970, ECLI:EU:C:1970:114.

101 Roellecke 2003, 549, 560, 566; Davies and Rasmussen 2014, 125.

102 European Parliament, 1976. 'Resolution on the Primacy of Community Law and the Protection of Fundamental Rights'. Official Journal of the European Communities (OJEC). C159, 12.07.1976: 13–14, 14 §1.

103 European Parliament, 1976. 'Resolution on the primacy of Community law and the protection of fundamental rights'. Official Journal of the European Communities (OJEC). C159, 12.07.1976.

protection. This would 'constitute an infringement of the Treaties'.[104] Accordingly the EP 'invite[d]' the Commission to keep a close eye on the further development and 'to ensure . . . full compliance with the principle of the uniform application of Community law'.[105]

This resolution was the outcome of a lengthy process of discussion in the Legal Committee and the plenary. Individual MEPs were concerned enough to pose parliamentary questions on the issue.[106] Already in October 1974, the French Gaullist MEP, Pierre-Bernard Cousté, at the time Vice-President of the EP,[107] had posed a question to the Commission concerning the *Solange* decision. He advocated decisive action to be taken vis-à-vis West Germany.[108] Apparently, the West German government was also embarrassed about its BVerfG's verdict and started a close exchange with the Commission on what to do, and how best to avoid setting a problematic example for other member states' courts.[109]

This concern was shared across the supranational institutions. Indeed, the Director-General of the Commission's Legal Service, Walter Much,[110] Gaudet's successor, viewed the decision as a 'significant attack' on the European legal system, and considered taking drastic action, such as and infringement procedure or a request for the national legislature to limit the Karlsruhe Court's power.[111] The concern also induced cooperation between the European institutions. Until his untimely death in April 1975, Much attended the Legal Committee meetings on the dossier.[112] The Director-General of the Council Legal Service, the West German lawyer Hans-Joachim Glaesner,[113] a veteran negotiator of the Treaties of Rome, also took part in some of the meetings.[114] This is suggestive of the importance they

104 European Parliament, 1976. 'Resolution on the primacy of Community law and the protection of fundamental rights'. Official Journal of the European Communities (OJEC). C159, 12.07.1976, 14 § 4.

105 European Parliament, 1976. 'Resolution on the primacy of Community law and the protection of fundamental rights'. Official Journal of the European Communities (OJEC). C159, 12.07.1976, 14 § 6.

106 E.g. Jahn, Hans Edgar. 'Written Question No. 545/75 to the Commission of the European Communities, 20 November 1975: 'Danger of Fragmentation of Community Law,' and Answer, 3 February 1976'. Official Journal of the European Communities (OJEC) C67, 22.3.1976: 23–24.

107 Cousté, Pierre-Bernard. 1920–1989, Assemblée nationale: www2.assemblee-nationale.fr/sycomore/fiche/(num_dept)/2043.

108 Cousté, Pierre-Bernard. 'Written Question No. 414/74 to the Commission of the European Communities, 10 October 1974: "Decision of the German Constitutional Court Limiting the Applicability of Community Regulations," and Answer, 29 January 1975'. Official Journal of the European Communities (OJEC) C54, 6.3.1975: 1.

109 Davies 2012a, 425–427.

110 On Much, see Davies forthcoming.

111 Davies 2012a, 425–427.

112 'Hommage à Paul Leleux' 1980.

113 Hans-Joachim Glaesner, Director-General (13.069-2), Personnel, 1975, Commerce Clearing House. http://aei.pitt.edu/75242/.

114 HAEP, PV!JURI.1961_JURI-19760920001oFR. European Parliament, Legal Committee. Procès Verbal de la Réunion du Lundi, 20 Septembre et Mardi 21 Septembre 1976, PE 45.925, 1–10.

attributed to the role of the formally powerless assembly in this context. On 7 February 1975, the Legal Committee started to discuss how the European institutions should respond to the BVerfG's decision. Some of the Committee members already highlighted what were to become the key arguments in the resolution, namely that the uniform application of European law was challenged by the Solange mechanism proposed by the BVerfG. There was consequently a need to emphasise the exclusive role of the ECJ to interpret European law. Other members flagged with glee that the judgment had explicitly mentioned the need for direct elections of the EP and the democratisation of the EC – in line with West German lawyers' structural congruence theory. Again, as in the 1950s and 1960s, the defence of the European legal order and the EP's institutional self-interest in direct elections went hand in hand.[115] Both aspects were raised as well in the plenary discussion on the eventual resolution on 15 June 1976.[116]

The Legal Committee clearly treated the BVerfG's decision as a major attack on the European legal system's key tenets, and considered whether it was feasible and opportune for the Commission to produce a reasoned opinion in line with Article 169 of the EEC Treaty.[117] Such a procedure would have brought the West German government into a difficult situation politically, given that it could be read as a challenge to very fundamental national constitutional principles of the separation of powers and judicial independence, in particular when coming from an institution – the Commission – with a less than spectacular record on democracy and human rights protection.

In October 1975, the Legal Committee officially appointed the French Gaullist politician, Hector Riviérez, who had already drafted the report, to the role of rapporteur.[118] As a former Conseiller at one of France's high courts, the Cour de Cassation, Riviérez was extremely well-qualified for the job.[119] Perhaps surprising due to his party affiliation, Riviérez was strongly committed to the primacy of European law: He pointed out that the Commission's timid response, namely to merely ask the West German for government for comments on the *Solange*

[115] HAEP, 1975. PV!JURI.1961_JURI-19750206001oFR. European Parliament, Legal Committee. Procès Verbal de la Réunion du Jeudi 6 Février et du Vendredi 7 Février 1975, PE/II/PV/75-2, 26.03.1975, PE 39.928, 1–6, 4 §6.

[116] European Parliament, Debates on 'Primacy of Community Law', Sitting of Tuesday, 15 June 1976, Official Journal of the European Communities, Annex: Proceedings of the European Parliament, June 1976, 53–62.

[117] HAEP, PV!JURI.1961_JURI-19750324001oFR. European Parliament, Legal Committee, Procès-verbal de la réunion du lundi 24 mars et mardi 25 mars 1975, PE/II/PV/75-5, 11.04.1975, PE 40.302, 1–6, 3–4 §4, 6 'Annex, Feuille de présence'.

[118] Hector Rivierez, Report Drawn Up on Behalf of the Legal Affairs Committee on the Primacy of Community Law and the Protection of Fundamental Rights, 26 November 1975, PE 41.913fin, European Parliament Working Documents 1975–76 390 (1975): 1–52.

[119] Rivierez was one of the few people of colour in the EP at the time and represented his native Guyana. NN, 'Hector Rivierez, ancien député de Guyane (obituary)', *Le Monde*, 30 May 2003, 7.

judgment, was not sufficient.[120] The Commission should instead make public its own position on this interference with the European legal order by the BVerfG.[121]

This report backed up an EP resolution by providing an overview of previous discussions in the EP of issues regarding fundamental rights and the conception of European law as an autonomous legal order.[122] It explicitly condoned the doctrine of primacy by referring to the 'celebrated decision of 15 July 1964' *Costa v ENEL.*[123] The ECJ was to be the sole arbiter of European law, in order to ensure the uniformity of its application:[124] 'These principles and rules are now universally recognized. Our Parliament has had occasion to proclaim them, too.'[125] The report discussed how the European institutions had so far tried to address the human rights within the emergent European legal order.[126] Meeting in Rome on 21 October 1975, the Legal Committee unanimously supported Riviérez's report with only one abstention and discussed how the protection of fundamental rights could be ensured in the future either by the ECJ or by the codification of a new 'code of Community rights'.[127] This presaged the strategy jointly pursued by the three institutions, namely, to proactively address the issue of human rights within the European legal system.

It proved a convenient coincidence that on 4 February 1976 the Commission eventually published its report 'The protection of fundamental rights as Community law is created and developed.'[128] This was written as a response to the EP resolution

[120] Hector Rivierez, Report Drawn Up on Behalf of the Legal Affairs Committee on the Primacy of Community Law and the Protection of Fundamental Rights, 26 November 1975, PE 41.913fin, European Parliament Working Documents 1975–76 390 (1975): 19 §34.

[121] Hector Rivierez, Report Drawn Up on Behalf of the Legal Affairs Committee on the Primacy of Community Law and the Protection of Fundamental Rights, 26 November 1975, PE 41.913fin, European Parliament Working Documents 1975–76 390 (1975): 20 §35.

[122] Hector Rivierez, Report Drawn Up on Behalf of the Legal Affairs Committee on the Primacy of Community Law and the Protection of Fundamental Rights, 26 November 1975, PE 41.913fin, European Parliament Working Documents 1975–76 390 (1975): 10 §11.

[123] Hector Rivierez, Report Drawn Up on Behalf of the Legal Affairs Committee on the Primacy of Community Law and the Protection of Fundamental Rights, 26 November 1975, PE 41.913fin, European Parliament Working Documents 1975–76 390 (1975): 8 §7.

[124] Hector Rivierez, Report Drawn Up on Behalf of the Legal Affairs Committee on the Primacy of Community Law and the Protection of Fundamental Rights, 26 November 1975, PE 41.913fin, European Parliament Working Documents 1975–76 390 (1975): 10 §9.

[125] Hector Rivierez, Report Drawn Up on Behalf of the Legal Affairs Committee on the Primacy of Community Law and the Protection of Fundamental Rights, 26 November 1975, PE 41.913fin, European Parliament Working Documents 1975–76 390 (1975): 10 §10.

[126] Hector Rivierez, Report Drawn Up on Behalf of the Legal Affairs Committee on the Primacy of Community Law and the Protection of Fundamental Rights, 26 November 1975, PE 41.913fin, European Parliament Working Documents 1975–76 390 (1975): 11–17.

[127] HAEP, PV!JURI.1961_JURI-197510200010FR. European Parliament, Legal Committee, Procès-verbal de la réunion du lundi 20 octobre 1975 et du mardi 21 octobre 1975, PE/II/PV/75-14, 31.10.1975, PE 42.462, 1–6, 4 §4.

[128] European Commission, The Protection of Fundamental Rights as Community Law Is Created and Developed. Report of the Commission Submitted to the European Parliament and the Council. COM (76) 37 Final, 4 February 1976, Bulletin of the European Communities, Supplement 5 (1976): 5–16. See on the background: Davies 2012b, 429.

of 1973 mentioned above, but was most timely considering the changing political context.[129] The Commission defended the delay in producing the report by reference to what had happened in the meantime: various judgments of national courts and the ECJ itself, as well as the Commission's general report on European Union of 1975.[130] The report on fundamental rights started out with a survey of the 'standard of fundamental rights in the Community', explained the 'position taken by the Commission on fundamental rights to date', including the role and position of the EP, notably in their response to the *Solange* judgment.[131] The Commission discussed various options for strengthening the role of human rights through research, by the EC joining the European Human Rights Convention (a proposal the Commission did not deem necessary), or by drawing up a fundamental rights catalogue of its own (an idea that the Commission did not think could be realised in the short term).[132]

What the Commission advocated to do instead was what could be called a 'light touch instrument', that could be realised rather quickly, without much controversy. For this purpose 'a solemn common declaration of the three political institutions of the Community' was drawn up. Such a – legally non-binding – declaration was 'to confirm' the institutions' 'respect for fundamental rights in the Community'. Clearly, what the Commission however wanted to avoid was 'long discussions on its content'. The idea for such a declaration has been traced by Bill Davies back to discussions between Helmut Schmidt and ECJ Advocate General Gerhard Reischl in 1974–1975.[133]

The Commission's worries that starting a debate on the scope and contents of European fundamental rights might lead to great controversy proved far-sighted and well-founded. Indeed, during the EP's plenary discussion on the EP's report and resolution on the Commission report on 12 October 1976, a number of MPs engaged in discussions on which types of rights should be included or not as European fundamental rights. Harking back to the controversies of the 1940s, and the conflict between basic rights and social rights, this debate touched upon a politically sensitive and potentially divisive issue in a Cold War context.

[129] European Parliament, Resolution Concerning the Protection of the Fundamental Rights of Member States' Citizens When Community Law Is Drafted, 4 April 1973, Based on Report by Mr. Jozeau-Marigné (Doc 297/72).

[130] European Commission, Report on European Union. COM (75) 400 Final, 25 June 1975, Bulletin of the European Communities, Supplement 5 (1975): 26–27 §82–85.

[131] European Commission, The Protection of Fundamental Rights as Community Law Is Created and Developed. Report of the Commission Submitted to the European Parliament and the Council. COM (76) 37 Final, 4 February 1976, 8, 11–12.

[132] European Commission, The Protection of Fundamental Rights as Community Law Is Created and Developed. Report of the Commission Submitted to the European Parliament and the Council. COM (76) 37 Final, 4 February 1976, 14–15.

[133] European Commission, The Protection of Fundamental Rights as Community Law Is Created and Developed. Report of the Commission Submitted to the European Parliament and the Council. COM (76) 37 Final, 4 February 1976, 16 §38; Davies 2012a, 421.

Deputy Rapporteur, Derek Walker-Smith, a British Conservative and former barrister, distinguished the civic and political rights protected by the European Convention on Human Rights, to which the member states were party already, and the 'political and socio-political matters'[134] that the EC was concerned with. While Walker-Smith's distinction remained largely academic, French MEP Gérard Bordu of the Communist and Allies Group used the opportunity to demand the inclusion of an entire catalogue of social rights notably 'to employment, education and occupational training, the right to better conditions of pay and work, the right to the satisfaction of major social needs – housing health, culture, public services, transport, etc. . . . the right to greater democracy in industry'.[135] Such rights were of course dear to the parties on the left, but anathema to most Christian Democrats, Liberals and more moderate Social Democrats. His fellow MEP from the Scottish Nationalists, Winifred Ewing, supported Bordu's views. Somewhat curiously, he linked the question of rights to the issue of Scottish independence: 'the right to join a Union or not to join a Union' should be among the protected fundamental rights.[136] In its plenary, the EP thus took the liberty to debate the much broader implications of the issue of fundamental rights in the context of the EC.

The EP Legal Committee, however, avoided such a politicisation of the issue, and collaborated very closely with the Commission and the Council, to fend off the admonition by the BVerfG. For instance, at the first Committee meeting to discuss the question on 29 April 1976, Peter Karpenstein from the Legal Service informed the Committee about the draft text of the joint declaration of the three institutions that the Commission was in the process of drawing up.[137] On 21 September 1976 the Committee discussed, adjusted and unanimously supported the text of an EP resolution and report in the presence of the Director General of the Council's Legal Service.[138] At about the same time, in October 1976, at a colloquium on basic rights at the University of Heidelberg, European law experts from relevant West German Federal ministries, leading figures from the BVerfG and the ECJ met and in a much more conciliatory atmosphere discussed and agreed on the joint declaration as the most suitable way forward.[139]

134 HAEP. PE0_AP_DE!1976_DE19761012-069900EN. European Parliament, Debates of the European Parliament, Tuesday, 12 October 1976, Intervention by Deputy Rapporteur Sir Derek Walker-Smith, 57.

135 HAEP. PE0_AP_DE!1976_DE19761012-069900EN. European Parliament, Debates of the European Parliament, Tuesday, 12 October 1976, Intervention by Gérard Bordu, 62.

136 HAEP. PE0_AP_DE!1976_DE19761012-069900EN. European Parliament, Debates of the European Parliament, Tuesday, 12 October 1976, Intervention by Winifred Ewing, 64. On the contemporaneous issue of Scottish independence see Nairn 1977.

137 HAEP. PV!JURI.1961_JURI-19760529001OFR. European Parliament, Legal Committee, Procès-verbal de la réunion du jeudi 29 et vendredi 30 avril 1976, PE/II/PV/76-5, 6.5.1976, PE 44.634, 7 §10.

138 HAEP. PV!JURI.1961_JURI-197609200010FR. European Parliament, Legal Committee, Procès-verbal de la réunion du lundi 20 septembre et mardi 21 septembre 1976, PE 45.925, 7–8 §10.

139 Davies 2012a, 430.

The EP report emphasised the importance of the ECJ's judgments between 1969 and 1975,[140] and concluded that the Court had thus acknowledged the role of fundamental rights in European law, thus disproving the concerns of the BVerfG that had led to the *Solange* judgment.[141] This – Committee members argued – should be highlighted in front of the EP plenary.[142] In its motion for a resolution, the Committee also explicitly supported the Commission's proposal of a joint declaration by the three political institutions of the EC.[143] Indeed, the subsequent report on this declaration, and the discussion in the Committee were very brief. There was no alternative for the EP but to accept the wording proposed by the (Commission and) the Council, to swiftly advance the joint effort. With three abstentions, and twenty-seven votes in favour, the Committee accepted the joint declaration in December 1976.[144]

The declaration constituted a polite, but explicit rejection by the three institutions of the BVerfG's scepticism concerning the EC: they highlighted the importance the European institutions attached to the protection of fundamental rights, 'derived in particular from the constitutions of the member states and the European Convention on the protection of human rights and fundamental freedoms' and reaffirmed that the institutions 'respect and will continue to respect these rights'.[145]

As in the mid-1960s, the EP and its Legal Committee thus closely cooperated with the other institutions to help resolve the challenge posed by the *Solange* judgment. The EP was an attractive partner for the other institutions for its moral claim in representing member state citizens and its function as a forum and link to the public. The EP used similar instruments, having information collected by the Secretariat, followed by an own-initiative report and resolution, but also reaching out to the public and the academic world at conferences. The EP was, however, not only at the service of its partner institutions, but used the opportunity to assert its role before direct elections.

140 29/69, *Erich Stauder v City of Ulm – Sozialamt*, 1969, ECLI:EU:C:1969:57; 44/73, *J. Nold Kohlen- und Baustoffgroßhandlung v Commission of the European Communities*, 1974, ECLI:EU:C:1974:51; 36/75, *Roland Rutili v Ministre de l'Intérieur*, 1975, ECLI:EU:C:1975:137.

141 Léon Jozeau-Marigné, Report Drawn Up on Behalf of the Legal Affairs Committee on the Report of the Commission of the European Communities on the Protection of Fundamental Rights, 4 October 1976, PE 43.967 Fin, European Parliament Working Documents 1976–77 321 (1976): 8–10 §6–9.

142 European Parliament, Procès-verbal de la réunion du lundi 20 septembre et mardi 21 septembre 1976, PE 45.925, 7–8 §10.

143 European Parliament, Procès-verbal de la réunion du lundi 20 septembre et mardi 21 septembre 1976, PE 45.925, 6 § 8–9.

144 HAEP. PV!JURI.1961_JURI-19761220010FR. European Parliament, Legal Committee, Procès-verbal de la réunion des lundi 20 décembre et mardi 21 décembre 1976, PE/II/PV/76-12, 7.1.1977, PE 47.369, 2 §6.

145 Léon Jozeau-Marigné, Report Drawn Up on Behalf of the Legal Affairs Committee on the Draft Joint Declaration by the European Parliament, the Council and the Commission on the Protection of Fundamental Human Rights, 10 February 1977, PE 47.848 Fin, European Parliament Working Documents 1976–1977 557 (1977): 3 §1–2.

RESPONDING TO *COHN-BENDIT*

Right after the first direct elections of 1979, the EP and its Legal Committee worked hard to fend off the challenges posed by the French Conseil d'État in their *Cohn-Bendit* judgment. The French high court rejected two key aspects of the constitutional legal order build by the ECJ, namely the principle of the direct applicability of directives that was the result of an audacious string of ECJ judgments in the 1970s and the obligatory practice of using the preliminary reference mechanism to obtain authoritative interpretations of European law from the ECJ (Article 177 of the EEC Treaty).[146] The EP continued to use its traditional instruments to address the new crisis, producing a report and a resolution based on its ample legal expertise. Again, the Committee operated in close conjunction with the Legal Service of the Commission.[147]

In France during the 1970s, the primacy and direct effect of European law, and the way the practice of preliminary reference fuelled the constitutional case law of the ECJ, was a divisive issue. It constituted a rift between the then dominant parties of the centre-right as well as across its court system. By 1974, the Cour de Cassation had accepted the primacy of European Law. However, during the second half of the 1970s, the other French high courts, the Conseil constitutionnel and the Conseil d'État, continued to reject the constitutional interpretation of European law and primacy in particular.[148] A showdown between France and the EC over the nature of European law was consequently looming (see Chapter 7 for the full story).

Daniel Cohn-Bendit was a West German citizen who had been born and grown up in France. He had reached fame as leader of the Paris student movement of 1968 and was subsequently expelled from France in May 1968. In the mid-1970s, Cohn-Bendit tried to return to France and went to court in France against the French Ministry of the Interior. He demanded re-entry with reference to European law, drawing on his right to use the freedom of movement of labour. The Tribunal administrative de Paris handled the case and found a contradiction between the French laws concerning the rights to residence of foreigners in France and the Council Directive 64/221 of 25 February 1964. Hence, the Tribunal sent a preliminary reference to the ECJ. This preliminary reference was intercepted by the French Ministry of Foreign Affairs, and instead, the Conseil d'État took the opportunity to consider the case. The government commissioner of the Conseil d'État (commissaire du gouvernement) was relatively sympathetic to

146 Pierre Pescatore and Court of Justice of the European Communities, References for Preliminary Rulings Under Article 177 of the EEC Treaty and Cooperation Between the Court and National Courts (Luxembourg: Office for Official Publications of the European Communities, 1986), 35.

147 Hellmut Sieglerschmidt, Bericht im Namen des Rechtsausschusses über die Verantwortung des Gerichtshofs der Europäischen Gemeinschaften für die einheitliche Anwendung des Gemeinschaftsrechts in den Mitgliedsstaaten, 1. September 1981, PE 67.004 Endg, European Parliament Working Documents 1981–1982 1–414 (1981): 1–28, plus annexes.

148 Alter 2001, 150–151; Rasmussen 2017, 300.

European law, and suggested sending a preliminary reference to the ECJ. However, the administrative Court of last instance rejected this proposal and took the interpretation of European law into its own hands, deciding that according to Article 189 of the EEC Treaty directives had no direct effect. This directly ignored ECJ case law, where the Court in Luxembourg had gradually extended direct effect to different types of directives based on an *effet utile* logic – the efficiency of the implementation of European law trumped the letter of Article 189 of the EEC Treaty.[149] Thus, Cohn-Bendit would have to submit to the French law and could not go back to the country where he had grown up. However, two days before the ruling, the French Ministry of the Interior revoked the extradition order, so Cohn-Bendit could safely ignore the Conseil d'État's verdict.[150]

While the material part of the case had thus been resolved, this was not the case at the doctrinal level. The ECJ, the Commission's Legal Service and the EP Legal Committee could not ignore the ruling. They viewed it as endangering the very coherence of the European legal order, just as the *Solange* ruling had done a few years earlier. Their reaction was in many ways similar to that towards West Germany. The ECJ responded by finally accepting that the *effet utile* could not alone define whether directives could have direct effect. Instead, the Court now admitted that it was states that were the destinataire of directives (Article 189 of the EEC Treaty). As a consequence directives could not produce direct effect horizontally, that is, between citizens.[151] As with West Germany previously, the Commission carefully considered the idea of an infringement proceeding or whether just to contact the French government for clarification. Eventually, they settled on the latter option and send a letter from Commission President Roy Jenkins to the French Minister of Foreign Affairs in March 1979. Again, from November 1979 onwards, the Legal Service cooperated closely with the EP's Legal Committee on the crisis.[152] However, in this case the Legal Service found it difficult to steer the Legal Committee of the EP towards a suitable report that took into account the serious political sensitivities involved.

Until early November the Legal Committee of the newly elected EP had primarily dealt with other issues relevant to a constitutional understanding of EC law. For instance, in October 1979 they continued to discuss human and civil rights protection in the EC.[153] However, even though almost a year had passed since the judgment, the Committee had not yet responded to the *Cohn-Bendit* decision.

149 33/70, *SpA SACE v Finance Minister of the Italian Republic*, 1970, ECLI:EU:C:1970:118; 41/74, *Yvonne van Duyn v Home Office*, 1974, EU:C:1974:133; 36/75, *Roland Rutili v Ministre de l'Intérieur*, 1975, ECLI:EU:C:1975:137. For a historical analysis of this case law see Rasmussen 2017.

150 Rasmussen 2017, 301.

151 148/78, *Criminal proceedings against Tullio Ratti*, 1979, ECLI:EU:C:1979:110.

152 Rasmussen 2017, 302–303.

153 HAEP. PE1.AP.JURI.1979.PV_JURI-19791009_0010. European Parliament, Legal Affairs Committee, Minutes of the Meeting of 9 and 10 October 1979, PE/VII/PV/79-9, 17.10.1979, PE 60.133, 7, §8.

It was only on 6 November 1979, that the West German Social Democrat member of the Legal Committee, Hellmut Sieglerschmidt, suggested discussing the case. The Committee endorsed this demand.[154] The Commission's Legal Service representative Deputy Director-General Giancarlo Olmi participated in the debate on 26 November, when the Committee decided to proceed in a comparable manner as at earlier instances, first, having the EP Secretariat collect relevant documentation as a basis for discussion before taking a decision. Collaboration with the Legal Service was apparently so close and seamless that the Italian Committee Chairman Mauro Ferri even asked for the Commission Legal Service's 'assistance' in drawing up these documents.[155]

Even MEPs who were not part of the Legal Committee voiced their concern about the challenges to the authority of the ECJ that the *Cohn-Bendit* judgment constituted. They used the instruments at hand to raise attention. In December 1979, the British Conservative MEP, the solicitor John Mark Taylor, sought to push the Commission on the issue and sent a parliamentary question, inquiring about any Commission proposals intended to ensure that the decisions of the ECJ were being respected and what kind of sanctions were foreseen.[156]

In late April, the Committee discussed the documents collected and decided to produce a parliamentary report and resolution. Invited by the Committee Chairman, Olmi from the Legal Service confided to the Committee members that the Commission had already addressed the French government on the issue.[157] Sieglerschmidt, appointed rapporteur, additionally emphasised the judgment's implications with a view to the 'observance' of the preliminary reference mechanism according to Article 177 of the EEC Treaty and the 'relationship between national legal systems and the Community legal system, in particular the problem of the consistent application of European law'.[158] When the Legal

[154] HAEP. PE1.AP.JURI.1979.PV_JURI-19791106_0010. European Parliament, Legal Affairs Committee, Minutes of the Meeting of 6 November 1979, PE/VII/PV/79-10, 15.11.1979, PE 61.013, 4, §4.

[155] HAEP. PE1.AP.JURI.1979.PV_JURI-19791127_0010. European Parliament, Legal Affairs Committee, Minutes of the Meeting of 27 and 28 November 1979, PE/VII/PV/79-12, 10.12.1979, PE 61.464, 6, §6 and Legal Service Archive (LSA). 07.763 Applicabilité des directives dans les États-membres. Affaire Cohn-Bendit European Commission, Secrétariat général, Commission juridique, compte rendu sommaire, Bruxelles, 3 décembre 1979, SP (79)2553.

[156] European Parliament, Question écrite no. 1316/79 de M. John Mark Taylor à la Commission des Communautés européennes: Autorité de la Cour de justice, 11 décembre 1979, Legal Service Archive 07.763 Applicabilité des directives dans les États-membres. Affaire Cohn-Bendit.

[157] HAEP. PE1.AP.JURI.1979.PV_JURI-19800428_0010. European Parliament, Legal Affairs Committee, Minutes of the Meeting of 28 and 29 April 1980, PE/VII/PV/80-7, 6.5.1980, PE 64.929, 4, §5, 9 and LSA.07.763 Applicabilité des directives dans les États-membres. Affaire Cohn-Bendit European Commission, European Commission, Secrétariat général, Legal Affairs Committee. Summary Record (Meeting, 28–29/04/1980), Brussels, 2.5.1980, SP (80)2024.

[158] European Parliament, Legal Affairs Committee, Notice to Members No. 32/79. Subject: Decision of the French Council of State of 22 December 1978 (Cohn-Bendit). Note by Mr. Sieglerschmidt and Documentation Compiled by the Directorate-General for Research and Documentation. Luxembourg, 6 February 1980, PE 62.430, European Parliament Working Documents 32 (1980): 2.

Committee – again including Olmi – discussed Sieglerschmidt's draft report in early December 1980, Committee members and Olmi in particular, insisted on moderating the somewhat aggressive tone vis-à-vis the member states and avoiding any insinuation of 'interference in the judiciary by national or Community authorities', namely the idea that the Commission could overrule national court decisions. Some of the rapporteur's suggestions seemed impractical, such as developing a blend between a directive and a regulation to ensure direct effect.[159] Before this meeting, in November 1980, Legal Service Director-General Claus-Dieter Ehlermann had written directly to Sieglerschmidt and recommended changes. Still in April 1981, the latest version of the report raised Olmi's concern: apparently Sieglerschmidt had only taken up a select number of Ehlermann's suggestions, and continued to suggest what he considered inappropriate ideas. These included introducing a provision granting a right of citizens to seek recourse by the ECJ against any European and national laws.[160] Hence, Olmi wrote to Sieglerschmidt asking for further changes after the meeting, highlighting – among other issues – that taking a member state to court for infringement based on the decisions of its independent courts would be problematic. He explained in detail the problems regarding the report's demand to define the directly effective parts of directives already in the law-making process.[161]

The Committee finally agreed at its meeting in Edinburgh at the end of June – again with Olmi attending – after some amendments were accepted, on the final text of the resolution.[162] The resolution adopted on 14 October 1981 made a number of references to earlier assertions of the autonomous nature and primacy of European law in its 'considérants': the reports by Dehousse on the application of Community Law, discussed above, and two further reports, on the application of Article 177 and on the individual right of action before the court, of 1969/70 and 1970, respectively. Thus, it rhetorically reconstructed a tradition and emphasised the continued constitutional understanding of European law. The resolution repeated the familiar arguments: the importance of the ECJ for the upholding of the legal order, the relevance of the preliminary reference mechanism to ensure the 'uniform application and interpretation of the law', and member states' courts' obligation to

159 HAEP. PE1.AP.JURI.1979.PV_JURI-19801204_0010. European Parliament, Legal Affairs Committee, Minutes of the Meeting of 4 and 5 December 1980, PE/II/OJ/80-17, 8.1.1981, PE 69.9963, 4, §4 (quote); LSA.07.763 Applicabilité des directives dans les États-membres. Affaire Cohn-Bendit. European Commission, Secrétariat général, Legal Affairs Committee. Summary Record (Meeting, 04–05/12/1980), Brussels, 10.12.1980, SP (80)5189.

160 LSA.07.763 Applicabilité des directives dans les États-membres. Affaire Cohn-Bendit. European Commission, Legal Service, and Peter Karpenstein, Note à l'attention de Monsieur Olmi, Rapport de Monsieur Sieglerschmidt sur la décision du Conseil d'État dans l'affaire Cohn-Bendit, Bruxelles, 8 avril 1981, JUR(81)D/01685 PKa/Dh.

161 LSA.07.763 Applicabilité des directives dans les États-membres. Affaire Cohn-Bendit. European Commission, Legal Service, Mr. Olmi to Hellmut Sieglerschmidt, Brussels, 15 April 1981, JUR (81) D/01806, PKa/Cs.

162 HAEP. PE1.AP.JURI.1979.PV_JURI-19810625_0010. European Parliament, Legal Affairs Committee, Minutes of the Meeting of 25–26 June 1981, PE/VII/PV/81-11, 7.7.1981, PE 73.912, 4–5.

participate in the mechanism. The resolution criticised the refusal of 'certain courts' to engage in this 'dialogue between . . . judges' and suggested that there was a lack of knowledge among national judges about European law. Furthermore, the resolution welcomed the ECJ's recent decisions regarding the direct effect of directives but deplored the lack of legal certainty this arguably created. Finally, the resolution made four concrete and ambitious proposals: first, a technological fix to the problematic lack of information on European law. In the nascent computer age, 'information centres' with 'terminals' providing 'access to data-retrieval banks' of ECJ rulings were to be set up in each member state.[163] Second, the EP demanded a formal commitment in the form of a 'joint statement' by the member states to ensure that their courts would submit relevant cases for preliminary reference. Third, they called for treaty reform, namely an adjustment of Article 173, to allow individuals to plea in front the ECJ, once 'they have exhausted all internal means of redress' regarding the implementation of European law in the member states. Fourth, again with a view to improving information about and a familiarity with European Law, 'training courses for judges in national courts' should be planned to enhance their 'familiarity with European law'.[164]

The EP continued to follow up on the issue of the implementation of and compliance with European law during the first term after direct elections. A resolution on this issue advanced by the Legal Committee in 1983 referred again in its 'considérants' to the 1981 resolution.[165] In early 1983, a scandal regarding lost barrels of toxic waste from Seveso alerted MEPs to the implementation problems of European law. Enforcement, compliance and application were issues that were increasingly being problematised by different EP committees, notably the Environmental Committee.[166]

With regard to the French resistance to the constitutional practice of European Law, the crushing defeat of the Gaullists in the 1981 elections resolved the conflict. The new president Francois Mitterrand was staunchly pro-European and in 1982 the

163 This was less futuristic than it seems in retrospect. In fact, on 1 July 1981, the French version of the CELEX computerised database of European Law, preparations for which had started as early as 1967, was made available to the public via the 'telecommunication network'. Publications Office of the European Union, ed., *25 Years of European Law Online* (Luxembourg: Publications Office of the European Union, 2006), 109–119.

164 European Parliament, Resolution on the Responsibility of the Court of Justice of the European Communities for the Uniform Application of Community Law in the Member States, Voted Upon on 14 October 1981, Official Journal of the EC C 287 (9 November 1981): 47–48.

165 European Parliament, Resolution on the Responsibility of the Member States for the Application of and Compliance with Community Law, Accepted on 9 February 1983, Official Journal of the EC C 68 (14 March 1983): 32–34.

166 European Parliament, Resolution on the Application of the Community Directives on Toxic Substances and the Shipment and Storage of the Seveso Dioxin (Own-Initiative Resolution, Voted Upon 14 April 1983), Official Journal of the European Communities (OJEC) 26, C 128 (16 May 1983): 60; Meyer 2021.

new Minister of Justice Robert Badinter introduced a circulaire that requested French courts to send preliminary references to the ECJ.[167]

CONCLUSIONS

During the first three decades of European integration, the EP and, particularly, its Legal Committee advocated for a federalist vision of European integration. This went hand in hand with staunch support for a constitutional interpretation of EC law. This finding is not particularly surprising against the backdrop of what we already know about the EP. Due to self-selection, only those committed to European integration voluntarily accepted the heavy burden of the dual mandate.[168] However, self-selection also mattered in a second respect: the Legal Committee attracted prominent law professors, former ministers and judges, who endowed the Committee with a high level of legal expertise and political acumen. Nevertheless, with characters like Sieglerschmidt – who was not a lawyer, but trained in business administration – and their self-understanding of their own role as representatives of the Europeans, federalist fervour at times outweighed legal, political and diplomatic concerns that, by contrast, the Commission's Legal Service had acquired over time.

The EP was part of a larger network – or even what political science has called an 'advocacy coalition'[169] – across different European institutions collaborating in favour of a constitutional understanding of European Law. While scholarly networks and the leading role of the Legal Service(s) therein are well known, this chapter demonstrates that the EP's Legal Committee was a veritable 'norm entrepreneur'[170] working in favour of development of a constitutional practice in European law to help facilitate the federalisation of the EC. At the same time, it always involved pursuing the EP's institutional self-interest in finally obtaining direct elections and in being accepted by the other institutions as a real parliament, on par with national parliaments.

As part of this cooperation, the EP served as a forum, where other actors – notably leading Commission figures like Hallstein – could present their message to a sort of proxy European public sphere. The EP as a representative body was able to lend democratic legitimacy to projects like the joint declaration on human rights. At the same time, the EP and its Legal Committee were actors, pursuing their own institutional interests next to those of the wider federalist project and that of a constitutional order.

Even though during the period covered by this chapter the EP was largely powerless in legislative terms, its members and the Legal Committee in particular

167 Rasmussen 2017, 305.
168 Knudsen 2012.
169 Sabatier 1998
170 Finnemore and Sikkink 1998.

skilfully used the instruments available – as noted already by Stein and Haas in the 1950s quoted above – 'performing' as a parliament:[171] posing parliamentary questions, having information gathered by the Secretariat, speaking at or organising conferences to spread the word, issuing reports to set the agenda and having debates and votes on carefully worded and often demanding, idealistic and at times radical resolutions. What this chapter demonstrates is an ongoing process of the rhetorical construction of a constitutional European legal order through the voices of the formally most powerless actors on the European playing field, the MEPs.

171 Krumrey 2018, 109–153.

4

Academic Allies: Transnational European Law Academia and the Development of the Constitutional Practice

Rebekka Byberg

This chapter[1] explores how a transnational European law academia was gradually established and played a leading role in legitimating and promoting the constitutional practice of European law. It demonstrates how the European supranational institutions in close cooperation with a small group of pro-European legal scholars and practitioners in the member states developed a transnational academic field dedicated to European law by the means of three central pillars: the Fédération Internationale pour le Droit Européen (FIDE) (from 1961), a number of European law journals (from the first half of the 1960s) with *Common Market Law Review* (*CML Rev*) as the frontrunner and the European University Institute (EUI) (from 1978). The chapter furthermore argues that the academic outlook of the transnational European law academia was shaped by its proximity to the supranational institutions of the EC, in particular the Commission and the European Court of Justice (ECJ). Following the wording of the ECJ, European law was promoted as a 'new legal order'[2] at FIDE conferences and in the European law journals from the mid-1960s onwards. While criticism of the ECJ's case law began to appear at the FIDE conferences in the 1970s, transnational European law academia was instrumental in developing and consolidating an outspoken constitutional discourse to legitimate and promote the ECJ, its case law and the ambitions for a federal Europe in the 1980s. Towards the 1990s, transnational European law academia reached a stage of professional maturity, which required a new degree of independence from the European institutions and allowed for more critical reflections on the jurisprudence of the ECJ. The chapter thus demonstrates just how entangled the development of the academic field of European law was with the political project of the constitutional practice until the late 1980s, while adding new nuances to its history.

As Bruno de Witte has pointed out, the academic field of European law has for years been composed by a transnational field of scholars and institutions with

[1] I would like to thank Claus-Dieter Ehlermann, Michel Waelbroeck, Stefan Vogenauer, and the research group 'Towards a New History of European Public Law' for comments, which improved this chapter significantly.

[2] 6/64 *Costa v ENEL*, 1964, ECLI:EU:C:1964:66.

a 'denationalised' outlook as well as national sub-fields that tend to fragment the discipline along national and linguistic lines.[3] While we do have the first thorough analyses of the national fields of European law academia, on respectively Germany and France,[4] the establishment and nature of what we call transnational European law academia have yet to be analysed in a coherent manner. The first venture into exploring European law academia as a social phenomenon was published in 1997 by two legal scholars with a sociological bend, Harm Schepel and Rein Wesseling. Focusing on the writing of legal doctrine in law journals, they documented the vital role played by the staff of the supranational European institutions using statistical methods. They concluded that the European legal doctrine in specialist journals were written to a relatively large degree by the staff from the administrative and judicial European institutions, and to a lesser degree by academics when compared to journals of national public law and national economic law.[5] Limited in scope and methodology, this initial analysis was followed by important contributions by Karen Alter and Antoine Vauchez, who both explored the formation and role played by FIDE in the development of European law. Alter and Vauchez agreed to highlight the role of this early umbrella organisation that organised both European law academics and professionals. They stated that the so-called 'FIDE entrepreneurs' played a major and successful role in developing European law through academic contributions and test cases. Vauchez in addition claimed that FIDE coordinated the mobilisation of the supranational institutions behind the seminal judgments of *Van Gend en Loos* and *Costa v ENEL* in the first half of the 1960s.[6] FIDE and the 'euro-law associations' were assumed to constitute an ideological cohesive network, which positioned itself in opposition to sceptical national observers of European law in a Bordieuan battlefield of European law.[7] To Vauchez transnational European law academia, including FIDE, was born as a by-product of the strategies for the institutionalisation of the Treaties of Rome, for instance promoted by Walter Hallstein, President of the EEC Commission 1958–1967, as an academic space with fuzzy borders between academic and extra-academic practice, science and reform, law and politics. He also highlighted how the EUI would come to play a role similar to FIDE from the late 1970s onwards. To Vauchez, the Department of Law of the EUI functioned as an interdisciplinary and trans-Atlantic hub, where the paradigm of constitutionalism emerged in the early 1980s in close connection with the plans of the Altiero Spinelli and the European Parliament (EP) to draft a Treaty on a European Union.[8]

3 De Witte 2013.

4 Mangold 2011; Bailleux 2014.

5 Schepel and Wesseling 1997.

6 26/62 *Van Gend en Loos v Nederlandse Administratie der Belastingen*, 1963, ECLI:EU:C:1963:1 and 6/64 *Costa v ENEL*, 1964, ECLI:EU:C:1964:66.

7 Alter 2009, 73; Vauchez 2010, 108–128; Vauchez and Mudge 2012; Vauchez 2008.

8 Vauchez 2015, 87–88 and 203–204.

Historians have already modified some of these results. Bill Davies, Alexandre Bernier and Morten Rasmussen have, for example, demonstrated that the European law associations were not very successful in promoting European law nationally, meeting both a lack of attention and occasionally stiff resistance of the conservative national legal elites to adapt to the brand-new world of European law.[9] Similarly, the theoretical assumption that FIDE functioned as a coherent and dynamic hub for coordinating support for the constitutional practice of European law has been shown to be misleading. It was rather the Legal Service of the Commission that occasionally played a coordinating role, as Rasmussen has convincingly demonstrated. Rasmussen furthermore suggests that in the 1970s European law journals such as the *Common Market Law Review* may have played a more significant role in the development of European law academia than FIDE.

Overall, existing research has offered several interesting insights about the historical roots of and roles played by European law academia in the development of European law. Indeed, the role of several institutional settings – all transnational in nature – such as the FIDE, European law journals and the EUI have been discussed. The chapter moves beyond existing research on the history and role of European law academy in the development of European law from 1950 to 1993. It also represents a major effort in terms of empirical research based on archival sources to substantiate and test earlier claims.[10] Finally, the chapter offers the first well-documented narrative about how the transnational dimension of European law academy was developed and the role it played in the battle over the constitutional practice in European law.

EUROPEAN LAW AT THE NATIONAL LEVEL IN THE 1950S

The historical roots of the constitutional practice in European law can be traced back to the political visions that flourished in the immediate post-war years where important popular movements advocated the establishment of a European federation based on a constitutional legal system.[11] In the 1950s, national governments, however, only took modest steps towards the federal objectives with the formation of the European Coal and Steel Community (ECSC), the European Economic Community (EEC) and the European Atomic Community (EURATOM). The Schuman Declaration did highlight a European federation as a distant goal. But in the negotiations on the Treaty of Paris, only the West German delegation promoted a federal organisation of the ECSC. The other delegations primarily aimed at

9 Bernier 2012; Davies 2012b, 46–88; Rasmussen 2013.

10 Most important archive are: Historical Archive of the European Union (HAEU), Archive of Mauro Cappelletti (AMC), Archive of Fédération Internationale de Droit Européen (AFIDE) and Archive of the Common Market Law Review (ACMLR). The latter two archives are held respectively by FIDE and privately.

11 Rasmussen 2008.

developing a tight legal and political control of the powers of the High Authority (HA), the supranational executive, which the French delegation led by Jean Monnet tried to defend. In the negotiations on the Treaties of Rome, all delegations except the Dutch shied away from the notion of a powerful supranational executive. Instead, they gave the main legislative role to a Council of Ministers, and the powers of the institutions were limited to the functional tasks required to fulfil the objectives of the Treaties. To a majority of the founding member states, the Treaties of Rome were considered a matter of international law with the sole exception of competition policy. Nevertheless, certain legal techniques beyond traditional international law found their way into the Treaties during the negotiations partly due to the far-reaching nature of the Common Market, and partly due to the role played by legal experts in drafting the treaties. Elements of administrative and constitutional law, therefore, became part of the Treaties.[12]

Consequently, the legal nature of the Treaty of Paris and the Treaties of Rome remained ambiguous, giving leeway to a battle over the nature of European law. Several key actors tried to champion a constitutional understanding of European law from the mid-1950s. Not least French member of the Legal Service of the HA, and later Director-General of the Legal Service of the EEC Commission, Michel Gaudet,[13] found it necessary that the ECJ should assume a constitutional role in the ECSC by using a teleological interpretive legal method, and not a textual method traditionally employed in international public law. In several cases before the ECJ, the Legal Service promoted this vision. But the ECJ of the ECSC refrained from adopting such an approach.[14] With the realisation that the fulfilment of his constitutional vision required a broader mobilisation of national legal academics and practitioners beyond the few actors sharing his vision such as Hallstein, Pierre Pescatore,[15] and Nicola Catalano,[16] Gaudet strategically turned elsewhere for support, not least to the academic field, where pro-European lawyers were already organising themselves from the mid-1950s onward.

In France, for example, an association of European law, the Association des juristes européens (AJE), was founded in 1954. The aim of the AJE was to organise jurists partial to the European idea not only in France, but across all the member

12 This section relies on Boerger and Rasmussen 2014, 201–203.

13 Michel Gaudet was first a legal counsellor of the Legal Service of the High Authority of the European Coal and Steel Community (ECSC). From 1958 to 1967, he was the director of the Legal Service of the Commission of the European Economic Community, and from 1967–1969 he was the director of the Commission of the European Community, as the European Coal and Steel Communities, EURATOM, and the European Economic Community were merged into the European Community with a unified Legal Service in 1967. Jean Rey was Commissioner in the Hallstein Commission 1958–1967 and President of the Commission 1967–1970.

14 See for example 1/54 *French Republic v High Authority of the European Coal and Steel Community*, 1954, ECLI:EU:C:1954:7. Cited from Boerger and Rasmussen 2014, 204.

15 Judge at the ECJ from 1967 to 1985.

16 Judge at the ECJ from 1958 to 1962.

states of the ECSC.[17] By studying how European law impacted both public and private law in the member states, the association hoped to provide the ECSC with crucial information that could help develop a genuine European legal order.[18] Despite the high ambitions, the AJE remained a modest association with few members until 1958.[19] In 1958, the association received new impetus by the establishment of the EC and decided to attempt the creation of a genuinely European association that would include all the member states. To this end, the AJE brought prominent European jurists together at international conferences that successfully motivated the establishment of new national associations.[20] In 1958, the Associazione Italiana dei Giuristi Europei (AIGE) was thus founded by eleven Rome-based jurists, primarily lawyers, who formally sought to establish an association similar to the AJE.[21] In Belgium, the Association Belge pour le Droit Européen was likewise established in 1958, by, among others, Walter Ganshof Van der Meersch, Advocate General at the Belgian Court of Cassation and later judge in the European Court of Human Rights (1973–1986).[22] The creation of the Association Luxembourgeoise des Juristes Européens followed in December 1959.[23] In the Netherlands, the Dutch Nederlandse Vereniging voor Europees Recht (NVER) was created on 24 September 1960 by thirty-seven jurists, primarily practitioners, including the president of the ECJ at the time Andreas Donner (President of the ECJ 1958–1964, ECJ judge 1964–1979), the former Dutch ECJ judge Jos Serrarens (ECJ judge 1952–1958) and the Director-General for Competition in the EEC, Pieter Verloren van Themaat (ECJ Advocate General 1981–1986).[24] Prompted by the West German Ministry of Foreign Affairs and the Ministry of Justice, as well as by Gaudet, a West German association followed, as German law professor Ernst Steindorff founded the Wissenschaftliche Gesellschaft für Europarecht (WGE) with ten fellow academics as a subgroup of the German Association for Comparative Law at the Max Planck Institute for Comparative and International Private Law in Hamburg on 26 April 1961. Among them were Hans-Peter Ipsen, Ernst Mestmäcker, Konrad Zweigert and Bodo Börner.[25]

These professional associations helped to consolidate and further develop the new academic fields of European law in the member states, where new university chairs, institutes and academic centres and law journals began to see the light from the

17 This aim was written in the AJE statues. Bailleux 2014, 277.

18 Bernier 2012, 401–402.

19 Bernier 2012.

20 Rasmussen 2012, 176.

21 Archive of the Associazione Italiana dei Giuristi Europei (AAIGE). Costituzione di Associazione Associazione Italiana dei Giuristi Europei, 27 November 1958.

22 Bailleux 2014, 278; Rasmussen 2008, 191.

23 Rasmussen 2008, 177.

24 I thank Karin van Leeuwen for pointing these facts out.

25 Archive of Walter Strauss (AWS), 328 and Mitgliederverzeichnis, 1 November 1964, AWS, 328. Referat IV 4, Aufzeichung in Stichworten für Herrn Staatssekretär betr. Wissenschaftliche Gesellschaft für Europarecht.

latter half of the 1950s onward.[26] An example was the founders of the Dutch association that knew each other from an informal working group which had existed since 1954, and was initiated by law professors C. H. F. Polak and F. M. von Asbeck as discussed in Chapter 8. In 1959 the group became a part of the new Europa Institute directed by the ubiquitous socialist politician Ivo Samkalden, Dutch Minister of Justice from 1956 to 1958, professor of international law, and outspoken federalist[27] with a close relationship to Gaudet. At the Institute, Samkalden founded the journal *Common Market Law Review*, which went on to become one of the most prominent European law journals.[28]

These early tentative developments towards establishing a new field of law did not have any profound impact on the academic field of international law in the 1950s. Scholars of international law found it difficult to endorse a constitutional approach to European law, as they generally understood international affairs in a Westphalian light that only recognised states, generally speaking, as subjects in international law.[29] In 1957, at a major international conference in Stresa organised by the ECSC Assembly in order to evaluate the achievements of the ECSC, a number of the most authoritative international law scholars of the time were invited to join a committee that would assess the progress made by European law. A key question was how to understand the legal nature of the ECSC. Was it a new autonomous legal order of a potentially federal character, or did the ESCS belong to the family of international law? Despite intense lobbying by Gaudet, the committee disappointingly concluded that the ECSC was by no means extraordinary and should merely be understood as a peculiar subset of international law. In the debate that followed, a number of younger scholars criticised the conclusion of the committee and argued that the notion that the ECSC was based on an autonomous European legal order was a more accurate description that matched the supranational setup of the ECSC.[30] After Stresa Gaudet had learned his lesson. It would take a comprehensive and sustained effort to secure the backing of legal academia for a more progressive understanding of European law and it would be crucial to separate the latter from international law.

THE FOUNDATION OF FIDE

Gaudet's idea was to create a European association of European law that could bring together legal scholars, lawyers and practitioners involved or interested in European law. With the formation of several European law associations beyond the original

26 With regard to the German and French experience please see Mangold 2011; Davies 2012b, 46–90; Bailleux 2014.

27 Interview with Laurens-Jan Brinkhorst, 6 December 2013.

28 Byberg 2017.

29 Vauchez 2015, 77–78.

30 For a detailed account of the Stresa conference see Bailleux 2014.

French one in 1958–1959, it seemed obvious that such an association could take the shape of an umbrella association that would bring together the new member state associations of European law. According to Gaudet, such a European association would have a significant effect on the implementation of European law in the member states not just by providing academic legitimisation, but by facilitating the penetration of European law into the national legal professions. It would thus be an indispensable tool for the realisation of the Common Market that depended on the correct implementation and application of the common European rules.[31] This was the background for Gaudet's engagement in the establishment of national associations of European law since 1958–1959. Although the associations differed in character and composition of membership, they were all based on the ideological support for European integration, and a belief in the potential of law in the integration process. On this basis, a federation was established at a Congress in Brussels 12–14 October 1961 which was organised by the Belgian association in close cooperation with the Directorate-General of Competition from the Commission. Despite the engagement by several current or former ECJ judges in the national associations, there were no judges in the leadership of the new federation, entitled the 'Bureau', the work of which was overseen by a Steering Committee (Comité Directeur).[32] A future permanent secretariat was planned but did not materialise.[33] These organs were supposed to ensure the aims of FIDE: first, to promote the objectives of the member associations, including joint events and exchange of information, second, to organise lawyers interested in European law, third, to study the legal problems of European law and, last, to raise awareness of these problems.[34] Concretely, FIDE would organise a number of events, such as the founding Congress, where national reports on topics chosen by the Bureau would be discussed, and a common resolution would be adopted.[35]

FIDE CONGRESSES IN THE 1960S

The founding Congress set a precedent for the format of FIDE activities. Based on national reports, participants from various backgrounds would discuss European law topics in a grand comparative law exercise. In 1961, 35 per cent of the 182 participants

[31] Archive of Michel Gaudet (AMG). Chronos 1961. Letter from Gaudet to Rey, 21 January 1961 and Bernier 2012, 401–402.

[32] AMG. Chronos 1961. Letter from Gaudet to Rey, 21 January 1961.

[33] Archive of Eric Stein (AES). Box 12 Pettiti. Compte-rendu de la réunion du bureau de la Fédération internationale pour le droit européen, 13 January 1962 in Paris and Archive of Dansk Forening for Europaret (ADFE). Letter from Pescatore to Lando, 9 November 1971.

[34] AAIGE. Statuts de la FIDE.

[35] Archive of the Legal Service of the European Commission (ALSC). 347.96 (100). Fédération internationale pour le Droit européen. Gaudet, Note concernant la fédération internationale pour le droit européen, undated.

were from national courts;[36] 18 per cent were private practice lawyers; 14 per cent were academics; 9 per cent were from the Commission; 6 per cent from national firms, 4 per cent were national officials (mostly from ministries), 3 per cent were judges or other kinds of personnel from the ECJ; and 2 per cent were from national banks.[37] The distribution of participants reflected to a large degree the institutional links of the Belgian association in charge of organising the event. The President, Louis Hendrickx, and most of the association's leadership had a relation to the Cour d'appel de Bruxelles. As a result, they were, therefore, able to attract a considerable number of participants whose work intersected directly and indirectly with the court. The topics discussed were company mergers, anti-trust laws and sales with promotional free gifts.[38]

In 1962, after pressure from Gaudet, the Legal Service was officially charged with the responsibility for managing the relationship with FIDE, which led to the development of a high degree of intimacy between the Service and FIDE. The latter agreed to draft reports on various aspects of European law for the internal use of the Commission, and in return, the Commission would fund not only the FIDE's basic running costs, but also provide subsidies for national associations, and FIDE working groups contributing to Commission reports.[39] Themes of the Congresses likewise reflected the interests of the Legal Service, as they typically centred on the most relevant questions of European law of the day. At the Hague Congress in October 1963, the theme was directly applicable provisions in international treaties and their application in the Treaties of Rome – a central topic after the ECJ's ruling in the *Van Gend en Loos* case.[40] The national reports demonstrated a significant difference in how the member states received international law. Where international treaties in principle, but not always in reality, were incorporated directly into domestic law in monist states (the Netherlands, France, Luxembourg and Belgium), in the dualist member states (West Germany and Italy) national parliaments were required to transform international treaties into internal law. Upon this comparative basis, a vast discussion among, for instance, former ECJ judge Catalano, future ECJ judge Pescatore, the Dutch lawyer Ter Kuile, the Belgian legal scholar Michel Waelbroeck, the German Permanent Representative in Brussels Carl Friedrich Ophüls and Ipsen led to the adoption of a resolution

36 This number however reflected the close connections between the leadership of the Belgian association and the Cour d'appel de Bruxelles.

37 The analysis is based on a participant list from the Congress in the Archive of Michel Waelbroeck (AMW). Programme, Colloque international de droit Européen, Bruxelles, 12–14 octobre 1961.

38 FIDE Congress report 1961. Rapport au Colloque international de droit européen organisé par l'Association belge pour le droit européen, Bruxelles, 12–14 October 1961, Bryant, Bruxelles 1962.

39 Rasmussen 2012, 179.

40 26/62 *Van Gend en Loos v Nederlandse Administratie der Belastingen*, 1963, ECLI:EU:C:1963:1. In addition, consequences of infringements of Community law were discussed see FIDE Congress report 1963: Deuxième colloque international de droit Européen organisé par l'Association Néerlandaise pout le Droit Européen, La Haye 24–26 Octobre 1963. N.V. Uitgeversmaatschappij W.E.J. Tjeenk Willink, Zwolle, 1966.

where direct effect but also the primacy of European law were generally supported.[41] A year later, in the *Costa v ENEL* judgment,[42] the ECJ was able to draw on the legitimacy that FIDE resolution provided for the doctrine of primacy. Some of the participants at the Congress, such as Waelbroeck, were very sceptical regarding the attempt to distinguish European law from international law. This was advocated by Ophüls, Ipsen, Gaudet and Paul Leleux from the Legal Service. It seemed clear that the political agenda of the Commission counted for more than purely legal considerations.[43]

The next FIDE Congress in Paris in 1965 focused on respectively how Council legislation entered national legal orders and the harmonisation of company laws. Here, the national reports on the first topic all concurred that regulations took effect immediately in the national legal systems, but the majority of the speakers at the Congress insisted that directives had to be transformed into domestic law by a national implementation act.[44] At a time when the Empty Chair Crisis had led to an abrupt halt in the progress towards a federal Europe at the political level, many delegates at the Congress apparently chose to shy away from legal activism, and instead relied on the wording of Article 189 of the EEC Treaty. This Article stated that regulations were directly applicable, whereas directives were binding with regard to the result, but left the implementation to national authorities.[45] A minority rejected this literal interpretation and held that directives could produce 'vertical' direct effect (they could be invoked as a defence by an individual in relations with the state), but not horizontal direct effect (could not be invoked in purely inter-individual relations).[46] In contrast to the two previous Congresses, no resolution was adopted at this time. However, a special FIDE commission, which included Ophüls and Donner, was established.[47] In its report it found that directives could in fact have direct effect to ensure the effectiveness (*effet utile*) of European law. When the question finally appeared before the ECJ in the *Grad* case in 1970,[48] the Legal Service considered carefully what position to adopt in an internal memorandum. It acknowledged that to attribute direct effect to directives would be very controversial. Both legal scholarship and national courts had conflicting views on the question. However, due to the conclusion of the FIDE report, the Legal Service argued that scholarly opinion was gradually shifting towards the endorsement of the

41 FIDE Congress report 1963, 287–288.

42 6/64 *Costa v ENEL*, 1964, ECLI:EU:C:1964:66.

43 I thank Michel Waelbroeck for pointing this out.

44 Bignami 2011, 22–23, and FIDE Congress report 1965: Trosième Colloque de droit Européen organise par l'association des Juristes Européens. Paris les 25, 26, 27 novembre 1965. Unpublished.

45 Article 189 of the EEC Treaty.

46 See, for instance, the Belgian report in FIDE Congress report 1965. 'Mécanismes juridiques assurantla mise en oeuvre de la législation communautaire par les autoritéslégislatives ou exécutives nationales by C. Cambier, M. Waelbroeck, J.V. Louis, and H. Desmedt.

47 Dumon, Rigaux, and Goffin from Belgium, Ophuls and Bulow from Germany, Labbé from France, Donner, Erades, and Ter Kuile from the Netherland, and Lapace from Greece. Bignami 2011, 22.

48 9/70 *Franz Grad v Finanzamt Traunstein*, 1970, ECLI:EU:C:1970:78.

direct effect of directives, and eventually that also became the position the service presented to the ECJ.[49]

The ECJ supported the position of the Legal Service in the *Grad* judgment and in two additional judgments *Sace* (1970) and *van Duyn* (1974), the Court established that directives could produce direct effect,[50] repeating the argument of *effet utile* from the FIDE commission report.[51] The Legal Service was correct when it considered the new doctrine controversial. In response to the new case law, legal and political elites in some member states protested vociferously. In Britain, a committee of the House of Lords reacted sharply to the 'legal uncertainty' created by the ECJ's approach and proposed that the Council routinely should state explicitly whether a directive could produce direct effect or not in future Community legislation. In France, the Council of State (Conseil d'État) openly rebelled against the ECJ's jurisprudence in the *Cohn-Bendit* case in 1978,[52] where the court in its own interpretation of European law held that directives according to Article 189 of the EEC Treaty had no direct effect. In 1979, in the *Ratti* judgment, the ECJ modified its approach and pointed out that while certain directives did produce direct effect they only did so vertically and not horizontally.[53] While the fate of the doctrine of direct effect for directives caused serious criticism of the ECJ and the Commission, the story clearly demonstrates the use of FIDE as a sounding board for ECJ case law.[54]

Regarding the organisation of FIDE, the plans of the early 1960s did not fully materialise. In the end, the federation did not manage to develop a coherent leadership at the European level. The Bureau quickly lost its momentum, and the secretariat was never established.[55] As a consequence, FIDE ended up as a loose framework consisting first and foremost of a rotating presidency that was primarily engaged in suggesting topics for, planning and conducting the next Congress,[56] and second of the Steering Committee consisting of representatives from the national associations, which decided all major questions including the topics of the Congresses. Consequently, FIDE lost its early dynamic.[57] Apart from the

49 Rasmussen 2017, 296.

50 9/70 *Franz Grad v Finanzamt Traunstein*, 1970, ECLI:EU:C:1970:78, 33/70 *SpA SACE v Finance Minister of the Italian Republic*, ECLI:EU:C:1970.118 and 41/74 *Yvonne van Duyn v Home Office*, 1974, ECLI:EU:C:1974:133.

51 Bignami 2011, 23.

52 Conseil d'État (Assemblée), 22 December 1978, *Cohn-Bendit*, n° 11604, published in *Recueil Lebon* 524, 1980.

53 148/78 *Criminal proceedings against Tullio Ratti*, 1979, ECLI:EU:C:1979:110 and 152/84, *M. H. Marshall v Southampton and South-West Hampshire Area Health Authority (Teaching)*, ECLI:EU:C:1986:84.

54 For a more detailed analysis of this story consult Rasmussen 2017.

55 Byberg 2017.

56 ADFE. Letter from Pescatore to Lando, 9 November 1971 and Archive of FIDE (AFIDE), Minutes, Steering Committee meetings.

57 AFIDE. Minutes, Steering Committee meetings.

Congresses, practically no activities took place under the auspices of the FIDE. Much depended on the national association in charge of the next Congress, which suggested the potential topics[58] and drew on its ties to the Community institutions, national institutions and business partners in preparing and financing the Congress. The organisation and particular shape of the Congresses thus came to vary greatly according to the preferences and abilities of the host association.[59]

THE IMPACT OF FIDE IN THE 1960S

When Gaudet stepped down as Director-General of the Legal Service in 1969, he could look back at the creation of a new field of European law, which was separate from international law, as well as a transnational federation of European law. The close ties between the Legal Service and FIDE meant that several of the FIDE Congresses dealt with crucial doctrinal developments in European law, including direct effect and primacy, and served a key legitimating role by endorsing the case law of the ECJ. There is, however, no evidence that FIDE was instrumental in aligning the supranational institutions and academics involved in European law behind the case law of the ECJ, as claimed by Antoine Vauchez. In fact, the lack of organisational development meant that the FIDE remained a loose association.[60] While FIDE was a success at the transnational level, Gaudet's ambition that FIDE would help European law have an impact in the national legal arenas was also not realised. One example of the limited impact of the national associations was the oldest one, the AJE. The AJE was well organised, expanded its membership base, published a bulletin several times a year and continuously held conferences and seminars on European law in the 1960s, 1970s and 1980s. These activities played a role in disseminating and legitimising European law in certain legal environments in France. However, the euro-sceptic Gaullist regime in the 1960s, as well as the long-lasting hostility of the French Conseil d'État, limited the general impact of the AJE on the French reception of European law. In West Germany, a much more pro-European member state, the WGE, with its academic character, also built up a well-functioning organisation with a solid power base in the German administrative and political elite. The association for instance received financial support from West German ministries.[61] Nonetheless, the scholars who supported the constitutional interpretation of European law promoted by the ECJ found it difficult to overcome the widespread scepticism in the German legal academy as well as among certain parts of the judiciary. It did perhaps not help that the WGE excluded judges from

58 Even though these topics were often adjusted or redefined at the Steering Committee meetings. AFIDE. Minutes, Steering Committee meetings.

59 AFIDE. Minutes, Steering Committee meetings.

60 This argument has already been put forth in Rasmussen 2017, 179–180. The present analysis supports Rasmussen's argument.

61 AWS. 237. Letter from Börner to C.H. Beck'sche Verlagsbuchhandlung, 12 February 1973.

participating in the association.[62] The journal *Europarecht* dedicated to European law was a good example of the lack of impact. It was established in 1965 by the WGE, but in the 1960s and 1970s, the journal was far from self-sustaining and in severe danger of having to close.[63] Another example of the same trend was the AIGE in Italy which never became a genuinely national association and was practically dormant already from the mid-1960s onwards,[64] a situation that even led to a lack of representation in the Steering Committee in the early 1970s.[65]

THE ESTABLISHMENT OF THE EUROPEAN LAW JOURNALS

With FIDE established as a first central pillar of a transnational European law academia in 1961, Gaudet sought to create another; a journal dedicated solely to European law, which should be available in all the community languages as well as English.[66] In 1962 Gaudet seriously began to examine this idea in close cooperation with Ivo Samkalden.[67] A few journals dedicated to European law already existed in some of the member states, but they did not fulfil the need for general information on the development of European law either because of the editorial conception of the journals, or because they only targeted practitioners. The information gap for researchers and practitioners, which existed according to Gaudet, posed 'des dangers sérieux' for the latter.[68]

Gaudet and Samkalden's journal never materialised, as the Commission found the undertaking too expensive.[69] In a parallel process initiated in 1961, however, Samkalden established the journal *CML Rev* at the auspices of the Europa Institute at Leiden University, which Samkalden directed at the time. The journal was to deal exclusively with European law and was eventually published in English by both a British and a Dutch publisher in a joint venture between the Europa Institute and the British Institute of International and Comparative Law. The British publisher at Stevens and Sons/Sweet and Maxwell initially doubted whether there would be a market for such a specialised journal in Britain or for that sake on the Continent.[70] In the end, Samkalden managed to convince the publisher to take the chance. The *CML Rev* thus became a suitable substitute to Gaudet's original plan. It was truly

62 Davies 2012b, 46–88.

63 AWS. 237. Letter from C.H. Beck'sche Verlagsbuchhandlung to Wissenschaftliche Gesellschaft für Europarecht, 25 July 1972.

64 Interview with Paolo de Caterini, 30 March 2016.

65 See, for instance AFIDE. Minutes, Steering Committee meeting 10 April 1973.

66 Gaudet's effort has been described in Bailleux, 2013.

67 AMG. Chronos 1961. Letter from Gaudet to Stein, 20 March 1961 and Interview with Laurens-Jan Brinkhorst, 6 December 2013.

68 AMG. Chronos 1962. Rapport sur la création d'une publication périodique concernant le droit des Communautés européennes by Michel Combarnous and Michel Gaudet, 15 May 1962.

69 Bailleux 2013, 366.

70 Archive of the Common Market Law Review (ACMLREV). Letter from Burke to De Flines, 2 May 1962.

a transnational journal with a broad appeal to both scholars and practitioners. The only downside seen from the perspective of Gaudet was perhaps that the journal was set up as a traditional academic-commercial enterprise, which limited the direct influence of the Commission or FIDE.

In the foundational years, almost all editors of *CML Rev* were academics. Faced with the challenge of identifying authors to write about European law in a field that was still small, the editors soon turned to their connections inside the institutions of the EC. Central personalities such as Gaudet, Donner and Pescatore were therefore heavily involved in the management of the journal with tasks such as identifying and proposing authors for specific tasks.[71] They were also active as editorial board members in the other academic journals dedicated to European law established around the same time such as *Rivista di diritto europeo* (1961), *Cahiers de droit européen* (1965) and finally *Revue trimestrielle de droit européen* (1966). Only *Europarecht*, established in 1966, did not involve Pescatore, Donner or Gaudet because only German members were allowed on the board. Although most of these journals had a national or regional orientation based on language, the involvement of central community actors in almost all the journals nevertheless suggests a close affiliation between the institutions of the EC and the emerging national field of European law in this period.

Among the law journals the *CML Rev* had a special status. It served as a model to the other journals,[72] and it helped define the academic field for European law as differentiated from international law. Most articles were doctrinal pieces attempting to clarify the latest ECJ judgments without explicit theoretical or contextual considerations. Implicitly, however, they followed the new constitutional interpretation of European law launched by the ECJ in the seminal *Van Gend en Loos* and *Costa v ENEL* judgments. In a limited number of significant articles and editorials this underlying view of the journal came out clearly typically when the more controversial ECJ judgments were treated.[73] By the end of the 1960s, the ECJ's doctrines and its proclamation of a new and special legal order seem to have been accepted by European law scholars. Along with the small circle of central Community actors, they constituted a tight power-knowledge nexus, which promoted an understanding in line with Gaudet's constitutional vision, although more cautious notions were used to describe it.

[71] See, for instance ACMLREV. Letter from Scheltema to Stein, 19 October 1965.

[72] ACMLREV. Letter from Rabe to Brinkhorst, 18 July 1966. Hans-Jürgen Rabe, editor of Europarecht wrote to Brinkhorst that they studied CML Rev. thoroughly, and that CML Rev. served as a model to Europarecht in some respects. Unfortunately, Rabe did not elaborate in the letter, and the contact between Europarecht and CML. Rev. was very limited. It is however reasonable to assume that CML Rev. was a source of inspiration to the founders and editors of Cahiers de droit européen also, since the profile of this journal resembled CML Rev.'s.

[73] For an analysis of the content of the journal, see Byberg 2017b, 53–55, 57–59, and 61–63.

THE TRANSNATIONAL ACADEMIC INSTITUTIONS OF EUROPEAN LAW IN THE 1970S

With the establishment of FIDE and several journals dedicated to European law in the 1960s, most importantly the *CML Rev*, key transnational academic institutions of European law were established. To these institutions, reaching agreement on the nature of European law was a primary concern. In the 1970s, the focus would change towards a defence of the constitutional interpretation against attacks from national legal scholars, who accused the ECJ of behaving as a 'gouvernement de juges', and by national courts that did not necessarily sympathise with the constitutional interpretation of the ECJ. This change was indirectly caused by the new activism displayed by the ECJ from 1967 onwards under the leadership of the new French President of the Court, Robert Lecourt (see more in Chapter 1).[74] In 1970, the ECJ challenged the boundaries between European and national law in the *Internationale Handelsgesellschaft* judgment,[75] when it ruled that the primacy of European law was unbound even by basic principles in national constitutions. This caused strong critique from both national academic circles and national courts.

The *CML Rev* was a constant and true companion of the ECJ. In the pages of the journal Donner, for instance, tried to meet the critique with a humble approach by stating that the ECJ and the interpretation of the Treaties by 'nine old men' should not be confused with the activities in the national constitutional courts.[76] However, it was perhaps more characteristic for the tone of the European lawyers, when Cesare Maestripieri, from the Legal Service of the Commission, described Italian courts' use of the lex posterior principle and their lack of use of preliminary references as heresy.[77] National courts that displayed hesitance towards the ECJ's case law on the direct effect of directives, which was applauded in the journal,[78] were likewise heavily criticised – especially the *Cohn-Bendit* ruling[79] by the French Conseil d'État in 1978.[80] The journal also strongly backed the *Internationale Handelsgesellschaft* judgment and showed little understanding for the *Solange* judgment by the West German Constitutional Court (Bundesverfassungsgericht (BVerfG)) in 1974.[81]

In this period, Claus-Dieter Ehlermann, the new German Director-General of the Legal Service of the Commission from 1977, became a very active and highly

74 For an analysis of the 'Court of 1967', see Davies and Rasmussen 2014.

75 11/70, *Internationale Handelsgesellschaft mbH v Einfuhr- und Vorratsstelle für Getreide und Futtermittel*, ECLI:EU:C:1970:114.

76 Donner 1974, 129–130.

77 Maestripieri 1975, 441; Bebr 1974; Forman and Stevens 1976.

78 'Editorial Comments', (1971) 8 *Common Market Law Review*, 1–4, at 3.

79 Conseil d'État (Assemblée), 22 December 1978, *Cohn-Bendit*, n° 11604, published in *Recueil Lebon* 524, 1980.

80 Kapteyn 1975; Bebr 1983.

81 Bebr 1973, 98; Bail and Lichtenberg 1975, 307.

regarded editor of the journal.[82] Similarly to Gaudet, his aim was the synchronisation between academic activities and practice, and he wanted to better inform the academic readers about the activities of the Commission in the field.[83] Ehlermann was engaged with other European law journals as well and participated regularly in meetings between executive editors from the late 1970s onwards. Here Ehlermann would inform the editors of the topic with which the Legal Service was concerned and encourage them to deal with them in the journal.[84]

Ehlermann was, however, not involved in FIDE to the same extent. He did not consider the FIDE Congresses to have the same operational or political importance as the European law journals. The organisational weaknesses of FIDE were so apparent that it did not constitute a viable tool for informing national legal communities about the progress of European law.[85] As a result, the ECJ became the major link between the EC and FIDE in the 1970s almost by default. The 1970s also saw a more pronounced participation of ECJ judges or advocates generals through membership of the national European law associations in the Steering Committee meetings. This was in line with the general campaign for stronger ties between the ECJ and national legal elites under the presidency of Lecourt.[86] Participation of ECJ judges in the national associations and FIDE allowed for the diffusion of knowledge of European law to national legal elites. Some of the ECJ judges, such as Pescatore and Thijmen Koopmans,[87] were heavily engaged in FIDE with the clear ambition of setting the agenda. Through participation in their respective national associations, they served as FIDE Presidents when their association held the presidency and enjoyed considerable esteem and authority at the Steering Committee meetings. Other ECJ judges were less involved and normally only participated in the Steering Committee meetings when their national association held the presidency of FIDE. However, compared to legal scholars and lawyers such as Börner from the WGE, Leon Goffin from the Belgian Association and Paul François Ryziger and Lise Funck-Brentano from the AJE, who participated in the Steering Committee for decades, the participation of ECJ judges was

[82] Ehlermann became the Director-General of the Legal Service of the European Commission in 1977. In 1987, he became special adviser for Institutional Questions of Commission President Jacques Delors, and from 1990–1995 he was the Director-General for the Directorate-General for Competition.

[83] Interview with Claus-Dieter Ehlermann, 29 June 2016.

[84] ACMLREV. Minutes, meeting of the Editors, 6 December 1979.

[85] Interview with Claus-Dieter Ehlermann, 29 June 2016 and interview with Claus-Dieter Ehlermann by Sigfrido Ramirez 16 September 2016 (carried out in cooperation with the present author). The Director-General of the Legal Service from 1969 to 1975, Walter Much, did not engage much with FIDE or academia in general.

[86] Prominent national judges were for instance invited to dinner in Luxembourg as a part of the recruitment campaign, which should mobilise national judges in the enforcement of European law (Invitation lists, kindly made accessible by Karen Alter).

[87] ECJ judge 1979–1990.

sporadic for most.[88] The involvement by the ECJ in FIDE did thus not amount to a long-term strategic involvement in FIDE.

In the 1970s, the debate in the FIDE Congresses was furthermore characterised by a gap between promoters of the constitutional interpretation of European law and national jurists who were critical about the direction ECJ case law followed. The question of national fundamental rights, which was on the agenda of several Congresses, created strong feelings. West German and Dutch scholars argued that the doctrine of primacy of European law did not apply with regard to national fundamental rights until that day where the latter were protected at the Community level.[89] They argued the ECJ's reluctance in recognising the European Convention on Human Rights (ECHR) as binding on the EC opened up for reactions like the *Solange* judgment by the BVerfG.[90] Pescatore responded vigorously to this critique. He described it as 'provincialisme juridique' and accused the opponents of in reality just wanting to challenge and undermine the achievements of European integration. To him, the defence of democracy and human rights was simply dishonest and worked as a cover for outright nationalism.[91] Nevertheless, the fact that the critique by national legal elites even made inroads into the transnational field of European law academy probably contributed to the ECJ's willingness to initiate an approximation of European law towards the ECHR with the *Rutili* (1975)[92] and *Hauer*[93] judgments (1979), where the ECJ now cited individual articles of the ECHR.[94] In addition, the political institutions of the EC bound themselves to the principles of the ECHR in a joint declaration of 1977.[95] Based on this development, the BVerfG declared a ceasefire in 1986, when in the *Solange II* judgment it stated that it would not review European legislation as long as effective protection of fundamental rights were guaranteed at the EC level, but that it could overrule the ECJ if protection of fundamental rights required it.[96] (See Chapter 6 for a detailed analysis.)

As banks and companies increasingly contributed financially to the FIDE Congresses, topics of relevance to these sponsors were on the agenda in the 1980s. These included in particular the legal underpinning of the Common Market and,

88 AFIDE. Minutes, Steering Committee meetings.

89 See, for instance Jahn, Gerhard, 1971. 'Eröffnungsansprache', *Gemeinschaftsrecht und Nationale Rechte. Das Zusammenwirken der Europäischen Rechtsordnung mit den nationale Rechtsordnungen. V. Internationaler Kongress für Europarecht com 23.–26. September 1970 in Berlin veranstaltet von der Fédération Internationale pour de Droit Européen*, E/I, 4–5 (Carl Heymanns Verlag) (FIDE Congress report 1970) and Harms, Wolfgang, 1970. 'Deutscher Bericht', Kommission II (Wettbewerb) (FIDE Congress report) especially at II/3 13.

90 Davies 2012b, 78–88; Alkema, Evert, A., 1975. 'The Judicial Protection of Fundamental Rights in the Netherlands' in Die Enzelperson und das Europäische Recht. FIDE VI (FIDE) (FIDE Congress report 1975), at II/11, 28–29.

91 Alkema 1974, at II/3, 27.

92 36/75 *Roland Rutili v Ministre de l'intérieur*, 1975, ECLI:EU:C:1975:137.

93 44/79 *Liselotte Hauer v Land Rheinland-Pfalz*, 1979, ECLI:EU:C:1979:290.

94 Davies 2012a, 457.

95 Davies 2016, 801–805.

96 BVerfGE 37, 271, 29.05.1974, *Solange I*, 2 BvL 52/71.

after 1986, questions related to the Single European Act (SEA). The number of participants at the Congresses had doubled since the first Congress,[97] but bearing the time gap and the progress of the EC in mind (thus also the relevance to a much broader scope of people), the number of participants was not necessarily a measure of success for the association. The Congresses still constituted a rather exclusive party of the already initiated, not least due to high Congress fees,[98] and the impact on national legal elites appeared to be quite limited.

THE EUI AND THE ITL PROJECT

Up until the late 1970s, FIDE and the European law journals constituted the key institutions in the transnational academic field of European law. Even though the resistance to the primacy of European law in several member states' law occasionally reared its head at FIDE congresses, the constitutional interpretation of European law generally enjoyed widespread support. Due to the activism of the ECJ in the 1970s, this support typically took the shape of legal formalism, that is, doctrinal analysis, without reference to the broader political context in which European law developed. It seems that the best way the pro-European legal scholars could support the ECJ was to treat it as just a normal court.[99] By the late 1970s, new institutions and research projects would stir things up in transnational European law academia. At the centre of this new dynamic movement was a project on European law at the Department of Law of the new European University Institute (EUI).

The idea to create a European university was first put forth at the Congress of Europe in 1948, but disagreements concerning the seat of the new university, the emergence of opposing views on the nature of the European construction, accession of third countries and so on blocked agreement in the following decades. It was not until 1976 that the new EUI opened its doors to students. The university was based on an intergovernmental convention outside, but in orbit around the EC, and its main object was to 'contribute, by its activities in the fields of higher education and research, to the development of the cultural and scientific heritage of Europe … pursued through teaching and research at the highest university level'.[100] One of the professors to join the Department of Law[101] was Mauro Cappelletti, a renowned Italian legal scholar of comparative law. Grounded in the experience of fighting fascism, as a young partisan during World War II, Cappelletti held a strong belief in the value of written constitutions and constitutional courts as a bulwark against

97 See for example the FIDE Congress in Rome in 1994, where 468 thus participated compared to 182 in 1961 (AAIGE, list of Participants, XVI Congres internationale de la FIDE, Rome, 12–15 Octobre 1994).

98 Von Bogdandy 2000, 212.

99 Boerger and Rasmussen 2014, 210–215.

100 For a detailed review of the prehistory of the European University Institute see Palayret 1996.

101 As of today, the EUI consisted of four departments: History and Civilisation, Economics, Law, and Political and Social Sciences.

attacks on the fundamental rights of the individual.[102] It was only in the last part of his career that he gained an interest in European law. He considered European law to have a great potential to secure individual rights at the national level in the same manner done by the United States' legal tradition.[103] On this basis, he initiated a grand research project entitled Integration through Law (ITL) at the EUI in the late 1970s, which examined basic legal developments, tools and potential for European integration in the light of the American Federal experience, using a comparative and contextual approach.

In the beginning, during the 1960s, American scholars hinted at the comparability between the legal system of the EC and the USA. The pioneers were a comparative law professor from the University of Michigan, Eric Stein, and his apprentice Peter Hay.[104] According to the recollections of Hay, they were unconsciously motivated by a dream of turning Europe into a new kind of USA. This normative starting point strongly influenced their writings on the nascent European legal system.[105] Additionally, Stein had a number of collaborators and friends in the European institutions, most prominently Gaudet, who deeply influenced his writings.[106] Most European law scholars shied away from bold references to the American legal system, but as a comparative law scholar with an outspoken belief in a converging world and in the importance of strong legal order to secure individual rights, it seemed self-evident to Cappelletti to conduct a survey comparing the new European legal order with the American legal counterpart. Seemingly by coincidence, Cappelletti developed the ITL project simultaneously with Stein working on his own grand comparative European-American study on the role of the judiciary in economic integration financed by the Ford Foundation, which resulted in the Bellagio conference in 1979, and the book *Courts and Free Markets: Perspectives from the United States and Europe* published in 1982.[107] Cappelletti initially planned some kind of coordination with Stein, given the similarity in content and focus of their projects,[108] but in the end it never took place.

Instead, Cappelletti built his own huge transnational network of researchers consisting of American and European legal, economic and political science researchers as well as key employees of the EC institutions.[109] Close cooperation with Ehlermann was established, and as a result, jurists from the Commission, the ECJ, the Council and the EP became massively represented in the project as informants, consultants, authors and visiting professors at the EUI in warm and beautiful Florence. Last but not least Pescatore joined the project. His philosophy of

102 Calabresi 1985; Grande 2006, 112.
103 Interview with Monica Seccombe, 11 May 2013.
104 See for instance Stein and Hay 1960.
105 Interview with Peter Hay, 17 March 2014.
106 Boerger and Rasmussen 2014, 216–17.
107 Stein and Sandalow 1982.
108 Archive of Mauro Cappelletti (AMC). Memorandum from Cappelletti to Kohnstamm, 16 July 1979.
109 Stein participated in the network by contributing with a chapter on European foreign policy.

integration was a major source of inspiration for Cappelletti.[110] Finally, Cappelletti had the luck to hire a young talented doctoral student originating from Israel, Joseph H. H. Weiler, as an assistant of the ITL project.[111]

Over the following years, the project developed into a three-level structure. The first level was constituted by a publication series that came out from 1985 to 1988. This series was divided in two parts, namely one on 'Methods, Tools, and Institutions for Legal Integration', and another including studies of substantive topics and areas in which a deepening of integration was considered crucial or especially needed.[112] Equally important to the project was the second level, which included an ongoing series of seminars and activities for research student,[113] encompassing practically the entire Department of Law of the EUI. Finally, the third level concerned externally oriented activities such as organising international conferences and meetings on European law. This level also included the direct involvement of Cappelletti and Weiler in the treaty revision project of the Institutional Committee of the EP, which aimed at establishing a European union based on a constitutional document that included fundamental rights.[114] In the following years, the Department of Law of the EUI evolved into something similar to a think tank on European integration and law.[115]

Encompassing all the levels, the basic understanding of the ITL project was the assumption that law was not only the object but also an instrument of integration. By the means of a constitutional interpretation of European law, the ECJ had fashioned no less than a 'federal' constitution of the EC and thus transformed law into a central tool for integration.[116] Stein had already set the agenda by forcefully stating the same conclusion in the *Courts and Free Markets* and in the article 'Lawyers, Judges and the Making of a Transnational Constitution' published in 1981, which would become one of the most popular articles on European law.[117] As the close connections between Cappelletti, the Legal Service and judges of the ECJ illustrate, Stein and Cappelletti both promoted academic expressions of a constitutional vision which had flourished in the Commission and the ECJ for decades. This was not openly discussed at in transnational European law academia, where most scholars subscribed to the careful characterisation of the ECJ in the *Van Gend en Loos* and *Costa v ENEL* rulings declaring a 'new legal order'.[118]

110 AMC. Letter from Cappelletti to Pescatore, 11 April 1979.
111 For Weiler's doctoral thesis consult: Weiler 1982a.
112 Cappelletti et al 1985–1988.
113 AMC. Seventh Report of Activities, Academic Year 1982–83.
114 AMC. Note from Cappelletti and Weiler to Maihofer, 21 June 1982.
115 Vauchez 2015.
116 Cappelletti et al. 1985–1988, 15 and 29.
117 Stein and Sandalow 1982; Stein 1981.
118 Byberg 2017b, 54–55.

CHANGES IN THE TRANSNATIONAL EUROPEAN LAW ACADEMIA IN THE 1980S

Cappelletti and Stein's projects had a deep and lasting influence on transnational European law academia which they propelled forwards with their explicit constitutional interpretation, contextualisation and critical approach. The European law journals, which had a significant impact in building up an independent academic field around an implicit and cautious promotion of a constitutional interpretation of European law, now found themselves behind the trendsetters and quickly adapted the explicit constitutional discourse promoted by Cappelletti and Stein. The new dynamics of European integration from 1984 onwards also made a more explicit appreciation of the constitutional interpretation of European law less contested. This was for instance highly visible in the *CML Rev*, where community actors,[119] law students,[120] established legal scholars[121] and even ECJ judges openly began to subscribe to the claim of the constitutional nature of European law.[122] The new explicit constitutional discourse became paradigmatic in the field to a point where the ECJ dared to openly refer to the constitutional nature of the treaties and describe them as the constitutional charter of European law in the *Les Verts* ruling in 1986.[123]

Weiler was a central figure in the wider popularisation of the constitutional discourse. In 1985, when the ITL project ended, Weiler went on to the University of Michigan to become a colleague of Stein, where he stayed until joining the Harvard Law School Faculty in 1992. In the USA, Weiler developed the ITL theory which culminated in the famous article 'The Transformation of Europe' in the *Yale Law Journal* in 1991. The time was marked by optimism about the future of the EC, following the SEA, which made young American political scientists, such as Anne-Marie Slaughter, Walter Mattli, Alex Sweet-Stone and Alter keen on studying Europe. They read the work of Weiler, became fascinated with the role of the ECJ, and adopted the ITL theory. Eventually, the assumptions of the constitutional nature of European law and law's centrality in the integration process would become the standard interpretations not only in European law scholarship, but also in European studies in general, where ITL became a guiding research hypothesis and a self-explicatory super-theory.[124] As a result, Weiler became the academic superstar of European law.

Paradoxically, the constitutional discourse went hand-in-hand with a contextual and, at least, potentially, critical approach to European law in Cappelletti and

119 See, for instance, Bieber 1984; Bebr 1988.

120 Dallen 1990.

121 Jacqué and Weiler 1990.

122 Mancini 1989.

123 Boerger and Davies 2017; 294/83, Parti écologiste "Les Verts" v European Parliament, 1986, ECLI: EU:C:1986:166.

124 The notion 'Integration through Law' is seldom defined by the authors, who subscribe to the theory and use the notion in their work. See for instance Alter 2001.

Stein's projects. This approach similarly had an important impact on the transnational, academic field. As an echo of the 1970s debate raging in FIDE on human rights, primacy and the ECHR, there was a push for a careful balance between the European legal order and the national courts. Additionally, legal scholars in the European law journals called for safeguarding institutions on the national level, such as the national constitutional courts,[125] or the European Court of Human Rights in the field of human rights.[126] The main editor of *CML Rev* in the 1980s, Henry Schermers, argued:

> When the Community was young and vulnerable and not yet generally accepted we fought for the powers of the Court of Justice. Uniformity of Community law, even the creation of Community law as a legal system required unrestricted authority of the Community Court. But has the situation not changed? Now that the Court of Justice has authority and a substantial amount of power, are there no reasons which may justify some control over it?[127]

The self-awareness of the field thus grew and prompted a new stage of professional maturity with a new distance and a higher degree of independence from the Community institutions. In 1992 the editors of *CML Rev*, for instance, agreed that they should be careful not to encourage people from the Commission to write for the *CML Rev*.[128] When the Danish legal scholar Hjalte Rasmussen argued that the ECJ engaged in policy-making without a legal or political mandate in the book *On Law and Policy in the European Court of Justice*,[129] he stunned the legal community. Despite the aspirations towards a critical stance, this kind of criticism was unparalleled in the transnational academic field which was still profoundly marked by adherence to the idea of the centrality of law in the integration process and the connections to the Legal Service and the ECJ.

CONCLUSION

This chapter has demonstrated that a transnational European law academia was gradually established from the early 1960s onwards by a loose network of pro-European legal scholars in close cooperation with the EEC Commission, but also to some extent with the ECJ. By exploring the history of its three main pillars (FIDE, European law journals and the EUI) it became clear that not all were equally successful, however, but taken together they offered a distinct transnational space where the terminology and parameters of a pro-constitutionalist outlook was established. The chapter furthermore demonstrated that transnational European law academia became a leading legitimiser and promoter of the constitutional

125 Frowein 1988, 204.

126 Schemers 1990, 104.

127 Schemers 1990, 103.

128 ACMLREV. Minutes, meeting of the Editors, 26 June 1992.

129 Rasmussen 1986.

interpretation of European law. In the 1980s, an explicit constitutional discourse eventually emerged from transnational European law academia that helped consolidate a veritable constitutional practice of the supranational institutions.

With the creation of FIDE in 1961 and the *CML Rev* in 1963 the backbone of transnational European law academia was established. Simultaneously, the ECJ launched a constitutional interpretation of European law with the doctrines of direct effect and primacy which provided the new academic field of European law with an extraordinary legal development to account for.

As most clearly seen in the *CML Rev*, this was done with a doctrinal methodology relying heavily on the ECJ's jurisprudence and an extraordinary dose of ideological dedication. The unquestioned academic support by authors and editors was central in carving out a transnational academic field for European law and legitimising the constitutional interpretation of European law of the supranational institutions (see Chapters 1, 2 and 3). Working closely together under an academic cover, academics, practitioners and actors from the supranational institutions joined forces in these efforts.

The same ideological engagement characterised FIDE, which endorsed direct effect and primacy at its Congresses in the mid-1960s. However, FIDE did not develop into a coherent organisational unity which would unconditionally back up the legal visions of the federalists. Nor was it instrumental in consolidating and legitimising the constitutional interpretation launched by the ECJ in 1963 and 1964 as earlier argued by Alter and Vauchez. Half embedded in national academic fields, FIDE could not completely escape the frequent criticism of the ECJ's jurisprudence from national legal scholars and elites, as the clashes in the mid-1960s, for instance on direct effect of directives at the Congress in Paris, and in the 1970s on fundamental rights exhibited.

In the 1970s, a third cornerstone of transnational European law academia was established with the EUI in 1976 and the signature undertaking of the Department of Law in the late 1970s and 1980s otherwise known as the ITL project. The project whole-heartedly embraced the constitutional understanding of European law, thus merging legal vision and academic representation. With the seal of approval by the scholarly 'stars' Stein, Cappelletti and Weiler, the scholarly milieu of students and researchers at the EUI as carriers, and the momentum in the EC with the SEA as tailwind, Gaudet's original hope for a constitutional understanding of European law was finally fulfilled in academia with the bloom of a proper constitutional discourse.

In the 1980s, the academic projects of Stein and Cappelletti drove the field forwards and set the agenda in transnational European law academia while the journals and FIDE dragged behind as trendsetters. The explicit theoretical approach of the ITL project was now generally adopted, and it unified not just transnational European law academia (which provided a strong theory as a scientific foundation and a common identity), but the entire transnational field of European law where all rejoiced in exalting law to the position of the very engine of the integration process.

Simultaneously, by the early 1990s, self-awareness in transnational European law academia reached a stage of professional maturity, which required a level of independence from the Community institutions. The constitutional understanding, however, remained paradigmatic at the transnational level.

With this history, the alliance between academics and the supranational institutions, and the shared aim of providing academic support to the constitutional interpretation of European law, has been carefully documented. This has brought out nuances such as the discontent with the jurisprudence of the ECJ at the display at the FIDE Congresses and the development towards scholarly maturity in the 1980s. However, it primarily documents that a transnational field of European law was built and developed through a circular attribution of legal ideas, legitimacy and self-image between the ECJ, the Commission and academia. The key academic institutions endorsed the jurisprudence of the ECJ, promoted the constitutional vision of European law and provided the entire legal field with a flattering image when the ITL narrative gained prominence in European law and beyond. To the judges and civil servants that participated heavily in the scholarly enterprise, academic institutions of European law were not isolated ivory towers; they were 'academic allies' in the contestation on the development and national enforcement of European law. The success at transnational level did not mean, however, that the legal elites and academics in the member states now subscribed to a constitutional discourse of European law. Far from it. With the establishment of the European Union in 1993, however, national legal elites and academics had to begin the long journey of coming to terms with the new European legal order, integrating it into the curricula of universities and critically engaging with the doctrines and interpretations of the ECJ.

5

Intergovernmentalism on the Rise: The Council in the Battle over the Constitutional Practice of European Law

Philip Bajon

While it is a core argument of this book that a constitutional practice of European law developed from the early 1960s to 1993, this chapter will argue that it was accompanied by the emergence of an equally if not even more important intergovernmental pillar in the European Communities (EC). The intergovernmental pillar of the EC gained in strength and centrality in all aspects of Community life from the first half of the 1960s onwards and included a consensus culture of national governments in the Council, the swift establishment of the Committee of Permanent Representatives (COREPER) and from 1974 also the European Council. In the end, the EC arguably was dominated by this pillar of collective state power.[1] Historically, the strengthening of the intergovernmental pillar became obvious with the Empty Chair Crisis of 1965 to 1966 and the establishment of an informal veto right through the Luxembourg Compromise of 1966. The Luxembourg Compromise postponed the transition of majority voting originally planned in the Treaties of Rome and meant that the Council, helped by COREPER, circumscribed the Commission's independence and agenda-setting role.[2] However, surprisingly the emergence of the intergovernmental pillar had relatively limited impact on the development of a constitutional practice in European law at least until the negotiations of the Maastricht Treaty in 1991.

In the recent surge of sociological research on the development of European law, this important dimension of European integration history has been underestimated. The most prominent sociological research has almost exclusively focused on the role of jurists in the supranational institutions such as the European Court of Justice (ECJ), the Commission and the European Parliament (EP).[3] Historians have begun to address the role of the intergovernmental pillar,[4] but they have generally not offered an overall narrative of the multiple connections between the rise of intergovernmentalism, and the

[1] For an interesting recent conceptualisation of the European Council as a collective government consult van Middlelaar 2013.

[2] Dinan 2010; Ludlow 2006a; 2008, 189–205; Knudsen and Rasmussen 2008, 51–68; Mourlon-Druol 2016; Bickerton et al. 2015.

[3] Crucially, the standout monograph by Antoine Vauchez neglects the rise of intergovernmentalism: Vauchez 2015. The main exception is an article by Michel Mangenot analysing the role of the legal service of the Council. See Mangenot 2004. It does not offer a more overarching interpretation of the role of the Council in the history of European law, however.

emergence of a constitutional interpretation of European law.[5] Instead, we need to go back to the work of Joseph H. H. Weiler, who already in his doctoral thesis in the early 1980s, but most forcefully in his article from 1991, 'The Transformation of Europe', offered an interpretation of the relationship between the Council and the ECJ. Weiler argued that member states accepted the constitutional interpretation of the ECJ, which gave European legal norms direct effect, and strengthened their enforcement in the member states, because the national veto right introduced by the Luxembourg Compromise in 1966 put them firmly in the driver's seat in the EC. While there were not necessarily any causal links between the two parallel developments, together they constituted a certain balance between law and politics which Weiler believed lay at the roots of the member state acceptance of the development of a constitutional practice in European law. When the Single European Act (SEA) was negotiated, and majority voting widely used after 1986, Weiler theorised that this would shake the balance, and might lead to a rebellion of the member states against the ECJ.[6]

This chapter offers the first empirically grounded explanation of what seems an unexplained paradox in the process of European integration. While the second section of the book examines how the member states broadly understood, received and responded to the development of a constitutional interpretation of European law at the national level, this chapter will focus more narrowly on how national governments responded at the European level, both individually as well as collectively – first in the Council and from 1975 onwards, also in the European Council. It will not only fill an important gap in recent sociological and historical literature, but also empirically evaluate the longstanding claims of Weiler.

The chapter will proceed in three steps. The first part of the chapter will analyse the rise of EC intergovernmentalism over time along the milestones of European integration history. In doing so, it will analyse the open nature of the founding treaties, the emergence of COREPER, the consensus culture, the battle over federalism leading to the Empty Chair Crisis, the Luxembourg Compromise, the establishment of the European Council in 1975 and finally the two treaty reforms of the 1980s – the Single European Act of 1986 and the Maastricht Treaty of 1992. The second part will focus more specifically on the Council and will illustrate how the national governments in the Council split over how to deal with the ECJ's constitutional case law, and its constitutional claim more widely. The third part will then explore how member state governments, the Council, the COREPER and the European Council specifically responded to key developments in ECJ case law.

The findings of this chapter seriously question Weiler's account of member state policies towards the ECJ. No empirical evidence supports the hypothesis that the informal veto right resulting from the Luxembourg Compromise of 1966 somehow

4 Rasmussen 2014; Fritz 2015; Rasmussen and Martinsen 2019.

5 The main exception is: Rasmussen and Martinsen 2019.

6 Weiler 1991; Weiler 1994.

moderated the response of the member states to the ECJ's constitutional case law. Instead, as this chapter demonstrates, a split occurred among member states over the ECJ's constitutional claim and practice, which resulted in a deadlock of the Council. Although some member states like France would have preferred, and attempted, to reform the ECJ, the national governments in the Council could neither agree to form a coalition to curb the Court, nor could they agree to codify the ECJ's constitutional doctrines. This chapter reveals how member states finely calibrated their resistance against the ECJ's constitutional claim in order to avoid an open breach with the EC. No member state was prepared to risk its membership in the battle over the nature of European law. At the same time, however, the scepticism of a number of national governments towards the ECJ's constitutional doctrines and interpretations were a long-term phenomenon and ultimately became one of he driving force of their resistance against the strengthening of supranationalism that the Jacques Delors Commission pursued during the negotiations on the Maastricht Treaty.

THE RISE OF THE INTERGOVERNMENTAL COUNCIL PILLAR

The rise of the intergovernmental Council pillar had historically four core elements: first, the relative openness of the founding treaties with regard to either a federal or an intergovernmental outcome, something which allowed the national governments to gradually seize control over the integration process and to reinforce the intergovernmental pillar of the EC. Second, the vast nature of integration in the European Economic Community (EEC), which urged member states to adopt a consensual approach to Community business and which resulted in the emergence of various committee structures under the umbrella of the Council pillar such as COREPER. Third, the complex political battle over federalism from 1963–1965, which locked in the consensus culture, and a trend towards strengthening intergovernmentalism. And fourth, the establishment of the European Council as lead institution of the EC, which further consolidated the intergovernmental dimension. Even during the *relance européenne* of the 1980s, core member states maintained their longer-term scepticism towards gradual federalisation, which led to a reinforcement of intergovernmental tendencies in the period between the SEA and the Maastricht Treaty.

THE OPEN NATURE OF THE TREATIES

The Treaties of Paris and Rome were, despite significant differences, relatively open-ended endeavours. At the time of negotiating the treaties, and during the first decades of European integration, it was impossible to forecast with any precision whether the new Communities would gradually federalise Europe or eventually become dominated by national governments. It would take a complex political battle in the first half of the 1960s to clarify the balance between the contradictory tendencies inherent in the treaties, and in some ways the battle between federalism and intergovernmentalism has continued to the present day.

In the negotiations over the Treaty of Paris, the West German delegation proposed a classical separation of powers with a common Assembly and a permanent Court of Justice because the dominating personalities Walter Hallstein and Carl Friedrich Ophüls regarded the emerging institutions as the embryo of a future federal organisation. Hallstein highlighted the benefits of a strong (constitutional) Court of Justice to Monnet in early July 1950.[7] The result of the negotiations was somewhat different, however, namely a court which included elements of international law, administrative law drawn from the French tradition and somewhat more discretely also constitutional law. Although the court fell short of what Hallstein had hoped for, the European Coal and Steel Community (ECSC) legal system had the potential to break with classical international public law.[8] As early as 1955, the High Authority's Legal Service adopted a federal understanding of the ESCS treaty and of the role of the Court of Justice of the ECSC. However, throughout the 1950s, this constitutional interpretation of European law was largely rejected by member state governments, experts, scholars and the ECJ itself.[9]

In the negotiations over the Treaties of Rome of 1957, the institutional questions had to be handled in a pragmatic way to ensure ratification in France. This was in line with a general trend to tone down the supranational dimension of European integration after the defeat of the European Defence Community (EDC) and European Political Community (EPC) projects in the French National Assembly in 1954. Therefore, the Spaak Committee – chaired by Belgian Minister of Foreign Affairs Paul Henri Spaak (who had to work out a roadmap for a Common Market and an Atomic Community) – proposed on 21 April 1956 a four-pillar structure, in which the Council was to become the decision-making centre and relegating the High Authority (HA) (now the Commission) to merely holding the legislative initiative, acting as a supranational co-executive. The Val Duchesse Intergovernmental Conference confirmed this institutional model, which then became part of the treaty. Though the committee of jurists, the Groupe de rédaction, was able to insert a small number of constitutional elements into the Treaties of Rome, the two new treaties were clearly designed to ensure the central position of the member states. At the same time, the EEC treaty was not a *traité de loi* providing for a well-defined roadmap (like the Treaty of Paris), but an open-ended and flexible framework treaty establishing the core principles, objectives and means to achieve them.[10]

7 Steinberg 2003, 104–109; Pernice 2003.
8 Boerger 2012; Davies and Rasmussen 2014.
9 Davies 2012b; Rasmussen 2012.
10 Boerger 2012 and Rasmussen 2023.

THE CONSENSUS CULTURE AND THE EMERGENCE OF COREPER

Flowing naturally from the above-described ambiguities of primary law, the strengthening of the intergovernmental dimension of the EC was a complex and wider development. At the core was a gradual expansion of the role of the Council pillar in the EC. The experience of the ECSC demonstrated that the supranational HA was highly dependent on member state support from the Council, with the latter blocking parts of the ECSC's agenda such as competition policy. Having learned this lesson, the treaty drafters gave the member states a more prominent role in the institutional set-up of the Treaties of Rome.[11] A central feature of the rise of the intergovernmental pillar was the emergence of a consensus culture among the member states. Since the EEC Treaty planned the establishment of major public policies, such as the Common Agricultural Policy (CAP), tariff harmonisation and a common competition policy, this required from the beginning a high degree of consensus among national governments concerning the objectives to be achieved, and the methods to be employed. Because the EC were still in their formative period, national governments were naturally reluctant to delegate full administrative tasks to supranational institutions and, instead, involved their national administrations to a very high degree. This was also necessary for purely technical reasons since only the national administrations had the resources and exercised the specific powers to deal with some of the technical tasks in building common European policies.

The consensual approach, practiced by national governments acting collectively in the Council, became particularly manifest in the committee structures developed within the intergovernmental pillar. To organise the work of the General Affairs Council, and to set up various working groups preparing European legislation, the Committee of Permanent Representatives (COREPER), was formally established on 24 January 1958. It was based on Articles 151 of the EEC Treaty and 121 of the EURATOM Treaty.[12] The Permanent Representatives of each member state placed in Brussels acted as deputies to the ministers of the member states. Furthermore, the Permanent Representatives were accompanied by national experts both serving in the Permanent Representation and in national ministries, to whom the difficult technical work was delegated in working groups and committees, where also the three executives, including the EEC Commission, were represented. COREPER thus counterbalanced the supranational executives and also the EP.

Soon and in reaction to the complexity of the Community agenda, a 'functional division of labour' became apparent with the creation of specialised Council compositions, such as the Council of Agricultural Ministers. In the area of agriculture, the Special Committee for Agriculture (SCA) was set up, which took up much

[11] Rasmussen and Martinsen 2019, 256; Witschke 2009.
[12] European Commission 2007, 38.

of the Council's workload in the field. Following this example, a lengthy list of other sub-committees and technical working groups – composed of supranational and national officials and experts – were established in the early 1960s, such as the Special Committee for Article 111, monitoring the EEC's Kennedy Round negotiations within the General Agreement on Tariffs and Trade (GATT) round. Not only under the auspices of the Council, but also in support of the Commission, management and advisory committees were set up to implement CAP legislation. These 'comitology committees' were composed of Commission officials, member state experts and social partners. The emerging committee structures integrated national administrations both in the agenda setting and the administrative tasks of the Commission, thereby de facto undermining the political and administrative autonomy of the latter. At the same time, they also facilitated a more deliberative and slightly less confrontational bargaining style between member states, which however could also be seen as part of the consensus culture cemented by the Luxembourg Compromise.

The increasing involvement of COREPER and of various other committee structures in Community affairs was not only a member state attempt to monitor the activist and dynamic Commission but is perhaps better understood as the member states' collective attempt to control what within the EEC quickly became a vast integration process which was so much broader (and confusing) than the highly specialised integration handled by the ECSC. The monthly Council meetings simply did not suffice to supervise the multiplicity of Community activities and tasks. Here, COREPER with its specialist expertise and seat in Brussels stepped in and facilitated the tasks of the Council. The rise of COREPER was criticised by supporters of the 'community method' – from the Benelux states in particular – who argued that the EC would 'slide into unaccountable technocracy'.[13] However, what was really at stake was the loss of autonomy of the Commission, which originally was considered as key in the protection of the interests of the smaller member states.

THE CONSOLIDATION OF STATE POWER IN THE EMPTY CHAIR CRISIS

From the outset of the integration process, federalist ideology significantly shaped the agenda of the newly created supranational executives and the worldviews of their members, in particular in the High Authority from 1951 and the Commission from 1958. Striking examples were the first President of the ECSC High Authority and 'statesman of interdependence',[14] Jean Monnet, and the first President of the EEC Commission, Walter Hallstein, who both held strong federalist assumptions about

[13] Ludlow 2005; 2008; Knudsen and Rasmussen 2008; Houben 1964; Hayes-Renshaw and Wallace 2006; Wessels 2000.

[14] Duchêne 1994.

the nature of integration, European institutions and European law.[15] Hallstein aimed at establishing and consolidating the EEC Commission as 'a new element in international diplomacy', at eye-level with the member state governments.[16] To him, the replacement of power politics with a European rule of law was one of the most fundamental and revolutionary qualities of the integration process. Therefore, he promoted a constitutional interpretation of European law and encouraged the ECJ to assume the role of a European Constitutional Court. He personally defended the principles of direct effect and primacy before the European Parliament (EP) in 1964, lobbied for the ECJ's new doctrines in a pamphlet published together with former judge Nicola Catalano soon thereafter, and welcomed the report by MEP and law professor Fernand Dehousse of 15 March 1965, which also came out in support of the new doctrines. Likewise, the EP legal committee in close cooperation with the Legal Service of the EEC Commission fully endorsed the new doctrines after the *Costa v ENEL* judgment.[17]

The importance of federalist ideology in the political centre in most Continental European countries also had a major impact on the EP. With no direct elections at the European level before 1979, a double-mandate system existed that selected national members of parliament to serve also in the EP. This system ensured that the political centre formed a majority of MEPs, while politicians from the political fringes tended to be excluded from the EP, leading to a much larger pro-European majority than seen in most national parliaments.[18]

At the national level, the support for federalisation of the EC was considerably more mixed in most member states. National parliaments in the Benelux countries and Italy were generally positive about institutional reform of the EC in a federal direction. However, governments, academics and lawyers from these pro-European countries were not always as supportive towards federal ideas as their parliaments. Despite the presence and strength of federalist ideology in the EC, the decisive reform towards political and institutional deepening of European integration in a federal direction failed to materialise. The political forces in favour of this were not – despite several attempts – able to overcome the resistance inside most member states, and consequently a clear majority of national governments in favour of federalist reform never emerged. Nevertheless, the support for federalisation inside the supranational institutions became a driving force for the constitutional interpretation of European law.[19]

Sharply contrasting with federalist tendencies in the European supranational institutions were the supporters of an intergovernmental European cooperation,

[15] Loth et al. 1995; Hallstein 1969; Noel 1995, 165–169; Narjes 1995.

[16] Bajon 2018b.

[17] For the support of the ECJ's new legal doctrines by Hallstein, Catalano, Gaudet and Dehousse, see Rasmussen 2013b, 1209–1210; Boerger and Rasmussen 2017, 25–26; Vauchez 2010a; Vauchez 2015, 133–146.

[18] Herman and Lodge 1978, 141–156.

[19] Rasmussen and Martinsen 2019, 257.

most prominently French president, Charles de Gaulle, and his various governments from 1958 to 1969. His proposals for Western European cooperation in the 1960s – whether it was the Fouchet Plans of 1960–1962, the French–West German Elysée Treaty of 1963 or his proposal to the West German government of July 1964 for participation in the 'force de frappe' – were designed as intergovernmental alternatives to the EC.[20] Around 1964 to 1965 West European economic integration quickly developed towards a point of no return when the CAP was completed with a hard fought agreement on the common price level in December 1964, the decision over the fusion of the executives in spring 1965 and the imminent transition to majority voting from January 1966. Over the preceding years, France benefitted enormously from the CAP and were able to dominate the agenda of the EC. However, the French dominance gradually led to a change in mentality of the other member states. They increasingly began to consider European integration in a strictly quid pro quo perspective.[21]

The tensions and overall distrust among member states aggravated when Hallstein launched an audacious attempt to exploit the spillover dynamic and strengthen the supranational institutions at the expense of the Council pillar in 1965. When the EEC Commission in spring 1965 had to make proposals for the financing of the CAP for the period from 1965 to 1970, Hallstein decided to link agricultural financing to a general strengthening of supranationality. No agreement over the EEC Commission proposals could be found in the Council throughout spring and summer 1965.[22] Provoked by the EEC Commission, annoyed by the other governments' quid pro quo politics and guided by his geopolitical vision of European cooperation on an intergovernmental basis, de Gaulle started a boycott of the EC at the beginning of July 1965, and withdrew France's representative in the Council and her EC ambassador.[23] This blockage became known as the Empty Chair Crisis. In a famous press conference, de Gaulle revealed that France would only return to the EC if, first, ambitious Commissioners like Hallstein were replaced by weak bureaucrats, and the EEC Commission turned into a European technical secretariat and if, second, the scheduled majority voting in the Council was replaced by a universal

[20] Some historical works tend to portray de Gaulle as a 'good' but misunderstood European and father of the EEC, who took over the European project from the founder generation and guided the EC towards a functioning reality, see Vaïsse 1998. Others remain sceptical and characterise de Gaulle as a distinct and early Eurosceptic whose obstructionist policy ran counter to the original federalist assumptions of the European project, see Roussel 2002; Lucas 1992; Loth 1991. Loth, while fully acknowledging the Gaullist challenge of the 1960s, insists that the political polarisation of the 1950s and 1960s largely contributed to the spiral of escalation, which finally led to the showdown between de Gaulle and Hallstein in the mid-1960s, see Loth 1995; Loth 1991.

[21] Ludlow 2006a, 52–58; Ludlow 1999.

[22] Bajon 2018a.

[23] Ludlow 2006a; Palayret et al. 2006; Newhouse 1967; Camps 1966; Bajon 2012.

national veto right.[24] When de Gaulle quickly realised that the other partners would protect the EEC Commission, the national veto in the Council became his primary concern.[25]

The unfolding Empty Chair Crisis accentuated the general trend of increasing state power in several respects. First, there was overall agreement that the crisis was deeply political in nature and could only be solved 'between the member state governments'. Early assessments by the Legal Service of the Commission under Michel Gaudet left no doubt that legal instruments, in particular taking France to the ECJ for treaty infringement, were inappropriate to deal with the Empty Chair Crisis.[26] Neither did de Gaulle make any claims regarding the European legal order or the ECJ during the crisis,[27] nor did France's partners attempt to bring France before the ECJ for breaching European law, although Dutch MPs publicly demanded this.[28]

Second, the crisis rapidly developed into a classical interstate power play, in which the supranational institutions were largely marginalised. Various politico-legal assessment from the West German government, and the Legal Service of the Commission suggested that qualified majority decisions and even unanimous decisions were possible and legitimate in France's absence.[29] This gave France's partners a perfect pretext to increase the political pressure on de Gaulle and to reaffirm their leadership in the EC. The Benelux and Italian governments asked the West German Minister of Foreign Affairs, Gerhard Schröder, to take the lead in blocking de Gaulle's brinkmanship and bringing him back to the negotiating table. Behind the scenes, Schröder built a coalition against de Gaulle, and he widely used the conclusions of the West German legal experts in his psychological campaign

24 De Gaulle 1970, 372–392.

25 Bajon 2012, 239–243.

26 Historical Archive of the European Union (HAEU).BAC 49 2013 18. Memo by Michel Gaudet, 'Absence d'un État membre . . . ', 12 July 1965; HAEU.BAC 49 2013 18. Michel Gaudet to Walter Hallstein, 'Annahme der Tagesordnung durch den unvollständig besetzten Rat', 26 July 1965; Hans-Peter Schwarz, ed., *Akten zur Auswärtigen Politik der Bundesrepublik Deutschland* 1965 (Munich: Oldenbourg, 1966), document 351, Telex 1403 Sachs (Brussels) to Carstens and Lahr, 15 September 1965, 1442; HAEU.BAC 49 2013 18. Record of Commission session of 30 January 1978, without date; also see Rasmussen 2012, 377, fn. 15.

27 Bernier 2017, 112–118.

28 See Archive of the German Ministry of Foreign Affairs (PAAA). B20 1321. Telex Obermayer (The Hague) to West German Foreign Office, 15 July 1965.

29 Hans-Peter Schwarz, ed., *Akten zur Auswärtigen Politik* 1965, document 303 on talks between Schröder and Spaak, 26 July 1965, 1275; PAAA. B20 1321. Note by Meyer-Lindenberg, 'Verfahrensfragen . . . ', 16 July 1965; PAAA. B20 1322. Note by Carstens, 'EWG', 7 September 1965; PAAA. B20 1323. Kölble (Ministry of Interior) to Foreign Office, 22 September 1965; PAAA. B20 1322, Memo by Ophüls, 'Fragen der Beschlußfähigkeit des Rates bei der EWG bei Mitwirkungs-Weigerung eines Ratsmitglieds . . . ', 16 September 1965; HAEU.BAC 49 2013 18. West German Foreign Office Memo, 'Die Rechtsfolgen des französischen Fernbleibens aus den Gemeinschaften', ca. autumn 1965; PAAA. B20 1325, Note of Ministry of Economics, 'Einstimmige Beschlußfassung im Rat der Fünf', 28 October 1965, 1; HAEU.BAC 49 2013 18. Memo by Hans-Joachim Glaesner, 'Beschlüsse des Rates bei Fernbleiben eines Mitgliedstaates', 12 November 1965.

designed to provoke and pressurise de Gaulle. Schröder briefed the partner governments about the various West German legal analyses of the crisis and urged them to consult each other and to resist French attempts to manipulate, confuse, weaken and split the so-called *bloc des cinq*.[30]

Third, in the conflict over the functioning of the EC, an anti-supranational consensus emerged among the member states, which confirmed and locked in the intergovernmental trend that had already characterised EC politics for years. The conflict was less about the EEC Commission, despite de Gaulle's initial demands for curbing this supranational institution. The intergovernmental style of the crisis management marginalised the EEC Commission anyway. Rather the conflict centred on how the Council pillar would function, more precisely on the transition to majority voting originally scheduled for January 1966 in the Treaties of Rome. While the Treaties of Rome generally emphasised the role of member states, the transition to majority voting, the potential direct election of the EP and the independence of the EEC Commission and the ECJ still constituted a federalising potential.[31] Voting became the point of contention, because it crystallised the question whether member states still had the last word in the legislative process, or whether they individually could be outvoted on 'vital' questions in the Council. Over weeks of negotiations and in particular at the Luxembourg conference in January 1966, which formally ended the Empty Chair Crisis, a surprising anti-supranational consensus emerged among France and its counterparts over how to handle voting. De Gaulle and the French diplomats gave up their original maximalist demand for formal treaty revisions. Instead, they agreed to negotiate a 'political arrangement', or in Couve's words: 'Le droit reste inchangé. Il y a les consequences politiques.'[32] French foreign policy experts told de Gaulle that a consensus trend already existed in Council decision-making, which was likely to prevail even after the formal transition to majority voting in 1966.[33] And the other governments, maybe with the exception of the Dutch, were more than willing to accommodate French concerns. They provided Paris with reassuring statements about the 'desirability of

[30] Bajon 2011; PAAA. B1 214. Schröder to Schmücker, 3 January 1966; Archives of the German Federal Parliament (ADBT), 3104, 4th Legislative Period, Protocol 87, 21 [Foreign Affairs Committee of 23 September 1965, Schröder speaking]; HAEU.BAC 49 2013 18. Article in *Europe* entitled 'La politique française de la chaise vide: Une analyse des problèmes juridiques', 20 November 1965.

[31] Boerger 2012.

[32] Archives of the French Ministry of Foreign Affairs (MAE). DE-CE, 1113. Memo 'Une réunion a eu lieu à Luxembourg [. . .]', 29 January 1966, 2. English translation: 'The law rest unchanged. But there are political concsequences.'

[33] MAE. DE-CE, 1111. Memo (presumably by Jean-Pierre Brunet) entitled 'Règles de majorité dans le Traité de Rome', 21 May 1965, 5: 'il est vraisemblable qu'un accord tacite s'établira entre pays membres pour que, comme par le passé, les décisions ayant une grande importance politique telles que le niveau des prix agricoles ou celui du tarif extérieur commun, soient prises d'accord entre les Gouvernements' (English translation: 'It is likely that a tacit agreement will be reached between member countries so that, as in the past, decisions of major political importance, such as the level of agricultural prices or the common external tariff, will be taken by agreement between governments'); also see Ludlow 2001, 248; Newhouse 1967, 67.

consensus' and made a number of proposals for strengthening unanimous decision-taking at the expense of qualified majority decisions.[34] Schröder in particular shared de Gaulle's preferences of maintaining the sovereignty of the nation state and agreed with de Gaulle that the national governments should ultimately control integration, while the independent role of the Commission had to be strictly limited.[35] Both the Commission and the EP were unable to play a significant role in the crisis management or in the conference at Luxembourg in January 1966, which formally ended the empty chair politics. The European Commissioners, most prominently Hallstein and Narjes, in their bilateral talks with the French and the West German governments, did their utmost to defend the voting principle and the supranationality of the EC, but without success.[36] In Luxembourg, France's partners tolerated the French unilateral declaration that no member state must be outvoted when 'very important national interests' were at stake, and that each member state was free to define its 'vital interests' independently.

The Luxembourg Compromise marked the locking in of an aggressive veto-culture in which a Council minority held the power to block new legislation favoured by a majority of the other member states.[37] Voting over important questions did not take place over the remaining years of the 1960s and was rarely used in the first half of the 1970s, despite the new dynamics the integration process experienced during this period.[38]

The predominance of state power in the settling of the Empty Chair Crisis ended the openness of the original treaties regarding the ultimate goal of the integration project. An immediate or mid-term federal outcome of European integration was not possible anymore. Crucially, the Empty Chair Crisis also confirmed the fading and eventual disappearance of the rhetoric of federalism, which national politicians and members of the supranational institutions employed throughout the 1950s and

34 PAAA. B20 1330. Note by Meyer-Lindenberg 'Vorschläge Außenminister Spaaks zur Mehrheitsregel', 26 January 1966; also see the decision for the 'stopping of the clock' regarding the Council agenda: Historical Archive of the Council of Ministers (HACM). CM2 1966 1. Protocol of EEC Council 17–8 and 28–9 February 1966, 29 April 1966, p. 120; HAEU.BAC 49 2013 19. Commission paper 'Décision ayant dû être prises en 1966 mais qui ont dû être remises en raison de la crise', 26 January 1966.

35 Bajon 2011, 253–269.

36 BArch. NH, 1187. Letter from Jazke to Narjes, 17 September 1965; BArch. NH, 1187. Letter from Lanzke to Narjes, 16 September 1965; HAEU. EN, 761. Manuscript Noel of Commission session of 26 January 1966; BArch. NH, 1119. Memo of Hallstein cabinet 'Ich danke sehr [. . .]', ca. mid-January 1966; Archive of Walter Hallstein (AWH). 1119. Letter from Narjes to Hallstein, 2 March 1965; BArch. NH, 1114. Memo Narjes 'Gespräch in Bonn vom 23.-26. November', 22 November 1965; BArch. NH, 1114. Note Narjes 'Gespräch mit dem Bundeskanzler am 10. Dezember', 9 December 1965; BArch. NH, 1090. Note Narjes 'Ihr Gespräch mit Bundesminister Schröder', 9 December 1965; BArch. NH, 1194. Hallstein to Wagner (BDI), 5 February 1966.

37 HAEU. EN 807. Memo, 'Effets indirects de la règle de la majorité', no date; Lahr 1983, 223–239; Streinz 1984; Palayret et al. 2006; Hayes-Renshaw and Wallace 2006; Nicoll 1984; Teasdale 1993; Heisenberg 2007; Bajon 2025.

38 Archive of Emile Noel (AEN). 807. Memo 'Nombre de décision . . . ', 9 March 1967; Memo UE(82)19 rev 'Vote à la majorité qualifiée dans le Conseil. Note du Secrétariat general', 22 March 1982.

in the early 1960s.[39] The formative years of European integration, ending with the Empty Chair Crisis, also produced clear winners and losers among the European institutions. The Council performed well, implementing most of the initial agenda like the CAP and the Customs Union. Nevertheless, the EC suffered from a lack of dynamic leadership. This was partly a result of the member states' disagreement over UK membership, but also because the efforts for negative integration which had characterised the early years of the EEC in particular, above all the tariff reduction, had been largely completed. In contrast, the EEC Commission's federal ambitions were frustrated and contained by de Gaulle. After the Empty Chair Crisis, the new merged Commission was forced to adopt a low profile and thereby lost its original impetus and daring spirit. It became significantly weakened as an agenda setter, far from Hallstein's original claim for the supranational executive to be an 'engine, guardian, and honest broker'.[40]

On the one hand, the informal veto power introduced in 1966 certainly had an impact on EC institutions, and the decision-taking procedure, especially in the 1970s – a period of great political and institutional challenges for the EC. Both the Commission and the Council adopted a more cautious approach to potentially controversial legislative proposals, so as to avoid the crystallisation of standpoints and the invocation of the Luxembourg Compromise.[41] Thus, EC institutions gave the impression of under-performing. This view in particular was held by federalist inclined observers, who identified the Luxembourg Compromise as the focus of all evil and as the main origin of the so-called 'Eurosclerosis' of the 1970s.[42] On the other hand, the malfunctioning of the EC institutional machinery due to the Luxembourg Compromise is difficult to substantiate empirically. Researchers have been unable to document a significant legislative setback as a result of invocations of the Luxembourg Compromise.[43] It is, therefore, today widely acknowledged that the EC institutional deficits and inefficiencies of the 1970s can hardly be reduced to the informal voting practices in the Council.[44]

REINFORCED INTERGOVERNMENTALISM: FROM THE EUROPEAN COUNCIL TO MAASTRICHT EUROPE

Since the late 1950s, the national governments reaffirmed their leadership role and increased their control of the process of European integration, which is best exemplified in their consensual approach to Community business, the rise of COREPER, the marginalisation of the EEC Commission in the Empty Chair Crisis and the

39 Ludlow 2006a, 122–124.

40 The Commission role as described by Hallstein, see: Hallstein 1969, 56.

41 Archive of Klaus Meyer (AKM). 220. Memo UE(82)19 rev 'Vote à la majorité dans le Conseil. Note du Secrétariat général', 22 March 1982.

42 As an example, see Nicoll 1984, 35–43.

43 Golub 2006.

44 Frowein 1973.

informal national veto right of the Luxembourg Compromise. The intergovernmental dimension of the EC was further reinforced after 1973 through the accession by United Kingdom and Denmark, and later by Greece. These three countries shared the French preference for an intergovernmental approach to European integration and, together with France, they became known as the 'Luxembourg Compromise Club', clearly endorsing and more frequently invoking the unconditional veto right. At the same time, the late 1960s and the 1970s saw a renaissance of summitry between member state governments and its ultimate institutionalisation in the European Council in 1974, which further strengthened the collective government of the member states in the Council pillar.[45] After sporadic summits with limited political agendas in the 1960s, the summit at The Hague in December 1969 aimed at overcoming the policy-making deadlock of the Gaullist era. Initiated by the new French President, Georges Pompidou, the summit addressed three major topics, namely the problem of enlargement, the policy fields of economic and monetary union, as well as European political cooperation.[46] After somewhat unsuccessful summits at Paris 1972 and at Copenhagen 1973, EC summitry was institutionalised in 1974 after Valéry Giscard d'Estaing and Helmut Schmidt came to power in France and West Germany.[47] The European Council did not only seize a large number of minor disagreements and leftovers from the Council. More importantly, it assumed a broader leadership role in the following decades and became the primary agenda setter and initiator of major reforms of the EC. Its importance in the institutional setting was confirmed both in the SEA and in the Maastricht Treaty.[48]

The SEA became the first major treaty reform since 1958 and proposed the creation of a Single Market by 1992. It formalised the European Political Cooperation initiated in the early 1970s, gave the EP genuine powers in the legislative process through the cooperation procedure and made majority voting in the Council the rule for future legislation within the field of the new Single Market program. Although significant, these reforms were very different from the wishes of some more federalist-inclined politicians, and they were crucially accompanied by a confirmation of the European Council, as the leading agenda-setting institution. Meanwhile, the French President François Mitterrand and government underlined their continued preparedness to invoke the Luxembourg Compromise even after the SEA, if needed.[49] With regard to the European legal order developed by the ECJ, the SEA was a game changer. Before the SEA, the EC's Common Market was deeply segmented because of national protectionism in the shape of different

45 Westlake 1995; Wessels 1980; Bulmer 1985; Mourlon-Druol and Romero 2014.

46 See the contributions in van der Harst 2003; van der Harst 2007.

47 Mourlon-Druol and Romero 2014; Mourlon-Druol 2016, 409–437.

48 Ludlow 2013; Ludlow 2015.

49 See e.g. the foreign affairs speeches of French President François Mitterrand and Foreign Secretary Jean-Bernard Raimond in the debate over SEA ratification by the French National Assembly or the National Assembly Plenary Debate on 24 October 1986. MAE. DE-CE. 2534 and 2535.

standards, taxation schemes and hidden state aid. Although the ECJ developed quite advanced case law on the four freedoms from the 1970s onwards, the case law had a limited impact since national administrations and courts could easily ignore the judgments emanating from Luxembourg. With the Single Market being established from 1987 onwards, member states suddenly found that the legal order built by the ECJ could not so easily be ignored anymore. The SEA legislative program caused a rise in litigation and confronted national administrations and courts with far-reaching consequences of European law. In addition, the political consensus in favour of the SEA and the Single Market made it difficult to oppose the SEA and the European legal order in the way possible before 1984.[50]

The second dynamic element of the 1980s became the Commission under Jacques Delors's presidency. Delors, who took office in 1985, swiftly built on the new political dynamic. His Commission was praised for its activism in policy fields such as budget, monetary union, competition or environment, as well as regional and social policy, and it gained international prestige, for example, by successfully handling West German reunification or acquiring a leadership role in the G7. This created hopes in some political circles for a move towards a more federal Europe through a reform that would also finally codify the ECJ's doctrinal advances and the proto-federal legal order, which the ECJ had established by the end of the 1980s. The 'Delors Committee' of the then twelve independent central bank presidents under Delors's chairmanship delivered a report on monetary union in April 1989, which clearly suggested the transfer of national sovereignty to a common monetary institute as a precondition for the subsequent creation of a single currency. Before the background of imminent German reunification from 1989 to 1990, Delors continued to publicly demand a substantial transfer of executive authority to the Commission. In February 1991, he formally submitted proposals to the intergovernmental conference for a significant strengthening of the Commission, the codification of the ECJ case law and an overall increase of supranationality in the new EU based on a single treaty. This was however rejected by the national governments. To further counteract Delors' claim for more Commission power, the French government introduced the idea of intergovernmental treaty pillars. This idea was picked up in a treaty draft by the Luxembourg Council presidency in April 1991. Delors was able to partially mobilise the Dutch, Belgian, German, Italian, Spanish, Irish and even Greek governments against the pillar conception. Yet, the revised presidency draft maintained the pillar structure, which excluded the Commission from the fields of foreign and security policy and justice and home affairs. An attempt by the succeeding Dutch Council presidency to bring the pillars back under the supranational Community umbrella (though weakening the proposals for a common foreign and defence policy) failed. Under pressure from France, the German

50 Rasmussen and Martinsen 2019, 265–266; for a special case see the analysis of Denmark by Pedersen 2016, 137–230.

government supported the original Luxembourg draft. The negotiations that led to the Maastricht Treaty placed the important policy fields of 'Justice and Home Affairs' as well as the 'Common Foreign and Security Policy' in the intergovernmental second and third pillar. Delors was able to prevent a downgrading of the Commission within the first pillar, but the member states clearly rejected the federalist treaty design he advocated.[51]

Added to the Maastricht Treaty were three protocols, among which the Barber protocol most forcefully raised the question as to whether the member states as 'Masters of the Treaty' had 'hijacked the Acquis Communautaire'.[52] In the *Barber* ruling of 17 May 1990,[53] the ECJ had decided that Article 119 of the EEC Treaty, which demanded equal pay for women and men, also applied to private pension schemes in the UK, which imposed considerable financial burdens on private pension funds. Because the ECJ failed to clearly define the retroactive effects of its ruling, four member state courts sent references to clarify this point. However, before the ECJ was able to respond, the Barber protocol was activated, stating that Article 119 was not to apply to private pension schemes for periods of employment before the *Barber* ruling. The governments thus interpreted a treaty Article and overturned the ECJ.[54]

The above section has demonstrated that despite the strong presence of federalist ideas and rhetoric in the supranational institutions and in national parliaments, especially during the formative years of European integration in the 1950s and 1960s, a critical mass of supporters in favour of federalising Europe never emerged among the national governments. On the contrary, the member states gradually reinforced their political control over the process of European integration and ultimately during the Maastricht Treaty negotiations decided not to base the new European Union on European constitutionalism as the legitimating principle.[55] With the pillar structure of the Maastricht Treaty and the Barber protocol added to it, member states clearly rejected the federalist vision of a substantial transfer of member state sovereignty to reinforced supranational institutions, as proposed by the Delors Commission.

Legal, political science and sociological accounts on the evolution of European law have mostly focused on the expanding role of the supranational institutions, the Commission and the EP, and how the federalist ideology of the supranational institutions shaped the emergence of a constitutional European legal order. This section, however, has illustrated that arguably the most remarkable and momentous development between 1958 and 1992 was the rise of the member states' collective

51 Ludlow 2013, 11–23; Loth 2013; Ludlow 2015, 173–196; Bickerton et al. 2015.

52 Curtin 1993, 44–61.

53 262/88, *Douglas Harvey Barber v Guardian Royal Exchange Assurance Group*, 1990, ECLI:EU:C:1990:209.

54 Curtin 1993, 17–69; Fitzpatrick 1992.

55 The member states did refer to the acquis communautaire in the Treaty of Maastricht, in Article B, 5th indent and thus acknowledged indirectly the case law of the ECJ.

government in the Council and more generally the cementation of state power in the intergovernmental pillar of the EC.

The following two sections will discuss how the Council and national governments responded to the development of a constitutional practice in European law while at the same time supporting the parallel rise of the Council pillar. As mentioned in the Introduction, Weiler's interpretation of this paradox was that a certain balance developed between the rise of intergovernmentalism and the development of a constitutional practice in European law, and that the member states accepted the latter without too much trouble. As the following sections demonstrate, this view must be revised.

THE SPLIT IN THE COUNCIL PILLAR OVER THE CONSTITUTIONAL INTERPRETATION AND PRACTICE

Member state governments already followed the development of ECJ case law closely in the 1960s, and a majority of them rejected the new constitutional doctrines developed by the ECJ. When they presented their positions in the key cases before the ECJ, they were typically opposed to any new doctrinal breakthroughs, like France in the *Bosch* case,[56] the Netherlands, Belgium and West Germany in *Van Gend en Loos*,[57] as well as Italy in *Costa v ENEL*.[58] From the 1970s onwards, when the Court extended its case law to new fields such as the external powers of the EC or human rights, national governments and administrations were aware of the dynamic nature of European law, and it was also in this period that several of the most important national courts began to react. But although the member states had been opposed to the first constitutional judgments in the first half of the 1960s, the Netherlands and Luxembourg in particular began to support the ECJ's new constitutional interpretation of European law based on the logic that a strong legal system would benefit the smaller member states. As a result, the Council remained split over how to evaluate the ECJ's constitutional case law with, in particular, France being very sceptical about the dynamic interpretations of the ECJ. In some cases, when the Council directly responded to the ECJ, a minority protected the Court, while another minority actually ensured that advances in ECJ case law would not be codified.[59] As a result, the ECJ was never threatened by any major reform at the hand of the Council.

The late 1960s and early 1970s were a period of great political upheaval – inter alia due to de Gaulle's resignation, the summit at The Hague and the coming enlargement negotiations of the EC with the UK, Ireland, Denmark and Norway. In this

56 13/61, *Kledingverkoopbedrijf de Geus en Uitdenbogerd v Robert Bosch GmbH et al.*, 1962, ECLI:EU:C:1962:11.

57 26/62, *Van Gend en Loos v Nederlandse Administratie der Belastingen*, 1963, ECLI:EU:C:1963:1.

58 6/64, *Costa v ENEL*, 1964, ECLI:EU:C:1964:66.

59 Rasmussen and Martinsen 2019.

context and encouraged by the revival of the integration process after De Gaulle left office in 1969, the newly composed 'Court of 1967', led by French judge and President Robert Lecourt, extended its case law and attempted to push the boundaries of European law.[60] The preliminary reference mechanism, which was so instrumental in the development of the ECJ's constitutional case law, became a point of contention.[61] The French government accused the ECJ of having instrumentalised the preliminary reference mechanism, and it was looking for a way to take action against the Court. The conflict escalated in the negotiations over the 1971 Luxembourg Protocol of the 1968 Brussels Convention on Jurisdiction and the Enforcement of Judgments in Civil and Commercial Matters. The Convention raised questions about whether the member states would give the ECJ authority over private international law agreements signed on the side of the EEC treaty. The 1971 Luxembourg Protocol attempted to define this.

Crucially, the member states split over whether the preliminary reference mechanism was to be extended to private international law agreements or not, and whether competencies in this field should generally be conferred upon the ECJ. On the one hand, the Dutch, Italian and Luxembourg governments agreed that a preliminary reference system modelled on Article 177 of the EEC Treaty could do the job, and they would accept the ECJ as the main authoritative interpreter of private international law agreements. On the other hand, France was, as a matter of principle, very hostile towards extending Article 177 to private law conventions. The French Ministry of Foreign Affairs sought to limit the national courts' recourse to the preliminary reference mechanism, and it regarded the revision of the mechanism as a first step towards an overall reform of the EC legal system. But Belgium and West Germany only could agree to involve the ECJ if its powers were limited and the preliminary reference system modified. The Belgian government proposed to preclude first instance courts from sending references or to allow references only from courts of last instance. The West German government shared the restrictive Belgian position, and the two governments presented a joint memorandum along these lines in June 1969. Pompidou's France (after the end of de Gaulle's presidency) now joined the sceptical but pragmatic Belgian and West German viewpoint. Behind the scenes, the ECJ lobbied hard against the three governments, the Belgian in particular, because it feared that national governments were creating a precedence for an overall revision of Article 177, so as to limit the ECJ's collaboration with national jurisdictions (see Chapter 1).

The Luxembourg Protocol of 3 June 1971 followed the Belgian–West German formula and provided for a preliminary ruling mechanism which indeed conferred jurisdiction upon the ECJ, albeit in a considerably modified formula compared to Article 177 of the EEC treaty; no first instance courts but only courts of appeal were

60 Davies and Rasmussen 2014.
61 Rasmussen 2017.

to send references, and the Supreme Courts listed in the protocol only had to do so if they considered it necessary for their judgment. The Protocol was a blow to the ECJ's ambitions in two respects. First, it resulted precisely in the loss of dynamic of the preliminary reference mechanism that the European judges feared. Second, instead of drafting one general protocol over the ECJ's jurisdiction with regard to international law conventions, as wished for by the European judges, the Luxembourg Protocol defined the ECJ's role individually by each agreement.[62]

Generally, European law and ECJ reform were never high on the agenda of any of the member states, with the only exception of the Maastricht Treaty negotiations. The limited saliency of ECJ reform at the European level also resulted from the fact that, first, the legal, political and economic consequences of the constitutional case law remained limited in the period before the SEA. Second, national administrations and courts could relatively easily contain the various consequences of ECJ case law until the 1980s as demonstrated in Chapters 7, 8 and 9 in this book. Even after the accession of the United Kingdom and Denmark, ECJ reform never became a central foreign policy objective of the United Kingdom or France, although the British government joined the sceptical French point of view, despite the governments in London and Paris occasionally raising the question of the ECJ doctrinal advances. As demonstrated in Chapter 1, the member states also never aimed at controlling the ECJ via the selection and appointment of new judges.[63]

At the same time, the Council divide over how to deal with the ECJ's constitutional case law continued far beyond the first EC enlargement of 1973 and into the late 1970s. Crucially, when larger member states attacked the Court, governments of smaller member states defended the ECJ against the assault. A striking historical example from the late 1970s aptly illustrates this finding: France had been provoked by a number of ECJ rulings, which placed restrictions on the member states' manoeuvring space in foreign policy and in the Common Market.[64] To the French government, this seemed to confirm that the ECJ had turned into a *gouvernement de juges* trying to replace the Council as legislator. Thus, the French government called for an informal minister of foreign affairs meeting at the Chateau Mercuès near Cahors to discuss the matter.[65] However, on the meeting

62 Fritz 2015.

63 See Chapter 1.

64 See the case of 'import restrictions on potatoes': 231/78, *Commission of the European Communities v United Kingdom of Great Britain and Northern Ireland*, 1979, ECLI:EU:C:1979:101.; the case of a 'unilateral signing of a draft convention': 1/78, *International Atomic Energy Agency*, 1978, ECLI:EU:C:1978:202.; the famous 'mutton and lamb' case: 232/78, *Commission of the European Communities v French Republic*, 1979, ECLI:EU:C:1979:215; and finally 48/74, *Charmasson v Minister for Economic Affairs and Finance*, 1974, ECLI:EU:C:1974:137. For details see Rasmussen 2017, 304–305; Bernier 2017, 222–224.

65 This meeting was part of the so-called Gymnich meetings which were informal and confidential gatherings of EC ministers of foreign affairs for discussion of larger topics and long-term strategies. The first such meeting had taken place in 1974 at West Germany's Gymnich Castle in the proximity of Cologne.

which took place upon French request on 12 and 13 May 1979, the smaller member states such as the Benelux countries, but also Denmark, actually rejected intervening against the ECJ.

Added to that fact, the smaller states occasionally defending the ECJ was the ostensive paradox – since the same smaller states were often at the same time containing the ECJ's constitutional case law on an administrative level. This resistance to European law – in particular in the Netherlands, Belgium and Denmark – was not only due to long-held traditions of parliamentary sovereignty and a lack of judicial review in those countries, but also due to a specific political culture of pragmatically addressing economic and political problems without intervention of national courts. In this regard, the Danish internal debates with regard to the above-mentioned Gymnich talks were particularly revealing, because Denmark normally supported the informal veto right resulting from the Luxembourg Compromise and tended to side with the Eurosceptic British and French governments on the matter of reforming the ECJ. However, even if the Danish Ministry of Foreign Affairs and administration strongly disliked the allegedly activist ECJ, they recognised Denmark's interest in a strong legal system and a Court, which had sufficient authority vis-à-vis the largest member states. This would in the view of the Danish diplomats and government to some extent able to compensate for the alleged Council's paralysis resulting from the general lack of voting caused by the veto right. Therefore, Denmark had no interest in weakening the Court by supporting the French initiative.[66] (See Chapter 9.)

Ambiguities did not only characterise the member states' behaviour in the Council throughout the 1970s, but they were a characteristic feature of the EC political system in the 1980s and at the turn of the 1990s. The European Union at the beginning of the 1990s was a hybrid system, consisting on the one hand of a proto-federal European legal order, locked in through the SEA, and on the other hand, the political dominance of the European Council. When the Single Market acquired more importance in the second half of the 1980s, member state governments were under mounting pressure to accept the way the constitutional legal order built by the ECJ functioned. The dualist attitude of the governments, which de facto accepted the legal order as a necessary foundation for the Single Market (while at the same time rejecting and containing the ECJ's constitutional claim) was reflected by Supreme Court judgments of three major EC member states between 1989 and 1993 – the Italian Constitutional Court (Corte Costituzionale) (1989), the French Council of State (Conseil d'État) (1989) and the German Constitutional Court (Bundesverfassungsgericht, BVerfG) (1993).[67] While accepting the operation of the

66 Pedersen 2016, 142–145.

67 Corte Costituzionale, *Fragd v Amministrazione delle Finanze*, judgment no. 232 of 13 April 1989; Conseil d'État (Assemblée), 20 October 1989, *Nicolo*, n° 108243, published in *Recueil Lebon* 190, 1990; BVerfGE 89, 155, 12.10.1993, *Maastricht*, 2 BvR 2134, 2159/92; Højesteret, 6 April 1998, *Treaty of Maastricht*, Case 361/1997. See also de Witte 1998, 277–304.

European legal order, the Supreme Courts rejected the ECJ's claim for constitutional autonomy by pointing out that the powers of the EU were delegated by the member states, based on their respective national constitutions.

The above analysis suggests that the reinforcement of intergovernmentalism in the post-SEA period was not a short-term reaction of Eurosceptic member states mainly to the introduction of qualified majority voting in the field of the Single Market, as argued by Joseph H. H. Weiler. Rather, the member state rejection of the federalist project around 1990 resulted from longer-term trends of resistance against the ECJ's constitutional claim by a number of member states and a deeply rooted scepticism with regard to the vision of a gradual federalisation of the EC through supranational institutions.[68] The split in the Council and the member states' ambiguities towards the ECJ had a major impact on the way national governments responded to the constitutional case law of the ECJ, as will be demonstrated in the following section.

MEMBER STATE REACTIONS TO ECJ CASE LAW

Classical accounts from legal scholarship hold that the Council and the member state governments tacitly accepted the ECJ's constitutional case law and that national administrations and courts progressively implemented it.[69] More recent social science and historical research has nuanced this traditional account, and demonstrated how critically and hesitantly the Council, individual governments, administrations, as well as national courts, reacted to the ECJ's constitutional case law.[70] As the four chapters on how key member states dealt with European law at the administrative and court level demonstrate, it was possible to mitigate the effects of ECJ case law administratively until the mid-1980s. This section will proceed to examine how national governments individually, but also collectively in the Council, reacted to some of the most important advances in ECJ constitutional case law. In the first step, it will analyse how national governments almost systematically rejected key doctrinal advances by the ECJ from 1961 to 1970, from *Bosch*, *Van Gend en Loos*, to the *European Agreement on Road Transport* (ERTA). In a second step, it will scrutinise how the major challenges of two national Supreme Courts to the ECJ played out in the 1970s. While the West German government had to address the Constitutional Court's resistance against the ECJ's doctrinal advances in the field of human rights protection, the French government had to deal with the Conseil d'État's opposition against the preliminary reference system.[71] Whereas the West German government successfully balanced its reactions to this in order to avoid a possible infringement proceeding, the conflict between the French

68 Rasmussen and Martinsen 2019, 266–268.
69 Stein 1981; Weiler 1982b.
70 Alter 2001; Alter 2010; Davies 2012b; Conant 2002.
71 Davies 2016, 801–805; Bernier 2017.

government and the ECJ only ended with the arrival of François Mitterrand at the presidency of the French Republic. During the two crises resulting from the intervention of the two national Supreme Courts, member states continued to disagree over the ECJ's constitutional case law. As will be demonstrated, this is why neither a codification of the constitutional case law nor a fundamental reform of the ECJ took place.

It is well known that national governments generally opposed the ECJ's doctrinal advances when involved in court cases already in the 1960s and 1970s, for example in key cases such as *Bosch*,[72] *Van Gend en Loos*,[73] *Costa v ENEL*[74] and *ERTA*.[75] However, they did not firmly respond to the legal revolution, first, as a result of their disagreement over how to deal with the ECJ constitutional case law and, second, because the ECJ constitutional case law largely depended on the cooperation of national courts and therefore typically only had domestic consequences in the long run. Despite these initial reactions by national governments that often were also shaped by the substance of the case, in particular the Netherlands and Luxembourg quickly came to support the constitutional case law of the ECJ from the mid-1960s onwards. However, even in the case of such general political support for a strong constitutional legal order, national administrations and courts still attempted to mitigate and contain the effects of ECJ case law as can be seen in the Dutch case in Chapter 8. As will be shown, member state reactions did not only come from national governments, but more often from the national parliaments and national courts that in various ways felt threatened by the advances of the ECJ case law.

The first major dispute among member state governments over the interpretation of a core occurred in a case involving the question of an opening up of the preliminary reference mechanism to private litigants in cases concerned with the application of European law in the member states. In the governments' original understanding, the EEC Treaty did not provide a basis for such an opening up.[76] The *Bosch* case dealt with the interpretation of Article 85 of the EEC Treaty, which prohibited all cartels and restrictive agreements.[77] Whereas most treaty articles were supposed to become member state law through the Council's subordinate legislation, Article 85 was regarded as directly applicable from the moment the EEC Treaty stepped into force. Dutch competition law did not outright forbid cartels, and therefore the Dutch planned to continue – through a special law called

[72] 13/61, *Kledingverkoopbedrijf de Geus en Uitdenbogerd v Robert Bosch GmbH et al.*, 1962, ECLI:EU:C:1962:11.

[73] 26/62, *Van Gend en Loos v Nederlandse Administratie der Belastingen*, 1963, ECLI:EU:C:1963:1.

[74] 6/64, *Costa v ENEL*, 1964, ECLI:EU:C:1964:66.

[75] 22/70, *Commission of the European Communities v Council of the European Communities*, 1971, ECLI:EU:C:1971:32.

[76] Stein 1981, 1–27.

[77] 13/61, *Kledingverkoopbedrijf de Geus en Uitdenbogerd v Robert Bosch GmbH et al.*, 1962, ECLI:EU:C:1962:11.

Sinterklaaswetje – the rules of the Dutch competition law until negotiations over the European Competition Policy administered by European authorities were completed. Dutch firms and lawyers systematically questioned the Dutch government's transitional special law and brought cases to Dutch courts in order to enforce Article 85. A first preliminary reference to the ECJ was sent when the *Bosch* case appeared before the Court of Appeal in The Hague and the latter requested a definitive interpretation of Article 85 on 30 June 1961.[78]

Member state opinions strongly disagreed on the direct applicability of Article 85. Both the Dutch and the French government challenged the direct applicability of Article 85. They both argued that the preliminary reference itself dealt with the application of European law in the member state and, therefore, was inadmissible. While Dutch competition law did not prohibit restrictive practices, as mentioned above, the French competition law was prohibitive but not applied systematically. On the opposite side, the West German and Belgian governments supported the direct applicability of Article 85, with West German legislation clearly prohibiting cartels.

In its judgment, the ECJ argued that Article 85 had direct effect and based its argument on the treaty's design, which outlined a common competition policy. On the one hand, the ECJ did not expand direct effect beyond Article 85, nor did it elaborate a wider vision of the standing of national citizens in relation to the application of the treaty. Therefore, the *Bosch* case cannot be seen as a precedent for *Van Gend en Loos*. On the other hand, the Commission Legal Service argued in the *Bosch* case that the EEC Treaty had a presumption in favour of being self-executing, given its constitutional nature. And the judgment contributed to a streamlined interpretation of the European competition policy and marked a major step towards opening the preliminary reference mechanism for a wider range of questions than perhaps originally envisaged.[79]

The dispute over the preliminary reference mechanism continued with the case that is most prominently associated with the ECJ's legal revolution, namely in *Van Gend en Loos*. It emanated from a tariff reform among the Benelux countries – the Brussels tariff nomenclature – which involved tariff increases for a number of products. While the Dutch government assured the Dutch parliament that the increases were justified by the overall objective of a Benelux tariff harmonisation, Dutch firms saw this as a breach of Article 12, which potentially had a direct effect. They challenged the position of the Dutch government, so that Dutch courts sent a number of preliminary references, among others *Van Gend en Loos*. Reacting to the *Van Gend en Loos* case, the Director of the EEC Legal Service, Michel Gaudet, proposed (for presentation before the ECJ) a system in which all clearly formulated treaty provisions were directly applicable in the legal orders of the member states if

78 Rasmussen 2014; van Leeuwen 2018.

79 Rasmussen 2014, 150, nt. 87; Davies and Rasmussen 2014, 105.

the ECJ interpreted them as such through the preliminary reference mechanism to ensure the uniformity of the interpretation of European law across member states. In its final judgment, the ECJ declared itself as having jurisdiction, largely adopted Gaudet's proposal and argued that Article 12 created rights that national citizens could pursue before national courts, given that European law constituted a 'new order of international law'.

However, West German, Belgian and Dutch governments rejected the direct effect of Article 12, with Belgium and the Netherlands also rejecting the ECJ's jurisdiction in a case, which from their view related to the domain of Dutch constitutional law, because it dealt with the application of European law. In the Netherlands, the Ministry of Foreign Affairs was willing to accept an ECJ judgment in favour of the direct effect of Article 12, although it was believed to be an unlikely outcome. However, the Ministry of Finance wanted to defend the Dutch tariff harmonisation. An argument was therefore developed which rejected the direct effect of Article 12, because its application was a matter for Dutch constitutional law. In the Federal Republic, *Van Gend en Loos* was received by Ulrich Everling of the law department of the Ministry of Economics. Everling took a restrictive view, later adopted by the West German government in its submission in the case, that Article 12 was directed to states only, and crucially that the ECJ had no competence to decide on the applicability of norms for citizens. The law section of the Ministry of Foreign Affairs and the other ministries agreed with Everling's view.[80]

In the early 1970s, the ECJ extended its constitutional case law to the field of EC external relations, more specifically to the EC's capacity to conclude international agreements, which provoked the first head-on clash between the Council and the ECJ. In the quarrel over the ERTA, the Commission for the first time brought a case against the Council before the ECJ. The resulting ECJ ruling extended the Community's powers in external relations beyond the explicit treaty text and created a third ground-breaking case after *Van Gend en Loos* and *Costa v ENEL*.[81] Thus, the judgment represented a crucial step towards a federalised Europe, and it backed the established practice of letting the Commission negotiate on behalf of the member state governments.[82]

In the Treaties of Rome, the EC had not received an international legal personality. Without approval by the international legal community, the EC was not an equal actor on the international stage, *pari passu*, for example, with the United States, with which the EC had negotiated in the Kennedy Round of the GATT during 1964–1967. In these negotiations over trade liberalisation, the Commission negotiated on behalf of the member states.[83] Five EC member states as well as other

80 Davies 2012b, 156–157.

81 22/70, *Commission of the European Communities v Council of the European Communities*, 1971, ECLI:EU:C:1971:32. See McNaughton 2017.

82 Bernier 2017. See also Chapter 2.

83 Coppolaro 2013, 119–204.

European governments concluded negotiations over ERTA in the framework of the United Nations at Geneva on 19 January 1962. However, ratification failed in some signatory states. Before the UN negotiations over ERTA were to be resumed, the Council authorised the member states in its Regulation 543/69 of 25 March 1969 to enter ERTA negotiations and sign the agreement as contracting party. The Commission reacted swiftly, arguing that the competence to conclude an agreement in the field of transport fell within the competence of the Community and could not be done by the member states individually. The Council ignored the Commission's view and accepted the results of UN renegotiations over ERTA, inviting member state governments to sign the agreement on 20 March 1970. Thus, on 3 April 1970 the member state governments contracted the renegotiated ERTA. The EP forcefully supported the Commission in requesting the ECJ on 15 May 1970 to cancel the Council declaration of 20 March 1970. The EC alone, and not individual member states, was able to conclude such an agreement.

Although the Council quickly reassured its declaration had no legal effect, the ECJ confirmed the Community's competence to conclude international agreements and thus its international legal personality, thereby developing the new legal doctrine of Community 'implied powers': an external dimension of the Community existed not only where the Treaties of Rome were explicit about it, but also where the Community acquired a competence for developing internal policies.[84] From the ECJ's perspective, the member state governments transferred their sovereignty and competence to the EC as a result of the Council Regulation 543/69 of 25 March 1969, which authorised the latter to conclude international agreements. Following the *effet utile* argument ('who was entitled to sign a treaty derived from the capacity to ensure its fulfilment'), the ECJ concluded that the implementation of the agreement could only be secured by the Community and its institutions, which were thus holding the contractual responsibility, and were thus entitled to sign the agreement. In contrast, member state governments were no longer competent to conclude agreements with third parties, neither individually nor collectively. However, the EC was free to delegate its contractual responsibilities to the Council acting as a supranational institution (and not as governmental conference). The Council Legal Service's Pierre Puissochet sanguinely criticised the ECJ for its allegedly ideological ruling, which was from his view inspired by US and West German federalist concepts. He feared that the ECJ judgment might damage the ECJ's reputation and aggravate member state resistance up to a point where the Community would lose its capacity to negotiate international treaties.

Again, member states disagreed over how to evaluate the ECJ's doctrinal advance. French Gaullist circles, but also French Minister of Foreign Affairs Maurice Schumann, and Minister of Justice René Pleven (both non-Gaullists), were deeply

[84] 22/70, *Commission of the European Communities v Council of the European Communities*, 1971, ECLI:EU:C:1971:32.2.

critical of the ECJ judgment. Thus, in early summer 1971, the French government, led by Jacques Chaban-Delmas, was searching for a common sense among the member state governments with regard to the *ERTA* case, which would enable a coordination of member state positions. This attempt was counteracted by the West German and the Italian governments, which resisted the French attempt to organise the coordinated adoption of future regulations. Furthermore, the Dutch government insisted that future agreements be negotiated case by case, thereby avoiding a central and privileged role for the Commission. While the ECJ was driven by the aforementioned *effet utile* argument and by the teleological assumptions of judge rapporteur Pierre Pescatore about the constitutionalising role of the ECJ, the member states remained split over how to deal with the ECJ doctrinal advance.[85]

MANAGING AMBIGUITY: THE BALANCING ACT OF NATIONAL GOVERNMENTS

The new dynamics of ECJ case law in the 1970s resulted in a number of complex crises related to European law that national governments had to deal with. The Court of 1967 led by President Lecourt from 1967 to 1976 and composed by more federalist-minded members pushed the boundaries of European law.[86] As a result, the member states became increasingly aware of the impact of the ECJ, in particular in the fields of enforcement through direct effect and primacy, implied powers of the institutions (ERTA), the Common Market more generally (*Dassonville*[87] and *Defrenne*[88]) and human rights protection (*Internationale Handelsgesellschaft*).[89] National constitutional courts opposed some of the ECJ's most daring advances and caused struggles, in which the governments and the Council were soon involved, and in which the ECJ had to react to specific national concerns, like in the case of West Germany.[90]

Despite the resistance of many of the national governments to the ECJ's constitutional case law, they made sure to avoid an open breach with the Communities and a questioning of their EC membership.[91] No government escalated its resistance to ECJ doctrinal advances to a point where membership was up to debate. Furthermore, the containment of European law by national administrations and courts documented in several chapters of this book never urged member state

[85] See Chapter 2.

[86] Davies and Rasmussen 2014, 97–130.

[87] 8/74, *Procureur du Roi v Benoît and Gustave Dassonville*, 1974, ECLI:EU:C:1974:82.

[88] 43/75, *Gabrielle Defrenne v Société anonyme belge de navigation aérienne Sabena*, 1976, ECLI:EU:C:1976:56.

[89] 11/70, *Internationale Handelsgesellschaft mbH v Einfuhr- und Vorratsstelle für Getreide und Futtermittel*, 1970, ECLI:EU:C:1970:114.

[90] Davies 2012b; Davies and Rasmussen 2014, 119–129.

[91] Only in the renegotiation debate of 1975 was UK membership seriously at debate.

governments to make ECJ revision a primary target of their European policy agenda. The balancing act of the national governments vis-à-vis the ECJ is perhaps best illustrated by the West German government's trouble with handling the question of human rights caused by the famous *Solange* judgment of the West German BVerfG, and the French government's difficulty in handling the domestic court and parliamentary opposition to the expansion of direct effect of European law that the ECJ pursued in the 1970s.[92]

The topic of building a human rights regime was discovered by European institutions in the 1970s as a means to compensate the shortcomings of European integration in times of 'Eurosclerosis', especially the perceived lack of supranational quality and democratic legitimacy. The human rights question crystallised an underlying conflict: as a result of the doctrines of direct effect and primacy, European law could sidestep the normal way national constitutions inserted international law into national constitutional orders. In addition, the primacy of European law potentially implied that national constitutions were normally subordinate to European legislation. Thus, the assertion of European law autonomy in the quarrel over human rights fundamentally questioned the integrity of national constitutions. This conflict escalated in the famous *Solange* case. The battle over a Community human rights regime does not only illustrate the resistance to the constitutional case law by national (constitutional) courts, but it also underlines the importance of governmental diplomacy in shaping the European legal system. Furthermore, it demonstrates that a total breach with European law was no option for national constitutional courts and governments, given the political implications this would have had.

Whereas West Germany and Italy had charters of fundamental rights in their constitutions and were full members of the European Council's European Convention on Human Rights (ECHR) the other two largest member states, United Kingdom and France, for various reasons remained highly sceptical with regard to developing an EC charter of human rights (with France acceding under conditions to the ECHR only in 1974). In its *Solange* ruling of May 1974, the BVerfG refused to accept the unconditional primacy of European law over national constitutional provisions and maintained its right to rule on this domain 'as long as' (in West German 'Solange') a system of rights protection endorsed by a democratic parliament was lacking in the EC.[93] The BVerfG ruling was designed to make the Commission, the ECJ and the West German government aware of the democratic deficit and the missing rights protection within the EC, and more generally it was one of the most important acts of national resistance against the ECJ's constitutional case law. At the same time, the judgment resulted in elevated levels of political pressure on the BVerfG itself to find a way to secure continued EC membership of

92 Davies 2016, 801–805; Bernier 2017.

93 BVerfGE 37, 271, 29.05.1974, *Solange I*, 2 BvL 52/71; followed more than a decade later by BVerfGE 73, 339, 22.10.1986, *Solange II*, 2 BvR 197/83.

the Federal Republic, something which the Court finally managed to do in its subsequent *Solange II* judgment.

The *Solange* judgment triggered a difficult process whereby the EC attempted to secure fundamental rights at the European level. Responding politically to the *Solange* ruling, the Council, Commission and EP issued a Joint Declaration in 1977 to respect the ECHR, while the ECJ responded on a legal level by citing the ECHR in its *Hauer* ruling of 1979.[94] We now know that the Joint Declaration was not an initiative of the EP, but rather that it originated in a series of meetings between West German Chancellor Helmuth Schmidt and ECJ advocate general Gerhard Reischl in 1974 and 1975, which underlines the importance of governmental politics in the solution of the crisis. The West German government aimed to domestically protect the BVerfG while at the same time addressing the controversies raised by its ruling.[95]

A second collision between the ECJ and a national supreme court resulted from the ECJ's policy during the 1960s and 1970s of expanding the principle of direct effect to an increasing number of treaty articles, thereby creating an alternative system of public enforcement, in which private litigants could police member state compliance through the preliminary reference mechanism of Article 177. National supreme and constitutional courts continued to resist the ECJ's doctrinal innovations, in the first half of the 1970s when the ECJ developed a controversial case law that extended direct effect also to Council directives. This touched upon the balance of competence between the European level and the member states, as the implementation of Directives had been the *domaine réservé* of national institutions. Preserving the original balance of power was a key concern for the French government in particular, so the ECJ case law on the direct effect of directives provoked serious reactions from the French government, the national assembly and courts, as shall be seen below.

The preliminary reference mechanism of Article 177 EEC was originally designed to secure the uniform interpretation of European law. However, the head of the Commission Legal Service, Michel Gaudet, proposed granting direct effect and primacy to 'immediately applicable' treaty articles to turn the preliminary reference mechanism into an alternative enforcement mechanism, added to the weak public enforcement system of the infringement procedure of Articles 169 and 170. Member state citizens should be able to rely on the direct effect and primacy of European law before national courts to systematically question national law that seemed incompatible with European legal norms. Although the ECJ in its seminal judgments *Van Gend en Loos* and *Costa v ENEL* followed Gaudet's advice and introduced the new doctrines of direct effect and primacy, the new enforcement system depended upon

94 44/79, *Liselotte Hauer v Land Rheinland-Pfalz*, 1979, ECLI:EU:C:1979:290.

95 Davies and Rasmussen 2014; Davies 2012a; Davies 2012b.

the cooperation of national courts, and its efficiency required an extensive case law of the ECJ to determine which European legal norms had direct effect.

The Commission and Council first formulated directives in such a precise manner as to minimise the member states' discretion when interpreting them. The third academic conference of the Fédération pour le Droit Européen (FIDE) in November 1965 in Paris split over the expansion of direct effect, but it set up a special committee to study the problem.[96] The FIDE committee issued a report, in which it recommended the expansion of direct effect to directives based on the argument of *effet utile*, that is, the effectiveness of the treaties. The Commission Legal Service followed this report in its recommendations to the Court. Thus, citing the *effet utile* argument the ECJ expanded direct effect in a number of cases – *Franz Grad v Finanzamt Traunstein* of 1970,[97] *SACE* of 1970[98] and most notably *Van Duyn* of 1974[99] – first to decisions and later to directives: citizens could now invoke clearly defined and unambiguous elements in directives before national courts.

When the *Grad* and *SACE* cases came up, the French and West German governments wished to discuss the topic of direct effect, but this was blocked by the Benelux governments. The *Van Duyn* judgment, however, provoked a serious reaction from the British House of Lords, the French National Assembly and the French Conseil d'État. The Committee of the European Communities of the British House of Lords issued a highly critical report on 26 November 1974.[100] Lord Diplock argued (prophetically in hindsight) that the direct effect of Directives could only bind the member states, and that directives could not produce direct effect horizontally between private individuals.[101] France however was the country to react most forcefully. Pro-European president Giscard d'Estaing's view regarding the ECJ hardened towards the late 1970s, best exemplified in the replacement of the European-minded Minister of Justice Jean Lecanuet by the Gaullist Alain Peyrefitte. Driven by their understanding of national and parliamentary sovereignty, the Gaullists brought the conflict over the ECJ into the public sphere when a majority in the National Assembly voted against adopting a Council directive in late 1978. The French Conseil d'État opted for open rebellion against the ECJ case law on the direct effect of directives in its famous judgment of 22 December 1978 regarding the expulsion of Daniel Cohn-Bendit from France.[102]

96 See Chapter 4.

97 9/70, *Franz Grad v Finanzamt Traunstein*, 1970, ECLI.EU:C:1970:78.

98 33/70 *SpA SACE v Finance Minister of the Italian Republic*, 1970, ECLI:EU:C:1970:118.

99 41/74, *Yvonne van Duyn v Home Office*, 1974, ECLI.EU:C:1974:133.

100 House of Lords, Tenth Report from the Select Committee on the European Communities: Direct Applicability of Directives, Session 1974–1975, Tuesday 4 February 1975.

101 Lord Diplock's memo on the Van Duyn case in the House of Lords Archive, PARLI.HL.PO.CO.EC.E.1.1 and PARLI.HL.PO.CO.EC.E.2.1, 'Direct applicability of Directives'.

102 Conseil d'État (Assemblée), 22 December 1978, *Cohn-Bendit*, n° 11604, published in *Recueil Lebon* 524, 1980.

Here the Conseil d'État declared that EC directives were not to have direct effect and that there was no need to send a preliminary reference to the ECJ.

Following the judgment, the Commission Legal Service and the ECJ feared two threatening scenarios: first, that a coalition of national courts across the EC rejected ECJ key doctrines and case law; and second, that France would opt for open rebellion against the ECJ and European law.[103] Thus, in the *Ratti* judgment, the ECJ gave up its maximalist interpretation of direct effect of directives and adapted its case law due to the pressure from member states.[104] The Commission Legal Service and the EP Legal Committee likewise discussed how to deal with the Conseil d'État's reluctance to apply the preliminary reference procedure. Despite an exchange of letters between the French government and the Commission, the Giscard government became increasingly frustrated with the ECJ due to a number of controversial judgments. Most notably, the potential opening of the French market of 'mutton and lamb' for British exports gave the French government a pretext to criticise the alleged *gouvernement de juge*. The conflict between France and the ECJ ended to a large extent with the presidential and general elections of 10 May 1981, which brought a socialist government to power and François Mitterrand to the presidency of the French Republic. The French government now saw European law in a much more positive light. However, the conflict between Paris and Luxembourg was now echoed in West Germany with the West German Bundesfinanzhof annulling a reference from a lower West German tax court.[105] Arguing that directives could not be instrumentalised to challenge national policy, the Bundesfinanzhof continued its rebellion against the ECJ until being stopped by the BVerfG in April 1987 in the *Kloppenburg* judgment.[106]

The above analysis of the Council pillar's reaction to ECJ case law, in conjunction with the national reception studies of this book, illustrate three core findings. First, the member states generally tended to reject the major key doctrinal advances of the ECJ, as demonstrated by *Bosch*, *Vand Gend en Loos* and *ERTA*. Second, though member states became increasingly aware that the Court of 1967 pushed the boundaries of European law, they remained split over how to deal with the ECJ's doctrinal advances. And third, when the ECJ was challenged by two national Supreme Courts in the controversies over building a human rights regime and extending direct effect to directives, the West German government balanced between protecting the BVerfG and addressing the doctrinal problems, while the Giscard government remained sceptical about the ECJ until being replaced by Mitterrand. Both governments, however, toned down their resistance against the constitutional doctrines so as to avoid a threat to their EC membership and a total breach with the EC. National administrations and courts could typically contain the

[103] Rasmussen 2017, 303.

[104] 148/78, *Criminal proceedings against Tullio Ratti*, 1979, ECLI:EU:C:1979:110.

[105] BVerfGE 75, 223, 08.04.1987, *Kloppenberg*, 2 BvR 687/85.

[106] Rasmussen 2017, 290–308; Prechal 2005; Bignami 2011.

most detrimental effects of European law. Therefore, governments rarely made ECJ revision or reform the primary target of their European policy. Despite highly sceptic attitudes in France and Britain, national governments generally mastered the balancing act between securing their EC membership, responding to ECJ's constitutional case law and absorbing negative reactions from member state courts and parliaments.

CONCLUSION

This chapter has offered an analysis of why member states have been seen as relatively passive with regard to the gradual establishment of the ECJ's constitutional case law from the 1950s through to Maastricht Europe. The first part of this chapter has focused on the reinforcement of the intergovernmental dimension of the EC over time. In response to the openness of the treaties and to the vast nature of EC integration, an intergovernmental and highly consensual approach emerged among member state governments, which led to consensus building structures like COREPER, and which culminated in the Empty Chair Crisis and the Luxembourg Compromise. The institutionalisation of summitry through the European Council in the mid-1970s and its formal recognition as the leading institution and driving force of European integration in the SEA, as well as in the Maastricht Treaty only confirmed the centrality of state power in the process of integration. Despite a parallel development of the supranational institutions, exemplified in the EP direct elections of 1979 and the introduction of qualified majority in the field of the Single Market, the national governments rejected the Delors Commission proposals for a move towards federal Europe in the Maastricht Treaty negotiations.

The second part of this chapter demonstrated that a split occurred between the EC Council members over the ECJ constitutional interpretation of European law, which resulted in a Council deadlock over the role and future of the ECJ. The member states could neither agree to revise the ECJ status and form a coalition to curb the Court nor to codify the ECJ constitutional case law when the Maastricht Treaty opened the door to placing new policy fields in the supranational pillar.

Finally, the third part of this chapter scrutinised the Council pillar's response to major ECJ case law, and to the ECJ's constitutional claim more widely. As seen above, member states opposed the ECJ's key doctrinal advances of the 1960s and 1970s but remained largely inactive vis-à-vis the Court due to the split in the Council. When two national Supreme Courts attacked the ECJ, the respective governments successfully balanced the problems raised by ECJ doctrinal advances and at the same time the pressures from sceptical member state administrations, parliaments and courts. They calibrated their reactions both at the European level and domestically, thus avoiding a total breach with the EC. Clearly, the scepticism of some governments towards the ECJ constitutional interpretation and the general containment of the constitutional case law by national administrations and courts were long-term phenomena stretching from early ECJ case law in the 1960s to the Maastricht Treaty of 1993.

This chapter has not only filled a gap in the recent sociological and historical literature, but it also served to test longstanding claims in the law and politics literature about the obvious paradox between rising intergovernmentalism and the increasing legal integration promoted by the ECJ. Joseph H. H. Weiler suggested an equilibrium between the ECJ's constitutional case law and the rise of the EC intergovernmental pillar, most prominently characterised by the informal veto right established in the Luxembourg Compromise of 1966. However, no empirical evidence could be identified so far which clearly supports the hypothesis that holding a veto right encouraged EC member state governments to tolerate the ECJ's constitutional case law. In fact, several member states, in particular France from 1963 to 1981, at various times wanted to reform the Court. This chapter suggests that the split in the Council over the ECJ and its constitutional case law was the key explanatory element why national governments did neither curb the Court nor codify the constitutional case law. Finally, it demonstrated that the rise of intergovernmentalism in the EC ultimately in the Maastricht Treaty led to a rejection of the federalist aspirations of the Commission and the codification of the constitutional legal order developed by the ECJ, even if the member states accepted how the latter worked as a basis for the Single Market.

PART II

Member State Reception of the Constitutional Practice of European Law

6

The Solange Admonition: The Necessity of Structural Congruence between Germany and Europe

Bill Davies

The purpose of this chapter is to address how West Germany received and responded to the constitutional interpretation of European law launched by the European Court of Justice (ECJ) in 1963–1964 with the doctrines of direct effect and primacy.[1] The reception of these doctrines by the highest levels of the West German judiciary and West Germany's legal academia has been surprisingly fraught against a context in which European integration has been a fundamental aim for the Federal Republic. These difficulties originate in the DNA of the West German Basic Law itself, as well as in response to the subsequent case law of the ECJ. The sometimes contested and often admonitory dialogue between the West German Constitutional Court – the (Bundesverfassungsgericht, BVerfG) – and the ECJ is the most keenly watched of all judicial relationships in the European public arena.

This chapter will provide a historical analysis of the reception of European law in West Germany, starting with the negotiations that led to the establishment of the European Coal and Steel Community (ECSC) in 1950–1951 through to the BVerfG's Maastricht decision of 1993. It will draw from my prior work on the West German reception, focusing especially on the interplay between legal academic debate and the back and forth of decisions emanating from the BVerfG and ECJ during this period.[2] Rather than restate archival research that has been done in my previous work (which demonstrated particularly forceful domestic government dynamics[3] and an unusually robust and early public discourse on European law[4]), this chapter will instead provide a summary overview of the West German legal academy's reception of European law. This will enable us to take a closer look at contemporary dynamics of the BVerfG-ECJ relationship. Adding historical context to that judicial relationship will possibly allow for the recasting of what is normally

1 26/62 *Van Gend en Loos v Nederlandse Administratie der Belastingen*, 1963, ECLI:EU:C:1963:1 and 6/64 *Costa v ENEL*, 1964, ECLI:EU:C:1964:66.

2 Davies 2008; Davies 2012a; Davies 2012b; Davies 2015; Davies 2016; Davies 2017; Davies and Rasmussen, 2014; Boerger and Davies, 2017; Nicola and Davies 2017, chapter 1.

3 Davies, 2008.

4 Davies, 2012b. See also Chapter 3.

considered a strained or admonitory dialogue into one that, while not perhaps easy, will require rights protections, democracy and the rule of law are central concerns of European governance.

To get to that point, this chapter will describe the competing currents of legal thought in the West German legal academy as it grappled with both the dynamics of a brand new domestic constitution and the impact of the ECJ's constitutional jurisprudence of the 1960s and beyond. Whilst open to the transfer of national competencies for the purpose of international cooperation, the Basic Law also contained elements, such as fundamental rights and democratic standards, that could not be amended by any public authority – national or beyond. What to do in the face of European laws that may supersede national constitutional rules? This tension found its first major expression in the BVerfG's *Solange* ruling in 1974 and continues in modified form until the current day. The *Solange* doctrine has been informed by the necessity of having sufficient 'structural congruence' in constitutional form between West Germany and Europe if a transfer of national sovereign competency to European institutions is to be considered legitimate. This chapter details the origin and impact of the structural congruence idea and how it continues to shape the judicial dialogue between the ECJ and BVerfG today. At its core, this was a battle of aspirations and of ideas about what a new Europe should look like and what West Germany's role in this might be. The core outlook presented in the chapter is that the BVerfG's jurisprudence on European law has been deeply shaped by legal academic argument and, due to the significance of the BVerfG-ECJ dialogue in shaping broader European legal governance, analysis of these positions within West German legal academia is crucial to understanding the historical development of European law as a whole.

WEST GERMANY IN EUROPE: A POSITIVE ENVIRONMENT

West Germany's participation in the European integration project has been a central plank of the country's post-war rebirth and the securing of its democratic institutions. In the political, diplomatic and economic dimensions, West German membership of the ECSC and the EC had a profoundly positive impact on West German society. A stable and peaceful Europe, as the new 'home' for the western half of the divided country, offered a strengthening alliance while steps to reunify the country stalled during the Cold War. Partnership within a process of European integration offered West Germans a way to overcome historical divisions and rebuild a new identity based on shared values and common goals. Diplomatically, the country's commitment to multilateral, peaceful international governance is anchored demonstrably in its commitment to a united Europe. European integration thus offered a new home for West German diplomacy. Even in the early years of integration, West Germany often supplied leading figures in the European project, such as Commission and ECJ Presidents like Walter Hallstein and Hans Kutscher.

West German officials appointed to the European institutions came to work side-by-side in a new spirit of collaboration and purpose with colleagues who had lived under occupation only shortly before.

From an economic perspective, the increasingly simplified access to the larger European market for West Germany's voluminous exports buoyed the 'Wirtschaftswunder' (Economic Miracle), itself a phenomenon which helped legitimate the institutions of the new Republic. West German businesses gained better access to a huge market of consumers, workers and investment, consolidating West Germany's position as a globally significant economy and leader in international trade. West German lawyers and judicial officials have engaged in a substantial amount of interaction with European law, exerting major influence on how European law is shaped within both the legislative and judicial systems. On the whole, West Germans have been broadly supportive of European integration and the many gains that it has brought to the country.

WEST GERMANY IN EUROPE: THE CONSTITUTIONAL DILEMMA

Notwithstanding the benefits of European integration, membership of the EC, particularly after the establishment of the ECJ's doctrines of direct effect and supremacy, has caused much consternation from a constitutional perspective. These difficulties are caused by a clash of competing dynamics present in the creation of the 1949 Basic Law. Under the scrutiny of the occupying Allies and in the environment of an increasingly tense Cold War, the framers of the new Constitution had to achieve multiple goals under difficult circumstances. Among these was ensuring the permanency of the democratic order, especially its protection of individual rights. Further, it was also necessary to ensure that West Germany could effectively take part in new forms of international cooperation that appeared in the post-war period.[5] These goals were achieved in constitutional requirements that sought to ensure the inviolability of the fundamental liberal democratic order (especially West German federalism and the protection of fundamental rights in Article 79.3) and to support openness to international integration by allowing for the transfer of sovereign powers to international institutions through legislation (and not constitutional amendment) (Article 24.1 of the original 1949 Basic Law).[6]

In theory, if not yet a fully fledged legal dilemma, this created a tension between the ability to initiate a legislative transfer of sovereign competency to non-domestic public authorities and the requirement of ensuring that all public authority,

5 Surveys of the work of the founding mothers and fathers of the Grundgesetz have proven that some of the constitutional authors had clear and well-defined concepts of future paths of European integration, even before the signing of the Treaty of Paris some years later.

6 Article 24.1 in the original Grundgesetz, prior to later amendments, read 'The Federation may, by legislation, transfer sovereign powers to international institutions.' A version of the 1949 document can be in English and containing the original language of the articles at www.cvce.eu/content/publication/1999/1/1/7fa618bb-604e-4980-b667-76bf0cd0dd9b/publishable_en.pdf.

domestic or not, be bound by inviolable domestic constitutional stipulations. Under what conditions could a transfer of West German public competency to external authorities be considered legitimate? West German legal scholars and practitioners already began trying to answer these questions right from the start of the 1950s. Finding a suitable response became more acute once the ECJ issued its constitutional jurisprudence in the early 1960s. The ECJ's claims in *Van Gend en Loos* and *Costa v ENEL* that the EC were a new kind of autonomous legal order, whose laws might have direct effect and supremacy over competing national norms, sharpened the debates and turned a theoretical question into one of genuine legal import. Further still, at the turn of the 1970s, the ECJ extended its claims that supremacy applied even against national constitutional standards.[7] What then was the relationship between this new autonomous legal order and the existing national system? Could European law have primacy over national laws, even inviolable constitutional standards? And who had the final adjudication on European law applied within West Germany?

The body that took on the responsibility for finding answers to this question was the Federal Constitutional Court (BVerfG). Beginning its work in September 1951, only shortly before the ECJ itself was born, the BVerfG rapidly became the pivotal voice in West German constitutional life. By the end of the 1950s, the BVerfG had moved to ban extremist political parties, weighed in on rearmament issues, and placed the protection of fundamental rights at the very heart of its purpose.[8] The BVerfG's responses to the constitutional dilemma of European integration became an enduring feature of the principle judicial dialogue in Europe.

STRUCTURAL CONGRUENCE AS A PRECONDITION OF EUROPEAN INTEGRATION

To understand this story, we must first abandon the constraints of historical chronology and begin the story at the *midway point* of our chosen period of analysis, namely in the 1970s, when the conflictual nature of the BVerfG-ECJ dialogue first began.

The West German word 'Solange', 'as long as' in English, frames the discourse between the two courts. It captures the conditionality placed on the BVerfG's acceptance of ECJ's doctrine. The *Solange* jurisprudence of the BVerfG began formally in a May 1974 decision, delivered by the court's Second Senate by a five to three majority.[9] This ruling was in response to a referral from the Frankfurt

7 11/70, *Internationale Handelsgesellschaft mbH v Einfuhr- und Vorratsstelle für Getreide und Futtermittel*, 1970, ECLI:EU:C:1970:114.

8 On the significance of human rights for the BVerfG, see especially BVerfGE 6, 32, 16.01.1957, *Elfes*, 1 BvR 253/56 and BVerfGE 7, 198, 15.01.1958, *Lüth*, 1 BvR 400/51. For a more recent history of the German Constitutional Court, see Collings 2015.

9 BVerfGE 37, 271, 29.05.1974, *Solange I*, 2 BvL 52/71.

Verwaltungsgericht (Administrative Court), which itself had referred the same case to the ECJ at an earlier stage. The ECJ had already ruled in the case, contributing to its growing case law at that time around fundamental rights.[10] The ECJ argued in its own interpretation of the case that:

> 'Respect for fundamental rights forms an integral part of the general principles of law protected by the Court of Justice', but that 'the protection of such rights, whilst inspired by the constitutional traditions common to the Member States, must be ensured within the framework of the structure and objectives of the Community'.[11]

While this position convinced three of the eight BVerfG Second Senate judges in their dissenting opinion, the ultimate *Solange* decision sought to strike and refine an acceptable equilibrium between the overlap of West German constitutional norms and European aspirations.

At its heart, the BVerfG has argued that its acceptance of the ECJ's primacy doctrine depends on the development of a European constitutional democracy that would be comparable with the one created nationally by the Basic Law. In the first *Solange* decision, the BVerfG decided that:

> The Community still lacks a democratically legitimate parliament directly elected by general suffrage which possesses legislative powers and to which the Community organs empowered to legislate are fully responsible on a political level; it still lacks, in particular, a codified catalogue of fundamental rights, the substance of which is reliably and unambiguously fixed for the future in the same way as the substance of the Basic Law.[12]

Framed as an admonition – 'as long as' these gaps in European system of governance existed – the BVerfG reserved the right to review the applicability of EU law in West Germany until such time its conditions for acceptance have been met at the European level. This would ensure that the fundamental principles of the West German legal order could be maintained in the face of binding public action not held to the same standards of democratic or rights scrutiny as those found nationally. It also meant, were European authorities keen to appease the Constitutional Court of its largest Member State (and the Italian Constitutional Court (Corte Costituzionale), which had issued a similar judgment the previous year),[13] the European legal order would have to be transformed to resemble more closely that of West Germany's. This is, as this chapter will show, what happened. This places

10 11/70, *Internationale Handelsgesellschaft mbH v Einfuhr- und Vorratsstelle für Getreide und Futtermittel*, 1970, ECLI:EU:C:1970:114.

11 11/70, *Internationale Handelsgesellschaft mbH v Einfuhr- und Vorratsstelle für Getreide und Futtermittel*, 1970, ECLI:EU:C:1970:114.

12 BVerfGE 37, 271, 29.05.1974, *Solange I*, 2 BvL 52/71.

13 Corte Costituzionale, *Frontini e a.*, judgment no. 183 of 18 December 1973. For context on the Italian Constitutional Court's jurisprudence in this case, see Cartabia and Lupo 2023.

the BVerfG on the list of formative agents in the creation of the European polity in effect today, a list typically reserved for the political and economic leaders of the Member States.

The *Solange* doctrine rests on the argument that sufficient 'structural congruence' between the West German constitutional order and European legal order is necessary for a transfer of West German public competency to European authority to be legally acceptable. The structural congruence argument is applied particularly in those areas of the West German constitution designated as inviolable and considered central to its identity, such as the fundamental rights provisions and the democratic and federal nature of the West German republic. In other words, a transfer of public authority to international or supranational organisations could only be considered legitimate if the receiving authority had standards, for instance, of democratic accountability and rights protection equivalent to that found in West Germany. It would be unacceptable to transfer public authority to an international agency that did not hold the same regard for democracy and rights protection as its constituent parts. Article 24 does not allow for the transfer of sovereignty without some reservation.

Structural congruence subsequently became such an essential part of West Germany's constitutional relationship with the EC and later EU that it was explicitly enumerated when the articles related to European integration of the Basic Law were amended in the early 1990s.[14]

CHOOSING STRUCTURAL CONGRUENCE

Structural congruence as a precondition of the BVerfG's acceptance of the ECJ's doctrine emerged as a legal position not in the 1970s when *Solange I* was delivered, but at a much earlier time, before even West Germany had joined the European project. From the very start of the Schuman Plan negotiations, the question of the relationship between national and European legal orders was keenly contested by legal academics and practitioners. The key venue for this early debate was in an Advisory Group of Judicial Experts, established in June 1950 to advise the West German negotiating team in Paris preparing the Treaty of Paris. Apparent within this Advisory Group were a spectrum of opinions on this question, ranging from those who believed the Treaty of Paris would be the first step towards a federal constitutional order for Europe to those who considered it an innovative, but nonetheless standard treaty under international law.

In between were the advocates of structural congruence in the Advisory Group, who conceptualised that the ECSC would be something less than a federation but more than an international organisation. This position, championed by the Chair of

[14] Bundesgesetzblatt. 1992. *Gesetz zur Änderung des Grundgesetzes*. BGBl. I Nr. 58, 24 December 1992, 2086. www.bgbl.de/xaver/bgbl/start.xav?startbk=Bundesanzeiger_BGBl&jumpTo=bgbl192s2086.pdf.

the Group, Herbert Kraus, drew heavily from West Germany's nineteenth-century constitutional past.[15] Kraus, fully cognisant of the terminology for describing federal and confederal entities, chose instead to employ the neologistic 'Überstaat' to describe the nascent ECSC. This neologism might be best translated as a kind of 'meta-state', above the member states, but dependent on the granting of their nationally sourced legitimacy for its own power.[16] In this model, sovereignty remained with the member states, who pooled and transferred parts of their sovereignty to the meta-state to serve predefined 'essential interests'.[17] For the transfer of sovereign competency to the meta-state to be legitimate, the meta-state must resemble the basic constitutional nature of its constituent parts, including 'the separation of powers, checks and balances, democratic legitimation, rights, the legality of administration, parliamentary control, etc'.[18] These points championed by Kraus came to define the 'structural congruence' paradigm in West Germany and, due to the significance of the contemporary BVerfG-ECJ relationship, to a large degree shape our contemporary understanding of the unusual nature of the EU today, particularly seen from the perspective of the BVerfG, which now uses another, but very similar neologism, *Staatenverbund*, to describe the European Union.[19]

The structural congruence position was just one of several arguments in West German legal academia that emerged during the initial period of West Germany's membership of the ECSC and later the EC, and it was by no means certain that the structural congruence paradigm would win the day in the West German legal community. A battle for the legal consciousness of the lawyers, academics and judges engaging in the system would have to be fought between groups with differing views on the nature and intentions of the Treaty of Paris. The status quo would be to recognise the Treaty of Paris as another addition to the growing number of international organisations established in the immediate post-war years to facilitate multilateral cooperation in Western Europe. Deviating from this regular understanding of the Treaty of Paris would require some persuasion. Some in the Advisory Group, for instance the acclaimed international law scholar Hermann Mosler did not recognise it as anything other than an international organisation, although admittedly of some innovation. This traditional position from international law was reflective of a West German legal academic community that would require some time to overcome the normal inertia required in grappling with something entirely new.

Yet more challenging to the structural congruence idea was that of the federal constitutionalist position. Championed by highly influential people like the

15 Davies 2015, 446–448.
16 Davies 2015, 447–448.
17 Davies 2015, 447.
18 Kraus 1952, 545.
19 The term is used in the BVerfG's Maastricht decision – BVerfGE 89, 155, 12.10.1993, *Maastricht*, 2 BvR 2134, 2159/92.

Head of the West German delegation in Paris, Walter Hallstein, and later Secretary of State of the Ministry of Foreign Affairs until 1957 as well as his right-hand man Carl Friedrich Ophüls, the constitutionalist position imagined that the Treaty of Paris was a new constitution for a federal Europe and the new Court of Justice of the ECSC a unifying European Supreme Court in the mode of the Marshall Court in the United States. It criticised the structural congruence position by arguing that the creation of the rule of law at the European level would better protect individual rights than any of its Member States could do individually.[20] Such a view was also dominant in the thinking behind the European Convention on Human Rights. Moreover, with their hands on the levers of political power, the federal constitutionalist group was able to have Herbert Kraus removed as chair of the group and replaced with Ernst Wolff, a close associate of Hallstein and more amenable to the constitutionalist's groups aims. Kraus resigned from the Advisory Group because of his demotion.[21] Hallstein's constitutional approach to European integration dominated West German European policy until 1956. Despite the disappointing result of the Treaties of Rome considered from a constitutional point of view, Hallstein used his position as President of the EEC Commission to promote the breakthrough for a constitutional interpretation of the Treaties of Rome. After the breakthrough in 1963–1964 with the decisions of the ECJ on *Van Gend en Loos* and *Costa v ENEL*, Hallstein defended the Court's new constitutional interpretation of European law as fundamental to the survival of the EC, dismissing structural congruence as political inopportune and dangerous. The ability of leading personalities such as Hallstein and Ophüls to push their particular vision of European law both from within West Germany and the supranational institutions gave them a powerful influence over the development of European law. Aided by the organisational support of the Fédération internationale pour le droit européen (FIDE), this strongly pro-European elite achieved some initial progress in the mid-1960s in convincing the generally traditionalist West German legal academy that the nature of European law was constitutional in nature.[22]

However, during the 1950s, the rather limited sectoral impact of the ECSC and the subsequent failure of the European Defence Community (EDC) (and thus also the European Political Community) in 1954 meant that the potential for discord between the BVerfG and ECJ was quite minimal. The public and political debates surrounding West German participation in the EDC issues, however, did allow for the structural congruence position to be argued before the BVerfG. Before his retirement, Kraus participated in a high-profile debate

20 Ophüls 1951, 291.
21 Davies 2015, 443.
22 For the role of the Commission, its Legal Service and allied academic associations, see especially Chapters 2 and 4 of this volume.

about West German rearmament before the BVerfG. In Kraus's report to the court, he detailed his thoughts about the limitations imposed on West German participation in international agreements. In language that foreshadowed the *Solange* ruling over two decades before its publication, Kraus argued that a transfer of West German public authority to international organisations utilising Article 24 meant that the international authority would be bound by the limits on public power created by the Basic Law, most especially the fundamental rights catalogue and the constitutional identity created by Article 79. Kraus concluded that, 'it was never, ever the intention of Article 24 to allow for the encroachments on fundamental rights provisions through the transfer of sovereign competency to international organizations'.[23]

While the impact of European law was quite limited during the 1950s, by the end of the decade, with the reimagining of integration through the EEC in 1958, the jurisprudential trajectories of the BVerfG and the ECJ made a potential conflict between the two courts more of a reality. Domestically, through its rulings in the *Elfes* (1957)[24] and *Lüth* (1958)[25] decisions, the BVerfG had developed its position on the impact of fundamental rights in the West German constitutional order. Reading expansively, the BVerfG described the Basic Law as an 'objective system of values',[26] in which fundamental rights permeated the entire body of West German law. This solidified the BVerfG's role as the final arbiter of fundamental rights issues in West Germany and put in place one of the necessary legal planks for the future *Solange* conflict. At the very same time, in 1958 and 1959, the ECJ, in its *Storck*[27] and *Ruhrkohlen-Verkaufsgesellschaften*[28] rulings, was distancing itself from considering national law provisions, specifically the fundamental rights provisions in the Basic Law in these cases. In *Storck*, arguing that it as a Court and the High Authority as the ESCS administration were bound only by European law, it refused to consider the plaintiff's arguments that Articles 2 and 12 of the Basic Law had been infringed by a High Authority decision. In the *Ruhrkohlen* cases, the ECJ was even more blunt, arguing that,

> it is not for the Court, whose function is to judge the legality of decisions adopted by the High Authority and, as obviously follows, those adopted in the present case . . . to ensure that rules of internal law, even constitutional rules, enforced in one or other of the Member States are respected.[29]

23 Kraus 1952, 837.

24 BVerfGE 6, 32, 16.01.1957, *Elfes*, 1 BvR 253/56.

25 BVerfGE 7, 198, 15.01.1958, *Lüth*,1 BvR 400/51.

26 BVerfGE 7, 198, 15.01.1958, *Lüth*,1 BvR 400/51.

27 1/58, *Friedrich Stork & Cie v High Authority of the European Coal and Steel Community*, 1959, ECLI:EU:C:1959:4.

28 36/59, 37/59, 38/59, and 40/59, *Präsident Ruhrkohlen-Verkaufsgesellschaft mbH et al. v High Authority of the European Coal and Steel Community*, 1960, ECLI:EU:C:1960:36.

29 36/59, 37/59, 38/59, and 40/59, *Präsident Ruhrkohlen-Verkaufsgesellschaft mbH et al. v High Authority of the European Coal and Steel Community*, 1960, ECLI:EU:C:1960:36.

THE GATHERING STORM

The subsequent and most famous jurisprudence of the ECJ in the early 1960s, establishing the doctrines of direct effect and primacy, sharpened the potential for conflict in the respective courts' interpretations of the role for national fundamental rights. In *Van Gend en Loos*, the ECJ claimed that the new community legal order was autonomous, independent and a new order of international law. The primary law of the Treaties of Rome when appropriately framed, could confer rights on individuals that member states were bound to respect. Moreover, in *Costa v ENEL*, the ECJ stipulated that for the EC to be effective and maintain their autonomous legal character, European law had primacy and could thus not 'be overridden by domestic provisions *however framed*' (emphasis added). The Court also found that European law now constituted a 'new legal order' omitting the reference to international law. The judgments amounted to a breakthrough for the constitutional interpretation of European law that Hallstein and his director of the legal service of the EEC Commission, Michel Gaudet, had pursued. It broke with the design of the Treaties of Rome where primary law, apart from competition policy, was supposed only to be fleshed into legislation through the decision-making of the Council of Ministers. Perhaps even more remarkably, the ECJ took upon itself the competence to decide how important parts of European primary law entered the member states, namely through its new design of direct effect and primacy, thereby controversially discarding the different constitutional clauses of the member states of how to receive international law.[30]

The political reaction in West Germany to the breakthrough of a constitutional interpretation of European law was largely muted, primarily due to the fact that the Ministry of Foreign Affairs had the 'Verfassungsressorts' to make decisions on European integration, thereby sidelining the more critical Ministries of Justice, the Interior and Economics.[31] The Ministry of Foreign Affairs continued to subscribe to the federal constitutionalist position, being heavily influenced by figures such as Hallstein and Ophüls, now Permanent Representative in Brussels, as well as Karl Carstens, State Secretary since 1958 and later Federal President. By controlling West Germany's European policy, around the time of the *Van Gend en Loos* ruling,[32] the Ministries of Foreign and Economic Affairs were able to exclude voices critical of the nature of the ECJ's jurisprudence. This is especially true of the Ministry of Justice, where concerns about getting the right balance between Articles 24 and 79 were being articulated from early in the period.[33]

The Ministry of Foreign Affairs however could not control how the West German legal community responded to the ECJ decisions. Two episodes from the 1960s

30 Rasmussen 2014.

31 Davies 2012b, 146–159.

32 Davies 2008, 63–65 and 68.

33 Davies 2008, 69.

demonstrate how the West German judiciary and legal academic community were grappling with the new reality created by the ECJ.

First, West German judges began almost immediately to face questions about the applicability of Treaties of Rome under West German constitutional law. Two cases of particular importance on the issue ended up before the BVerfG in this period. The first was a referral to the BVerfG by the Rhineland-Pfalz Finanzgericht (Tax Court) from November 1963.[34] In this referral, the Tax Court asked the BVerfG for clarification if EC regulations could be applied with direct applicability (defined as such under Article 189 of the EEC Treaty) in the West German constitutional order and if that was the case whether membership in the Treaties of Rome could be considered constitutional in the face of the Basic Law's fundamental rights, especially Article 20, which guarantees the democratic and republican structure of the constitution. In other words, the Treaties of Rome had created European Communities that were not democratic enough to be congruent with the Basic Law and therefore could not be allowed to move beyond a traditional intergovernmental international organisation. The Second Senate of the BVerfG delivered its decision in this case only after a long four-year period of consideration, ultimately ruling in 1967 that the Tax Court's referral was inadmissible. In doing so, it criticised the Tax Court for not laying out its case clearly enough.

The second case emerged from a constitutional complaint (Verfassungsbeschwerde) delivered to the First Senate of the BVerfG.[35] In this EC regulations case, several West German firms raised a complaint against directly applicable European regulations, which, the firms argued, restricted their fundamental rights granted by the Basic Law. Again, the BVerfG decided the case was inadmissible. This time the BVerfG posited that it could only consider constitutional complaints against acts of West German public authority, and that European regulations emanated from a 'separate and independent', non-West German power. Mirroring the language of the *Van Gend en Loos* ruling, the First Senate wrote that, 'The community itself is not a state, not even a federal state. It is a community of its own kind in the process of progressive integration . . . To a certain extent, the EEC Treaty represents the constitution of this community.'[36] This ruling understandably provided much cheer for the federal constitutionalist position. However, quite tellingly, the BVerfG made clear that its ruling applied only to constitutional complaints, a distinct process of appeal in the Basic Law. It was withholding judgment on the more 'far reaching' question of the general relationship between the West German constitution and European authority and the extent to which the ECJ doctrine of primacy that meant that European would trump West German law within the competences of the EC necessitated a defence of the Basic Law to ensure that West German citizens rights were not ignored indirectly through the activities of the EC. While respecting the autonomy and independence of the Community legal order, in

34 BVerfGE 22, 134, 05.07.1967, *EWG-Recht*, 2 BVL 29/63.

35 BVerfGE 22, 293, 18.10.1967, *EWG-Verordnung*, 1 BvR 248/63, 1BvR 216/67.

36 BVerfGE 22, 293, 18.10.1967, *EWG-Verordnung*, 1 BvR 248/63, 1BvR 216/67.

line with *Van Gend en Loos*, the BVerfG pushed its judgment down the line until a consensus could be reached in the West German legal community about this question.[37]

The West German legal academic community was indeed grappling with this question. Again, two episodes stand out as particularly enlightening about the parameters of the academic discussion. The first was the 'Bensheim Colloquium' in 1964 – held just a short while before the *Costa v ENEL* ruling was delivered. The Bensheim Colloquium was an academic conference organised with support of the European Commission under Hallstein to both gauge opinion in West German legal academy and help to push the federal constitutionalist agenda.[38] The conference was attended by ECJ President André Donner and West German Advocate General Karl Roemer, as well as a number of other leading political officials, including the ubiquitous Ophüls, and academics. One of the major questions it proposed was that of the relationship between national and European law. Hans-Peter Ipsen, one of the academic leaders in the field of European law throughout this period, argued that direct effect but also primacy that was being considered by the ECJ at the time in the ongoing *Costa v ENEL* case were both necessary for the EC to function and that even if there were conflicts between European law and West German fundamental rights, Article 24 enabled European law to come out on top. Ministry of Justice official, Erich Bülow, argued instead that while the autonomy of the European legal order was clear, the case for primacy was yet to be fully persuasive. Ultimately, in memos flowing back to Hallstein about the conference, Commission attendees reported back that the majority of participants had sided with Ipsen at the end of the day. This was potentially due to the fact that many attendees were Community employees. This support at least had the appearance of another victory for the federal constitutionalist position.

However, just as was the case with the two BVerfG rulings, this victory was illusory. In the same year, another academic conference, the meeting of the premier West German public lawyers' association, the Congress of West German Public Law Teachers, was held in Kiel under the title 'The Preservation and Alteration of Democratic and Legal Constitutional Structures through International Communities'. Unlike Bensheim organised by the WGE, this conference was not promoted by the Hallstein Commission and was attended by a much broader range of West German lawyers and academics. Interestingly, the conclusions reached at the Kiel conference differed significantly from Bensheim, strongly emphasising the fact that the Bensheim colloquium's impact was limited to a self-selecting group of already strongly pro-European lawyers. From Kiel, several conclusions were drawn. First, there appeared a growing acceptance that total structural congruence between the EC and the Federal Republic was

[37] Mann 1972, 184, 420–421.
[38] Davies 2012b, 86–87, 91–96.

impossible but that even if the democratic control was qualitatively weaker at the supranational level, this was a 'sacrifice' that West Germany had to make in the name of integration.[39] Second, while the weakness of parliamentary control of executive power in the EC was below the standards of the national level, it was accepted that national standards were not appropriate as a benchmark for the EC level. But when it came to the democratic accountability of the supranational institutions, agreement existed that it still had to evolve significantly. Third, it was accepted that European law was independent and not under the scope of national judicial review, but at the same time European law still had to be bound by the same basic constitutional principles as national law. Finally, European law was subject to national constitutional control, in that it was agreed that the BVerfG had the right to measure the constitutionality of the national laws transforming European primary law into West German law against the Basic Law and to rule them unconstitutional if necessary. The problem was of course that this could only apply to Community directives and not to European primary law with direct effect or regulations with direct applicability.[40]

These conclusions aligned much more closely with the structural congruence paradigm than the federal constitutionalist. They also demonstrated that the traditionalist international law paradigm, personified by Mosler in the 1950s Advisory Group, had largely disappeared and that the West German legal academy, in light of the constitutional breakthrough of European law, had come by this point to accept the special and independent nature of European law. In fact, Mosler himself wrote in 1968 about his surprise at the huge growth in scholarship on European law and admitted that the literature on the topic had become unmanageable.[41] Of noteworthiness in the Kiel conference conclusions was especially the new emphasis placed on democratic accountability and its perceived absence at the European level. Until this point, much of the structural congruence perspective had focused on the question of infringements of fundamental rights by European law. While this remained central to the argument going forward, from Kiel onwards, the question of the qualitative nature of European democracy was now of joint concern. This would only intensify towards the end of the 1960s as questions about the nature of democracy at the national level came to the fore in the generational changes occurring across Europe in and around 1968.

Herbert Kraus, the leading proponent of the structural congruence position in the 1950s, had retired in 1953 and passed away in 1965. The mantle for the structural congruence argument during this period was taken up by another younger member of the 1950 Advisory Group, Hans-Jürgen Schlochauer. Schlochauer, like Kraus, had a significant reputation as both an international jurist and scholar of international law. He published several articles during the 1960s reaffirming – like much of the

39 Davies 2012b, 84. See also Erler and Theime 1959, 48.

40 Davies 2012b, 84.

41 Mosler 1968, 482.

West German legal academy at this point – that European law was separate and distinct, but that a satisfactory answer was yet to be found to how the West German commitment to fundamental rights could be honoured vis-à-vis a non-domestic legal system whose powers were directly effective and had primacy. Schlochauer attempted to offer a range of possible political and legal processes that he believed would avoid potential conflicts between European law and national fundamental rights on a case-by-case basis.[42] Other scholars were neither as pragmatic nor as optimistic about the potential to avoid a clash of systems. As one such example, Wilhelm Wengler, a Professor of International Law at the Free University in Berlin, provocatively questioned in 1968 why West German competencies could be transferred to a set of European institutions that had no basic rights protection, if they could not be transferred to institutions who would undertake wars of aggression – another constitutional stipulation of the Basic Law?[43]

Certainly, empowered by the positive recognition of its claims to an autonomous and new legal order as well as aware of national concerns about the nature of democracy and rights protection at the European level, the ECJ attempted at the end of the 1960s to further supplement its rights jurisprudence to pre-empt conflicts with West Germany and Italy. Using two cases, both involving West German plaintiffs, the ECJ outlined in *Stauder* in 1969 that 'fundamental human rights [were] enshrined in the general principles of Community law and protected by the Court'.[44] Further still in *Internationale Handelsgesellschaft* in 1970, the ECJ described these fundamental rights as being 'inspired by the constitutional traditions common to the Member States'.[45] However, these fundamental rights were not tied to any particular constitution or tradition because 'recourse to the legal rules or concepts of national law in order to judge the validity of measures adopted by the institutions of the Community would have an adverse effect on the uniformity and efficacy of Community law'.[46] Therefore, 'the protection of such rights ... must be ensured within the framework of the structure and objectives of the Community'.[47] The ECJ had made it clear that it did not consider itself compelled to adhere to or be bound by the fundamental rights of the Basic Law. But what was unclear still was what the formulation of 'common' constitutional traditions meant more precisely and whether this would be sufficient appeasement for the growing concerns not only in West Germany, but also Italy too.

42 Davies 2012b, 86–87.
43 Davies 2012b, 101–102.
44 29/69, *Erich Stauder v City of Ulm – Sozialamt*, 1969, ECLI:EU:C:1969:57.
45 11/70, *Internationale Handelsgesellschaft mbH v Einfuhr- und Vorratsstelle für Getreide und Futtermittel*, 1970, ECLI:EU:C:1970:114.
46 11/70, *Internationale Handelsgesellschaft mbH v Einfuhr- und Vorratsstelle für Getreide und Futtermittel*, 1970, ECLI:EU:C:1970:114.
47 11/70, *Internationale Handelsgesellschaft mbH v Einfuhr- und Vorratsstelle für Getreide und Futtermittel*, 1970, ECLI:EU:C:1970:114.

PUSH BACK AND REACTION

By the start of the 1970s, it was becoming ever clearer that the ECJ's rights jurisprudence was indeed insufficient within the West German context. Going even further than the critique delivered by Wengler in 1968, Mainz Professor Hans-Heinrich Rupp launched a polemic attack against the deficiencies in the European legal system in a speech to the West German Academy of Judges in January 1970.[48] Rupp strongly criticised the transfer of public authority to structurally incongruent European institutions, observing that the integrity of the Basic Law had been sacrificed in the process and the ECJ's aspirations to become a European Constitutional Court were a 'farce'.[49] Rupp continued to famously declare the EC constituted 'not only a regime without a master, the use of power without a democratic sovereign, but also a regime without fundamental rights'.[50] Moreover, he claimed the declining popular support for integration at the end of the 1960s was due to the recognition that democratic traditions were being sacrificed to a non-democratic European technocracy. Rupp's strongly worded condemnation of the current state of integration captured both the long-standing concerns about rights protections, and – in the broader context of the 1968 movement – the growing saliency of the nature of democratic participation across Europe. Rupp's speech made a splash. The Frankfurt Verwaltungsgericht, which had initially referred to the ECJ in the *Internationale Handelsgesellschaft* case, re-referred the case to the BVerfG and cited Rupp in the process. It was this second referral by the Administrative Court that became *Solange I*, which was discussed at the beginning of this chapter. It is evident at this point that the structural congruence conditionality had become the most persuasive approach to European law among significant parts of West German legal academia, but also for a majority of the BVerfG's judges. The decision rested on the argument framed by 'the concordance of the two [Community and West German] legal orders' and the fact that the fundamental rights formulated in the Basic Law were an 'essential ... constitutional structure of the Basic Law'. As a result, the BVerfG would allow constitutional scrutiny of questions of European law until such point that the EC possessed a proper rights catalogue and sufficient democratic accountability. While no rights breach was found in the case at hand, the BVerfG had laid out an admonition and challenge to ECJ. It had now made explicit the constitutional limits of Article 24 and provided a warning to its European counterpart that it was committed to holding those lines.

The ECJ had attempted to forestall a national judicial mutiny in its *Nold* ruling, delivered just two weeks before *Solange I*. Here the ECJ elaborated on its understanding of nationally 'inspired' rights traditions by stating that 'the Court is bound to draw inspiration from constitutional traditions common to the member states, it

48 Davies 2012b, 106–108.

49 Rupp 1970, 353–359.

50 Rupp 1970, 354.

cannot therefore uphold measures which are incompatible with fundamental rights recognized and protected by the Constitutions of those states'. Moreover, it was inspired not only by national rights traditions, but also 'international treaties for the protection of human rights on which the member states have collaborated or of which they are signatories'.[51] This was likely too little, too late to pacify the BVerfG's judges.

Faced with a challenge from the Constitutional Court of the largest member state required the Commission to both defend the European legal system publicly and consider ways in which the concerns of the BVerfG could be allayed. This urgency was reaffirmed by the fact that the BVerfG's *Solange* admonition was, as mentioned previously, joining in chorus with the Italian Corte Costituzionale, which had issued a similar ruling, *Frontini*, on fundamental rights and structural congruence the previous year.[52]

Publicly, the West German government was faced with calls from the European Parliament for the Commission to commence an embarrassing infringement proceeding, even though the government's position in the Solange ruling was ardently pro-European.[53] Jan-Henrik Meyer's chapter in this book (Chapter 3) neatly captures this narrative from the European Parliament's perspective. Behind the scenes though, multiple forces were acting in a much more conciliatory manner, perhaps even sharing the BVerfG's concerns about the deficiencies in Community governance. For instance, central to the diplomatic efforts to respond to the BVerfG's admonition was the Director-General of the Commission's Legal Service at the time, the West German Walter Much.[54] Much had also been part of the negotiations on the Treaty of Paris and was familiar with the debates in the West German Advisory Group. It was telling that when he completed his doctorate at the University of Frankfurt after the negotiations were complete, Much selected Hans-Jürgen Schlochauer, longtime proponent of structural congruence, as his supervisor. Equally important to these discussions was the newly appointed West German Advocate General at the ECJ, Gerhard Reischl. It was Reischl who visited Bonn in late 1974 to suggest a feasible way out of the judicial bind – an agreement to bind the EC to the European Convention on Human Rights (ECHR).[55]

The West German government and the Commission positively received the Reischl Compromise, but it also raised some challenges. Full accession to the ECHR was deemed too problematic given that France had not yet abolished the death penalty and still limited individual petition rights (until 1981). Moreover, the BVerfG's stipulation in *Solange I* had been that the fundamental rights

[51] 44/73, *J. Nold Kohlen- und Baustoffgroßhandlung v Commission of the European Communities*, 1974, ECLI:EU:C:1974:51, case summary, paragraph 2.

[52] Corte Costituzionale, *Frontini e a.*, judgment no. 183 of 18 December 1973.

[53] Davies 2012b, 235–236.

[54] Davies 2012a, 425–426.

[55] Davies 2012a, 427–428.

catalogue for Europe should be drawn up by a parliamentary body. It would take some clever diplomacy[56] and some good fortune[57] to ensure that the Reischl Compromise at least *looked* like the European Parliament had initiated it. Nonetheless, after said wrangling had taken place, in 1977, a Joint Declaration by the three political institutions of the Community – the Commission, Parliament and Council – was issued, which voluntarily bound them to the standards of rights protection found in the ECHR. While assessed to be not fully comparable to the rights of the Basic Law by the West German Ministry of Justice, this was at least a move in the direction demanded by the BVerfG.

The second condition of *Solange I* was about democratic accountability and having a parliamentary body elected by general suffrage. The European Parliament had, historically since its inception as a Common Assembly in the ECSC, been underwhelming in both its powers and democratic credentials. This changed drastically in 1979, when the first direct elections to the European Parliament were held. The move towards direct elections certainly preceded the *Solange* ruling and cannot be definitively tied to the BVerfG's decision, unlike the Reischl Compromise, but nonetheless, the timing of the electoral changes was fortuitous. By the end of the 1970s, the EC had taken significant steps in rights protection safeguards and democratic governance.

What then of the ECJ? It was conspicuous in its absence from the 1977 Joint Declaration and, in fact, it was opposition to the proposal from the ECJ Presidents past and current, Robert Lecourt and Hans Kutscher, which stymied an attempt at the end of the 1970s to push for the full accession of the EC to the ECHR. In a dynamic that foreshadowed the ECJ's later Opinion 2/13 (2014), Kutscher expressed the ECJ's concern at no longer being the last resort in issues of European law and feared being overruled by the European Court of Human Rights. When Commission President Roy Jenkins took Kutscher out for lunch in November 1978, it was reported that Kutscher's discomfort at the idea of ECHR accession was only relieved when Jenkins conceded that the Commission was merely testing the waters and accession would probably never happen for another 'twenty years'.[58]

Instead of accession, the ECJ instead worked to further build out its right jurisprudence to address the challenge from the BVerfG. In the *Rutili* decision from 1975, the ECJ consolidated on its general reference to the ECHR after having

56 For instance, the West German government decided to use a working group on European rights established by the 1974 Paris Summit to push the issue of improving basic rights in the then Community. This was not really the intention of the committee when established. See Davies 2012a, 429.

57 Here, an example of the good fortune, was the convenient timing around the publication of a three-year long study into basic rights protection in the Community by the European Commission. See Davies 2012a, 429–430.

58 Davies 2016, 809.

cited Protocol 4 of the ECHR in the Nold decision of 1974.[59] Then, in *Hauer* – issued incidentally just a few weeks after the Jenkins-Kutscher lunch – the ECJ went further still.[60] After recounting the court's own development of rights jurisprudence since *Internationale Handelsgesellschaft* and *Nold*, as well as the 1977 Joint Declaration, the ECJ went on to discuss specific constitutional rules and practices found in the West German, Italian and Irish constitutions, and directly cited Article 1 of Protocol 1 of the ECHR. The ECJ reasoned, that

> thus it may be stated, taking into account the constitutional precepts common to the Member States and consistent legislative practices, in widely varying spheres, that the fact that Regulation . . . imposed restrictions on the new planting of vines cannot be challenged in principle. It is a type of restriction which is known and accepted as lawful, in identical or similar forms, in the constitutional structure of all the Member States.

It appeared that, in the face of possible accession to the ECHR and pressure from the BVerfG and Italian Corte Costituzionale, the ECJ wanted to use the *Hauer* ruling to demonstrate that it was given concrete form to its claim to be inspired by member states' constitutional traditions. It is also worthy further consideration that the ECJ also used its case law to further strengthen the constitutional position of the European Parliament in this period, notably in the *Luxembourg*[61] and *Les Verts*[62] rulings of 1983 and 1986, respectively. All in all, the ECJ managed to further build and refine the constitutional approach to building the European legal order by including fundamental rights, promoted by the BVerfG and the Italian Constitutional Court, but in a way that kept its authority intact and the European legal order autonomous and self-sufficient.

RAPPROCHEMENT AND CONSOLIDATION

In 1986, the BVerfG was faced with another case originating in the Frankfurt Administrative Court on the constitutionality of European law.[63] It had been twelve years since *Solange I* had been delivered and the new dynamics of European integration surrounding the Single European Act and the plans for a Single Market had fundamentally changed the fortunes of European integration. The new referral, much like *Solange I*, had already gone to the ECJ for preliminary ruling as well as the West German Bundesverwaltungsgericht. By the time the BVerfG issued its decision, the case had been rolling around the various levels of the European and West German legal system for a decade. A few years earlier, the

59 44/73, *J. Nold Kohlen- und Baustoffgroßhandlung v Commission of the European Communities*, 1974, ECLI:EU:C:1974:51 and 44/73, *J. Nold Kohlen- und Baustoffgroßhandlung v Commission of the European Communities*, 1974, ECLI:EU:C:1974:51.

60 44/79, *Liselotte Hauer v Land Rheinland-Pfalz*, 1979, ECLI:EU:C:1979:290.

61 230/81, *Grand Duchy of Luxembourg v European Parliament*, 1983, ECLI:EU:C:1983:32.

62 294/83, Parti *écologiste 'Les Verts' v European Parliament*, 1986, ECLI:EU:C:1986:166.

63 BVerfGE 73, 339, 22.10.1986, *Solange II*, 2 BvR 197/83.

BVerfG had withheld judgment on whether the developments in Community rights protection till that point had satisfied its concerns in *Solange I*.[64] Therefore, the BVerfG's decision in this new referral was much anticipated by those following the evolution of European law.

In a reversal of the *Solange I* ruling, the BVerfG argued that the changes wrought in the European legal system since 1974 were sufficient for it to withdraw its scrutiny of European law in West Germany. This new direction – *Solange II* – rested on the BVerfG's analysis of the ECJ's *Nold* and *Hauer* decisions, as well as the extra security offered by the 1977 Joint Declaration. The BVerfG's musings on these developments revealed that its exploration of 'the general principles of Community law' showed that its 'requirement of a catalogue of fundamental rights decreed by a parliament . . . [had] been satisfied in all the circumstances'. Moreover, the BVerfG's concomitant demand for a parliament elected by general suffrage and with legislative powers was not entirely necessary for the BVerfG to remove its review of European law. As such, the BVerfG considered its demands in *Solange I* met. In *Solange II*, a new equilibrium between the ECJ and BVerfG was achieved. But the seeming calm brought about by the *Solange II* ruling was in retrospect short-live. The BVerfG soon felt the need to address the extraordinary dynamics of European integration from 1989 to 1992 and help define the basic relationship of the united West Germany in the new European Union.

REIGNITING THE CONSTITUTIONAL CONFLICT: CHANGES AT THE START OF THE 1990S

In the early 1990s, the tension between the BVerfG and ECJ returned in full force and remains in place today as the two courts continue to negotiate, judicially, the parameters of European integration and the balance between the member states and European government. It is now arguably one of the most important dynamics within the entire integration process. Crucial areas of European public life are shaped by the BVerfG-ECJ dialogue, including the 'old' issues of democratic legitimacy[65] and rights protections,[66] but also now incorporating new areas such as monetary policy,[67] fiscal governance[68] and 'ultra vires' review.[69] How do we explain this new dynamic in what seemed, in the mid-1980s, like a settled issue? Again, we must turn to the structural congruence paradigm for our answer.

64 BVerfGE 52, 187, 25.07.1979, *Vielleicht*, 2 BvL 6/77.

65 BVerfGE 123, 267, 30.06.2009, *Lisbon*, 2 BvE 2/08, 2 BvE 5/08, 2 BvR 1010/08, 2 BvR 1022/08, 2 BvR 1259/08, 2 BvR 182/09.

66 BVerfGE 129, 300, 09.11.2011, *5% Threshold decision*, 2 BvC 4/10, 2 BvC 6/10, 2 BvC 8/10 and BVerfGE 135, 259, 26.02.2014, *3% Threshold decision*, 2 BvE 2/13, 2 BvE 5/13, 2 BvE 6/13, 2 BvE 7/13, 2 BvE 8/13, 2 BvE 9/13, 2 BvE 10/13, 2 BvE 12/13, 2 BvR 2220/13, 2 BvR 2221/13, 2 BvR 2238/13.

67 BVerfGE 154.17, 05.05.2020, *PSPP Decision*, 2 BvR 859/15, 2 BvR 1651/15, 2 BvR 2006/15, 2 BvR 980/16

68 BVerfGE 132, 195, 12.09.2012, *ESM Decision*, 2 BvR 1390/12, 2 BvR 1421/12, 2 BvR 1438/12, 2 BvR 1439/12, 2 BvR 1440/12 und 2 BvR 6/12 and BVerfGE 157, 332, 15.04.2021, *NGEU Decision*, 2 BvR 547/21.

69 BVerfGE 142, 123, 21.06.2016, *Gauweiler Decision*, 2 BvR 2728/13, 2 BvR 2728/13, 2 BvR 2729/13, 2 BvR 2730/13, 2 BvR 2731/13, 2 BvE 13/13.

Within three short years after the *Solange II* ruling, the geopolitical landscape for both West Germany and Europe changed in the most dramatic and fundamental fashion. The collapse of the Iron Curtain and the reunification of the two halves of West Germany became a reality and raised questions of genuine constitutional significance for both West Germany and the EC. At the European level, keenness to incorporate the reunified, larger and more influential Germany ever closer into the EC led to a push for an expansion in European governance that would bind the new Germany even more strongly to Europe. The result of this was the Maastricht Treaty, creating the European Union (EU) in 1993. While the new Union would place the European Council at the centre of power and not make European constitutionalism its legitimating principle, it did involve a very significant expansion of competences. Most importantly it planned the creation of an Economic and Monetary Union that would curb Germany's monetary supremacy in Europe, it added a package of home and justice affairs including a loosely defined and modest notion of European citizenship and finally created a distinct if again modest cooperation on foreign and defence policy. The two latter policy areas would be established on an intergovernmental basis. Nevertheless, the momentous and swift expansion of the competences of the EU created opposition in several member states, including the new united Germany. Uniquely, in the German political elite the main problem seemed to be that the EU did not build on European constitutionalism as a legitimating principle and that the political system prioritised the European Council and did not introduce sufficient democratic guarantees even if the European Parliament had now been given a limited form of co-decision.

German opponents of the Treaty of Maastricht raised a constitutional complaint to the BVerfG about the expansion of the competences of the new Union at the expense of the member states despite the 'lack of democracy' of the European political system.[70] This, it was claimed, violated their fundamental rights as well as notions of democratic accountability and as a result, German participation in the Maastricht Treaty should be denied. In response, the BVerfG reiterated its decision in *Solange II* that fundamental rights were now suitably protected by European law and rejected much of the separate complaints delivered by the Maastricht opposition. Instead, it narrowed its focus to one particular article of the Basic Law – Article 38, which determines the right to vote. In this, the BVerfG stated:

> Art 38 GG bars European integration from rendering the legitimation of state authority and the influence on the exercise of this authority, both of are provided by elections, void of meaning by transferring the functions and powers of the German *Bundestag* to the European level in a way that violates such elements of the principle of democracy that are considered inalienable under the Basic Law.[71]

[70] BVerfGE 89, 155, 12.10.1993, *Maastricht*, 2 BvR 2134, 2159/92.

[71] Federal Constitutional Court. 1995. *Statement by the Press Office of the Federal Constitutional Court.* Press Release No. 39/1995, 12 October 1995.

Furthermore, the BVerfG held that if EU law was to be directly applicable, the legislation transferring competency to the European authorities must be clear and precise, and 'if it remained unclear to which extent and scope the German legislature had approved the transfer of sovereign powers to be exercised at the European level, this would amount to a blanket authorisation and thus result in the disposal of sovereign powers'.[72]

However, the court ultimately held that the Maastricht Treaty did not meet these criteria and held the Treaty compatible with the democracy principle in Article 20. There were, however, further thoughts. While not in general rejecting the possibility of democratic participation in what it called a '*Staatenverbund*' (association of states), the BVerfG underlined that further transfer of member state sovereignty had to be carefully managed and only ensured through a legitimate transfer agreed to by the national parliament. The Maastricht Treaty had granted further substantial functions and powers to the EU which had 'not, as yet, been supported at the treaty level by a corresponding intensification and extension of the principles of democracy'.[73] Further, the BVerfG argued '*obiter dicta*' that

> it is therefore crucial, both from the point of view of treaty law and that of constitutional law, that the principles of democracy upon which the Union is based are extended in step with its integration, and that a living democracy is retained in the Member States while the process of integration is proceeding.[74]

Furthermore, the constitutional landscape within Germany was also changed fundamentally. The Basic Law had been thought of, in a way, as a temporary document in place until reunification was achieved. Now that this goal was met, constitutional changes were required. In 1992, a constitutional commission was established to address issues of constitutional significance. One of the many changes to the Basic Law that came about in this period coincided with Germany's signing of the Maastricht Treaty and saw a notable change to the 'European' articles of the Basic Law, particularly Article 24. As above, Article 24 had allowed for the transfer of sovereign competencies to international organisations and had long been the lever used for legitimating European integration. Structural congruence had come about as a result of the discussions around the conditions that would need to be met to allow Article 24 to be used for this purpose within the context of a partly inviolable constitution (Article 79.3). The constitutional amendments of the early 1990s saw the displacement of Article 24 with a newly crafted Article 23. Article 23 had previously been the 'reunification' article and had been fulfilled through for the establishment of a unified state in 1990. Symbolically, in its place, the new Article 23

72 Federal Constitutional Court. 1995. *Statement by the Press Office of the Federal Constitutional Court.* Press Release No. 39/1995, 12 October 1995.

73 Federal Constitutional Court. 1995. *Statement by the Press Office of the Federal Constitutional Court.* Press Release No. 39/1995, 12 October 1995.

74 Federal Constitutional Court. 1995. *Statement by the Press Office of the Federal Constitutional Court.* Press Release No. 39/1995, 12 October 1995.

was added in 1992 to redefine domestic constitutional stipulations related to European integration. Primarily, Article 23 addressed long-standing grievances of the German federal states about their lack of prominence in European policy formation. However, notably, Article 23 included a plain and undeniable affirmation of the structural congruence paradigm. The new text stated:

> With a view to establishing a united Europe, the Federal Republic of Germany shall participate in the development of the European Union, which is committed to democratic, social, and federal principles, to the rule of law, and to the principle of subsidiarity and guarantees a level of protection of basic rights essentially comparable to that afforded by this Basic Law.[75]

Structural congruence was no longer just a position held by some inside the German legal academy or a small majority of BVerfG judges. It was now a constitutional stipulation and ensuring that the Union's constitutional structure matched up to these standards became a mandate for the BVerfG.

The combination of a clearly laid out set of constitutional conditions for the transfer of competencies to European authorities combined with an expansive new treaty at the start of the 1990s ensured that the admonitory relationship between the BVerfG and ECJ would continue into the 2000s and beyond. How to allow for deeper European integration whilst maintaining the standards and identity of the domestic constitutional order? The generation of German Constitutional Court judges who would come to write the answers to this dilemma in the contemporary period have been influenced not only by the structural congruence paradigm, but by the writings of Herbert Kraus himself.[76]

CONCLUSION

The acceptance of European law by the highest level of the German judiciary has been a positive but conditional one. The BVerfG has accepted the autonomy and primacy of the EU's legal system, but not without conditions that protect the national constitutional identity. This conditionality has led to changes in the European legal system, such as clearer rights standards and increased democratic accountability. In this way, the BVerfG (along with other national courts) has been a co-constitutive player in the formation of the constitutional practice described in this book. West German governments in the post-war period had been a constant supporter of European integration, with enormous political, diplomatic and economic benefits gained by West German participation in European institutions. It is

[75] Article 23 West German Basic Law at www.gesetze-im-internet.de/englisch_gg/englisch_gg.html.

[76] See, for instance, the writings of Constitutional Court judges who have been particularly influential in European related decisions of the BVerfG since the 1990s. See the multiple references to Kraus's writings of the 1950s in Di Fabio 1993 or the terminology employed in Hommelhoff and Kirchhof 1994.

also without question that West German courts and litigants have been among the most prolific users of the European legal system. However, the highest levels of the West German judiciary have often articulated concerns about the nature of European democracy, governance and rights protections, particularly as the impact and authority of Community institutions increased through the jurisprudence of the ECJ. The conditionality of this acceptance is based on the structural congruence argument championed by scholars such as Herbert Kraus, Hans-Jürgen Schlochauer and Hans-Heinrich Rupp. This is ultimately a pro-European, pro-integration position, but not one that accepts 'more Europe' at the potential cost of national democratic and constitutional standards. This is the position ultimately adopted as a framework for judicial interpretation by the BVerfG.

Different interpretations can be given to explain the BVerfG's willingness to accept the structural congruence argument and condition its acceptance of the ECJ's jurisprudence. These can be legal or political in nature.

Legally, the West German Constitution prior to its revision in 1992 contained a tension between the immutability of its fundamental structure and provisions (Article 79.3) and its openness to transfer sovereign competencies to international institutions that may, in theory, not share the same qualitative democratic nature (Article 24). This tension was sharpened by the ECJ's constitutional interpretation of European law in the 1960s and 1970s, particularly its reluctance to have European law limited by national (constitutional) law. When assessing the validity of the ECJ's aspirational claims, the West German legal academy and judiciary largely decided that fundamental rights and democratic accountability in European governance were insufficient to go without some kind of safeguarding at the national level. Introducing direct effect and primacy into what was initially thought of as an international treaty with little to no fundamental rights protection or democratic accountability was a step too far for the West German legal academy. This prompted the BVerfG to articulate where it drew the boundaries of its willingness to cooperate by the mid-1970s (alongside its Italian counterpart).

Such a blow from two large member state constitutional courts forced real and substantive changes not only in the way the ECJ developed its proto-federal European legal order but also for the development of the EC institutions more generally. To temper the judicial conflict, there were changes in the ECJ's case law in order to secure that fundamental right were integrated in the European legal order (Hauer, etc.), as well as the joint declaration of the political institutions binding themselves to the ECHR in 1977 (even if the ECJ rejected the possibility of joining this declaration in a historical foreshadowing of its later Opinion 2/13.)[77] Finally, the constant pressure to increase the legislative role of the European Parliament from 1979 onwards should also be considered in this light. These changes at first appeased the BVerfG sufficiently, as expressed in its *Solange II*

77 Davies 2016, especially 810–814.

ruling, but the changes in both European and West German politics at the turn of the 1990s opened the potential for conflict again.

Politically, we also find two courts born at the same time and seeking to consolidate their institutional existence, but with widely differing and, in some part, competing 'teloi': the ECJ being driven by its teleological choice to deepen and further European integration and promote its claim for constitutional autonomy of the European legal order; and its West German counterpart's task centred on the securing of the national constitutional order which it based on the basic rights and the compliance of all public authorities with its tenets against the background of overwhelming political and economic support for European integration. In more recent years, the BVerfG's tone has been sharper and the details around which it is willing to set boundaries on European authority have become narrower and more technical in nature. It is therefore reasonable to describe the inter-court dialogue captured in the 1974–1986 *Solange I* and *II* period as qualitatively different and more cooperative in nature than the more recent, post-Maastricht relationship.

***

In the overall narrative offered by this volume – that the aspirational constitutional practice pursued by the ECJ and allied Community institutions, such as the European Parliament, Commission and its Legal Service ultimately floundered at the Maastricht Treaty and in the face of national judicial opposition – the West German component of this story offers some important nuance. It is clear that the competing currents in post-war West German European policy have at the same time resisted and shaped the development of a federalist vision of Europe. West German politicians, from Adenauer on, have often pushed for this outcome, largely supported by a West German populace recognizing Europe as their new multilateral, peaceful home. However, the conflict between the BVerfG and ECJ over the years has raised the spectre of national judicial revanchism, particularly when other higher national courts have emulated the *Solange* doctrine. Requiring Europe to meet West German standards of rights protection and democratic accountability could certainly be interpreted as a form of West German 'rights imperialism'[78] or the imposition of a constitutional 'Modell Deutschland' on the rest of Europe. The Maastricht decision was heavily criticised at the time.[79] However, the transition between the *Solange I* and *Solange II* decisions, with the willingness of European institutions to genuinely listen to national judicial concerns and the proven openness of national judicial authorities to accept the adaptations in European governance reminds us of the possibility that even an admonitory dialogue can ultimately be positive.

78 Tomuschat 1990, 351.

79 Weiler 1995.

7

To Be or Not to Be: France and European Law

Alexandre Bernier and Morten Rasmussen

France has occupied a vital role in the history of European integration due to the size of its economy and its geopolitical importance. However, French European policy has always been deeply ambivalent.[1] In contrast to West Germany and Italy, that were thoroughly defeated during the Second World War, and consequently found it easier to embrace the delegation of powers to a new supranational European political system, French political parties and state elites found it much more challenging to accept any diminution of the power of the French state. This meant that European federalism, despite important French supporters, found its most vehement opponents in France, in particular from the right wing of the political spectra. It is thus not surprising that the strongest opposition to the constitutional practice of European law would come from France during the period explored in this book.

Within the field of law and politics studies, the French reception of European law has long figured as a prominent case. Scholars have highlighted the importance of the strong notion of state power in French politics and in the French court system and delivered intricate analyses of how the relationship between French courts and the European Court of Justice (ECJ) was slow to develop compared to other member states.[2] As demonstrated by Jens Plötner, the French higher courts (Council of State (Conseil d'État), Cour de cassation and Conseil constitutionnel) adopted divergent positions on European law according to their nature, mutual interrelation and relationship with the legislative and executive powers. Plötner also delivered an excellent sociological analysis of the different courts in order to explain their position, and highlighted the agency of a handful of key actors.[3] Karen Alter based her eminent study of the contested national reception of European law from 2001 partly on the French example and argued that despite resistance at the political level and from the guardians of state sovereignty, the Conseil d'État, several French lower courts collaborated willingly through the

[1] We would like to thank Laurent Warlouzet for his comments on this chapter.

[2] The first comprehensive analysis which remains useful was Buffet-Tchakaloff 1985.

[3] Plötner 1998.

preliminary ruling procedure under Article 177 of the European Economic Community Treaty (EEC Treaty), as they had an interest in circumventing French higher courts. By the means of a large number of interviews, Alter managed to identify additional actors in her analysis, however, her narrative generally takes the shape of an institutional analysis.[4]

This chapter offers a new account of the French reception of the constitutional practice of European law based for the first time on systematic archival research.[5] By placing the history of French reception of European law in a broader political and social context than done in prior research and using new primary sources found in private, state and European archives, it is possible to offer an analysis that combines political and institutional history with a more fine-grained understanding of the agency of the many actors involved than the state of the art.

We argue that the French reception of European law can in fact best be understood as a broad political battle over the nature of European integration and France's position in Europe. This political battle played out between two informal and loosely organised groups – or 'trends of thoughts' – of politicians, civil servants and judges, almost all of them jurists by education. On the one hand, were the 'supranationalists' who predominantly came from the ranks of French Christian Democracy and fully supported the strengthening and even federalisation of the European institutions. On the other hand, the 'souverainistes' (supporters of national sovereignty), who were overwhelmingly Gaullists, fought against the constitutional practice of European law that was launched from the early 1960s onwards, and in general opposed strong supranational institutions and plans for a federal Europe. These two groups engaged in a long-term confrontation against the backdrop of not only European integration, but also the broader development of French society and France's place in the world.

It is a central argument of the chapter that this long-time struggle between supranationalists and souverainistes not only came to determine the French reception of European law, but it also shaped the development of European law at the European level. French civil servants and judges in the European institutions played a vital role in facilitating the breakthrough of a constitutional interpretation of European law and over time consolidating it into a broader practice. France thus played a double role in the making of European law. Finally, it is important to underline that the chronological narrative exploring this battle, divided into five sections, is multi-causal and includes numerous examples of how varying contexts, contingencies and unintended consequences shaped the interaction between French and European law.

4 Alter 2001.

5 The present chapter draws primarily upon the research undertaken by one of the authors within the framework of a PhD thesis defended in 2018. Bernier 2017.

THE FOURTH REPUBLIC AND THE FOUNDATION OF EUROPEAN INTEGRATION, 1945–1958

France was the key driving force of European integration in the late 1940s and first half of the 1950s. In a post-war world, where France could not compete with the superpowers, and where the decolonisation process first with Indochina and later with Algeria led to a gradual diminishment of French international power, European integration was widely regarded in the French political and administrative elite as a key strategy for consolidating French power and independence.[6] This went hand in hand with the need to reinvigorate the French economy and establish strong political links with the new West German Federal Republic founded in 1949.[7]

In 1950, the Christian Democratic (Mouvement républicain populaire – MRP) government, guided by Minister of Foreign Affairs Robert Schuman, launched the Schuman plan that led to the establishment of the European Coal and Steel Community (ECSC) – a new supranational organisation that involved the surrendering of national sovereignty – in 1952.[8] This was quickly followed by another French initiative to create a European army, due to the intensification of the Cold War caused by the outbreak of the Korean war, that led to the negotiation of a European Defence Community (EDC) in 1952 and intense debates on the possible establishment of a European Political Community (EPC) in parallel.[9] Although a majority of the French National Assembly ratified the Treaty of Paris in 1951, the prospects of a supranational, or even federal, EPC was far from uncontroversial in France. With the electoral fortunes of the MRP deteriorating in the first half of the 1950s, the majority in favour of supranational integration evaporated and in the summer of 1954, the National Assembly rejected a proposal to consider the ratification of the EDC (and consequently also the EPC).[10] When a relaunch of European integration was attempted from 1955 to 1957 by the Benelux countries, it was a new government coalition led by the socialist Guy Mollet that successfully negotiated and obtained the ratification of the Treaties of Rome that established the European Communities (EC).[11] However, the EC, now adding a European Economic Community (EEC) and Euratom to the already existing ECSC, toned down the supranational element and placed national governments at the centre of decision-making in order to ensure that the plans could pass the test of the French National Assembly.[12]

French influence was deeply felt in the various initiatives and projects of European integration that took place from 1950 to 1958. The ECSC was very

6 Lequesne 2015.
7 Milward 1992; Lynch 1997.
8 Milward 1984; Gillingham 1991.
9 Griffith 2000.
10 Parson 2003.
11 Milward 1992, 196–224; Warlouzet 2011a, 35–101.
12 Boerger 2012, 341–355; Boerger and Rasmussen 2014.

much shaped by the ideas of Jean Monnet, the leader of the Planning Commission (Commissariat du plan), who wanted to establish a strong technocratic executive – the High Authority (HA) – with genuine supranational powers to organise the European markets of coal and steel. The French government and Monnet nevertheless had to compromise during the negotiations with the Benelux countries, West Germany and Italy on the nature of the institutional system, adding a Council of Ministers, an Assembly and a Court of Justice to the proposed HA. However, with regard to the Court at least, the French influence meant that it was largely modelled on the French Conseil d'État, as an administrative court that would ensure the legality of the actions of the HA.[13]

Overall, the ECSC became less important economically than expected and as a consequence the Common Market of Coal and Steel was only partially established with the member states having limited interest in creating a genuine competition policy.[14] The relative lack of importance of the organisation after 1954 was also evident in its legal dimension, where the new Court of Justice of the ECSC (ECJ) that began to pronounce its judgments only in 1954 focused mainly on technical and economic questions and seldom ventured into doctrinal questions nor considered the deeper nature of the legal order created.[15] Nevertheless, French civil servants and Christian Democrats, such as a young legal councillor Michel Gaudet, who was employed in the legal service, and Advocate General Maurice Lagrange did test controversial ideas about the constitutionality of European law and the potential status of the ECJ as a future European Supreme Court. Such notions did not gain any acceptance beyond a very narrow circle of employees of the legal service of the HA, the Court and a few academics.[16] Nor were they supported by the French judge in the ECJ, Jacques Rueff, who as a prominent economist with a strong neoliberal outlook, was much more interested in the economic and technical aspects of the ECSC.

THE POLITICAL BASIS OF EUROPEAN POLICY IN FRANCE: TWO OPPOSING POSITIONS

Inside France, the political importance and dynamics of European integration during the 1950s increasingly led to a politicisation of the question and the development of two distinct positions, 'supranationalists' and 'souverainistes'. After General Charles de Gaulle had helped liberated France, as leader of the Free French Forces, and formed a provisional government in 1945 that oversaw the first free election of a Constituent Assembly, he withdrew from political life in January 1946. The Constituent Assembly was dominated by three equally strong political parties in

[13] Boerger 2012.
[14] Witchke 2009.
[15] For an empirical analysis consult the excellent Scheingold 1965.
[16] For a biographical study of Michel Gaudet consult Boerger and Rasmussen 2017.

France, the MRP (150 seats), Socialists (146 seats) and Communists (159 seats), which together drafted the Constitution of the Fourth Republic. In reaction to the new Fourth Republic with its emphasis on the Parliament, the supporters of de Gaulle created a new party in 1947, the Rassemblement du peuple Français (RPF). However, since the RPF failed to obtain a substantial number of seats in the National Assembly in the 1951 election, it ended up exercising most of its influence in the upper house of the French Parliament, the Council of the Republic (Conseil de la République). Here the senatorial elections of November 1948 had offered the RPF 57 out of 301 seats compared to the only 22 seats to the MRP. The new Fourth Republic continued the tendency of its predecessor of unstable governments, caused by deep splits in French society over the role of the Church, social and economic questions, decolonisation and European policy.[17]

As the question of France's position in Europe came to the fore in the 1950s, two opposing positions emerged in a debate. In the MRP, a strong support for European unification, and even European federalism, had been dominant since the war and French politicians participated in a broader transnational network between Christian Democratic parties in continental Europe from the late 1940s onwards.[18] Here the view was that even if the creation of a Federal Europe required the surrendering of national sovereignty to new supranational or federal institutions,[19] the result would be the overall strengthening of French power through Europe. Key Christian Democratic politicians such as Robert Schuman, Pierre-Henri Teitgen, Robert Lecourt and Alain Poher took the lead, backed by Socialist politicians such as André Philip or Guy Mollet. There were also a number of important French jurists: judges, lawyers and European civil servants that over the next decades would work in favour of this position such as Maurice Rolland, Adolphe Touffait, Paul-Francois Ryziger, Maurice Lagrange, Paul Coste-Floret, George Vedel and Michel Gaudet.

Confronting the MRP and the pro-European coalition in the national debate on European integration, were members of the RPF and none more so than Michel Debré, a close associate of de Gaulle. The latter thundered against the political class of the new Republic, whom he considered as incompetent as that of the Third Republic. This incompetence was perhaps most evident according to Debré in the willingness of the MRP to give away French sovereignty to a vague, technocratic European elite in supranational institutions.[20] To Debré and other Gaullists, French sovereignty was sacred and could not be shared. European cooperation was certainly important, but it ought not entail what they believed would be the gradual dissolution of the French nation-state into a united Europe. Debré considered for example the Treaties of Rome to be unconstitutional and illegitimate as they aimed 'for national sovereignty to be abrogated [by granting] excessive legal

17 A standard introduction to this period remains Berstein and Milza 1991.
18 Kaiser 2007.
19 Larqué and Lusson 2006, 209–218.
20 Bernier forthcoming.

powers to supranational authorities'. The force of law could only find its expression in the 'liberty, the Nation and the Republic' and certainly not in an artificial process of European integration.[21] This was a position that would be shared by a number of Gaullists over the coming decades, including Paul Reuter, André Gros, Jean Foyer, Alain Peyrefitte, Jean-Jacques de Bresson, Michel Aurillac and Etienne Burin des Roziers. However, a certain number of socialists also shared the same scepticism of a supranational Europe, including Nicole Questiaux.

The deep divide between the MRP and the RPF was in some ways paradoxical. During the war many of the most bitter opponents over the European questions had worked together either in the Resistance or in the Free French.[22] Some of them had developed strong personal ties, for example Debré and Teitgen. But disagreements had long been simmering since the constitution-making process of post-war France in 1946. Tensions were already considerable at the time of the creation of the ECSC in 1951. However, the proposal to create a European army led to a complete polarisation of the debate in 1953–1954.[23] Disagreements became so heated that it severed the friendly links between Debré and Teitgen and finally consolidated the two opposing positions, that is, the supranationalists and the souverainistes.[24]

EUROPEAN LAW AND THE FRENCH LEGAL SYSTEM

The legal roots of French European policy arguably began with adoption of the new Constitution of the Fourth Republic in 1946. In a post-war world where a reinvigorated United Nations and multilateral cooperation were to reshape international politics, the relationship between national constitutions and international law was crucial. Since the Constituent Assembly was dominated by a coalition of MRP and the socialists, side-lining the Communist Party, their vision on international and European cooperation very much shaped this question. Two Christian Democratic law professors, Teitgen and Coste-Floret drafted the two Articles, 26 and 28, that defined how France would receive international law, following a monist model that gave international law primacy over national law.[25]

Although the constitutional reform constituted an important step towards opening France to international and future European law, alone it remained insufficient.[26] The French legal system had since the French revolution been

[21] M. Debré, 'Intervention of 19 July Regarding Discussion of a Draft Law Concerning the European Economic Community and the European Atomic Energy Community'. *Journal officiel du Conseil de la République* 45 (1957): 1626–1636.

[22] Bernier 2017, 70–72.

[23] M. Debré, 'Intervention of 12 May Relating to Filing a Motion for a Resolution Regarding a Possible Revision of the Constitution Prior to the Discussion of the EDC Draft'. *Journal officiel du Conseil de la République* 30 (1953): 1024; M. Debré, Intervention of 25 May Relating to the Constitutionality of the EDC Draft Treaty'. *Journal officiel du Conseil de la République* 32 (1954): 1026–1027.

[24] Bernier forthcoming.

[25] Bernier 2017, 62–64. See also Bougrab 2002, 410.

[26] Plötner 1998, 41.

designed to reflect the subordinate role of French courts towards the Parliament.[27] The highest court in private law and criminal matters the Cour de cassation and the highest court of administrative law the Conseil d'État were consequently not inclined to engage in judicial review of the conformity of French law with international treaties, a tendency strengthened by the fact that the Conseil d'État had no formal basis in the French Constitution and could be eliminated by parliament by the means of a simple law.[28] In the 1930s, both the Cour de cassation with the *Sanchez* decision (that gave rise to the Matter doctrine taking the name of the procureur général performing in the case) and the Conseil d'État's *Arrighi* decision established a precedent that in practice gave subsequent French law precedence over international treaties.[29] Although the Cour de cassation had begun to question this practice with the 1950 *Hauck* judgment,[30] the doctrine remained particularly strong within the Conseil d'État. Finally, the centralised French administration, dating back mostly from Napoleonic times, with few powers left to local authorities, had little concept of what a federal organisation of law and administration would imply and as a consequence had found it difficult to adjust to the new supranational Europe.[31]

THE GAULLIST REPUBLIC AND THE REJECTION OF EUROPEAN LAW, 1958–1969

With the collapse of the Fourth Republic over the Algerian war and the ascendance of de Gaulle to power in what would become the Fifth Republic, French participation in the new European Communities planned in the Treaties of Rome seemed quite unlikely. However, to the surprise of most observers, de Gaulle opted for the EC as the most suitable framework for the modernisation of the French economy, which was essential to reassert French power in the world again.[32] During this decade, de Gaulle would continuously pursue a policy of developing the Common Market, including the Common Agricultural Policy (CAP) outlined in the EEC Treaty. However, at the same time, he also rejected British attempts to join the EC in 1963 and 1967 and harboured a deep reluctance and even opposition to the role of the supranational institutions, in particular the EEC Commission

27 Reuter 1968, 27.

28 Although established by the revolutionary Constitution of 13 December 1799 (First Republic) and granted an existence in the Constitution of 28 October 1848 (Second Republic), the Conseil d'État was deprived of any constitutional guarantee in the three following Constitutions (Third, Fourth and Fifth Republics).

29 Cour de cassation (Chambre civile), 22 December 1931, *Sanchez*, *Dalloz* 1932.I.131; Conseil d'État (Sections administratives), 6 November 1936, *Arrighi*, n° 41221, published in *Recueil Lebon* 966, 1936.

30 Cour de cassation (Chambre criminelle), 3 June 1950, *Hauck*, *Dalloz* 1950.I.521. See also Bernier 2017, 74–75.

31 Bjøl 1966.

32 Warlouzet 2011b.

under the leadership of the German law professor and federalist Walter Hallstein.[33] The effects of this European policy were hugely beneficial to the French economy that now grew at high rates, expanding industrial exports both inside the EC and internationally, and consolidating the agricultural sector by means of the CAP.[34] At the political level, de Gaulle's sceptical stance towards supranational institutions culminated with the Empty Chair Crisis in the autumn of 1965, where France boycotted the Council as a reaction to the EEC Commission's plans to expand the powers of the supranational institutions in relation to the creation of the EC's own finances. The Empty Chair Crisis ended with a great defeat of the EEC Commission and clearly broke the back of any federal ambitions Hallstein may have had for the remaining of the 1960s. However, although France obtained an informal veto right in the Luxembourg Compromise that solved the crisis, de Gaulle did not manage to change the Treaties of Rome, and consequently the partly supranational institutional and legal nature of the EC remained intact.[35]

Despite the Gaullist European policy during the decade, French supranationalists, in the shape of two Christian Democrats, Michel Gaudet and Robert Lecourt, would deeply influence the development of European law. In fact, Gaudet and Lecourt were arguably instrumental in the breakthrough of the constitutional interpretation of European law that the ECJ launched in the *Van Gend en Loos* (1963) and *Costa v ENEL* (1964) judgments. This breakthrough happened despite the fact that the Treaties of Rome had been a great disappointment to European federalists. It placed national governments at the centre of decision-making in the Council, reduced the role of the EEC Commission to initiate legislation and administer certain policies and did little to enhance the powers of the European Parliament (EP) and the ECJ. The primary law of the treaties was to be translated into concrete action through the proposals of the EEC Commission followed by Council legislation and then enacted by national administrations and applied by national courts. Any member state infringement of the treaty was to be handled by a politicised mechanism run by the Commission (Articles 169–171 of the EEC Treaty) that might end up before the ECJ; there were however no penalties. Similarly, a preliminary reference mechanism (Article 177 of the EEC Treaty) to ensure the uniform interpretation of European law across member states, where national courts sent questions to the ECJ, rested in practice solely on the active cooperation of national judges. Overall, national constitutional and administrative orders were kept intact, the treaties were formulated as international law, with the exception of competition policy, and Community action required the active cooperation of national administrations and courts. Despite this rudimentary institutional and legal setup that was based on active member states cooperation, the ambitions of economic integration of the EEC were sweeping and potentially transformative for

33 Ludlow 2006a.

34 Warlouzet 2011a and 2011b; Knudsen 2009.

35 Ludlow 2006a; Palayret et al. 2006; Bajon 2012.

the societies of the six member states, namely the European organisation of a common market (including agriculture, fishery and transport), a common competition policy and a common external trade policy.[36] Gaudet participated in the negotiations of the Treaties of Rome as legal expert of the ECSC in the Groupe de rédaction, but the committee worked under serious political constraints and only to a very limited extent was it possible to push the treaty texts in a constitutional direction.[37] Nevertheless, to Gaudet the task ahead was to make the case that 'there is something federal, if not a federal State, in our Communities'.[38]

To Hallstein and the EEC Commission, the modest institutional and legal blueprint of the treaties was not considered any hindrance in pursuing a gradual federalisation of the EC. While France blocked the strengthening of the EEC Commission and EP in the reform of community finance during the Empty Chair Crisis, the legal sphere was another important arena for the federal initiatives of the Commission. Here Hallstein nominated Gaudet as new director of the legal service of the EEC Commission and the latter would pursue a constitutional interpretation of European law already in the first preliminary reference submitted to the ECJ in the Bosch case in 1961.[39] Although unsuccessful at first, Gaudet managed to convince the ECJ in the *Van Gend en Loos* case and the *Costa v ENEL* case to adopt a new constitutional interpretation of European law. Here Lecourt, who paradoxically had been nominated as new French judge in 1962 by Gaullist Prime Minister Debré,[40] played a leading role in cajoling the majority in the Court to take such a daring and revolutionary step.[41]

The immediate effect beyond the doctrinal realm of European law was fairly limited, however, as long as national administrations and courts did not cooperate with the EC. The question was, consequently, how did Gaullist France react to the new constitutional interpretation of European law, and did it allow national courts to cooperate with the ECJ?

The answer to this question is complex. At the European level, Gaullist France did not develop a coherent policy to address the legal revolution. However, at the domestic level, the different Gaullist governments of the decade relatively effectively ensured that French courts would not accept the constitutional interpretation of European law and abstain from cooperating with the ECJ through the preliminary reference mechanism. Nevertheless, supranationalist lawyers and judges did manage to make some limited inroads into this Gaullist blockade against European law in particular through the Cour d'Appel de Paris and eventually the Cour de Cassation.

36 Boerger 2012; Rasmussen 2014.

37 Rasmussen 2023.

38 Archive of Eric Stein (AES). Box 6. Letter from Michel Gaudet to Eric Stein on 18 March 1958.

39 Rasmussen 2014, 156–163, 150–151.

40 French National Archives (FNA). Collection 'Michel Debré' (2DE11). Letter from Debré to Lecourt on 1 March 1962.

41 Davies and Rasmussen 2014.

Why did Gaullist France not develop a more sustained effort at the EC level to counter the legal revolution? What is discovered from careful archival research is that de Gaulle and the top political leadership were generally not much concerned with the legal development of European integration. The main reasons for this were probably the somewhat theoretical nature of the constitutional interpretation at the time, but also because the consequences of European law cases could relatively easily be contained in France. The main exception to this trend was Debré, who was Prime Minister from 1959 to 1962, only to return first as Minister of the Economic and Finance from 1966 to 1968 and then as Minister of Foreign Affairs in 1968–1969. His background as administrative lawyer and Conseiller d'État probably made him much more aware of the potential importance of the legal dimension of European integration. As a result, the formulation of French foreign policy with regard to European law was largely left to the legal service of the Ministry of Foreign Affairs and the General Secretariat dealing with European economic cooperation (SGCI), although government ministers occasionally became involved in important cases before French courts. Both seemed more concerned with the material part of ECJ cases and perhaps as a result of this, possible reform of the ECJ did not figure among the French demands during the Empty Chair Crisis of 1965.

The lack of involvement of the political leadership was evident in the inconsistent French response to the seminal cases that launched the constitutional interpretation of European law. The French approach to European law followed the original understanding of the Treaties of Rome, when tested in the first preliminary reference that reached the ECJ in 1961. The *Bosch* case dealt with competition policy and the possible direct effect of Article 85. The French representatives Gros and de Bresson, from the legal service of the Ministry of Foreign Affairs, assisted by a former legal expert negotiating the Treaty of Paris and the EDC Treaty, Reuter, believed the case should be declared inadmissible by the ECJ because it dealt with the application of European law in a member state, which fell within the competence of national courts.[42] If accepted the ECJ would misuse the preliminary reference mechanism to circumvent a politically sensitive set of negotiations by the Council that in parallel were developing the new European competition policy. In the end, the judgment of the ECJ avoided intervening directly in the ongoing negotiations on competition policy, but by accepting the case, the preliminary reference mechanism could now be used indirectly to check the application of European law in the member states before the ECJ.[43] Neither the ECJ nor the French representatives commented upon the first attempt by the Commission to propose a constitutional interpretation of European law during the case.[44]

42 FNA. Collection 'Premier ministre – SGCI – Affaire Bosch' (19771466/244). Letter from Secretary General François-Xavier Ortoli to Head of the Legal Service André Gros on 27 October 1961.

43 13/61, *Kledingverkoopbedrijf de Geus en Uitdenbogerd v Robert Bosch GmbH et al.*, 1962, ECLI:EU:C:1962:11.

44 The argument was that the Treaties of Rome had constitutional features, created obligations directly for citizens and thus had a presumption for being self-executing.

In light of the intervention in the *Bosch* case, it could be expected that the legal service of the Ministry of Foreign Affairs would also have intervened in the *Van Gend en Loos* case and the *Costa v ENEL* case. However, in both cases France did not submit positions before the ECJ. The departure of Gros to become judge at the International Court of Justice in 1964 as well as Reuter's involvement with the *Shell Berre* case, to which we shall return, meant that the legal service was already functioning at full capacity in 1963–1964. The *Van Gend en Loos* case apparently went under the radar of Gros and was handled by Lucien Hubert, who did not believe an intervention was necessary.[45] When Gros left the legal service Hubert took over as new director. Whereas the *Van Gend en Loos* case was not seriously discussed in the French administration, the implications of the *Costa v ENEL* case were carefully considered by the SGCI in correspondence with several ministries to assess whether France should submit a position. The focus was on what possible consequences the Italian nationalisation of a major energy firm could have for the rules of the Treaties of Rome, but there was also an awareness of the doctrinal importance of the case, in particular by de Bresson. In the end, the technical ministries as well as the Ministry of Foreign Affairs did not believe a French intervention was necessary, and de Bresson did not manage to change the decision despite several attempts.[46]

If France did not manage to intervene decisively in the seminal cases that introduced the constitutional interpretation of European law, to what extent did the Gaullist governments and administration attempt to influence the ECJ by the means of nominations of judges? Again, the evidence suggests a lack of strategic use of the nominations on the side of France. The first nomination of the Gaullist regime was remarkably of Lecourt, to replace Jacques Rueff, who despite French insistence could not continue as a judge while also serving as a key economic advisor of de Gaulle.[47] Lecourt had left the Debré government in August of 1961, and Debré and de Gaulle wanted to find a suitable position for the troublesome Christian Democrat. Clearly, even Debré did not at the time fear the damage Lecourt could do in the ECJ to Gaullist European policy.[48] Despite the fact that Lecourt had been publicly vocal about the importance of the legal revolution,[49] his mandate was renewed in 1964, and he ascended to become President of the ECJ from 1967 to 1976. In 1964, the mandate of Advocate General, Maurice Lagrange, also ended and this time the Conseil d'État and the Gaullist government found a new member,

45 Lucien Hubert had been part of Jean Monnet's team during the proposal of the Schuman Plan and was likely more pro-European than the other members of the legal service of the Ministry of Foreign Affairs. See Bernier 2017, 112.

46 See Bernier 2017, 113–118 for the detailed analysis.

47 Cohen 2013a.

48 Rasmussen 2010a.

49 Lecourt 1963.

Joseph Gand, who they believed could defend the interest of France.[50] Nevertheless, with the nomination and renewal of the mandate of Lecourt, Gaullist France ironically made a major contribution to the development of a constitutional practice in European law.

Only by the end of the 1960s did the Gaullist regime seriously consider a reform of the ECJ. This happened during the negotiations on the Luxembourg protocol of the Brussels Convention on jurisdiction and the enforcement of judgments in civil and commercial matters that was ultimately signed on 3 June 1971.[51] The Luxembourg protocol was supposed to confer jurisdiction on the ECJ within the Convention by means of a preliminary reference mechanism. During the negotiations it turned out, despite informal protests of the ECJ judges, that the Belgian, German and French governments wanted to limit the preliminary reference mechanism to courts of appeal (Belgian and West Germany) and supreme courts (all three countries). Negotiations culminated in 1969–1970, and both the legal service of the Ministry of Foreign Affairs and Minister of Foreign Affairs Debré considered using a revised preliminary reference mechanism in the Luxembourg protocol as a template for a future EC reform of Article 177. However, in the end, the resignation of de Gaulle in 1969 and the new more pro-European policy of his successor George Pompidou meant that such plans never materialised. However, despite renewed attempts by the President of the ECJ, Lecourt, the French position was only partially revised. France continued to support the Belgian-German position. In the end, only courts of appeal were included, specified with a precise list the courts involved, and in addition these were not necessarily obliged to refer cases to Luxembourg.[52] The ambition of Debré to seriously reform the ECJ was, nevertheless, defeated by the resignation of de Gaulle.

To conclude, de Gaulle and his government did not manage to counter the legal revolution. The question never entered the highest political level despite the fact that de Gaulle prioritised the battle against the supranational institutions of the EC. The consequences of the legal revolution were still limited and could not compete with more urgent political questions that crossed the desk of the General at the Elysée Palace.

If the Gaullist regime generally did not prioritise countering the development of a constitutional interpretation of European law at the European level, its dominance of national politics during the 1960s were massive. The Gaullist governments and the state administration generally tried to secure a high degree of freedom of manoeuvre for the French state on economic questions even when in contradiction with European legislation or the Treaties of Rome. This was perhaps not so different

[50] FNA. Collection 'Conseil d'État – Dossier Joseph Gand' (20040382/78). Note of 31 July 1964 from Parodi to Couve de Murville.

[51] Fritz 2015; Fritz 2017.

[52] Fritz 2015.

from the policies of other member states during the 1960s, but in the French case it was coupled with a willingness on the side of the executive to promote before French courts an explicit rejection of cooperating with the ECJ.

Winning both the first and second presidential elections in 1958 and 1965, de Gaulle and his newly reconstituted Gaullist party – Union pour la nouvelle République (UPR) – dominated French politics during the 1960s. The main opposition force became the Socialist Party and while the MRP participated in the Gaullist government until 1962 it became increasingly marginalised, only maintaining some influence in the Senate, before being disbanded in 1967. Following this, MRP members would join other parties including the UPR. Nevertheless, the supranationalists did their best to promote European law in France and achieved some limited success.

The framework for their activities was the Association des Juristes Européens (AJE) that had been established in 1954 by a number of pro-European jurists including Maurice Rolland, Touffait (who worked as chef de cabinet of Coste-Floret, Lecourt and Teitgen in the several ministerial positions they held), the important socialist politician André Philip, and a small group of lawyers from the Cour d'Appel de Paris. In 1961 the AJE director Rolland assisted by Gaudet established the European umbrella organisation Fédération Internationale pour le droit Européen (FIDE) that brought together legal associations on European law from all the member states to facilitate the reception of European law in the member states and work closely with the Commission (see Chapter 4).[53] During the 1960s, the AJE brought together key supranationalists who worked with European law including Rolland (who during the 1960s was director and judge in the Criminal Chamber of the Cour de Cassation), Touffait (President of the Cour d'Appel de Paris), Paul-Francois Ryziger (lawyer), Lagrange, Teitgen and Vedel and tried to inform both academics, lawyers and judges about European law. In 1965 for example, Gaudet and the AJE organised a General Assembly in order to discuss the preliminary reference mechanism (Article 177 of the EEC Treaty) with the judges from the Conseil d'État.[54] While the AJE's promotion of European law through conferences and information probably had a limited effect, certain members of the association did attempt to promote the use of European law in France in their capacity as lawyers or judges and often informally cooperating with Gaudet.[55]

The Gaullist regime held a firm grip over the way French courts could receive European law. In the Constitution of the Fifth Republic, the monist clause on the introduction of international law in the French constitutional order (Article 55) had been revised by introducing a clause of reciprocity. This meant that French courts could hardly argue in favour of the primacy of international (European) law without at minimum consulting with the Ministry of Foreign Affairs. Moreover, the Matter

53 Bernier 2012; Rasmussen 2013a; Byberg 2017a.

54 Archive of Michel Gaudet (AMG). Chronos 1964. Letter from Gaudet to Rolland 14 December 1964.

55 See Bernier 2012 for a detailed analysis.

doctrine was still in place. In addition to this, the Gaullist regime not only centralised the court system by abolishing 15 per cent of the lower courts, but there were also repeated attacks on the new Conseil constitutionnel that were unpopular in the Gaullist dominated parliament. The most serious attacks, however, were reserved for the Conseil d'État after its decision in the Canal affair to abolish a special military court in Algeria in 1962. To de Gaulle, this decision felt like 'daggers in the back' and he therefore demanded a thorough reform of the Conseil d'État.[56] His entourage included many members of the Conseil d'État however and they managed to eliminate the danger by setting up a Commission that ended up only making a change in personnel and some minor administrative reforms.[57] Given the new Constitution of 1958 and the serious Gaullist pressure on the French court system, it is hardly surprising that French courts were hesitant about accepting the constitutional interpretation of European law.

The Conseil d'État would take the lead with regard to rejecting cooperation with the ECJ in three different cases: *Shell Berre* (1964), *Petitjean* (1967) and *Semoules* (1968).[58] Confronting them was the Gaullist government that was not going to accept any European intervention against the French oil monopoly (*Shell Berre*) or the management of agricultural imports (*Petitjean* and *Semoules*) nor the acceptance of the Conseil d'État of the new constitutional interpretation of European law.[59] In *Shell Berre* and *Petitjean*, the Conseil d'État refused to avail itself of the preliminary reference mechanism, adopting instead the doctrine of 'acte clair' which implied that the law could be interpreted by the Court itself. In the last case on *Semoules*, the Conseil d'État was confronting a situation in which a French statute that allowed the old bilateral rules of exchange between France and Algeria during the transition to independence of the latter, but which was clearly illegal under European law. The Conseil d'État could have applied European law over the statute. However, the Commissaire du Government, Nicole Questiaux, who presented the three cases before the Conseil d'État, warned that it would endanger its very existence if it confronted the executive and Parliament. In addition, Questiaux expressed a disregard for the relevance of European law and lack of willingness to use the preliminary reference mechanism because it would undermine the authority of the - Conseil d'État. While conscious that this may break French treaty obligations, the Conseil d'État decided that it could hardly be expected to solve this question. Instead, the EEC Commission could launch an infringement procedure, or the

56 Foyer 2006a, 6.

57 For a detailed account, see Alter 2001, 138; Foyer 2006a, 6–12.

58 Conseil d'État (Section), 19 June 1964, *Société des pétroles Shell-Berre et autres* (*Shell Berre*), n° 235345, published in *Recueil Lebon* 344, 1964; Conseil d'État (Section), 10 February 1967, S.A. *des Établissements Petitjean et autres* (*Petitjean*), n° 59125, 59126, 59329, published in *Recueil Lebon* 63, 1967; and Conseil d'État (Section), 1 March 1968, *Syndicat Général de Fabricants de Semoules de France* (*Semoules*), n° 62814, published in *Recueil Lebon* 149, 1970.

59 Plötner 1998, 57.

doctrinal dilemma could be addressed by the French Parliament or the Conseil constitutionnel.[60] Concluding on the doctrinal dimension of the three cases, the Conseil d'État clearly did not want to take upon itself a role that would involve judicial review and thus break the longstanding French tradition for parliamentary sovereignty.

The *Shell Berre* case represented a high-profile foreign attack against the French oil monopoly by international petroleum firms. The lawyer, Jean Coutard, was not only a political opponent of the Gaullist regime, but had a record for opposing state monopolies in favour of the organisation of a Common Market for oil at the European level.[61] Coutard was in close contact with Gaudet during the case since the EEC Commission at first had adopted a sceptical position towards the continued existence of the French oil monopoly.[62] *Shell Berre* was without comparison the most important legal challenge of French state interests in the 1960s. As a result, French Minister of Foreign Affairs Maurice Couve de Murville quickly became involved and told the Vice-President of the Conseil d'État,[63] Alexandre Parodi, that the case was a question of French foreign policy. He also pointed out that the use of a preliminary reference to the ECJ would diminish the powers of the Conseil d'État.[64] When the attack against French oil interests continued through the Italian court system that then led to a preliminary reference from the Tribunale civile e penale di Roma to the ECJ in the *Albatros* case,[65] Couve de Murville made clear to the Italian government that it should abstain for presenting a position before the court. Likewise, Gaudet and the legal service also ended up showing restraint in the Commission submission, a fact much appreciated by the SGCI.[66] In addition, both Parodi, Minister of Justice Jean Foyer and Couve de Murville had made sure that the new French Advocate General, Joseph Gand, who had just been nominated to the ECJ, was a jurist who would work for 'the benefit of France and the proper functioning of the ECJ'.[67] It was Gand who emphasised to the ECJ in his presentation during the *Albatros* case, that it was crucial that the Court made a decision 'within the limits of [its] jurisdiction and within the framework of the

[60] For an excellent overview of the cases consult: Alter 2001, 140–142.

[61] AMG. CD 1955–1969.C. Note of 17 May 1960 from Coutard to Gaudet. Notes of 2 July 1953 and 2 February 1957 from Gaudet to Pierre Ducrot. See also Coutard 1946.

[62] European Commission 2007, 310.

[63] The acting leader of the Conseil d'État is called Vice-President, while its formal President is the Chief of Government (Premier ministre).

[64] Archives of the French Ministry of Foreign Affairs (MAE). Collection 'Couve de Murville' (12QO/70). Letter of Maurice Couve de Murville to Head of Conseil d'État Alexandre Parodi on 7 October 1963 and Note of 31 July 1964 from Parodi to Couve de Murville.

[65] 20/64 *SARL Albatros v Société des pétroles et des combustibles liquides (Sopéco)*, 1964, ECLI:EU:C:1965:8.

[66] FNA. Collection 'Premier ministre – SGCI – Affaire Albatros' (19771467/22), ECJ ruling 20/64 – Meeting between the representatives of all relevant French ministries on 12 February 1965.

[67] FNA. Collection 'Conseil d'État – Dossier Joseph Gand' (20040382/78). Note of 31 July 1964 from Parodi to Couve de Murville.

actual dispute' and thus refraining from addressing a case that dealt with the application of European law in the member states.[68] While the ECJ reiterated its *Costa v ENEL* doctrine, it strategically chose not to intervene in one of the most politically loaded cases of the first decades of its existence. The French press covered the drama intensely and concluded that the government had successfully defended the oil monopoly against foreign attacks.[69]

In parallel with *Shell Berre*, another supranationalist lawyer, Ryziger, had taken up the *Petitjean* case, and also coordinated closely with Gaudet in a broader campaign to move the Conseil d'État towards an acceptance of the new constitutional interpretation of European law. One could perhaps have expected the Gaullist governments to be less active regarding a case on canned tomatoes. However, Parodi consulted closely with the government, which assured him about the legality of the French position and recommended the use of 'acte clair' in order to reject the case and avoid a preliminary reference.[70] Ryziger on his side was in close contact with Gaudet,[71] who attempted to approach de Bresson, whom he knew from the negotiations of the Treaties of Rome, to discuss how a common ground could be found to solve the question but to no avail.[72] Gaudet's attempt to convince the Commissaire du Gouvernement, Questiaux, to recommend the use of a preliminary reference to avoid political pressure also came to naught.[73]

After the failure of the *Petitjean* judgment, Ryziger and Gaudet continued to coordinate in the *Semoules* case. Here Agricultural Minister, Edgar Pisani, had blatantly ignored European law (Regulation 19/62) in a series of governmental decrees that allowed the import of semolina from Algeria to France free of all Community levies. This time Gaudet believed a breakthrough could happen and former Advocate General Lagrange, who had now been reintegrated into the Conseil d'État tried to influence Questiaux, who again opposed all attempts from the 'supranationalists' to change her position.[74] Again she recommended that the Conseil d'État ignore European law, even in a case in which French law was

68 MAE. Collection 'Conseil d'État – Dossier Joseph Gand' (20040382/78). Conclusions of Advocate General Joseph Gand before the ECJ on 2 December 1964.

69 'La Cour de justice des Communautés européennes se refusent à condamner le contingentement des importations de pétrole en France', *Le Monde* (8 February 1965).

70 Conseil d'État Archives (CEA). Collection 'Section du contentieux' (ACE 19810252 – Article 28). Memorandum of 11 February 1963 from special counsel Ryziger in case 68684: Establishment Petitjean & others vs. Governmental decree of 23 August 1962 and Letter from Pisani to Parodi on 26 December 1963; Letter from Giscard to Parodi on 12 May 1964; Letter from Couve de Murville to Parodi on 23 November 1964: Letter from Pompidou to Parodi on 24 December 1964.

71 AMG. Chronos 1964. Letter from Gaudet to Ryziger on 25 January 1964 and CEA. Collection 'Section du contentieux' (ACE 19810252 – Article 28). Applicant's reply of 26 February 1966.

72 AMG. Chronos 1967. Note from Gaudet on 5 January 1967.

73 AMG. Chronos 1967. Letter from Gaudet to Maurice Lagrange on 24 January 1967.

74 AMG. Chronos 1968. Letter from Gaudet to State Councillor Pierre Ordonneau on 5 March 1968 and interview by Alexandre Bernier with Questiaux in April 2012.

obviously incompatible.[75] As we have seen, the strong informal interventions of the Gaullist governments were crucial in determining the position of the Conseil d'État. The administrative court was clearly put in its place by the executive and acted accordingly. At the same time, the three cases were clearly driven by Christian Democratic lawyers coordinating with Gaudet and the Legal Service of the Commission and thus represented a first stage of the battle over how France would receive European law.

While the Conseil d'État refused to enter into dialogue with the ECJ, European law fared better at the Cour de cassation and at lower courts. All in all, French courts sent seven preliminary references between 1958 and 1969, which only surpassed Luxembourg (three) and Italy (three) and was much lower than West Germany (thirty) and the Netherlands (twenty-two).[76] De Bresson from the legal service of the Ministry of Foreign Affairs attempted from July 1965 onwards to control the sending of preliminary references from French courts by asking them first to inform the Ministry of Justice's Direction des affaires civiles et du sceau (DACS) if they considered using the procedure, and second send any preliminary reference first to the Ministry of Foreign Affairs.[77]

The Cour d'Appel de Paris was really the vanguard for European law. This was no accident. The Court had been the birthplace of the AJE in the mid-1950s, and from September 1962, Touffait, became court president. Touffait was an expert in competition law and had participated in the Hamel committee that explored the legal challenges posed by the application of the Treaties of Rome from 1958–1963.[78] Despite his Christian Democratic background he quickly rose in the ranks of the Gaullist administration after he served as Public Prosecutor in a case against French Algerian supporters accused of having attempted to murder President de Gaulle on 8 September 1961.[79] The very same day Debré left his duties as Prime Minister on 14 April 1962, he appointed Touffait to Director of Personnel and General Administration at the Ministry of Justice.[80] As part of his tasks, he served as Inspector General of Judicial Services, and had to sort out the consequences for French judiciary personnel in Algeria pending the decolonisation process.[81] His vehicle was mistakenly machine-gunned at a roadblock in Algiers on 18 May 1962.[82]

75 Conseil d'État (Section), 1 March 1968, *Syndicat Général de Fabricants de Semoules de France (Semoules)*, n° 62814, published in *Recueil Lebon* 149, 1970.

76 Buffet-Tchakaloff 1985, 109.

77 FNA. Collection 'Ministère de la Justice' (19950411/206). Note of 19 April 1968 from Couve de Murville to Louis Joxe.

78 FNA. Collection 'Ministère de la Justice' (19950411/15). Dossier Comité Hamel.

79 'Martial de Villemandy mis à disposition du procureur de la République Touffait', *L'Impartial* (9 September 1961).

80 FNA. Collection 'Michel Debré' (2DE15). *Letter from Touffait to Debré on 15 April 1962.*

81 Foyer 2006b, 260.

82 L. Bodard, 'Le conseiller Touffait grièvement blessé à Alger', *France Soir* (21 May 1962).

Hospitalised for months, Touffait was promoted again this time to become President of the Cour d'Appel de Paris, undoubtedly a mark of gratitude for his service.[83]

Touffait was still recovering from his serious injuries, when the Cour d'Appel de Paris as the first French courts addressed the relationship between European law and French law and thus Article 55 of the French Constitution, by acknowledging that the two were part of the same hierarchy and the former had the same force as French law. This happened in the *UNEF v Consten* decision of 26 January 1963,[84] an appeal from the Tribunal de commerce de Paris on the application of Articles 85 and 86 of the EEC Treaty. Apart from its doctrinal remarks, the Cour d'Appel de Paris declared itself powerless, and stayed the proceedings, in order for the EEC Commission to decide on the application of the two treaty articles. Behind the scenes, the Debré government had intervened against the original judgment of the Tribunal de commerce de Paris, which had allowed an exclusive dealing agreement with a ban on parallel import, because Debré prioritised the fight against inflation and wanted increased competition in the French economy.[85] The legal consequences were apparently less important to Debré in this case.

The side effect of the *UNEF v Consten* decision was that other lower French courts could use the precedent established on the relationship between European and French law. Thus, the Tribunal de commerce de Marseille in a judgment of 13 May 1964, for example, cited word for word the terms of the now famous Paris judgment.[86] However, even if Touffait was not part of the judgment that for the first time took a position on the role of European law in the French legal order, the Cour d'Appel de Paris would under his leadership begin to send preliminary references to the ECJ from 1965 onwards, although they were all of minor importance both in terms of content and doctrine. The Maschinenbau Ulm case, which had Jean Louis Aujol (Vice-president of the AJE), as lawyer of one of the parties, led to a preliminary reference where the Cour d'Appel de Paris used the standard procedure and sent it to the Ministry of Foreign Affairs on 7 July 1965 where it was delayed for four months before the EJC received it.[87] However, this would be the only time a lower court used the procedure prescribed by de Bresson from the Ministry of Foreign Affairs. Other preliminary references from the Cour d'appel de Paris, Cour d'Appel de Colmar and Cour d'appel d'Orléans were sent directly to Luxembourg.[88]

If the Cour d'Appel de Paris and a few other lower courts thus tested the patience of the Gaullist administration, the Cour de cassation was less active. Rolland, who was judge of the Criminal chamber (there were six different chambers) witnessed

83 FNA. Collection 'Adolphe Touffait' (19820583/136). Medical record 33/77 B1132.

84 Cour d'Appel de Paris, 26 January 1963, *UNEF v Consten*, *Dalloz* 1963.189.

85 Warlouzet 2017.

86 Tribunal de commerce de Marseille, 13 May 1964, *Telefunken v Aubin et Pucci*, *Gaz. Pal.* 1965.3.

87 Cour d'Appel de Paris, 7 July 1965, SA *La Technique Minière LTM v Maschinenbau Ulm*, *Gaz. Pal.* 1965.2.90.

88 Cour d'Appel de Colmar, 1 June 1965, *La Hessische Knappschaft v La Maison Singer et fils*, *Gaz. Pal.* 1965.2.102 and Cour d'appel d'Orléans, 9 November 1967, *Stanislas Ciechelski v CRSS Centre d'Orléans*.

how difficult it was to convince his colleagues to avail themselves of the preliminary reference mechanism. Rolland and Gaudet discussed how to facilitate a change in the attitude of the court and in early 1967 organised a series of conferences and debates on 'the current issues related to the application of European law'.[89] The promotion paid off almost immediately, when the Cour de cassation sent its first preliminary reference in the *Goffart* case on 27 April 1967 directly to the ECJ. This caused quite some uneasiness in the Ministry of Foreign Affairs because the DACS had not informed the Ministry about the case. As a result, de Bresson attempted to tighten the surveillance system of the French courts.[90] This did not help. When Touffait was nominated procureur général at the Cour de cassation in early 1968, this coincided with the sending of yet another preliminary reference, the *Torrekens* case, again directly to the ECJ.[91] Because Debré was worried about this 'abusive and harmful use in a national perspective of Article 177', he required shortly after that any preliminary ruling to the ECJ should first pass through his Ministry of Foreign Affairs.[92] However, the massive social protest of May 1968 unleashed a new political climate that led to de Gaulle's resignation from power in June 1969 and thus marked the end of this first 'souverainiste attempt' to stop any further adaptation of French law to European law.

FROM ACCOMMODATION TO REBELLION: THE ERA OF POMPIDOU AND GISCARD D'ESTAING, 1970 TO 1981

The period from 1969 to 1981 was dominated by a French re-engagement with European integration. While the Gaullist era had seen France involved in developing the various policies of the EC, the opposition to supranational institutions as well as the rejection of British EC-membership had increasingly alienated France from the other member states.[93] The new Gaullist president George Pompidou (1969–1974) was in favour of British membership and the first enlargement, in order to create a breakthrough for French priorities with regard to EC policies, such as the establishment of own resources of the EC, the creation of an Economic and Monetary Union and the launch of European cooperation in the field of foreign policy. Pompidou was thus willing to engage much more positively with the development of the EC, but as a Gaullist also had to balance this wish with the conservatism of his own party.[94]

His successor President Giscard d'Estaing (1974–1981) came from the Independent Republicans of the centre right and was more pro-European than

89 AMG. Chronos 1967. Letter from Gaudet to Rolland on 24 January 1967.

90 FNA. Collection 'Ministère de la Justice' (19950411/210), Note from de Bresson to Jacques Lemontey Head of European and International Law Office in the Ministry of Justice on 13 January 1967.

91 Cour de cassation (Chambre sociale), 24 October 1968, *Torrekens*, n° 568, *Dalloz* 1965.II.956, p. 677.

92 FNA. Collection 'Michel Debré' 5DE2-3. Note to General de Gaulle on 11 February 1969.

93 Ludlow 2006a, 146–174.

94 Joëlle 2020, 135–164.

Pompidou but also had to secure the support of the Gaullists in the National Assembly. Giscard d'Estaing used the EC as a framework for finding solutions to the economic challenges of the 1970s. His main contribution was the establishment of the European Monetary System in 1979, which he developed together with the West German Chancellor Helmut Schmidt.[95] Institutionally, he followed in the footsteps of Pompidou and de Gaulle with a focus on intergovernmentalism. He proposed the establishment of the European Council in 1974 to strengthen the role of state leaders in the EC. While he was willing to accept the introduction of the direct election of the European Parliament as a quid pro quo for establishing the European Council, a step strongly opposed by the Gaullists,[96] he was not entirely happy about the supranational institutions and became particularly frustrated with the case law of the ECJ during the last part of his presidency.

The 1970s constituted a decade of serious economic crisis in Europe, which made it difficult for the European institutions to maintain the momentum of the integration process. In the field of European law, however, the decade was in contrast unusually dynamic. The main reason for this was the composition of the ECJ during this period. One of the key proponents of a constitutional interpretation, Lecourt, became president from 1967 to 1976 and was followed by a German President, Hans Kutscher, with similar views. In addition to this, the two new judges from respectively Luxembourg and Belgium, Pierre Pescatore and Joseph Mertens de Wilmars changed the balance of the Court further in the direction of a federalist approach to European law.[97] This was reflected in the case law of the Court, which continued to build on the legal revolution of the 1960s that aimed to produce an autonomous, proto-federal legal order. The ECJ thus extended the external powers of the EC in commercial policy. It continued to support and extend the principle of primacy, expanded direct effect to new treaty articles, as well as the implementation of directives, which according to Article 189 of the EEC Treaty belonged to the national authorities. Finally, it pushed for the removal of obstacles to trade and free movement for labour and finally introduced fundamental rights.[98] The ECJ also played a much more active role in relation to both the member state governments and national courts under the leadership of Lecourt. From the early 1970s, annual meetings were held in Luxembourg to inform national judges about European law. Lecourt also worked hard to improve the cooperation of the member states with the Court.[99] He thus addressed the Council of Ministers of Justice in November 1974 and asked for an improvement in the use of the preliminary reference mechanism in national courts.[100] He also intervened directly to convince

95 Mourlon-Druol 2012a; Warlouzet 2018.
96 Mourlon-Druol 2016.
97 Davies and Rasmussen 2014.
98 Dehousse 1998.
99 Fritz 2018.
100 FNA. Collection 'Ministère de la Justice' (19950411/206). Note from the EEC Council on 12 February 1975.

the new French Minister of Justice at the time, an old Christian Democratic friend, Jean Lecanuet (1974–1976), to finally improve the French use of the preliminary reference mechanism.[101]

In comparison to the 1960s, the Legal Service of the Commission took more of a backseat compared to the dynamism of the ECJ. The departure of Gaudet from the legal service in 1969 led to the nomination of the German jurist Walter Much as new director. Much had been in the service since 1952 but remained somewhat sceptic towards the constitutional interpretation of European law.[102] By 1975, Lecourt, consequently expressed his dismay to the Secretary-General of the Commission, Emile Noël, stating that he believed the Legal Service had lost its way.[103] Ultimately, Much fell ill during his mandate and died in 1975. He was followed by a caretaker, Giancarlo Olmi, from 1975–1977 before the appointment of the German jurist Claus-Dieter Ehlermann in March 1977.[104] The directorship of Ehlermann that continued until 1986 returned the Legal Service to the position it had occupied under Gaudet. Ehlermann modernised the working of the Service, emphasised the importance of monitoring the compliance of member states by emphasising the use of the infringement procedure under Article 169 of the EEC Treaty and continued to support the constitutional interpretation of European law.[105]

FRENCH RESPONSES TO EUROPEAN LAW AT THE EC LEVEL

French policies towards the ECJ clearly differed between the two presidential periods. Pompidou engaged positively with the EC from 1969 to 1974, a period which saw the first enlargement of the EC as well as the launch of several new policies. The new Minister of Foreign Affairs Schuman and Minister of Justice Pleven abandoned the plan to use the Luxembourg protocol to reform the ECJ after the intervention of Lecourt in late 1969. Pleven also showed a new willingness to ensure that French courts actually applied European law.[106] He made sure that a close Cristian Democratic co-operator, Dutheillet de Lamothe from the Conseil d'État, was nominated as Advocate General in 1970 and thus added yet another 'supranationalist' to the Court.[107] Despite this openness to engage with the EC, Pompidou never desired the strengthening of the supranational institutions. In fact, even to the generally pro-European ministers, Schuman and Pleven, the case law of the ECJ was so audacious from the early 1970s that it caused serious concern in the French government and administration. With controversial ECJ judgments from the early 1970s such as the

101 Bernier 2017, 206.

102 Davies 2015, 449–451.

103 Archive of Emile Noël (AEM). D.447, Memo of 12 May 1975.

104 Vauchez 2015, 172–185.

105 See Chapter 2.

106 FNA. Collection 'Premier ministre – SGCI' (19900642/2). Note from Pleven to Jean-René Bernard on 10 October 1969.

107 Fritz 2018, 122–123.

Franz Grad case[108] on the direct effect of directives and the *ERTA* case[109] on the external powers of the EC in commercial policy, France supported German attempts to set up a working group at COREPER level to consider how to respond, but this was blocked by the Dutch and Luxembourg governments.[110]

The administration of President Giscard d'Estaing from 1974 onwards first continued a more lenient policy towards the ECJ. The Minister of Justice from 1974–1976, Lecanuet, who had been part of several Christian Democratic cabinets' during the 4th Republic, first visited the ECJ in Luxembourg to signal an improvement in the cooperation between France and the Court. After an intense dialogue with Lecourt, he introduced a circulaire in 1975 that obliged French lower courts to reduce the recourse to 'acte clair' and instead send preliminary references directly to the ECJ.[111] But later the attitude of Giscard d'Estaing to the ECJ changed drastically and he nominated a Gaullist Minister of Justice, Alain Peyrefitte in 1977 who quickly buried the circulaire. What rattled Giscard d'Estaing and the French administration was a string of judgments from the mid-1970s onwards that not only continued to expand the powers of EC but systematically intervened in various domestic market organisations in France. This included the *Charmasson* judgment by the ECJ in 1974,[112] which ordered France to open its national market to the import of bananas from Dutch Suriname although no common organisation of the banana market existed in the EC. Another example was the *Commission v French Republic* judgment in September 1979 that potentially opened up the French market for lamb and mutton to British exports before a common policy had been adopted (which was incidentally blocked by Britain).[113]

The French Advocate General Henri Mayras, who had been seconded to the ECJ from 1972 by the Conseil d'État, had warned his fellow European judges that such judgments could easily be interpreted by member states as undue activism. But the warning fell on deaf ears.[114] Inside the French administration these judgments were considered examples of how the ECJ behaved as a 'gouvernement des juges'.[115] The legal advisor of the SGCI, Marc Dandelot, concluded in a critical note in May 1979 that the Court had developed an alternative enforcement system designed around the

108 9/70 *Franz Grad v Finanzamt Traunstein*, 1970, ECLI:EU:C:1970:78.

109 22/70 *Commission of the European Communities v Council of the European Communities*, 1971, ECLI:EU:C:1971:32.

110 Archives of the Belgian Ministry of Foreign Affairs (ABMFA). Collection 'CEE. Service Europe 1964–1970'. 6641.1.i.1. Réunion n° 577 du COREPER du 17 au 20 nov. 1970, XVII. Création d'un Groupe de travail pour examiner les répercussions de l'arrêt rendu par la Cour de Justice dans l'affaire 9/70.

111 FNA. Collection 'Ministère de la Justice' (19950411/210). Circulaire no. 75–7 of 24 March 1975.

112 48/74, *Charmasson v Minister for Economic Affairs and Finance*, 1974, ECLI:EU:C:1974:137.

113 232/78, *Commission of the European Communities v French Republic*, 1979, ECLI:EU:C:1979:215.

114 FNA. Collection 'Premier ministre – SGCI' (19900642/2). Note of the Permanent Representative of France Luc de La Barre de Nanteuil on 5 February 1980.

115 FNA. Collection 'Ministère de la Justice' (19950411/208). Internal note of 9 May 1979 on the ECJ's case law.

system of preliminary reference mechanism by the means of the doctrines of direct effect and primacy. Where the Court had been prudent until 1970, the last decade had seen a much more aggressive approach. The incoherent approach by the member states to the ECJ had allowed for this development. The only real threat to the ECJ was if national courts stopped their cooperation.[116] By 1979, Giscard d'Estaing had enough and complained directly to the President of the Commission, Roy Jenkins, and refused to respect the ECJ decisions.[117] In late May 1979, Minister of Foreign Affairs Jean François-Poncet raised the question of radical reform at the informal 'Gymnich' meeting of the EC Ministers of Foreign Affairs, held at Chateau Mercuès near Cahor. Here, the Netherlands and Denmark once again protected the Court and rejected to discuss any reform.[118]

If direct reform of the ECJ ultimately failed, Giscard d'Estaing did attempt to instrumentalise the nomination of judges to influence the ECJ during this period. The results were mixed, however. In 1976, Lecourt stepped down as president and judge and France had to appoint a replacement. Giscard d'Estaing preferred first a political candidate instead of a legal one from the Conseil d'État. However, his candidate, Foyer, did not accept the appointment because he was not keen on the idea of becoming 'a kind of useless hostage in the most supranational of all European institutions'.[119] As a result, the pendulum swung in the opposite direction. The new Minister of Justice from 1976 to 1977, the Gaullist Olivier Guichard, wanted to get rid of the troublesome procureur général of the Cour de Cassation, Touffait, who had played a crucial role for promoting European law in the French court system, by promoting him to Luxembourg.[120] Again France sent a 'supranationalist' judge to Luxembourg. By 1981 the lesson seemed to have been learned. After years of dissatisfaction with the ECJ, a more careful selection process took place. In early 1981, a member of the Conseil d'État opposed to the activism of the European judges was identified in Conseiller d'État, Fernand Grévisse.[121] The profile of Grévisse was prominent enough to secure the new eleventh post of ECJ judge that had been announced in December 1980 due to the enlargement of the EC with Greece.[122] While Grévisse was a convinced pro-European, he despised any bouts of legal innovation or political ideologies and repeatedly argued that the ECJ had to take the legal traditions of the member states into account.[123] All in all, French policies towards the ECJ thus became increasingly sceptical in the last half

116 FNA. Collection 'Premier ministre – SGCI' (19950411/207). Note of 10 May 1979 regarding the ECJ.

117 FNA. Collection 'Valéry Giscard d'Estaing' (5AG3/920). Audience of M. Jenkins on 23 September 1979.

118 See Chapters 8 and 9.

119 Foyer 2006b, 410–411.

120 Foyer 2006b, 411.

121 FNA. Collection 'Premier ministre – SGCI' (20010085/39). Note from Chief Legal Officer at the Legal Service of the French Ministry of Foreign Affairs Gilbert Guillaume to Jacques Viot Chief of Staff of Minister of Foreign Affairs Jean François-Poncet on 15 September 1980.

122 Combrexelle 2004, 102–107.

123 Maidani 2004, 108–113.

of the 1970s and early 1980s under Giscard d'Estaing, who publicly had an image of a pro-European, but behind closed doors launched one of the most important attacks on the ECJ in the history of European integration.

Where Gaullism had dominated French politics before 1969, the political scene of the 1970s was much more complex with varying successes of different political parties. A dominant feature was the gradual weakening of Gaullism first with the ascendency of Giscard d'Estaing to the presidency in 1974 and later with the defeats of both Jacques Chirac and Michel Debré as presidential candidates in 1981. This impacted the way France received European law. The increased fluidity of the political scene meant that the battle between the 'supranationalist' and the 'souverainiste' involved in shaping French reception of European law intensified, with the result that the status of European law in France and the way the national court system was supposed to handle it shifted several times during the period. It is thus unsurprising that the reception of European law by French courts was highly contradictory in this turbulent decade. We shall take a closer look at the first major breakthrough for European law in the French court system, namely the *Jacques Vabre* decision of the Cour de cassation in 1975 that accepted the core constitutional doctrines of European law and the obligation of French courts to cooperate with the ECJ. Second, we will explore in some detail what would amount to the most serious rebellion against the ECJ in any member state, namely the *Cohn-Bendit* decision in 1978 of the Conseil d'État.[124] Finally, we shall return to the political level and analyse how Debré and the 'souverainiste' attempted a political revolution of French European policy that would have rejected not only the introduction of direct election of the European Parliament, but also led to a break with the ECJ and European law.

THE COUR DE CASSATION AND THE FIRST ACCEPTANCE OF THE CONSTITUTIONAL INTERPRETATION OF EUROPEAN LAW

With the nomination of Touffait as Prosecutor General at the Cour de Cassation in late 1967, three key members of the AJE were brought together in this highest civil court. Maurice Aydalot had been appointed First President of the Court in October 1967 and had earlier been considered for a post in the ECJ by Debré in 1962, who nevertheless wanted him to stay in France, because he was a 'great servant of the state'.[125] The second was Rolland, the co-founder of the AJE who was the oldest judge of the Criminal Chamber of the Court. It was indeed from this Chamber that the first step towards acknowledging the direct effect and primacy

[124] Conseil d'État (Assemblée), 22 December 1978, *Cohn-Bendit*, n° 11604, published in *Recueil Lebon* 524, 1980.

[125] FNA. Collection 'Michel Debré' (2DE21). Letter from Debré to Couve de Murville on 22 February 1960.

of European law came with the *Ramel* judgment in 1970.[126] Based on Article 55 of the Constitution, this decision remained nevertheless of limited doctrinal value, as it came from only one of the six regular Chambers of the Court. Only a case brought before 'full Court' (the six Chambers) or 'joint benches' (at least three Chambers) could ensure a uniform interpretation for all Chambers.[127] To take this crucial step, the Cour de cassation needed an additional impetus. This came in 1974 when the Conseil constitutionnel finally decided to engage with Article 55 of the Constitution and thus indirectly touched upon the question of how European law would enter the French legal order.

The members of the Conseil constitutionnel had listened to the winds of change that had manifested itself with the departure of de Gaulle and the cultural revolution of 1968. De Gaulle had failed to cement a dominant Gaullist voice in the Conseil constitutionnel after Debré had refused to become President in 1964, he refused again in 1973 to join the Court when asked by Pompidou.[128] With the nomination of Francois Luchaire in 1965 and Coste-Floret in 1971, important voices of the left and centre right and two 'supranationalists' were now part of the Conseil constitutionnel.[129] From 1971, the Conseil constitutionnel took the first historical decision to gain its independence from the state executive.[130] The Court incorporated the preambles of all French Constitutions and statutes into the French doctrine, including the 1789 Declaration of Rights of Man and of the Citizen, thereby creating a veritable bill of rights. This offered the Conseil constitutionnel new opportunities to develop French constitutional law and perform judicial review.

The first step of the Conseil constitutionnel towards assessing the old Matter and Arrighi doctrines of the 1930s would remain ambiguous, however. Ironically, the move came in a case close to the heart of the Gaullists namely their opposition to the possible introduction of abortion in France. Foyer used his position as President of the Law Commission of the French Parliament to gain support of eighty MPs in order to challenge the bill on Voluntary Termination of Pregnancy before the Conseil constitutionnel as unconstitutional (Article 61 of the Constitution), alleging it was in violation with the European Convention on Human Rights. During the internal debates of the Conseil constitutionnel, Coste-Floret had pushed for a discussion whether the primacy of international law also applied to French law enacted subsequently.[131] However, instead of addressing this key question head on, the Conseil constitutionnel adopted a deeply ambiguous position. The Court

126 Cour de cassation (Chambre criminelle), 22 October 1970, *Ramel*, n° 2776, *Dalloz* 1970.276 and FNA. Collection 'Cour de cassation' (19770037/89). Dossier 'French Indirect Taxes Administration & Interprofessional Committee for Natural Sweet Wines vs. Pierre Ramel'.

127 Tallon and Gaudemet-Tallon 1971, 363; Alter 2001, 147.

128 FNA. Collection 'Georges Pompidou' (5AG2/1073). Letter from Pompidou to Debré on 9 January 1974 and from Debré to Pompidou on 19 January 1974.

129 Bernier 2017, 175–176.

130 Conseil constitutionel, 16 July 1971, *Liberté d'association*, n° 71–44 DC.

131 Conseil constitutionel, 15 January 1975, *Case IVG*, n° 74–54 DC.

refused to control the conformity of the pending bill with the Convention because the supremacy of an international treaty did not necessarily imply that a national law did not apply or was unconstitutional. This was partly due to the contingent (and unstable) nature of international law and partly because the supremacy of international law according to Article 55 depended on reciprocity.[132] Instead of addressing the problem itself, the Court delegated the interpretation of Article 55 to the individual courts.[133] The Conseil constitutionnel had managed to square the circle. Gaullist commentators praised it for respecting the spirit of Article 55. At the same time, it was recognised that the decision could be construed as an invitation to the other courts of last instance to take the task of interpreting Article 55 upon themselves.[134]

This green light from the Conseil constitutionnel was just what the Cour de cassation needed. An appeal by the French customs administration from a judgment by the Cour d'Appel de Paris in the *Jacques Vabre* case from 7 July 1973 offered just the right opportunity.[135] Having ensured that the case would be handled before joint benches in the Cour de Cassation,[136] Prosecutor General Touffait turned for advice to the Belgian jurist Ganshof van der Meersch, who as Belgian Prosecutor General had been a key figure behind the famous *Le ski* judgment by the Belgian Cour de cassation,[137] which had accepted the primacy of both international and European law in 1971 based on a monist interpretation.[138] Now Touffait attempted to make a similar argument in a French context. Following the core argument of the ECJ in the *Costa v ENEL* judgment and the approach by Ganshof van der Meersch, he proposed that the Cour de cassation gave European law primacy due to the special (constitutional) nature of European law. Touffait's proposal was, however, rejected by the joint benches presided over by Aydalot. Instead, the Cour de Cassation concluded that European law did have primacy but on basis of Article 55 of the French Constitution not the ECJ's *Costa* doctrine.[139] Anecdotal evidence suggests that Aydalot was behind this more cautious decision. He accepted the political

132 Plötner 1998, 43.

133 FNA Collection 'Conseil constitutionnel' (20040168/7), *Report of the Session of 15 January 1975 on Abortion Law.*

134 Plötner 1998, 44.

135 Cour d'Appel de Paris, 7 July 1973, *Jacques Vabre*, n° 4164.

136 As seen earlier a ruling from joint benches, or Chambres mixtes in French, is generally binding for the six different Chambers of the Cour de cassation ensuring thus the settlement of a jurisprudence in the case in point.

137 Belgian Cour de cassation, 27 May 1971, *État belge, Ministre des Affaires économiques v Société anonyme Fromagerie franco-suisse* (Le Ski), 1672484252.

138 Archive of Ganshof van der Meersch (AGVM). 180PP.040.000. Letter from Touffait to Meersch on 24 January 1975. The President of the *Cour de Cassation* R. Polet wrote afterwards a letter to Ganshof van der Meersch where he praised his contribution and called it essential for the later judgment. He emphasised in particular that due to Ganshof van der Meersch, the Cour de Cassation not only granted primacy to European law but also included international law. AGVM.180PP081.1971–1972. Letter from Polet to Ganshof van der Meersch.

139 Cour de cassation (Chambre mixte), 24 May 1975, *Jacques Vabre* n° 73–13.556, *Dalloz* 1975.

necessity of the principle of the primacy of the Treaties of Rome on subsequent internal French laws, but he was also a pragmatic man and wanted a solution based on the French Constitution.[140] Similarly, Aydalot was not supportive of the aspiration of Touffait to become the next First President of the Cour de cassation in 1976,[141] and instead the latter became, as we saw above, the next French judge of the ECJ. Nevertheless, the judgment was a significant breakthrough that fundamentally changed the way France received European law, and it was all the more controversial because it had significant financial consequences for the French Ministry of Finance that now had to pay back an important sum to the coffee merchant (Jacques Vabre) that had originally filed the suit.[142]

THE CONSEIL D'ÉTAT REBELS AGAINST EUROPEAN LAW

The road of the Conseil d'État to the acceptance of European law was in contrast much longer. The response to the *Semoules* judgment from the Commission came only after de Gaulle had stepped down. Gaudet still believed that what was needed was 'more education than proceeding' and that the Conseil d'État still did not find itself empowered to engage in judicial review.[143] Gaudet accordingly invited the members of the Conseil d'État to Brussels in June 1969 to visit the Commission and its Legal Service.[144] While Gaudet stepped down from his post on 1 November 1969, the Commission would follow his recommendation when challenged by the German member of the European Parliament, Arved Deringer, who urged intervention against the Conseil d'État.[145] With Much in place as the new director of the legal service, the lenient policy towards the Conseil d'État was thus continued.

With Gaudet out of the picture, Lecourt now took the lead and contacted the new Minister of Justice Pleven in order to address the limited use of the preliminary reference mechanism by French courts and in particular the Conseil d'État.[146] The Legal Committee of the EP had in coordination with the Legal Service published a report on the problems related to the non-use of the preliminary reference mechanism of national courts.[147] As a result, Pleven invited in December 1969 Parodi and all the section presidents of the Conseil d'État and impressed on them

140 FNA. Collection 'Michel Debré' (2DE21). *Note from Debré to Couve de Murville on 22 February 1960.*

141 P. Boucher, 'Schmelck et Sadon appelés à la tête du parquet de Paris' (1975) 25 June, *Le Monde*.

142 Plötner 1998, 59.

143 AMG. Chronos 1969. Note from Gaudet to Schoenbaum on 18 March 1969.

144 AMG. Chronos 1969. Note from Gaudet to Denoix de Saint Marc on 16 June 1969.

145 'Written question n° 349 to the Commission delivered on 10 November 1969 by Tjerk Westerterp regarding the compatibility with European law of the French Conseil d'État's judgment of 1 March 1968. Written answer from the Commission on 30 January 1970' (14 February 1970) 20 (13) *Official Journal of the European Communities*, 4–5.

146 FNA. Collection 'Ministère de la Justice' (19950411/210). Note from Yves Cotte to Dutheilet de Lamothe on 28 November 1969.

147 L. Merchiers, 'Report drawn up on behalf of the Legal Committee on the problems posed by the application of EEC Article 177', (15 September 1969), European Parliament's room paper n° 94.

the need to update their case law and avail themselves of the preliminary reference mechanism when relevant. If this were not done, France would soon violate her obligations in the EC.[148] Six months later the Conseil d'État decided to send its first preliminary reference to Luxembourg in a case of little doctrinal importance as a gesture of cooperation to the ECJ.[149]

If the Conseil d'État had thus timidly opened for cooperation with the ECJ, relations soon deteriorated. In the case from 1974 dealing with the French regulation of its market for bananas, raised by a French importer, André Charmasson, with the assistance of Ryziger as lawyer,[150] the Conseil d'État sent a new preliminary reference to Luxembourg. The Court had cleared the step with the French government that had felt certain that its protection of the banana import from the French Antilles, was compatible with European law. However, much to the surprise of the French government and the Conseil d'État, the ECJ ruled that French sovereignty over bilateral trade agreements had ended when the transitional period of the EEC Treaty had lapsed, even if that did not apply to the concrete case that had emerged before 1970.[151]

There is little doubt that the shock of the *Charmasson* judgment contributed to the renewed scepticism of the Conseil d'État towards the ECJ. Although the first Minister of Justice of the new President Giscard d'Estaing, Lecanuet, would continue the policy of cooperation pursued by Pleven, this would finally change after 1977. Now both the President and the French administration grew increasingly hostile to the ECJ.

The focus of this new hostility was directed towards a particularly controversial part of the case law of the ECJ: the attempt to expand the doctrine of direct effect to also cover Council directives, which according to Article 189 of the EEC Treaty were addressed to member states and gave national authorities the choice of means with which to reach the objectives set out in the directive. In a series of judgments, *Grad* (1970), *SACE* (1970), *Van Duyn* (1974) and *Rutili* (1975), the ECJ applied a teleological reading that prioritised the efficiency (*effet utile*) of the Treaties over the treaty text.[152] The aim was to ensure the enforcement of directives in the member state. But the consequence was a direct challenge to the balance between the powers of the EC and the member states: their parliaments, administrations and courts.[153]

148 Bernier 2017, 172.

149 34/70, *Syndicat national du commerce extérieur des céréales et al. v Office national interprofessionnel des céréales et Ministère de l'Agriculture*, 1970, ECLI:EU:C:1970:119.

150 The French administration would eventually categorise Ryziger as somebody who knew the inclinations of the ECJ well and would stop at nothing in pushing French courts to exploit this. FNA. Collection 'Ministère de la Justice'. (19950411/207). Note from Marc Dandelot on 10 May 1979.

151 48/74, *Charmasson v Minister for Economic Affairs and Finance*, 1974, ECLI:EU:C:1974:137. See also Alter 2001, 152.

152 9/70 *Franz Grad v Finanzamt Traunstein*, 1970, ECLI:EU:C:1970:78; 33/70 *SpA SACE v Finance Minister of the Italian Republic*, ECLO:EU:C:1970.118; 41/74 *Yvonne van Duyn v Home Office*, 1974, ECLI:EU:C:1974:133 and 36/75 *Roland Rutili v Ministre de l'intérieur*, 1975, ECLI:EU:C:1975:137.

153 Rasmussen 2017, 290–308.

Strong reactions came from the British House of Lords in 1974 and was followed by the French parliament, which passed a law in 1976 that would allow it to nullify European laws and ECJ judgments that undermined its authority. The first annulment took place in 1978, where the French parliament refused to adopt an EC directive to reform the system of value added tax.[154] Combined with the hostility of Giscard d'Estaing and the French administration to the ECJ in the late 1970s, it is easy to understand why the Conseil d'État felt ready to take on the ECJ on this particular question.

In the famous *Cohn-Bendit* judgment on 22 December 1978, the Conseil d'État finally rebelled openly against the ECJ's case law on the direct effect of directives.[155] In the concrete case the (in)famous youth rebel from 1968, German citizen Daniel Cohn-Bendit, who had been expelled from France, wanted to be able to return. The case thus dealt with the access of the citizens of one member state to another member state, a principle where the ECJ had moved decisively towards non-discrimination in its judgments in the *Van Duyn* and *Rutili* cases. Given the strong dissatisfaction with the ECJ case law in the French administration,[156] it was perhaps not surprising that the preliminary reference sent by the lower court in the case, the Tribunal administratif de Paris on 21 December 1977, had been held back by the Ministry of Foreign Affairs. With the storm coming, several attempts were made to temper the response of the Conseil d'État. The pro-European Commissaire du gouvernement, Bruno Genevois, took a positive stance towards European law when advising the Conseil d'État and recommended that the Conseil d'État should send a preliminary reference to the ECJ. He recommended dialogue with the ECJ instead of outright confrontation. Likewise, the Minister of the Interior relaxed the contested decision with regard to Cohn-Bendit a few days before. Nevertheless, it took the opportunity to completely reject the case law of the ECJ.[157] It annulled the preliminary reference sent by the lower court, and then interpreted European law itself by declaring that according to Article 189 of the EEC Treaty directives had no direct effect.

In the European institutions, the judgment of the Conseil d'État was considered an outright attack on the European legal order and the EC. The response came in two steps. First, the ECJ now moderated its interpretation of the direct effect of directives in the *Ratti* judgment on 5 April 1979.[158] Here the ECJ broke with the interpretative principle of *effet utile* and accepted that directives differed from regulations by being addressed to the member states and that they could consequently only have direct effect after the expiry of the period prescribed for their

[154] Alter 2001, 152–153.

[155] Conseil d'État (Assemblée), 22 December 1978, *Cohn-Bendit*, n° 11604, published in *Recueil Lebon* 524, 1980.

[156] FNA. Collection 'Premier ministre – SGCI' (19870407/45). Relevé de conclusions de la réunion du 12 janv. 1976. Interdiction de séjour. Conséquence à tirer de l'arrêt Rutili.

[157] Alter 2001, 154.

[158] 148/78 *Criminal proceedings against Tullio Ratti*, 1979, ECLI:EU:C:1979:110.

implementation. This was a decisive step towards addressing the complaints from the member states, including France.[159] Second, the Commission decided after careful consideration to address the French government about the judgment. In the Legal Service it was believed that the Conseil d'État judgment was even more dangerous than the *Solange* judgment by the German Constitutional Court (BVerfG) in 1974 because it had immediate consequences and potentially concerned all aspects of ECJ case law which the Conseil d'État disagreed with. If the attitude spread to other member states, the entire European legal order would collapse. However, just as in 1974 the recommendation was to deal with the challenge informally, and not immediately pursue an infringement case.[160] A letter was consequently sent from President Jenkins to the French Minister of Affairs on 7 March 1979 asking for clarifications on the judgment.[161] The letter did not receive any response, however, probably due to the French plans for a reform of the ECJ that were proposed at the annual 'Gymnich' meeting held at the Chateau Mercuès near Cahors. The Commission President consequently had to send a new letter in January 1980.[162] (See also Chapter 2 for details on this story.)

In the meantime, the legal committee of the European Parliament led by German Christian Democrat, Hellmut Sieglerschmidt, prepared a report that condemned France and introduced far-reaching proposals to address the fact that France and other member state continued to ignore the preliminary reference mechanism[163] (for details see Chapter 3). This finally prompted a French response on 23 March 1980, which assured the Commission President that France supported the integrity of European law and the problem raised by the *Cohn-Bendit* judgment was merely a procedural one.[164] This response was not considered satisfactory by the Commission and a new letter from Jenkins was sent on 8 October 1980 underlining that although an intervention from the French government against its own courts was not possible, it was obliged to ensure that the preliminary reference mechanism was respected and used by French courts.[165] The new legal advisor of the SGCI, Thierry Le Roy, a socialist and close associate of Questiaux,[166] found the

159 Rasmussen 2017.

160 Archive of the Legal Service of the European Commission (ALSC). Compte rendu de la réunion du lundi, 1978–1981, *Réunion du 15 janvier 1979*.

161 ALSC.07.763. Directives. Applicabilité des directives dans les E. M. Affaire 'Cohn-Bendit'. Letter from R. Jenkins to J. Francois-Poncet on 7 March 1979.

162 For further details consult Rasmussen 2017.

163 H. Sieglerschmidt, 'Report n° 1–414/81 on the responsibility of the Court of Justice of the European Communities for the uniform application of Community law in the member states' (9 November 1981) 287 (24) *Official Journal of the European Communities* 21.

164 ALSC.07.763. Directives. Applicabilité des directives dans les E. M. Affaire 'Cohn-Bendit'. Letter from J. François -Poncet to R. Jenkins on 23 March 1980.

165 ALSC.07.763. Directives. Applicabilité des directives dans les E. M. Affaire 'Cohn-Bendit'. Letter from Jenkins to François-Poncet on 8 October 1980.

166 Both Questiaux and Le Roy were members of the editorial board of the socialist periodical 'Non – Repère pour le socialisme' the aim of which was among others to spread Socialism in a 'souverainiste' perspective. 'La vocation de Non', *Le Monde* (19 June 1980).

unpublished draft of the Sieglerschmidt report and the action of the Commission absolutely unacceptable. Nevertheless, with the upcoming presidential election, the French government decided to do nothing. The main reason for this inaction was partly that Giscard d'Estaing had not achieved ECJ reform at the European level, but also because he had finally had to make a choice with regard to the ECJ when confronting an even more serious rebellion against European law that took place in parallel with the *Cohn-Bendit* judgment.

THE SOUVERAINISTE REBELLION

In order to establish the European Council in 1975, Giscard d'Estaing had accepted that the EP could finally introduce direct elections in 1979. The prospect of lending popular legitimacy to the EP represented in the eyes of the 'souverainistes' a most dire threat to French sovereignty. Combined with the increasingly activist ECJ, Debré believed direct political action was necessary. In July 1977, the National Assembly debated and adopted the law that introduced direct elections of the EP in France[167] and Debré did his best to underline the dangers to French sovereignty this implied. He also pointed out how the ECJ constantly endorsed the superiority of international legal rules and stressed the negative impact on French courts, pointing out the *Jacques Vabre* decision of the Cour de Cassation.[168] After his defeat in Parliament, Debré founded in November 1977 the Comité pour l'Indépendance et l'Unité de la France (CIUF), which included other Gaullists such as de Bresson, Etienne Burin des Roziers and Michel Aurillac. The aim was to hold public meetings across France.[169] Debré's initiative was typical among the Gaullists that did not share the liberal policies of the Giscard d'Estaing administration. In 1976, Jacques Chirac founded the Rassemblement pour la République (RPR), and together with the CIUF a common list was produced for the election of the European Parliament in 1979. The election ended up in a catastrophic defeat, even if Debré obtained a seat in the EP, only winning 16.3 per cent of the votes. As a result, Chirac soon moved towards the centre on the European question, marginalising Debré within the Gaullist camp. This was finally accomplished when Debré as a presidential candidate in 1981 suffered a devastating defeat obtaining only 1.66 per cent of the votes in the first round, whereas Chirac came in third.

Before this final defeat of the 'souverainiste' part of the Gaullist movement, Debré and Aurillac, who after having been promoted as Conseiller in the Conseil d'État and was elected as member of the RPR to the National Assembly

167 'Law n° 77–729 of 7 July 1977 on the election by direct universal suffrage of representatives to the European Parliament' (8 July 1977) 157 *Journal Officiel de la République française*, 3579.

168 M. Debré, 'Resume debate of 14 June 1977 concerning the draft law on the election by direct universal suffrage of representatives to the European Parliament' (15 June 1977) 54 *Journal Officiel de la République française*, 3742.

169 Debré 1994, 176–180.

in March 1978, launched a major attack on the ECJ. Debré, who had repeatedly criticised the ECJ in parliamentary debates, organised a conference in September 1980 entitled the 'Sovereignty of French Law'. The conference included former members of the Conseil constitutionnel and concluded that the ECJ had gone beyond the mandate of the Treaties of Rome and beyond Article 55 of the French Constitution.[170] Three weeks later, during deliberations on a law from the government that intended to complete the 'code d'organisation judiciaire', Aurillac launched an amendment that in his view reaffirmed the Republican sentiment of 1790, wherein judges cannot construe laws.[171] The explicit purpose of the amendment was to force national courts to both apply national law and reject the primacy of European law, and in particular, as pointed out by Aurillac before the National Assembly, the Cour de cassation's *Jacque Vabre* decision.[172] The Gaullist Minister of Justice, Peyrefitte, supported the amendment and the law was passed overwhelmingly by the National Assembly.

By the end of 1980, France was consequently seriously challenging the legal dimension of its EC membership. The highest administrative Court had rejected the exclusive competence of the ECJ to interpret European law and would not send preliminary references to Luxembourg and the National Assembly had passed a law that would force French courts to reject the primacy of European law. However, despite the frustration that Giscard d'Estaing felt about the ECJ, the failure to reform the ECJ at the Gymnich meeting meant that France could not continue to ignore European law without creating the most serious crisis since the Empty Chair Crisis of 1965. As a result, the legal advisors of the SGCI, Le Roy, and the Ministry of Foreign Affairs, Gilbert Guillaume, recommended that the French government dissociated itself from the Aurillac amendment.[173] There was no way around it. With the intervention of the executive, the Aurillac amendment was not passed in the Senate in December 1980. The great coup against European law led by the 'souverainiste' had failed.

1981–1989: A PYRRHIC VICTORY FOR THE SUPRANATIONALISTS?

The election of the socialist candidate François Mitterrand at the presidential elections in May 1981 did not at once lead to a more engaged European policy than during the years of Giscard d'Estaing. In fact, the opposite was the case from 1981 to 1983, when a coalition government between the Socialist Party and the Communist Party produced a full-blown socialist policy in France. Policies such as reducing working time, introducing a fifth week of pay holidays, reducing the

170 Alter 2001, 156.

171 Archive of the National Assembly. Amendment to the bill of the Peyrefitte reform of the Code of Judicial Organization, meeting of 9 October 1980.

172 Alter 2001, 156.

173 FNA. Collection 'Premier ministre – SGCI' (20000292/38).

retirement age to sixty instead of sixty-five and launching a comprehensive scheme of nationalisation of almost all important companies and banks led to several currency crisis that threated French participation in the European Monetary System. By 1983, Mitterrand changed course, following the advice of his Finance Minister Jacques Delors, in favour of austerity and liberalisation of the economy combined with a new emphasis on European integration. With Delors installed as President of the Commission from 1985 to 1995, the EC embarked on a number of reforms driven in particular by close cooperation between Mitterrand and the new German Christian Democratic Chancellor, Helmuth Kohl. The Single European Act of 1986 launched a programme to establish a truly Single European Market and finally introduced majority voting in the Council to improve efficiency. This was followed by the Maastricht Treaty of 1991 that created a European Union (EU), including an Economic and Monetary Union and intergovernmental cooperation on Home and Justice Affairs as well as Foreign and Defence Policy.[174]

With the renewed dynamics of the integration process, the ECJ's endeavour to gradually create a proto-federal legal order felt justified. New case law consolidated the four freedoms, enhanced the powers of the supranational institutions and helped improve the implementation of European law by the member states.[175] From 1986 onwards, the Court even followed in the footstep of a trend within European law academia and began to explicitly characterise the legal order built as one of constitutional and proto-federal nature.[176] The Legal Service of the Commission under the leadership of Ehlermann until 1986, together with the EP, also continued to promote a constitutional interpretation of European law. The influence of French supranationalists at European level continued to make its mark with the Delors Commission, where both the President and his legal advisor François Lamoureux promoted a gradual federalisation of the EC in the last half of the 1980s.[177]

To France, the rapid development of European integration during this period partly promoted by Mitterrand necessitated an adaptation and more loyal engagement of the French administration and legal system with the EC in order to build the Single Market. At the same time, an intensive political and legal battle over to what extent the EC should move in a federal direction was still being fought from 1986 to 1991 and offered opportunities for both 'supranationalists' and 'souverainistes'.

FRENCH RESPONSES TO EUROPEAN LAW AT THE EC LEVEL

With the victory of Mitterrand at the Presidential election, the French attitude to the ECJ changed markedly for the better. On the one hand, while France was central

[174] Warlouzet 2018, 180–213.
[175] Dehousse 1998.
[176] Boerger and Davies 2017; Boerger and Rasmussen 2014.
[177] See Chapter 2.

after 1984 in invigorating the EC and with the establishment of the Single Market from 1986–1992, the French court system and administration had to respectively apply and implement European law much more systematically and loyally than before. On the other hand, Mitterrand, although perhaps the most pro-European president of the Fifth Republic yet, did not necessarily support the strengthening of the supranational institutions or the federalisation of the European project. His approach was more pragmatic and very much shaped by a traditional French preference for intergovernmental solutions.

The adaptation of the French court system to the ECJ will be discussed in detail in the next section, but the Mitterrand administration intervened in important ways to force the Conseil d'État to engage with the ECJ through the preliminary reference mechanism and accept the primacy of European law. At the same time, the Mitterrand administration also addressed the dismal implementation of European legislation and ECJ case law in the national legal order. France had one of the worst records for implementing European law, leading to one of the highest rates of infringement cases launched against it.[178] By mid-1984 Pierre Morel, the technical advisor for European Affairs at the French Ministry of Foreign Affairs, gathered several studies and notes to collect better knowledge about the ECJ and its judicial procedure system.[179] This survey proved useful when the French Permanent Representative to the EC, Jacques Leprette, in June 1984 warned Minister of Foreign Affairs, Roland Dumas, about the deteriorating relations between France and the Commission. Since 1980, the latter had indeed brought infringement cases against France five times (in the estimate of Leprette) more than compared to other member states. To bring down the number of cases before Court, the government had to resolve disputes during pre-litigation procedures. Clear cut cases lost in advance should not be supported, or – if possible – not at all be brought before the Court in Luxembourg.[180] However, despite this innovative approach to implementation and infringement cases, Dumas and the Ministry of Foreign Affairs often found it difficult to gain the cooperation of other ministries, for example in competition policy.[181]

[178] 'First Annual Report to the European Parliament on Commission Monitoring of the Application of Community Law -1 1983' (11 April 1984) *COM* (84) 181 Final, 32–47.

[179] FNA. Collection 'François Mitterrand – Archives de Pierre Morel' (5AG4/PM34). See here the note of Jean-Pierre Spitzer technical adviser of French Minister for European affairs, Roland Dumas, produced on 21 June 1984 and entitled 'Note sur la séquence d'une procédure devant la Cour de Justice' and the document produced in September 1983 and entitled 'Le respect des règles communautaires par les États membres des Communautés européennes (éléments de comparaison)'.

[180] FNA. Collection 'François Mitterrand – Archives de Pierre Morel' (5AG4/PM34). Note of 8 March 1984 from French Permanent Representative to the European Communities Jacques Leprette to French Minister for European affairs Roland Dumas regarding recent trends in infringements of European law.

[181] Warlouzet, 2018, 170–174.

If France adapted to the requirements of EC membership in the legal arena during the two periods of the Mitterrand presidency[182], this did not necessarily imply any support for the strengthening of the supranational institutions or federalist reform of the EC. The Delors Commission did its best to exploit the new dynamics of European integration from 1984 onwards to strengthen the powers of the EC and the supranational institutions. During the negotiations on the Maastricht negotiations in 1990–1991, the Commission had pressed for a constitutional treaty that would codify the legal order the ECJ had built, strengthen the supranational institutions and ultimately set the new European Union on track towards a federal destination. However, France and a majority of member states did not want to place all the new policy fields under the EC and instead opted for a treaty that included two intergovernmental pillars of Home and Justice Affairs and Foreign and Security policy. A European Council would run the new European Union. The establishment of the EU thus represented a severe defeat to European federalists and the ambition of the ECJ that had created a proto-federal legal order of European law in the expectancy that a federal European Union would eventually be created.[183]

THE FRENCH RECEPTION OF EUROPEAN LAW

If the 1960s had witnessed a Gaullist monopoly of power at the Presidential level and in the National Assembly, the period from 1981 to 1993 was more volatile, despite the fact that Mitterrand was President for two terms. The parliamentary election in 1986 led to the formation of a right-wing government led by the Gaullist, Jacques Chirac, who was Prime Minister until 1988. Compared to the 1970s, there were few attempts by the souverainistes to push for a break with the ECJ and European law. In October 1981, an opportunity to lure the Conseil d'État towards an even more radical position on European law presented itself with the Service techniques d'assurance case. Aurillac, who was rapporteur on the case, believed this was a great opportunity to address the *Jacques Vabre* doctrine and push for a final rejection of the ECJ and European law by the Conseil d'État. He thus wished to convince the Court to ask the French government to push for an amendment of the Treaties of Rome. In the end, the case was withdrawn by the applicant and the Conseil d'État did not have to decide on the merits of Aurillac's argument.[184] It was only when Chirac became Prime Minister that the souverainistes tried again. This time, it was Debré, who in August 1986 managed to pass an amendment to a bill debated in the National Assembly to further limit the scope of application of Article 55 of the Constitution. The aim was to restrain foreign legal entities from interfering

182 This was eventually expressed in Treaty of Maastricht, Article B, 5th indent which made clear that member states would work on basis of the acquis communautaire to ensure the efficiency of the EU and thus implicitly respect the case law of the ECJ.

183 Ludlow 2013; Loth 2013.

184 FNA. Collection 'Michel Aurillac' (365AP84).

in French internal law. However, a group of socialist MPs challenged Debré's amendment before the Conseil constitutionnel on the basis of non-conformity with the French Constitution. Less than a month later, the Court delivered a report stating that Debré's amendment did not conform with the French Constitution since it represented a direct violation of Article 55. The drafter was no other than Lecourt, who had been promoted to the Conseil constitutionnel in 1979 as a replacement for the diseased Coste-Floret.[185] This was the final legislative attempt to safeguard French sovereignty against the encroachment of the ECJ. Now the souverainistes had to hope that the position of the Conseil d'État would not change.

The Conseil d'État was, however, under increased pressure to do just that. The Mitterrand administration had demonstrated from 1982 a new willingness to cooperate with the ECJ. The new Minister of Justice, Robert Badinter, reintroduced the circulaire on preliminary references and asked French courts to use the mechanism systematically, with the result that the number of preliminary references rose significantly in the 1980s. Convincing the Conseil d'État to change its stance proved much more difficult. The Mitterrand administration was hampered by the fact that it had to cohabitate with the Chirac government from 1986 to 1988. Nevertheless, the Mitterrand administration made a concerted effort to gradually pave the way for a reversal of the position of the Conseil d'État. Here the nomination of judges to the key French courts as well as the ECJ played a significant role in particularly by prompting the Conseil constitutionnel to take a more active role in promoting European law. In addition to this, several direct initiatives of the government led by Michel Rocard from 1988 onwards forced the Conseil d'État to finally make a decision.

The Conseil constitutionnel had been dominated by Gaullist appointees, but this gradually changed from the late 1970s with the nominations of Lecourt in 1979 and George Vedel in 1980, as well as additional socialist nominations after 1982. From 1986, Genevois was nominated as Secretary-General of the Conseil constitutionnel and quickly established himself as an outspoken promoter of the European cause. Against the backdrop of the active French European policy from 1984, the new Conseil constitutionnel began to adapt to the new political context. There had been academic critique of the unrealistic claim that international law was merely contingent in the famous 1975 decision in which the Court had declined to apply the primacy of European law. It was now obvious that neither the European Convention on Human Rights nor the EC could be considered contingent, as recognised publicly by Genevois. However, the procedural limitations of the Conseil constitutionnel remained. They could only address laws that were not yet promulgated and therefore did not want to enforce European law primacy. However, in a 1986

185 FNA. Collection 'Conseil constitutionnel' (20140168/12), Report of the Session of 3 September 1986 – Decision n° 86–216 DC.

judgment, the Conseil constitutionnel finally explicitly endorsed the *Jacque Vabre* precedent, pointing out that French courts were obliged to apply international conventions within their respective powers.[186] The following year the Conseil constitutionnel also delivered another crucial judgment, when it decided that the separation of powers of the French state depended on the existence of the Conseil d'État and thus finally offered it a constitutional basis.[187] Genevois was not slow to point out that the ball was now in the court of the administrative judge.[188]

By 1988, it was high time that the Conseil d'État changed its position considering the importance of the establishment of the Single European Market to the French economy. When the socialists won back the National Assembly, the new government led by Michel Rocard (1988–1991) launched a veritable offensive to finally push the Conseil d'État towards cooperating with the ECJ and accepting the primacy of European law. The Conseil d'État was consequently commissioned to study the relationship between international, European and national law and Rocard stressed the importance of the report for European integration and the realisation of the Single European Market.[189]

The political pressure was now immense. The Conseil d'État looked increasingly isolated, and several factors placed it under extraordinary pressure. At the European level, the Italian Constitutional Court's *Granital* judgment in 1984 and the German Constitutional Court's *Solange II* judgment in 1986 signalled a clear willingness to cooperate with the ECJ and apply European law.[190] Moreover, the creation of the Single European Market from 1986 onwards created a significant stream of new European legislation that posed a serious challenge to the French legal order. If the Conseil d'État continued to not apply European law, it would have important legal consequences to French firms that would operate under different rules than in the rest of the EC. Finally, the Conseil d'État had become isolated in the French court system.

Inside the Conseil d'État, the nomination of Marceau Long as Vice-President in 1987, but also the return of the socialist nominated ECJ judge, Yves Galmont in 1988, helped to improve the understanding and appreciation of European law considerably. Long in particular was explicit about his open mind regarding cooperation with the ECJ: 'one should not be cold in the face of European law, but come to know it and contribute to its creation'.[191] The result of this pressure was that the Conseil d'État finally reversed its *Semoules* doctrine in the *Nicolo* decision in 1989

186 Conseil constitutionel, 3 September 1986, *Loi relative aux conditions d'entrée et de séjour des étrangers en France*, n° 82–216 DC.

187 Conseil constitutionel, 23 January 1987, *Loi transférant à la juridiction judiciaire le contentieux des décisions du Conseil de la concurrence*, n° 86–224 DC.

188 Alter 2001, 160–161.

189 Alter 2001, 162.

190 Corte Costituzionale, *Granital v Amministrazione delle Finanze*, judgment no. 170 of 5 June 1984 and BVerfGE 73, 339, 22.10.1986, *Solange II*, 2 BvR 197/83.

191 Cited in Alter 2001, 162.

and started to cooperate with the ECJ by the means of the preliminary reference mechanism thus accepting the primacy of European law.[192] However, as was the case with the Cour de Cassation *Jacques Vabre* judgment, the basis for the *Nicolo* decision was not the special (constitutional) order of the European law, but Article 55 of the French constitution. The Commissaire du gouvernement Patrick Frydman did not hide his disdain for the ECJ's constitutional claim. In his view the ECJ's primacy jurisprudence had 'no legal basis whatsoever'.[193]

The decision of the Conseil d'État thus made it clear to all that it had to cooperate with the European legal order, however, at the same time, the Court rejected the constitutional claim of the ECJ. This position, although predating the Maastricht negotiations from 1990–1991, very much aligned itself to the French government's position on the nature of the new European Union. Ultimately, the new European Union would not be based on European constitutionalism as legitimating principle, while the codification of the acquis communautaire represented an explicit acceptance of the member states that they would work on basis of the acquis and thus also respect the case law of the ECJ.[194] In this sense, the *Nicolo* decision was a Pyrrhic victory for the supranationalists. It reflected a long trajectory of scepticism of the French political, administrative and legal elites towards the development of European integration, while at the same time reconciling France with the Single European Market and the EC.

CONCLUSION

This chapter has offered a new history of the relationship between France and European law. Earlier accounts focused mainly on French court's reception of European law, exploring the process as predominantly an institutional and legal history. Several of the key conclusions of this earlier research have been confirmed here. There is no doubt that the French proclivity for a preference of state power and the structure of the French court system shaped French reception of European law. Indeed, this chapter has confirmed that the closeness of the Conseil d'État to the executive and its lack of constitutional basis made it very difficult to accept the constitutional interpretation of European law, even if it had wanted to before the 1980s. Likewise, the chapter also confirmed that the relations between the Conseil constitutionnel established in 1958 and the Conseil d'État and the Cour de cassation were important. It was the development of the Conseil constitutionnel into a proper constitutional court from 1971 onwards that eventually broke the deadlock. By the mid-1970s, the Court gave its first ambiguous nod to engage with European law in the mid-1970s and eventually, in the 1980s, it began to push French

192 Conseil d'État (Assemblée), 20 October 1989, *Nicolo*, n° 108243, published in *Recueil Lebon* 190, 1990.

193 Cited in Alter 2001, 165.

194 Treaty of Maastricht, Article B, 5th indent.

courts hard towards accepting European law, while laying part of the groundwork for that acceptance by securing the constitutional position of the Conseil d'État.

This chapter has nevertheless gone significantly beyond existing research. By placing the story in a broader political and social context, while systematically using relevant private, state and European archival sources, the chapter has demonstrated that the French reception of European law was part of an intensive political battle over the nature of the EC and the French role in the process of European integration. This battle involved the French Presidents, their governments and administrations from 1958 onwards. However, it primarily played out between two 'trends of thought' or loose networks of politicians and jurists, of respectively Christian democratic or Gaullist background, with the socialists more split between the two positions. It was this political battle that accounts for the twists and turns of the French reception of European law, the pro-European actions of several lower courts and the Cour de Cassation, the launch of key court cases (by pro-European lawyers), the ups and downs in the use of the preliminary reference mechanism and ultimately explain the conditional acceptance of European law that the *Nicolo* decision entails.

The analysis of the battle between the two 'trends of thought' demonstrated the extent to which both the development of European law and its reception were part of a broader political battle over the nature of the EC and France's place in Europe. The 'supranationalistes' worked at both national and European level, and they crucially played a central role in launching the constitutional interpretation of European law in the first place. As Christian Democracy finally lost political power in France in 1958 and only occasionally would gain a foothold in French governments before the 1970s, the national arena was much more difficult to navigate. However, through the organisation of the AJE, close contacts and coordination with the European Commission and the ECJ, 'the supranationalistes' could use their positions as lawyers and judges to promote European law even under the constraints of the Gaullist republic. In the 1970s and 1980s, they occasionally held ministerial power and could actively promote a more positive French stance towards the ECJ and the use of the preliminary reference mechanism, or they were nominated to the Conseil constitutionnel like Coste-Floret, Lecourt and Vedel, and could shape the French reception of European law in the court system. However, it was only in the 1980s that the new dynamics of European integration more fundamentally changed the French position versus the ECJ and as a result it was mainly socialist politicians and jurists that overcame the last obstacles towards a more comprehensive, if conditional, acceptance by France of the European law.

The story of the 'souverainiste' was to a higher degree one of missed opportunities. During the 1960s, they did not pursue a wholesale reform of the ECJ at the European level, perhaps because they domestically could ensure the non-application of European law and limit cooperation through the preliminary preference mechanism in the French court system. In the 1970s, Debré and Foyer perhaps unwisely chose not to enter respectively the Conseil constitutionnel and the ECJ, instead preferring to fight the battle against the ECJ in the political arena. This offered in particular Peyrefitte the opportunity to stall the acceptance of the preliminary reference mechanism by French courts when he became Minister of Justice under Giscard d'Estaing. However, when the rebellion of the Conseil d'État in 1979 did not escalate and the Aurillac amendment was rejected by the Senate in 1980, the 'souverainiste' movement suffered a final defeat of hope to fundamentally break with the ECJ and the EC's legal system. When the integration process accelerated and deepened under the leadership of Mitterrand from 1984 onwards, even the entrenched position of the Conseil d'État would eventually have to give way.

8

Blazing a Trail: The Netherlands and European Law

Karin van Leeuwen

In 1963, a ruling of the European Court of Justice (ECJ) in a dispute between NV Algemene Transport- en Expeditie Onderneming Van Gend en Loos and the Nederlandse Administratie der Belastingen laid the foundations for what is generally considered a revolutionary development in European law.[1] At question was Article 12 EEC treaty, prohibiting the introduction of or increase in customs duties on trade between member states. Concluding that the Netherlands had, in fact, raised duties in the specific case brought before it, the ECJ reprimanded the Netherlands – the main protagonist behind the creation of a Common Market since the early 1950s – for violating a rule that only seemed to benefit its intra-European trade-oriented economy.[2] More importantly however, the ECJ confirmed that this particular Article did not only address the member state governments, but that it could also be invoked by citizens and companies against their national governments. This doctrine of direct effect was ground-breaking. Together with the *Costa v ENEL* of 1964 ruling establishing the supremacy of European law, Van Gend en Loos introduced a constitutional understanding of the Treaties of Rome, or, as the ECJ more cautiously described it, an understanding of European law as introducing a 'new legal order'.[3]

In the rich scholarship analysing the emergence of this constitutional interpretation, it has not gone unnoticed that, by bringing the *Van Gend en Loos* case before

[1] Rasmussen 2014. In this chapter I draw on van Leeuwen 2012; van Leeuwen 2018.

[2] 26/62 *Van Gend en Loos v Nederlandse Administratie der Belastingen*, 1963, ECLI:EU:C:1963:1. In 1955, Dutch export to ECSC countries amounted to 38.3 per cent of the total export, and import from the ECSC member states was 40.7 per cent. This was well above the figures of the other future EEC member states and only increased after 1962. See full figures in van Leeuwen 2018.

[3] 6/64 *Costa v ENEL*, 1964, ECLI:EU:C:1964:66. Recent scholarship however has revised this 'constitutional' narrative of European law, arguing that a constitutional interpretation was far from self-evident in 1963–1964, but instead was deliberately developed as a 'legitimating strategy' by a narrow group of 'Euro-lawyers' seeking to define integration in legal terms (Vauchez 2015). In addition, scholars such as Peter Lindseth and Will Phelan have offered alternative interpretations of European legal doctrine, pointing out its close relationship to national administrative law and international law respectively: Lindseth 2010; Phelan 2016. Also see Davies and Rasmussen 2012. By further analysing the construction of the constitutional narrative, this chapter will contribute to this more critical scholarship.

the ECJ, Dutch courts and companies crucially blazed a trail for this famous ruling.[4] This was no coincidence. Remarkably, *Van Gend en Loos* was only the second case that reached the ECJ via the preliminary reference procedure of Article 177 EEC treaty. *Van Gend en Loos* was also the second case to be filed by a Dutch court. In fact, Dutch courts were responsible for a large share of the first preliminary references sent to Luxembourg (fifteen out of the first eighteen cases). How can this exceptionally active contribution of one of the smaller member states to the development of European law be explained? And what does it tell us about the Dutch interaction with European law more generally?

In scholarly analyses of the Dutch contributions to the development of the European legal system, *Van Gend en Loos* is regarded as an example of the exceptionally pacific and smooth interaction between the Netherlands and European law.[5] Legal scholars, political scientists and sociologists pointed out how this exceptional cooperation was encouraged by the 'traditional openness' of the Dutch legal system to international law, while Dutch companies' and scholars' active engagement with European law followed from their commercial interests and ideological orientations respectively.[6] However, another look at *Van Gend en Loos* suffices to demonstrate that the Dutch interaction with European law cannot exclusively be described as smooth. The case also establishes how the Dutch government hesitated to fully implement the obligations created by the EEC Treaty in regard to customs duties – obligations which were at the same time accepted with open arms by businesses such as, in this case, a well-known national transport firm. If the Dutch government would not have contained the effect of these treaty clauses to begin with, the N.V. Algemene Transport- en Expeditie Onderneming Van Gend en Loos would have lacked the opportunity to start its famous court case. Thus, in this case, Dutch containment of the effects of European law was just as constitutive in shaping the European legal order as the cooperative patterns and practices that eventually enabled a Dutch court to refer the case to Luxembourg.[7]

In analysing the interaction of the Netherlands with European law between the 1950s and the early 1990s, this chapter aims to open up the narrative of this interaction to include both cooperation as well as resistance – here used for instances where the principles of a constitutional interpretation were challenged – and containment – indicating an unwillingness to fully comply with the effects of the new legal order. It does this by widening the scope of actors included in the narrative. Drawing on a wide range of archival sources, interviews as well as on

[4] Claes and de Witte 1998; Rasmussen 2014; Vauchez 2015.

[5] Claes and de Witte 1998; on a more recent period also van Harten 2015. This understanding resonates in for example the important work of Alter 2001.

[6] Claes and de Witte 1998, 189; Sweet 2004, 86; Vauchez 2015.

[7] On the key importance of national resistance for the shaping of European law see Davies 2012b; Davies 2015; Davies 2017.

parliamentary proceedings, press reports and journal articles, this chapter looks at courts as well as at politicians, legal scholars and litigants. On the other hand, it reconnects this legal history to the broader historiographies on Dutch foreign and European policy; it points out how the Dutch positioning vis-à-vis European law was not only steered by legal considerations, but also by economic interests, notions of smallness and a deeply ingrained sense of Atlanticism that some actors translated into a rather sceptical stance towards European integration.[8] Moreover, insights from political history help to understand how the Dutch political culture of accommodation generally precluded the use of court procedures to solve political disputes – until European law fundamentally changed it.[9]

Two chronological phases are discerned, separated by the breakthrough of the constitutional understanding of European law in 1963–1964. As the first two sections of this chapter demonstrate, the years prior to 1963 are marked by broad support for a supranational or constitutional European Community both in parliament and in scholarly debates, for example in the context of the Dutch constitutional reforms in the early 1950s. At the same time however, the Dutch government blatantly resisted attempts to radically open the Dutch legal order for international and European treaty clauses directly binding its citizens, as the first section establishes. Moreover, the second section demonstrates how the Dutch government, as well as courts, in this phase did not hesitate to contain the effects of European law where this was considered opportune for domestic interests – as the *Van Gend en Loos* case already suggests. In the second phase, beginning in the mid-1960s, this deliberate failure to fully implement treaty obligations had not changed, which an increasingly well-organised academic field started to point out from the 1970s onward. As demonstrated in the third section of this chapter, at the same time, this phase marked the end of the Dutch government's resistance to a constitutional understanding of European law. Instead, taking over academic arguments regarding the importance of a powerful legal order for small states such as the Netherlands, it became official government policy to support the understanding of this legal order developed by the ECJ well into the 1990s.

OPENING THE CONSTITUTION 'FOR A BETTER ENFORCEMENT OF INTERNATIONAL LAW', 1950–1957

'Leading the way' – with those words the New York Times opened its reporting on Dutch affairs in December 1952.[10] At first sight, the headline seems particularly ill fit for Dutch European policy at the time. In 1950, a Dutch plan for a European Common Market (the so-called Stikker plan) lost out against the French plans for a European Coal and Steel Community (ECSC) that caught the Dutch government

8 Kruizinga 2016; Segers 2013.

9 Andeweg and Irwin 2014; van Waarden and Hildebrand 2009, 263.

10 'Leading the Way', 1952, 4 December. *New York Times*.

by surprise.[11] And while the Netherlands had joined the ECSC, it only did so after securing the introduction of a Council of Ministers limiting the supranational character of the new community. In November 1952, during the negotiations on a European Political Community, the Netherlands appeared to again obstruct further integration with its demands that political integration needed to be accompanied by simultaneous economic integration.[12] Yet, as the *New York Times* highlighted, in one respect, Dutch politics was ready to take unprecedented steps towards international cooperation. A constitutional reform promised to remove all possible impediments with regard to the conferral of powers on 'organizations based on international law'.[13] In addition, new clauses were introduced regulating the interaction between the Netherlands and international legal orders. Although similar provisions on treaties and the transfer of sovereignty could be found in the new constitutions of France, West Germany and Italy, the Dutch clauses gave much more authority to international law.[14]

A PIONEERING CONSTITUTIONAL REFORM

The constitutional reform initiated in Spring 1950 by the establishment of two advisory committees was originally intended as a general modernisation of the nineteenth-century Dutch constitution.[15] The rapid emergence of international organisations such as the United Nations, the Council of Europe, NATO and the Benelux, however, resulted in a particular emphasis – embodied by a separate committee – on the democratisation of foreign policy. This second committee, consisting of legal scholars and politicians specialising in foreign policy, took the initiative to draft provisions on treaties and the transfer of sovereignty. The proposal was initiated by emeritus professor of international law, Willem van Eysinga, chair of the second committee.[16]

Earlier in the twentieth century, Van Eysinga and other prominent Leiden professors such as Cornelis van Vollenhoven and Hugo Krabbe rejected the strict separation of national and international law as it had been developed mainly in

11 Kersten 1988.

12 Harryvan 2009, 42–47; Griffiths 2000, 96–101.

13 Article 67.1: 'Aan volkenrechtelijke organisaties kunnen bij of krachtens een overeenkomst bevoegdheden tot wetgeving, bestuur en rechtspraak worden opgedragen.' [By or in virtue of an agreement certain powers with respect to legislation, administration and jurisdiction may be conferred on organizations based on international law.] Translation from van Panhuys 1953, 540.

14 De Witte 1998.

15 On this constitutional revision and the plans that preceded it see van Leeuwen 2013.

16 First report Van Eysinga committee Plenary committee 16 September 1950, 14–16, via http://resources.huygens.knaw.nl/grondwetscommissies/onderzoeksgids; National Archives, The Hague (NA-NL), Foreign Affairs 1945–1954 (2.05.117), inv. no. 27297. Memorandum by Van Eysinga, 20 May 1951 ('doc. 70') and memorandum-Van Eysinga 'inzake document 77', June 1951. Van Eysinga published a slightly altered version of these memoranda as 'De praktijk sedert de wedergeboorte van de verhouding tussen grondwet en tractaat'. *Nederlands Juristenblad* 27.10.1952.

German legal doctrine. Alternatively, these Dutch scholars pushed for an understanding of what they referred to as 'community law', perceiving the newly developing international communities as new and autonomous legal orders with sovereign powers and powers. However, that presumed a direct relation between these communities and individual citizens.[17] In accordance with this emerging trend in academic debate, the Hoge Raad, the Dutch Supreme Court, seemed to have embraced monism as early as 1906 by rejecting the opposing transformation doctrine.[18] And although the lawyers disagreed on whether the Hoge Raad adjudicated on the question of primacy of international law over subsequent legislation, a small majority of Dutch lawyers in the late 1930s had supported the doctrine of primacy.[19]

In its 1951 proposals for constitutional reform, the Van Eysinga committee suggested confirming existing doctrine on this matter by proposing a clause regarding the primacy of international law provisions. Building on his authoritative status as one of the country's key experts in international law, Van Eysinga had no difficulty in convincing the other committee members that the proposal would merely confirm a standing practice in Dutch doctrine, and that their main aim was to regulate in a more precise manner the consequences of this primacy for citizens and companies.[20] Marked by the experiences of the world crises of the 1930s, the Second World War and the painful decolonisation of Indonesia in the late 1940s, the notion of national sovereignty in Dutch political debate was understood as something inherently limited. Nonetheless, Van Eysinga's proposal was met with resistance from experts in constitutional law, including professors Louis Beel, George van den Bergh, André Donner (the future president of the ECJ) and Pieter Oud. As they

17 Van Eysinga 1950, 34–35. Van Eysinga pointed at van Vollenhoven 1932 and Krabbe 1906. The idea of 'mundiaal recht' was embraced by politicians such as P. Cort van der Linden. NA-NL, Staatscie. Grondwetswijziging 2.04.53.09 inv. no. 2. Minutes Th. van Heemskerk constitutional committee, 11 September 1911, pp. 459–460.

18 Hoge Raad (HR) 25 May 1906, *Weekblad van het Recht* (1906) 8383. At the same time, monism was acknowledged in parliament: Fleuren 2004, 98–109. Cf. van der Pot and Telders 1937 and Erades 1950, 217, who deny that the 1906 Hoge Raad ruling addressed monism.

19 The Hoge Raad dealt with the issue in two rulings on the Rhine Navigation Treaty on 17 December 1934: *Nederlandse Jurisprudentie* (1935) 5 and 11. The (temporary) High Court on Special Justice Concerning the Second World War (*Bijzondere raad voor cassatie*) had recognised the primacy of international law in 1949: Bijzondere Raad van Cassatie 12 January 1949, *Nederlandse Jurisprudentie* (1949), 87. In 1952, the Hoge Raad still avoided a clear ruling: HR 25 January 1952, *Nederlandse Jurisprudentie* (1952), 125. In the 1937 annual meeting of the Dutch lawyers' association (Nederlandse Juristenvereniging: NJV), only a small majority of lawyers voted in favour of the proposition that treaty law 'binding in the national sphere' should be given priority over national law whether antecedent or subsequent: 1937. 'Verslag eerste zitting'. *Handelingen NJV* 67: 96. In 1952, Rotterdam Judge Erades calculated that, of the law professors who had recently addressed the issue, fifteen supported the primacy clause, where three did not: Erades 1952, 228.

20 *Eindrapport van de Commissie nopens de samenwerking tussen regering en Staten-Generaal inzake het buitenlands beleid (9 July 1951)*, The Hague: Staatsdrukkerij- en uitgeverijbedrijf, 20–21, however, see the resistance from constitutional law professor C.W. van der Pot: NA-NL, Foreign Affairs 1945–1954 (2.05.117), inv. no. 27297. Memorandum 'doc. 77', 11 June 1951.

pointed out, the primacy clause would be incompatible with the traditionally rather restricted role of the judiciary in Dutch society. The core legal norm that best expressed this was the prohibition on reviewing the constitutionality of national legislation.[21]

While these concerns did not prevent Van Eysinga's proposal from finding a majority in both constitutional committees, the reservations with regard to the role of the judiciary provided useful fuel for its main opponents in the government. In particular, Labour Party (Partij van de Arbeid, PvdA) leader and Prime Minister Willem Drees expressed fear that the primacy clause would introduce as binding law many treaty provisions that the Netherlands (a small country in international politics) could only influence to a limited extent.[22] Apart from a general scepticism of European cooperation – for which Drees was known – this argument reflected a serious concern for the role of parliament and government (in the Dutch system known as 'the legislator') vis-à-vis the judiciary. Similar concerns had also been raised in internal discussions on the European Convention on Human Rights, where the Drees cabinet expressed fears that the Dutch state would become the hostage of 'querulous' individuals using litigation to push their interests.[23] Hence, the government decided to leave the primacy clause out of its reform proposals.[24]

In parliament, the primacy clause reappeared on the constitutional reform agenda due to an amendment drafted by Jos Serrarens, MP for the Catholic People's Party (Katholieke Volkspartij, KVP) and leader of the Dutch European Movement.[25] Together with then PvdA group leader Marinus van der Goes van Naters, Serrarens had already led the pro-European majority in parliament for some years. For example, he had tabled the resolutions which pushed the more sceptical government to take a similarly positive position on international cooperation.[26] When defending the amendment of the constitutional reform, Serrarens invoked both the broad parliamentary support for international cooperation expressed in these resolutions, as well as the claim to (doctrinal) continuity made by Van Eysinga. In addition, building on his experience as Secretary of the International Labour

21 NA-NL, General Affairs AZ/AOK/KMP (2.03.01), inv. no. 1124. Minutes Van Schaik committee Subcommittee III 8 November 1950; Draft W.C.L. van der Grinten 2 November 1950 and NA-NL, General Affairs AZ/AOK/KMP (2.03.01), inv. no. 1124. Memorandum Van Schaik committee Subcommittee III 'Samenvatting van de bezwaren' 23 January 1951; Minority report Van den Bergh and Donner in 1951. *Interim-rapport van de Staatscommissie tot Herziening van de Grondwet,* The Hague: Staatsdrukkerij- en uitgeverijbedrijf, p. 43.

22 NA-NL, Council of Ministers (2.02.05.02) inv. no. 395. Minutes Council of Ministers 1 October 1951. On Willem Drees consult Segers 2013, 79.

23 Klerk and Poelgeest 1991, 225; Hommes 2023.

24 Erades 1952, 232–233. See van der Pot 1952, 37–38 for a sharp criticism on this allegedly hasty decision by the government.

25 *Handelingen Tweede Kamer der Staten-Generaal* (Proceedings of the Lower House, *HTK*) 1951–1952, Bijlage 2374 no. 17. On Petrus Serrarens as 'pioneer' see van Heerikhuizen 1998.

26 *HTK* 1947–1948, Bijlage 761; *HTK* 1948–1949, Bijlage 1247. Robin de Bruin has recently argued that the remarkable support for integration in parliament was highly 'elastic': almost any political group could mould it to their own ideal shape. See de Bruin 2014.

Organisation during the interwar years, Serrarens also deliberately framed the amendment as a decisive political choice in favour of a better enforcement of international law. He argued that the Netherlands simply needed to set the good example in order to overcome the difficulties caused by the reliance on intergovernmental methods that so clearly had failed in the 1930s. Thus, Serrarens referred to the alleged Grotian tradition in Dutch foreign policy, which understood a pioneering role in international law as an important means to achieve foreign policy objectives.[27] Opponents of the amendment, including KVP Minister of Internal Affairs Beel, were remarkably keen to explain that they actually adhered to the same Grotian tradition; the difference was merely that they believed that the legislature should guarantee the enforcement of international law, not the courts. Serrarens, afterward appointed judge in the new Court of Justice of the ECSC (1952–1957), countered that government and parliament might still ultimately choose to defend national interests, whereas courts were in theory impartial.[28]

Eventually, Serrarens and his allies convinced a narrow majority of deputies to vote in favour of the amendment that gave treaty law 'binding in the national sphere' priority over prior and subsequent national law.[29] Confronted with the amended proposal, the government gave up its resistance on this point and defended the entire constitutional reform in the Senate before it entered into force in 1953. Apart from the controversial primacy clause and a long-expected democratisation of the procedure for treaty ratification, the 'leading' constitutional reform also introduced a provision authorising the transfer of power to international organisations and a special procedure for the ratification of treaties found deviating from the constitution.[30] In 1954, the new primacy clause however, was reviewed again during a second, 'technical' revision of the 1953 constitutional clauses which, as a result of the many parliamentary amendments, were found difficult to work with in practice.[31] The resulting 1956 revision limited the primacy of international law to international legal norms that were self-executing, or in

27 *HTK* 1951–1952, 1877–1962. On this Dutch 'tradition' consult Corduwener 2012, 202.

28 *HTK* 1951–1952, 1946, 1958.

29 The Serrarens amendment was passed with a forty-six to forty majority: *HTK* 1951–1952, 1959. Article 65: 'Binnen het Koninkrijk geldende wettelijke voorschriften vinden geen toepassing, wanneer deze niet verenigbaar zou zijn met overeenkomsten, die hetzij vóór, hetzij na de totstandkoming der voorschriften zijn bekend gemaakt overeenkomstig artikel 66.' [Legal provisions in force within the Kingdom shall not apply if the application should be incompatible with agreements which have been published in accordance with Article 66 either before or after the enactment of the provisions.] Article 66: 'De wet geeft regels omtrent de bekendmaking van overeenkomsten. De overeenkomsten verbinden een ieder, voorzover zij zijn bekend gemaakt.' [Rules with regard to the publication of agreements shall be laid down in the law. Agreements shall be binding on anyone insofar as they will have been published.] Translation from van Panhuys 1953, 540.

30 When 'demanded by the development of the international legal order', such treaties could be ratified by a 2/3 majority in both houses of parliament.

31 Instalment speech minister of Interior Affairs L.J.M. Beel, 1 October 1954. Kranenburg committee report, 21, via http://resources.huygens.knaw.nl/grondwetscommissies/onderzoeksgids. See for this criticism e.g. Duynstee 1954; van Panhuys 1955, 28.

Dutch legal language: 'binding upon anyone', meaning that they directly addressed the rights and duties of citizens.[32]

Presenting the 1956 revision as a 'technical' revision, the government emphasised that this revision was not to be considered as a limitation of the 1953 clause, as Van Eysinga had suggested in a critical discussion of the proposals.[33] Indeed, already in 1953, discussing the Serrarens amendment in the Senate, Minister Beel had differentiated between 'self-executing' and 'non-self-executing' provisions, the latter of which 'only regarded instructions to legislative and administrative organs' and hence could not be challenged in court.[34] Nonetheless, by ruling out the possibility that citizens would invoke vague or indirect policy objectives in court, the new 1956 phrasing did reflect some of the objections the government had made vis-à-vis the 1953 primacy clause. The pro-European majority in parliament however, agreed to the new phrasing after being reassured that, 'a broader understanding of "binding upon anyone" would be possible in the future'.[35]

. . . BUT NO 'CONSTITUTIONAL' UNDERSTANDING OF EUROPEAN INTEGRATION

In parliament, the new constitutional clauses were immediately understood as a key guideline in the ratification of the subsequent European treaties. In 1952, the special clause that had been heralded by the New York Times paved the way for a successful ratification of the European Defence Community (EDC) Treaty – as this treaty required the transfer of a 'constitutional' power, the new clause required a two-thirds majority for its ratification.[36] In 1957 however, no such special procedure was deemed necessary for the EEC treaty. Instead, the 1953/1956 constitutional reforms were cited only in general terms to argue that even a far-reaching treaty as the one founding the EEC agreed with the 'text and spirit' of the Dutch constitution.[37] At the same time, in its presentation of the EEC treaty, the government deliberately downplayed the constitutional implications of the new Community in order to avoid the special ratification procedure. Generally eager to ratify a treaty that satisfied both Dutch commercial interests and pro-European ambitions, Parliament did not

32 The new Article 66 stated: 'Binnen het Koninkrijk geldende wettelijke voorschriften vinden geen toepassing, wanneer deze toepassing niet verenigbaar zou zijn met een ieder verbindende bepalingen van overeenkomsten, die hetzij vóór, hetzij na de totstandkoming der voorschriften zijn aangegaan.' [Legislation in force within the Kingdom shall not apply if this application would be incompatible with provisions of agreements which are binding upon anyone, and which have been entered into either before or after the enactment of such legislation. Translation from van Panhuys 1953, 107].

33 Van Eysinga 1955, 615–20. Indeed, see the Hoge Raad Nyugat II ruling (Hoge Raad, 6 March 1959, *Nyugat II ruling*, *Nederlandse Jurisprudentie* 1962, 2), where the Hoge Raad acknowledged that no primacy could be assumed for unwritten international law anymore.

34 *HEK* 1952–1953, B 2700 no. 63a, 3.

35 *HTK* 1955–1956, 802.

36 *HTK* 1952–1953, B 2911 no. 6, 2; *HTK* 1952–1953, 1027.

37 Hollander 2013, 110–111, uses the term '*fait accompli* line of reasoning' here.

contest this decision. Instead, it repeated the arguments that had helped Serrarens defend his amendment five years earlier to justify the expected legal implications of the treaty. In particular, the preliminary reference procedure established in Article 177 of the EEC treaty was praised as a 'guarantee for the uniform application of the treaty'.[38] Concerns regarding the limitations this procedure placed on the independence of national courts were brushed aside by the claim that the Netherlands as a small state should welcome measures securing a more equal standing of all member states.[39]

The rhetoric used in Parliament suggested that it also supported even more far-reaching steps in the direction of supranationalism, for example where it came to the powers conferred to the ECJ. The position of the Dutch government during the actual negotiations however had been more reluctant – mirroring its earlier positioning on the constitutional reform. During the negotiations on the Treaty of Paris, the Dutch delegation on the one hand supported the establishment of a permanent Court of Justice that could protect member states against a too powerful High Authority. On the other hand, it had opposed to opening access to this Court for citizens or companies. During the negotiations on the Treaties of Rome, which followed a Benelux initiative, the Dutch delegation often found itself defending a more supranational institutional framework against other options, for example with regard to the powers granted to the Commission. Yet, it resisted attempts to widen access of private litigants to the Court.[40]

In the meantime, outright resistance to strong supranational institutions, and indeed to European federalism, was found with Willem Riphagen, the Ministry of Foreign Affairs' long time (1954–1983) jurisconsult. Allegedly, merely to invite him for a meeting of the Leiden University 'Europa working group' – a study group of law professors, practitioners and students – caused controversy.[41] Riphagen, member of the Dutch delegation at both the negotiations on the Treaty of Paris and Treaties of Rome, had indeed vehemently argued against 'state-like' understandings of the Treaty of Paris, which, he argued, could be found in their 'purest form' in a report prepared by some of his fellow negotiators for the ECSC's Common Assembly.[42] Referring to recent rulings by the ECSC's Court of Justice as well as to the ECSC's functioning in practice, Riphagen claimed that sovereignty at most was 'delegated'

38 *HTK* 1957–1958, B 4725 no. 9, 60.

39 Such concerns had explicitly been raised by the *Raad van State* (Council of State), the long-standing advisory council to the Dutch government, but were not even voiced in the parliamentary debate. Hollander 2013, 97.

40 Boerger 2012; Harryvan 2009.

41 Interview of the author with P. J. G. Kapteyn, The Hague 15 October 2013. The Europa working group met irregularly and discussed topics such as 'the constitutional developments in the ECSC', the Benelux protocols on agriculture or the Warsaw Pact.

42 Riphagen 1955. Riphagen referred to the 'Avis' prepared by Ophüls, Reuter and De Rossi for the General Assembly in December 1952: 'Avis sur la participation des observateurs du Conseil de l'Europe à l'Assemblée commune et sur la conclusion d'un accord à cet effet', Council of Europe doc. S.G. (52) 10.

to the ECSC, not 'transferred'.[43] Shortly before, the Ministry of Foreign Affairs had argued along the same lines when the Netherlands stood before the ECJ for the first time in 1954, challenging a price decision of the High Authority that it deemed unfounded in the Treaty. In his defence of the Dutch position, Utrecht international law professor Verzijl had contended that the ECSC was an organisation based on international law.[44]

In 1955, Riphagen's interpretation of the ECSC was fiercely attacked by Ivo Samkalden, a law professor who had served as a legal adviser in the Ministry of Agriculture under Sicco Mansholt, the renowned federalist and later President of the European Commission. Pointing at the underlying political intentions that guided the establishment of the ECSC, Samkalden argued that an alternative interpretation of its legal character would have been possible as well.[45] In 1960, in his inauguration speech as the first Dutch professor of 'the law of international organisations', Samkalden pointed out how in his view, the new European organisations of the 1950s had to be regarded as a 'jump towards more closely arranged communities between states' and even as 'the foundations for a European legal order'. Illustrative for Samkalden's approach to realising this legal order is that these observations were followed by a call for active engagement of his audience: 'whether on these foundations a building will emerge, is yet unclear. The answer depends more on the people than on the treaties.'[46]

Indeed, in the years following the establishment of the EEC, Samkalden and the small number of scholars pioneering the field of European law in the Netherlands actively 'brokered' their new field among their colleagues.[47] In this process of shaping the legal dimension of the integration process, exchanges of information between legal practitioners, courts, but also businesses were deemed crucial.[48] In the Netherlands, such exchanges in the early 1950s were concentrated in journals such as *Sociaal Economische Wetgeving* (*Social Economic Legislation*), established in 1952 to report on the 'new' field of economic law, and around the Leiden working group. In 1959, the latter under Samkalden's lead was transformed into a formal institute (Europa Instituut). Financed by the Ford Foundation, it provided graduate and postgraduate education in European studies, as well as a meeting ground for Dutch lawyers and law students interested in European law.[49] Further, the pioneers

43 Riphagen 1955, 45–49; Lindseth 2010.

44 6/54, *The Netherlands v ECSC High Authority*, 1955, ECLI:EU:C:1955:5.

45 Samkalden 1955, 813.

46 Samkalden 1960, 203.

47 Vauchez 2015.

48 Samkalden 1957, 121–132.

49 Samkalden sat on the editorial board of *SEW* for most of its first decade – he only left during his appointment as Minister of Justice (1956–1958) – and wrote almost all comments on ECJ case law in this period. The privately held archive of the Europa Institute (Leiden) contains material on the working group, the establishment of the institute and correspondence on its finances. Also: P. J. G. Kapteyn, 'De oprichting van de Europese studiegroep, de Europese kartelgroep en het Leidse Europa Instituut in de jaren vijftig' (unpublished, I thank P. G. J. Kapteyn for sharing it

actively reached out to other associations such as the Dutch Bar Association, encouraging lawyers to use the EEC treaty in their daily practice.

Remarkably, these early publications and activities in the field of European law usually focused on the practical implications of specific treaty aspects, rather than on theoretical disputes on the nature of the legal order. For example, when speaking before the Dutch Bar Association, Samkalden not only referred to the 'grand scheme of a new legal order that needs to be elaborated', but also to possibilities to enforce compliance for Dutch business vis-à-vis more powerful member states.[50] This practice-oriented approach would dominate Dutch discussions on European law in the first years after 1957. Clearly, larger questions about the nature of this new field of law were at stake. They were, however, addressed via more technical issues that due to the recent constitutional reforms, soon found their way into court rooms. The first of these questions regarded an EEC Treaty clause on competition agreements. Could this clause under the Dutch constitution be assumed to be 'binding on everyone', and hence have primacy over national legislation? And, more importantly, the fundamental question of the relation between legal orders: who was to decide on this? Was this still a matter for national courts, or was the ECJ to have a final say via the preliminary reference procedure established in Article 177 EEC treaty?

BREAKING RESISTANCE: PIONEERING A CONSTITUTIONAL INTERPRETATION IN EUROPEAN LAW, 1957–1963

In March 1957, only one week before the EEC treaty was to be signed in Rome, Samkalden, now Minister of Justice, drew the attention of his colleagues to what might be a problematic clause for the Netherlands: draft Article 85.2 of the EEC Treaty regarding competition agreements 'preventing, restricting or distorting competition in the trade between member states'. The phrase explicitly banning such agreements would most likely be understood as 'binding on anyone'. According to the constitution, Article 85.2 would, therefore, necessarily prevail over national legislation. However, the Dutch government only just passed a national competition bill that was considered more favourable on cartels than the above EEC clause. How would courts deal with this, knowing that in the other member states, a strict observation of the clause would probably only be demanded once a common European legislation would have been agreed on?[51]

with me); interviews of the author with L. J. Brinkhorst (23 August 2013, The Hague), B. H. ter Kuile (23 September 2013, The Hague) and P. J. G. Kapteyn (15 October 2013, The Hague).

50 Samkalden 1960, 348. Also see the most likely pre-arranged questions asked to Samkalden by W. L. Haardt at the same meeting, who as an example used the heavily subsidised automobile producer Renault in France that assumedly created unequal competition for Dutch firms: Samkalden 1960, 385.

51 NA-NL. Council of Ministers (2.02.05.02) inv. no. 405. Minutes Council of Ministers 18 March 1957; On the preparations of the national bill see van Leeuwen 2024.

Soon after the publication of the Treaties of Rome, the same question was raised by Dutch businesses that were bound to be affected by the new rules – cartel agreements still being widespread in for example the market for electronic equipment. Publishing in a leading law journal, company lawyers P. W. L. Brijnen (Bataafse Petroleum Maatschappij, currently part of Shell) and Hein Wertheimer (Philips N.V.) called for clarification.[52] At the European level, the heads of delegation of the member states confirmed in a public statement that the clause was to be understood as directly applicable.[53] The Dutch government, however, resisted this interpretation. Eager to ratify the EEC treaty, and to protect its national legislation as long as other member states also were not affected, it proposed a new law to mitigate with the consequences of this particular treaty Article, maintaining that the precise interpretation of the Article was still to be defined in common European legislation.[54]

The special law regarding the competition clauses was accepted in Parliament even though various delegates pointed out that national courts might eventually regard this new law as invalid vis-à-vis European primary law (with direct applicability) that according to the constitution had primacy.[55] Whether national courts would actually go that far was not clear, however. Until then, rather than setting aside national law in favour of international law, Dutch courts usually sought to reconcile the two in conformity with their restricted role, reflected by the constitutional ban on judicial review.[56] However, specialists soon questioned whether a similar reticent approach would be applied with regard to this new cartel clause, considering that a particularly dynamic jurisprudence on cartels was evolving in the Netherlands at the time.[57]

As Brijnen and Wertheimer anticipated, it did not take long before Dutch companies started to refer to Article 85 of the EEC Treaty before national courts when accused of bypassing distribution agreements.[58] The Dutch courts hesitated, however, to agree with their claim that Article 85 rendered the bypassed agreement invalid. Instead, most rulings followed the interpretation of the aforementioned special law: until a common competition policy was established, Article 85 ought to be read not as directly applicable, but as general principles guiding national

52 Brijnen and Wertheimer 1957, 253. On cartels in the Netherlands see Bouwens and Dankers 2011, 751.

53 Public statement of the head of delegations 6 May 1957 as cited in Rasmussen 2014, 143. At the time of the negotiations, it was not at all certain which interpretation of Articles 85–86 would prevail: Ramírez Perez and van der Scheur 2013, 19.

54 *HTK* 1956–1957, Bijl. 4778, no. 1–2. The special law was dubbed 'Sinterklaaswetje' since it was accepted on 5 December 1958, when the Dutch celebrate the patron's day of St. Nicolaas.

55 *HTK* 1957–1958, 28–29; *Handelingen Eerste Kamer* (proceedings of Senate, *HEK*) 1957–1958, 46, 84.

56 De Wit 2012.

57 As a consequence of the so-called 'Kolynos-jurisprudence' developed in the late 1930s under tort law, companies could be brought to court for deliberately making use of the contract violation by the official reseller.

58 Zutphen District Court, 11 July 1958, *Tuberies Louis Julien S.A. v N.V. Van Katwijk's Papier en Cartonverwerkende Industrieën*, *Nederlandse Jurisprudentie* 426.

policy.[59] Scholars were quick to observe that this Dutch interpretation diverged from the course taken by the German competition authorities.[60] While studying the diverging interpretations in various working groups, conferences and publications, both cartel specialists and more generalist scholars of European law arrived at the conclusion that courts had to use the preliminary reference procedure of Article 177 of the EEC treaty and ask the ECJ for a definitive interpretation of Article 85.[61]

Using the preliminary reference system was by no means obvious in the late 1950s – not even the ECJ itself agreed on its functioning.[62] Until 1960, the various Dutch courts that had been presented cases with respect to Article 85 refrained from invoking it. Apart from the fact that in most cases they had not been asked to do so, they argued that the procedure was incompatible with the procedural nature of the cases, which so far all had been so-called summary proceedings (*kort geding*). In the Dutch system, a summary proceeding is not only supposed to be fast, but it also does not allow the court to make irreversible decisions such as nullifying cartel agreements unless the case was unambiguous – and it was very clear that the interpretation of Article 85.2 was not.[63] At the European Commission's Legal Service, Gerhard Bebr had been given the task of monitoring how national courts received European law and interpreted this argumentation as a sign that Dutch courts were 'conveniently avoiding' a difficult ruling that might set aside national law.[64] From their side, Dutch lawyers in their comments mainly argued for 'better cases', that is,

59 This was the case in *Tuberies* (see note 58) as well as in Rotterdam District Court, 9 July 1960, *Linde's Eismaschinen Aktiengesellschaft and Heybroeck Zelander N.V. v v.o.f. Kledingverkoopbedrijf De Geus en Uitdenbogerd, Sociaal-Economische Wetgeving* 180; Rotterdam District Court, 26 October 1960, *Robert Bosch GmbH and W. van Rijn N.V. v v.o.f. Kledingverkoopbedrijf De Geus en Uitdenbogerd, Nederlandse Jurisprudentie* 159; The Hague District Court, 14 December 1960, *Aarts v Vereniging van Fabrikanten van Plakband en Parafinepapier, Sociaal-Economische Wetgeving* 265; Amsterdam District Court, 21 March 1961, *Bosch & Van Rijn v KIM & Slootmans*. Unpublished; retrieved in Noord-Hollands Archief, Haarlem (NHA), Arrondissementsrechtbank Amsterdam 1960–1969 (593) inv. no. 938; Arnhem Court of Appeal, 28 June 1961, *Tuberies, Sociaal-Economische Wetgeving* 125.; The Hague District Court, 24 November 1961, *Graetz N.V. Haarlem v J. Kadee, Voorburg, Nederlandse Jurisprudentie* (1962) 57.

60 Baardman 1960, 71 refers to a decision of the Bundeskartellamt on 19 February 1959, published in 1959. *Wirtschaft und Wettsbewerb*, 305.

61 Samkalden 1960, 334; Sk., case note Rotterdam District Court, 9 July 1960, *Linde's Eismaschinen Aktiengesellschaft and Heybroeck Zelander N.V. v v.o.f. Kledingverkoopbedrijf De Geus en Uitdenbogerd, Sociaal-Economische Wetgeving* 180; earlier also Brijnen and Wertheimer 1957, 257. Under the umbrella of Leiden University's newly established Europa Instituut, a special working group on cartel law had been established, financially supported by Philips: Archives of the Europa Instituut, Leiden (AEI). Letter C. H. F. Polak to J. R. Schaafsma 25 November 1958, Philips Company Archives (PCA) inv. no. 4281; Interview of the author with B. H. ter Kuile, The Hague 23 September 2013. Also, various annual legal conferences were dedicated to the subject: Dutch Association for International Law (*Nederlandse Vereniging voor Internationaal Recht*) in 1959 and the very well attended meeting of the Association for Company Law (*Vereniging Bedrijfsrecht*) in 1960.

62 Rasmussen 2014, 146.

63 Amsterdam Court of Appeal 3 March 1960, *K.I.M. Rijwielfabriek N.V. v Sieverding*, SEW Europa. 80. I thank Michel Waelbroeck for pointing out the consequences of a *kort geding* procedure.

64 Bebr 1962, 197; as cited in Rasmussen 2014, 136.

full proceedings, which, unlike summary proceedings, would leave no doubt on the possibility of using the preliminary reference procedure.[65]

In early 1961, a more fundamental debate on the use of the preliminary reference procedure was stirred when a case was referred to the Hoge Raad. In the case at hand, a dispute between two companies, K.I.M. and Sieverding, the Hoge Raad eventually avoided adjudicating on the matter by ruling that the interest of one of the parties to the case was not sufficiently established.[66] More provoking than the ruling however was the opinion published by Advocate General Pieter Eijssen. Here, Eijssen strongly opposed using the preliminary reference procedure, arguing that the question of whether treaty clauses were 'binding on anyone' was purely a matter of domestic law. Thus, according to Eijssen, the question whether Article 85 had primacy under Dutch constitutional law, should be decided by Dutch courts and not the ECJ.[67]

Eijssen's opinion – which seems to have been influenced by informal intervention from the side of the administration[68] – clearly diverged from the calls made by the lawyers based at the Europa Instituut and the new association on European law the Nederlandse Vereniging voor Europees Recht (NVER) that would soon join the umbrella organisation Fédération Internationale pour le Droit Européen (FIDE) covering all six member states.[69] For example, Leiden professor of administrative law Carel Polak, in a joint appearance with his colleague and friend Samkalden before the Dutch Bar Association in September 1960, had suggested that in order to clarify how Article 177 should be used, that a preliminary reference could be sent to the ECJ.[70] And upon its publication, Samkalden fiercely attacked Eijssen's 'firm but vulnerable' reasoning regarding the use of preliminary references in *Sociaal Economische Wetgeving*.[71] More importantly, Samkalden, since September 1960 combining his Leiden professorship with a seat in the Senate, provoked the government to openly disagree with Eijssen. In a June 1961 parliamentary debate, Samkalden made a non-expert State Secretary confirm his view that deciding whether treaty clauses are 'binding on anyone' was not purely a matter of domestic

65 Mok 1961, 98; Geertman 1961, 379. Also, Rotterdam district court President J. G. L. Reuder sent the parties back to start a full proceeding. He had seen them before in various summary proceedings on the illegal sale of refrigerators to start a full proceeding: 'Koelkastgeschil'. 1961. *Het vrije volk*, 11 January, p. 4.

66 Hoge Raad, 13 January 1961, *K.I.M. Rijwielfabriek* N.V. *v Sieverding, Nederlandse Jurisprudentie*, 1962, 245.

67 Eijssen's opinion was published in *Sociaal-Economische Wetgeving*, 1961, 319.

68 NA-NL Economic Affairs (2.06.087), inv. no. 2896. Letter from Alphen de Veer to A. Mulder, 13 May 1960.

69 Minutes NVER founding meeting 24 September 1960, held by the association in The Hague (private). When Director of the European Commission's Legal Service Michel Gaudet visited a NVER-meeting in Spring 1961, he was pleasantly surprised by the level of discussion: AMG. Chronos 1961. Letter from Gaudet to Samkalden on 5 May 1961.

70 Polak 1960, 362.

71 Sk., case note Hoge Raad (1961) *K.I.M. Rijwielfabriek* N.V. *v Sieverding (13 January 1961)*. Sociaal-Economische Wetgeving, 324.

law – as Eijssen had claimed – but instead depended on the intentions of the parties involved.[72]

Ten days later, the first preliminary reference in Europe was a fact. As before, the case – that already was pending since summer 1960 – dealt with the violation of a distribution agreement. The Rotterdam clothing seller V.o.f. Kledingverkoopbedrijf De Geus en Uitdenbogerd was brought to court by the German manufacturer Bosch for selling refrigerators that were imported in parallel to the official distribution agreement.[73] Unlike earlier cases, this time Bosch started a full proceeding, which allowed for the matter to be discussed more fundamentally. While the Rotterdam district court had simply rejected the direct applicability of Article 85 EEC treaty, the Hague Court of Appeal decided to refer the *Bosch v De Geus en Uitdenbogerd* case to Luxembourg.[74] Although its brief published considerations do not give any insight in the court's motivations to move beyond the Eijssen opinion, it is difficult to imagine that the statements made in the Senate quarters only a few kilometres away from its own premises had not yet reached the Court of Appeal.

In its very first preliminary ruling, the ECJ confirmed that the EEC treaty indeed 'empowered, or obliged' national courts to request a preliminary ruling also on questions of interpretation that indirectly dealt with the application of European law in the member states. Thus, it provided quite an expansive understanding of what kind of questions national courts could ask. With regard to the substance of the case, the ECJ was much more cautious. After having postponed its judgment until the new competition regime had become effective with Council Regulation 17/62, it eventually acknowledged the restrained attitude of Dutch courts. While ruling that Article 85 EEC was indeed directly applicable, it added that for the transition period preceding Regulation 17/62, only those agreements expressly declared by member states' authorities to come within the realm of Article 85.1 EEC were to be considered void.[75]

More importantly in the Dutch context, the Hoge Raad ruled on the Hague Court's decision to refer the case to Luxembourg, in an appeal which Bosch had lodged parallel to the ECJ judgement. Here the central question was whether the Hague Court had the competence to use the preliminary reference procedure in a case that clearly dealt with the application of European law inside a member state. In other words, the case prepared by a prominent member of the NVER addressed

[72] *HEK* 1960–1961 (20 June 1961), 401–403. The draft law under discussion more generally regarded the publication of international treaties and decisions of international organisations: *HTK* 1959–1960, Bijlage 5784, no. 2.

[73] It followed a summary proceeding from Bosch subsidiary Linde: Rotterdam District Court, 9 July 1960, *Linde's Eismaschinen Aktiengesellschaft and Heybroeck Zelander N.V. v v.o.f. Kledingverkoopbedrijf De Geus en Uitdenbogerd*, *Sociaal-Economische Wetgeving* 180.

[74] Rotterdam District Court, 26 October 1960, *Robert Bosch GmbH and W. van Rijn N.V. v v.o.f. Kledingverkoopbedrijf De Geus en Uitdenbogerd*, *Nederlandse Jurisprudentie* 159 and Hague Court of Appeal, 30 June 1961, *Bosch & Van Rijn v De Geus en Uitdenbogerd*, *Nederlandse Jurisprudentie* 375.

[75] 13/61, *Kledingverkoopbedrijf de Geus en Uitdenbogerd v Robert Bosch GmbH et al.*, 1962, ECLI:EU:C:1962:11.

the controversial Eijssen opinion. In May 1962, the Hoge Raad approved the use of Article 177 in this case, considering that the 'anyone binding' character of treaty provisions could, according to Dutch law, only be established by an interpretation of that treaty.[76]

As prominent lawyers already anticipated, the Hoge Raad ruling contributed to the eagerness of Dutch courts to request the ECJ for preliminary references. In fact, only a few days after the Hoge Raad had approved the use of Article 177 in *Bosch v De Geus en Uitdenbogerd*, a special court for tariff matters, the Tariefcommissie, decided to use the preliminary reference procedure to enquire about the 'internal effect' of Article 12 of the EEC treaty. Thus the Tariefcommissie, which as a court of first and last instance formally stood in no hierarchic relation to the Hoge Raad, shook off early hesitations to use the procedure in cases concerning the interpretation of this treaty article. The answer given by the ECJ would soon turn the Tariefcommissie's question into the most famous request made by a Dutch court: in its *Van Gend en Loos* ruling, the ECJ formulated its well-known doctrine on the direct effect of European law.

VAN GEND EN LOOS AND THE DOCTRINE OF DIRECT EFFECT

In 1957, during the ratification of the EEC Treaty, discussions concerning the possible 'any one binding character' of treaty provisions exclusively focused on Articles 85 and 86 regarding competition. Around 1960, however, Dutch academics started to debate whether the Treaties of Rome contained other norms of primary law, such as Article 85.2, that could be considered 'binding on anyone,' that is, creating rights for national citizens. In November 1961, while the Bosch cases were still pending before both the ECJ and the Hoge Raad, the NVER set up a working group to explore this question of 'direct applicability' of the EEC treaty more broadly. Soon, the issue of the 'direct applicability' was also chosen as a central theme for the second conference of FIDE, which was to be organised in The Hague in October 1963.[77]

The report of the Dutch working group, which would serve as the Dutch contribution to this conference, only briefly covered the doctrinal question of the possibility of direct effect, which was the main subject in most other national reports presented at the FIDE conference.[78] That does not mean that the question of direct effect was not contested in Dutch scholarly debate: the report described how in fact

[76] Hoge Raad, 18 May 1962, *Bosch & Van Rijn v De Geus en Uitdenbogerd*, *Nederlandse Jurisprudentie* (1965) 115. NVER-secretary C.R.C. van Wijckerheld Bisdom represented Bosch.

[77] See the introduction in the Dutch version of the 1963 FIDE report: 1963. 'Welke artikelen van het verdrag tot oprichting van een Europese Economische Gemeenschap moeten als een ieder verbindende bepalingen worden beschouwd?', *Sociaal Economische Wetgeving* 11: 545; Rasmussen 2013a, 180–182.

[78] The reports were published as 1966. *Deuxième colloque international de droit européen / organisé par l'Association Néerlandaise pour le Droit Européen, La Haye, 24–26 oct. 1963*, Zwolle, Tjeenk Willink.

some members of the working group adhered to a dualist point of view, while others defended the interpretation that European law directly applied 'by its own nature'. All members agreed however that these doctrinal differences did not matter for the Dutch constitutional context. Therefore, in a very practical manner, the working group focused on providing an extensive list of EEC treaty provisions for each of which the possible direct effect was discussed.[79]

One of the provisions standing out in this list was Article 12, stating that 'member states shall refrain from introducing between themselves any new customs duties on imports and exports ... and from increasing those which they already apply in their trade with each other'. As the working group underlined in its introduction, the phrasing of this prohibition was so clear that, seen from the perspective of the Dutch constitution, it most certainly granted rights to private actors.[80] Most likely, this is why some members of the working group actively engaged in starting court cases focusing on Article 12. In particular, its member J. A. van de Ven was involved a preliminary reference on Article 12 that was sent to Luxembourg by the College van Beroep Voor het Bedrijfsleven – the court of last instance in matters of trade and industry – in January 1962. This case however was withdrawn when the parties reached a settlement out of court.[81] Consequently, working group secretary Frits Salomonson was involved in a case filed later in 1962, regarding the interpretation of Article 12, leading to the ECJ's 1964 *Internatio-Puttershoek* ruling.[82] This latter case, however, was overtaken by a case that had started without any involvement of prominent working group members: the *Van Gend en Loos* case.[83]

As a case that emerged from 'below', in a field illustrative of the Dutch commercial interests in the developing common market, the *Van Gend en Loos* case is a reminder of the prominent role of companies in the development of European law. It also gave another example of how the Dutch government deliberately resisted the consequences of the EEC treaty. The case concerned the implementation of a new tariff law in March 1960 which harmonised tariffs among the Benelux countries. As this new law would raise import tariffs of a number of products,

79 Veegens et al. 1966.

80 Veegens et al. 1966, 61. By the time the report was presented, this interpretation of Article 12 had been confirmed by the ECJ in the *Van Gend en Loos* ruling.

81 College van Beroep voor het Bedrijfsleven, 10 January 1962, *NV Maatschappij voor Vee- en Vleeshandel Meattrading, Rotterdam v Produktschap voor Vee en Vlees, 's-Gravenhage, Sociaal-Economische Wetgeving* 65; NA-NL, College voor Beroep van het Bedrijfsleven (2.09.77), inv. no. 221. NA-NL, Foreign Affairs 1955–1964 (2.05.118), inv. no. 21195. Memorandum to W. Riphagen dated 19 February 1962. Ministry of Foreign Affairs official C. W. van Santen deemed this withdrawal 'sad for academia'.

82 73/63 and 74/63, *NV Internationale Crediet- en Handelsvereniging 'Rotterdam' et al. v Ministry of Agriculture and Fisheries*, 1964, ECLI:EU:C:1964:8. The involvement of Salomonson was first noticed in Vauchez 2008b, 9.

83 This finding contests the suggestion that *Van Gend en Loos* originated as a test case, as has been argued by Vauchez 2010a, 10–11; similarly Alter 2009b, 74; Rasmussen 2013b, 183. Eventually, two lawyers from the working group (L. F. D. ter Kuile and H. G. Stibbe) took over the defence in the *Van Gend en Loos* case before the ECJ.

questions were raised in Parliament with regard to the possible violation of Article 12 of the EEC treaty. The answer by the government referred to the conciliatory and pragmatic way of handling legal inconveniences ingrained in Dutch political and legal culture. In such an exceedingly complex technical operation as a tariff reform, some leeway could be expected from the EEC.[84] As a transport company that specialised in the administration of customs formalities and tax procedures, *Van Gend en Loos* was in the perfect position to question the government's decision of non-compliance.[85] It hired tax law expert Piet Droog to challenge the implementation of the law with regard to one of these exceptional cases: the import of Harnstoffharz, a substance usually used as a glue for wooden doors.

Droog was a regular at the Tariefcommissie, a court specialising in tariff matters. Thus, he was well aware that this particular substance had already been the object of several disputes before the Tariefcommissie in the past, as taxation officers and transport companies disagreed on whether it had to be classified as a glue or as a liquid.[86] This knowledge fed into his central argument. Claiming that Van Gend en Loos was taxed too much, Droog argued that the government in its new tariff classification not only deliberately raised the tariffs, which was to be considered a violation of Article 12, but also that it had knowingly ignored previous rulings of the Tariefcommissie, settling the disagreement on this substance.[87] This made the case different from the various earlier cases in which Droog invoked the EEC treaty. In these cases, the Tariefcommissie refrained from starting a preliminary reference procedure. Instead, it solved these cases in its normal way which meant finding its own conciliatory interpretation of the EEC treaty.[88] In *Van Gend en Loos*, however, as Droog argued, the government appeared to have deliberately used the tariff reform to counter earlier decisions of the Tariefcommissie. Thus, this hardly left any room for an interpretation based on the trust in the good intentions of the government that had guided its normal, conciliatory approach.[89] Whether it was indeed this argument that made the Tariefcommissie change its mind on the

84 The concerns expressed in Parliament in late 1959 were documented in the case file: NA-NL, Foreign Affairs 1955–1964, inv. no. 21197. Annex IV of the request dated 14 August 1962. In his opinion, Advocate General Roemer explicitly referred to these concerns.

85 Dankers and Verheul 1996, 124.

86 Copies of these earlier cases were added to the case file of the *Van Gend en Loos* case. NA-NL, Foreign Affairs 1955–1964, inv. no. 21197. Decisions 6 May 1958 (no. 6639 T) and 2 May 1960 (no. 8095 T). These cases had also been defended by Droog.

87 NHA, *Tariefcommissie* (609), inv. no. 148. Minutes *Tariefcommissie* 12 May 1962, First Chamber.

88 The first of these cases, which all were filed by Droog, regarded the direct effect of Article 95 on internal taxation. Here, the Tariefcommissie considered that the Article the foresaw a transition period before it would turn into effect: NHA, *Tariefcommissie* (609), inv. no. 139. no 8115 T 11 September 1961 Van Es&Van Ommeren. In a second set of cases, discussed on 15 and 22 January 1962, Article 12 was discussed but here the matter of the case seemed clear enough. NHA *Tariefcommissie*, inv. nos. 2 and 107. Jacob Meijer e.a.

89 Indeed, Droog found a weak point here: at its meeting of 15 January 1962, the Tariefcommissie internally discussed its discontent with this particular raise of tariffs. NHA, *Tariefcommissie* (609), inv. no. 2.

preliminary reference procedure is hard to tell from the minutes. In addition, it likely was inspired by the recent *Bosch* ruling, in which the Hoge Raad approved the use of this procedure. Although it was not mentioned in the Tariefcommissie's deliberations, it seems no coincidence that the Tariefcommissie decided to refer the *Van Gend en Loos* case to Luxembourg only three days after this *Bosch* ruling was issued.[90]

The reply of the ECJ constituted a breakthrough for the constitutional interpretation of European law. By ruling that the EEC treaty 'is more than an agreement which merely creates mutual obligations between contracting states', the ECJ concluded that the EEC constituted a 'new legal order', in which not only these states, but also their citizens, were conferred 'individual rights which national courts must protect'.[91] The ECJ famously referring to individual 'rights' to explain 'internal effect' was to a large extent due to the terminology in which the Tariefcommissie had phrased in its request asking whether Article 12 had 'internal effect, in other words whether individuals can directly derive rights from the Article that are enforceable by the judge'.[92] The Tariefcommissie followed Droog, who in his plea specifically emphasised the lack of alternatives for citizens to have their rights protected.[93] Moreover, the terminology was directly rooted in the Dutch constitutional reforms. In the parliamentary discussions on the 1953 constitutional reform, direct applicability of treaty provisions was explicitly translated as provisions creating rights for individuals.[94]

By referring *Bosch* and *Van Gend en Loos* to Luxembourg, Dutch courts did exactly what Samkalden had called for in 1960: they helped to elaborate the 'grand scheme of a new legal order'. Clearly Samkalden, as well as other professors and private lawyers, through associations such as the NVER importantly contributed to this development by debating the possibilities of this new legal field, and by pushing for acceptance of the preliminary reference procedure both in the political realm

90 NHA, *Tariefcommissie* (609), inv. no. 148. Minutes *Tariefcommissie* 21 May 1962, First Chamber. Soon, the Tariefcommissie decided to also refer one of its earlier cases (Jacob Meijer N.V.), as well as later, similar cases filed by Da Costa en Schaake N.V. and Hoechst-Holland N.V. to the ECJ. (See 28–30/62 *Da Costa en Schaake NV and Others v Netherlands Inland Revenue Administration*. 1963, ECLI:EU:C:1963:6). In order not to overstate the importance of this 'permission' of the Hoge Raad, it is important to keep in mind that the Meattrading case had already been referred to the ECJ in January 1962. (College van Beroep voor het Bedrijfsleven, 10 January 1962, *NV Maatschappij voor Vee- en Vleeshandel Meattrading, Rotterdam v Produktschap voor Vee en Vlees, 's-Gravenhage, Sociaal-Economische Wetgeving* 65.)

91 The mentioning of individual 'rights' to explain 'internal effect' was precisely the type of language proponents of a constitutional approach to EEC law could use to defend their case. Rasmussen 2014, 153.

92 Translation by Claes and de Witte 1998, 178; the phrasing used by the Tariefcommissie was criticised by e.g. international law specialist Erades 1964, 22. In the *Bosch* case, the defendants (Bosch c.s.) had used the term 'direct applicability to nationals of signatory states', a terminology that was then adopted by the Hoge Raad (but not by the ECJ).

93 NHA, *Tariefcommissie* (609), inv. no. 148. Minutes *Tariefcommissie* 12 May 1962, First Chamber.

94 *HTK* 1952–1953, B 2700 no. 63a.

and in the Hoge Raad. By doing so, these lawyers knowingly built on the unique constitutional context that made the enforcement of the new European norms before a national court much more feasible than elsewhere. At the same time, however, the pioneering preliminary references were also spurred by the fact that the Dutch government did not necessarily fully comply with the legal obligations outlined in the EEC Treaty – the result not only of diverging political interests, but also of a conciliatory political culture in which the possibility of national legislation being challenged in court was hardly considered. The challenges that surfaced were by no means purely due to a small group of pioneering lawyers. Instead, the ongoing disputes regarding competition agreements and tariff classification from which the famous *Bosch* and *Van Gend en Loos* cases arose are reminiscent of the key contribution of Dutch businesses to the emergence of these cases.[95]

For Dutch courts, *Bosch* and in particular the Hoge Raad's *Bosch* ruling marked the start of an overall active role in the development of European law. The number of preliminary references requested by Dutch courts until the 1980s went far beyond other member states, if measured per inhabitant.[96] Due to the themes covered by EEC law, administrative courts took the largest share of these references, but general courts also did not hesitate to use the mechanism.[97] Further, although figures show that most cases came from lower courts, the Hoge Raad occasionally took a firm lead. For example, in a test case on tax harmonisation in the 1970s, the Hoge Raad cleared the way for a preliminary reference on the VAT directive which the Tariefcommissie had refused.[98] In spite of the exemplary cooperation, scholars continued to find reasons for critical comments. They observed how in the difficult issue of competition law, Dutch courts remained hesitant to involve the ECJ in the remainder of the 1960s.[99] Also, the question whether the preliminary reference procedure could be reconciled with summary proceedings remained the subject of heated discussion.[100] Overall however, they had to acknowledge that Dutch courts overcame their initial hesitation to comply to the treaty despite the constitutional ban on judicial review and the fact that it changed the relatively consensual Dutch legal culture. In fact, the substantial number of preliminary references following *Bosch* made observers wonder whether the Dutch judiciary should not take better notice of the 'acte clair' theory.[101]

95 Van Leeuwen 2018.

96 Alter 2001, 35.

97 Overviews of Dutch jurisprudence until 1977 were published by Lauwaars et al. 1973; Tromm 1981. For an evaluation of all preliminary references see Korte and Kellermann 1991.

98 Tromm 1981, 444; Jans 2010, 136–142. The case meant here is 51/76, *Verbond van Nederlandse Ondernemingen v Inspecteur der Invoerrechten en Accijnzen*, 1977, ECLI:EU:C:1977:12. See for the Hoge Raad ruling of 9 June 1976, *BNB: Beslissingen in belastingzaken* 1976/168.

99 Brinkhorst 1966, 92 lists the cases of Nibeja-Graetz, FIVA II, Linde-De Geus.

100 Meij 1999; VerLoren van Themaat et al. 1998, 137.

101 Brinkhorst 1966, 84. The acte clair theory had been introduced in the European legal debate by Advocate General Maurice Lagrange in 28–30/62, *Da Costa en Schaake NV and Others*

Meanwhile, also the Dutch government shifted towards a more active support of the European legal order. First of all, it needs to be highlighted that, unlike in other member states dealt with in this volume, policymakers did not intervene in any fundamental way to stop the new cooperative mode of Dutch courts. Moreover, the formal opinions it sent to the ECJ with regard to *Bosch* and *Van Gend en Loos* reflected concrete policy objectives rather than abstract doctrinal concerns. In its *Bosch* opinion, which was primarily drafted by the Ministry of Economic Affairs, the Dutch government did not challenge the ECJ's competence to rule on this matter, but instead concentrated on explaining its interpretation of Article 85–88 of the EEC Treaty.[102] In *Van Gend en Loos*, it firmly rejected the possible direct effect of Article 12 of the EEC Treaty along with the Belgian and German governments.[103] As the internal considerations show however, this resistance regarded the consequences for the particular case at hand, rather than a principled rejection of a 'constitutional' interpretation of European law. In fact, the jurisconsulte office did not intend to send in an opinion at all, arguing that 'even the unlikely interpretation of Article 12 as having direct effect ("rechtstreeks bindend") would be acceptable to the Dutch government'.[104] It was instead the Ministry of Finance that pushed for an official Dutch position in the case in order to support the tax officials against whom this case was filed.[105]

In the years that followed, this practice-oriented approach would continue to dominate Dutch positioning towards new European legislation and case law. At the same time, the *Costa v ENEL* ruling provoked the Dutch government to redefine its stance with regard to the developing 'common legal order'.

PRINCIPLES AND PRAGMATISM: DEFENDING AND IMPLEMENTING COMMUNITY LAW, 1964–1992

From 1963 to 1964, the ECJ's *Van Gend en Loos* and *Costa v ENEL* rulings went largely unnoticed in the Netherlands. Obviously, specialist journals such as *Sociaal Economische Wetgeving*, and the newly established *Common Market Law Review*, extensively discussed the implications of the rulings with regard to the direct effect and primacy of European law. Newspapers however, which in the early 1960s reported on most cartel cases and other economically relevant legal developments,

v Netherlands Inland Revenue Administration. 1963, ECLI:EU:C:1963:6. According to Brinkhorst, it was (implicitly) applied by the Court of last instance in matters of trade and industry (CBB) in the *Internatio-Puttershoek* cases (that for other reasons were referred to the ECJ as cases 73–74/63, see note 80).

102 Memorandum 16 September 1961, Hubée to plv. Jura. NA-NL, Foreign Affairs 1955–1964, inv. no. 21194.

103 26/62, *Van Gend en Loos v Nederlandse Administratie der Belastingen*, 1963, ECLI:EU:C:1963:1.

104 NA-NL, Foreign Affairs 1955–1964, inv. no. 21197. Memorandum 31 August 1962, plv JURA (Hubée) to DIE (Directie integratie Europa).

105 NA-NL, Foreign Affairs 1955–1964, inv. no. 21197. Memorandum 25 September 1962 plv JURA to DIE.

generally ignored these doctrinal developments.[106] Similarly, Parliament only took an interest in the rulings after the publication of a critical review in 1967 claiming that the Dutch government in its positioning before the ECJ 'went against its own constitutional beliefs' of strengthening the international legal order.[107] In his response, Minister of Foreign Affairs Joseph Luns stated the Dutch government's rejection of direct effect in Van Gend en Loos and similar cases had only aimed at sharpening the ECJ's jurisprudence.[108] Apparently satisfied by this reply, a still outspokenly pro-integration Parliament dropped the issue.[109]

Clearly, Luns' explanation, which followed the advice of former Leiden professor, now Minister of Justice, Carel Polak, did not match the internal deliberations regarding the *Van Gend en Loos* opinion cited above.[110] Nevertheless, the suggestion that the government actively promoted what was now understood as a 'constitutional interpretation' of European law did have some truth in it – even though this promotion usually took other forms than the opinions presented before the ECJ. In particular after the *Costa v ENEL* ruling, the Dutch government started to defend the new constitutional interpretation of the ECJ vis-à-vis other more sceptical member states more actively in the Council. At the same time, however, the Dutch implementation of EC legislation and ECJ case law remained piecemeal and hesitant. When this was exposed by parliament and academics in the late 1970s, it became clear that the Dutch government in terms of compliance with European law hardly did better than the other member state.

DEFENDING THE 'DEVELOPING COMMON LEGAL ORDER'

Although not entirely accurate on the details retrospectively, Luns's account of the government's position with regard to the European legal order marked an important policy shift. Where the Dutch government from the early 1950s to the early 1960s had

106 A search on keywords such as 'Costa' and 'Europees Hof' for the period 1964–1966 in the newspaper database Delpher gave no results (kranten.delpher.nl). This is particularly striking when compared to Germany, where the case received quite some coverage in larger newspapers, but also to the considerable attention for 36/74, *Walrave and Koch v Association Union Cycliste Internationale and Others*, 1974, ECLI:EU:C:1974:140, on Dutch pacers given in the Dutch press. Cf. Davies 2012b, 114–115 and (on *Walrave&Koch*) for example 'Gangmakersproces'. 1974. *Het Vrije Volk*, 30 March, p. 13.

107 *HTK* 1967, B 9080; *HTK*, 1967, C60-C61. For the critical review see Salomonson 1967, 431.

108 *HTK* 1967, C60-C61. Similarly: Patijn 1967, 926. Patijn was official at the NA-NL. Ministry of Foreign Affairs.

109 The parliamentary questions also concerned the Dutch opinion in 57/65 *Alfons Lütticke GmbH v Hauptzollamt Sarrelouis*, 1966, ECLI:EU:C:1966:34, on which unfortunately no files have been found in the Foreign Affairs Archive. In the *Lütticke* case, which challenged a widely applied German tax system, the Netherlands contested the direct effect of Article 95 of the EEC treaty. The financial and societal stakes of the case were very high: Alter 2001, 80–82; Rasmussen 1986, 454–455.

110 NL-NL Foreign Affairs 1965–1974 inv. no. 16663. Memorandum June 1967. Polak served as minister from 1967 to 1971.

considered European law just another branch of international law and had resisted the direct effect of specific treaty provisions during the *Van Gend en Loos* case, from the mid-1960s onwards it explicitly acknowledged and supported the ECJ's new constitutional interpretation. Yet, this shift merely took place on the political level, such as in the government's interaction with Parliament or with the Council of the EC. At the same time, a more practice-oriented approach was preserved with regard to the actual implementation of European law as well as concerning the opinions sent to the ECJ.

Most activities in the latter regard fell under the coordination of the interdepartmental 'Committee for the uniform interpretation of the treaty' (CUI), which was established in 1959 to assist the politically important 'Coordination committee for European and association affairs' on legal questions. Typically, this committee proudly described its own position as 'pragmatic' even when its discussions concerned issues of some theoretical weight, such as the matter of the EEC's competencies regarding external relations.[111] Comparing its own position with the 'more theoretical approach' taken by the ECJ in its famous 1970 *ERTA* ruling regarding the European Agreement concerning the work of crews of vehicles engaged in international road transport,[112] the CUI moreover found that the essence of both interpretations was very similar.[113] The committee's reticent positioning reflected that of its chairman, Foreign Affairs Legal Advisor Willem Riphagen. In a 1964 memorandum describing the government's policy with regard to opinions sent to the ECJ, Riphagen stated as his general aim to keep the number of opinions as low as possible.[114] Indeed, not only had the government almost not sent in an opinion on *Van Gend en Loos*, but it also refrained from intervening in *Costa v ENEL*. Moreover, in those cases in which it did present an opinion – often at the instigation of the technical ministry involved – it focused on material interests rather than on doctrinal issues. Thus, the Dutch opinion in the later famous case of *Internationale Handelsgesellschaft* (1970) mainly regarded agricultural matters, leaving the doctrinal debate to other member states.[115]

111 NA-NL, Foreign Affairs 1965–1974 (2.05.313) inv. no. 16672. 'Rapport inzake de externe betrekkingen van de EEG', 26 June 1970; in the 1970s, this committee developed into a mere intermediary for distributing the documents sent from Luxembourg on newly opened court cases – only to become more active again upon the admission of European law experts from the Ministry of Justice such as Rob Mok and Ad Geelhoed. During his short period in office (1965–1966), Minister of Justice Samkalden had not yet been allowed such position for his department in the committee. NA-NL, Foreign Affairs 1965–1974 inv. no. 16672. Memorandum A. Bos 15 January 1965.

112 22/70 *Commission of the European Communities v Council of the European Communities*, 1971, ECLI.EU:C:1971:32.

113 NA-NL, Foreign Affairs 1965–1974 inv. no. 16672 'Aanvullend rapport Commissie voor uniforme interpretatie EEG-verdrag inzake externe betrekkingen EEG', 6 May 1971. As a consequence, the committee advised the government not to back a French 'démarche' inviting the governments of the other member states to draft an 'interpretative agreement' in the Council 'bending' the ECJ ruling. NA-NL, Foreign Affairs 1965–1974 inv. no. 17188. Memorandum A. Bos 25 June 1971.

114 NA-NL, Foreign Affairs 1955–1964, inv. no. 21203. Letter W. Riphagen to Ministry of Economic affairs 2 April 1964.

115 11/70 *Internationale Handelsgesellschaft mbH v Einfuhr- und Vorratsstelle für Getreide und Futtermittel*, 1970, EU:C:1970:114. The case in which the Dutch government did participate was 31/

Meanwhile, from 1964 onwards, in the context of the Council, the Dutch government evolved into an important advocate of the 'common legal order'. Reflecting the more progressive attitude of the Ministry of Foreign Affairs' political departments – in particular, its European integration office (Directoraat Europese Integratie, DIE) – Dutch representatives here increasingly found themselves pushing for acceptance of the ECJ's constitutional interpretation of European law by the other member states. Thus, in 1964, when the Council was preparing a common answer to questions asked in the European Parliament about the judgment of the Italian Constitutional Court on the *Costa v ENEL* case that preceded the later ECJ judgment, DIE officials argued in favour of a progressive attitude of the Councils (sic) regarding the 'developing common legal order'.[116] They had a clear reason for doing so: for a small member state that already by its constitution accepted direct effect of certain treaty provisions, supremacy of European law meant that the other member states would finally be bound by treaty obligations to the same extent. This became even more clear in another matter in which the Dutch government considered defending that legal order: the cases regarding the much-disputed French oil market regulations which effectively kept non-French companies out of the industry. When the French Conseil d'État in June 1964 refused to start a preliminary reference procedure in a case concerning these regulations started by Shell-Berre, the French branch of a Dutch oil company, the Dutch government asked the Commission whether the presumed interference of the French Ministry of Foreign Affairs in this case should not be regarded as non-observance of treaty obligations.[117] At the same time, indirectly supporting the interests of Shell, the Dutch government submitted an opinion in a parallel case that did reach the ECJ the case through an Italian court (the *Albatros/SOPECO*) case.[118] Eventually, after a meeting with the French ambassador, the Ministry's top officials decided to refrain from repeating the same arguments at the oral hearing however.[119] The Conseil d'État's protection of French oil interests nevertheless remained under

70, *Deutsche Getreide- und Futtermittel-Handelsgesellschaft mbH v Hauptzollamt Hamburg-Altona*, 1970, ECLI:EU:C:1970:108. NA-NL, Foreign Affairs 1965–1974 inv. no. 17185.

116 Eventually, the reference to the 'common legal order' was again removed from the memorandum at the instigation of the Dutch Permanent Representation. NA-NL, Foreign Affairs 1955–1964, inv. no. 20997. Telex Minister of Foreign Affairs Luns 102 876 to 'g.n.v. Brussel', 3 July 1964; Memorandum mr. H. H. Maas to 'Z. E.' (minister Luns), 13 July 1964 and Telex Minister of Foreign Affairs Luns 102 889 to 'g.n.v. Brussel, 15 July 1964. See van Leeuwen 2014.

117 (In Dutch: 'niet nakoming van verdragsverplichtingen'.) NA-NL, Foreign Affairs 1955–1964, inv. no. 20997. Telex Minister of Foreign Affairs Luns 102 918 to 'g.n.v. Brussel', 8 September 1964. Unfortunately, no follow-up to this telex is preserved in the archival files. The Dutch suspicion was well founded as demonstrated by Bernier and Rasmussen in Chapter 7.

118 20/64, *SARL Albatros v Société des pétroles et des combustibles liquides (Sopéco)*, 1964, ECLI:EU:C:1965:8.

119 NA-NL, Foreign Affairs 1955–1964, inv. no. 21202. French aide memoire with handwritten notes, 10 November 1964. ECJ Case 20/64.

close Dutch scrutiny, also through critical questions of Dutch MEP Tjerk Westerterp and in academic publications.[120]

The intensified policy of the Dutch government in defence of the 'common legal order' in the mid-1960s was mirrored by a quiet breakthrough in Dutch academic debate. Initially, the academic field of European law was dominated by the Leiden Europa Institute, and its professors Samkalden and Polak, who already in 1960 had argued that the Treaties of Rome were a special, new legal order separate from international law.[121] Until the mid-1960s, their position was still far from common. Amsterdam-based professor, A. J. P. Tammes, for example, defended the position that European law was not special at all since many of its characteristics could be found, or would be useful, in other international legal orders.[122] And Leiden PhD Jos Kapteyn, who was appointed professor of European law in Utrecht in 1963 – a stronghold of the international law school – experienced that it was by no means obvious for his colleagues to accept European law as a new legal discipline.[123] Yet, especially after *Costa v ENEL*, both sides soon agreed that due to the Dutch constitution, their disagreement had no other practical consequences than maybe for the organisation of the academic field or the sale of textbooks.[124] In the years that followed, the understanding of European law as a new legal order gradually became the dominant interpretation of Dutch legal academia – a development presumably supported by the appointment of Leiden-bred lawyers in the new chairs of European law.[125]

While the Dutch reception of European law thus hardly presented an occasion for fierce doctrinal debates, the academic 'pioneers' instead focused their discussions on the nature of European law on the situation in other member states. After the first FIDE conference in 1961, *Sociaal Economische Wetgeving* reported that in other member states, national interests seemed to prevail over 'pure' legal considerations.[126] Dutch academics therefore focused their work on how to develop a compromise between the different national constitutional models, and traditions that would ensure the implementation and application of European law. Especially

[120] Bernier 2014; Conseil d'État (Section), 19 June 1964, *Société des pétroles Shell-Berre et autres (Shell Berre)*, n° 235345, published in *Recueil Lebon* 344, 1964. *Common Market Law Review*, 1965, 22. See also Chapter 7.

[121] For example: Samkalden 1960, 334; Samkalden 1966, 161–174. Also see other 'Leiden' lawyers such as Polak 1960, 349; Brinkhorst 1963; van Panhuys 1966.

[122] Tammes 1966, 113. The 'Leiden' interpretation of the ECJ's *Costa v ENEL* ruling was also challenged by the Amsterdam (UvA) PhD candidate Meuwissen, who took a firm dualist point of view, as well as the Utrecht PhD candidate P. van Dijk: Meuwissen 1965, 66; van Dijk 1969.

[123] Interview of the author with P. J. G. Kapteyn, The Hague 15 October 2013.

[124] Tammes 1966, 113. Remarkably, a point that according to Claes and de Witte was often made in later discussions on whether primacy of European law was based in the Dutch constitution or in the ECJ doctrine – the point being that the former allowed the Dutch to withdraw by constitutional revision – lacked from these discussions. Claes and de Witte 1998, 185.

[125] Examples are P. J. G. Kapteyn in Utrecht, L. J. Brinkhorst and C. Timmermans in Groningen and B. H. ter Kuile in Rotterdam.

[126] Salomonson 1961, 228 describes how (French) lawyers tried to defend national interests especially in discussions on competition law. Similarly: van Emde Boas 1963, 604.

the question of primacy of European law was considered a key challenge for the other member states. Thus, shortly before the ECJ published its *Costa v ENEL* ruling, Samkalden for example explored whether the primacy of European law could become more palatable in the German and Italian dualist systems if it was based on the constitutional clauses allowing the limitation of national sovereignty in favour of international peace organisations.[127] Another example of the outward-oriented nature of Dutch academic debate was the launch of the first transnational academic journal on European law, the *Common Market Law Review*. Established by the Leiden Europa Instituut in cooperation with the British Institute of International and Comparative Law, this journal, through its European team of editors, would take up a significant role in promoting knowledge on European law across Western Europe, and more particularly, in endorsing the new constitutional interpretation of European law.[128]

For the government, in the meantime, defending the constitutional interpretation had taken the shape of defending the position of the ECJ. In the late 1960s, the status of the Court came under serious discussion during the negotiations on the Luxembourg Protocol.[129] This protocol conferred new powers upon the ECJ regarding the interpretation of the 1968 Brussels Convention on jurisdiction and the enforcement of judgments in civil and commercial matters. France – supported by Belgium and West Germany – threatened to water down these new ECJ powers as much as possible by limiting the preliminary reference mechanism only to courts of last instance. The Dutch government refrained from any such 'rebellion' against the newly claimed role of the Luxembourg court. On the contrary, throughout the discussions, it kept in close communication with the ECJ judges, for example by inviting the three 'Benelux' judges to an informal meeting of the three Benelux governments on the matter and in correspondence with the Dutch judge, André Donner. In terms of content, the Dutch government favoured the solution proposed by the ECJ, that is, to simply extend the procedure of Article 177 to other treaties. Yet, in the end the preferred solution was not feasible politically due to especially French and Belgian resistance.[130] Considering that the persistent non-observance of Article 177.3 in some states made the functioning of the preliminary reference procedure 'hardly ideal,' the Dutch government chose to resign themselves to this situation. Meanwhile, it continued to involve the ECJ in the discussions until June 1971, when the protocol was signed.[131]

127 Samkalden 1964, 11–13. This seems a variant to the '*Durchgriff* thesis' developed by German law scholars Carl Friedrich Ophüls and Hans-Peter Ipsen. Similar: Erades 1964, 494. On Ipsen: Boerger and Rasmussen 2014, 206–207 and Davies, 2012b, 57–70.

128 Byberg 2017b.

129 Fritz 2015; Fritz 2017.

130 NA-NL, Foreign Affairs 1955–1964, inv. no. 15266. Memorandum A. Bos for DIE, 10 December 1968; letter M. R. Mok to A. M. Donner, 13 December 1968; memo M. R. Mok 9 January 1969.

131 NA-NL, Foreign Affairs 1955–1964, inv. no. 15266. Memo M. R. Mok 9 January 1969; NA-NL, Nederlandse Permanente Vertegenwoordiging bij de EG Brussel (PV Brussel) (2.05.281), inv. no. 3. Instruction telex for PermRep meeting 28–29–30 October 1970. From a different position, MEP and

A similar, pro-ECJ position was taken in 1978, when the ECJ, pending the establishment of a 'court of first instance' that dragged out in negotiations between the member states, presented the Council with some reform plans of its own. Concerned by the increasing workload of the court, ECJ president Hans Kutscher urged the Council to extend the number of judges and advocates general and speed up the introduction of a court of first instance, which in principle was already agreed upon in 1974.[132] In response to the Kutscher memorandum, the British government proposed to enhance the role of the member states in court procedures. From these proposals, especially the idea to introduce an extra step in preliminary reference procedures allowing the ECJ to consider the relevance of the reference – if necessary in dialogue with member states – immediately caught the attention of the Dutch press as well as the Parliament.[133] The Dutch press fiercely criticised what they understood as a possibility 'to withhold cases from being sent to Luxembourg' as an 'attack on the European court'.[134] At the same time, the Dutch government, supported by Belgium amongst others, argued that the British proposals should not delay the discussions on a court of first instance that was 'urgently' needed to safeguard the speed and quality of the administration of law.[135] Again, the Dutch government presented itself as a strong supporter of 'the essential role played by the Court in the development of European legal order'.[136] At the same time, it also acted as the guardian of the interests of private litigants across the Community against the more powerful member states, warning that the reforms proposed by the United Kingdom – and later also by France – 'would give European institutions and member states a privileged position vis-à-vis other parties in procedures before the court'.[137]

MP Henk Vredeling critically followed the negotiations by asking questions both in the Dutch and the European Parliament: see NA-NL, Foreign Affairs 1955–1964, inv. no. 15266.

132 Archives Ministry of Foreign Affairs, The Hague (MinBuZa) 1975–1984, inv. no. 19035. Memorandum Hans Kutscher 21 July 1978 to H. D. Genscher, President of the Council. The earlier idea on a court of first instance that was to hear litigation between the institutions and her staff was scheduled in the conference of ministers of Justice on 26 November 1974, which asked the Commission to submit a proposal: see COM (78) 395.

133 The other proposals concerned extending the possibilities for member states to participate in preliminary reference cases in opinions and replies and creating the possibility for intervention in direct cases of individuals against EC institutions. Telex with summary of meeting of Justice council 9 October 1978, NA-NL, PV Brussel, inv. no. 4.

134 'Britten doen aanval op Europese Hof'. 1978. *NRC Handelsblad*, 10 October. This led to questions in parliament: *HTK* 1978–1979, Aanhangsel nr. 340 (written question A. Vrijlandt-Krijnen, 18 October 1978).

135 Minutes Coordinatie-commissie 3 October 1978, in MinBuZa 1975–1984, inv. no. 19035.

136 In an internal memo 30 January 1979, DIE described Dutch position as 'in favour of good functioning of law and the practice of the law': MinBuZa 1975–1984. inv. no. 19035. The quote on the 'European legal order' is derived from the reply to the written question by Vrijlandt-Krijnen: HTK 1978–1979 Aanhangsel nr. 340.

137 By this time, proposals similar to the earlier British ones were defended by France. NA-NL, PV Brussel, inv. no. 4. Summary of meeting ad hoc group Justice Council 25/26/27 June 1979. On a smaller scale, the Dutch government had a political agenda of its own as well, hoping that the new, fifth position of advocate general that was to be created by the reform would be rewarded to a Dutch jurist. NA-NL, PV Brussel, inv. no. 4. Summary COREPER meeting 4 July 1979; MinBuZa

Finally, in 1979, when the ECJ came under attack again from France, after several controversial ECJ rulings,[138] Dutch policymakers did not hesitate to describe their own position vis-à-vis the Treaties of Rome in terms that could hardly be found in other member states. Reporting on a discussion on the role of the ECJ held during the informal council meeting in Mercues in May 1979, Dutch minister of Foreign Affairs Chris van der Klauw related his disagreement with French minister of Foreign Affairs Jean-François Poncet on this matter to a 'fundamentally different approach of the treaties: intergovernmental vs. supranational'.[139] Internally, Dutch officials seconded the position taken by Commission president Roy Jenkins: if the Court engaged in any activism so despised by the French government and Poncet, it only resulted from the failure of the Council to make decisions itself.[140]

INTEGRATION HITTING HOME: THE PROBLEM OF COMPLIANCE

The principled positioning of the Dutch government in the Council corresponded well with the progressive understanding of Dutch policy with regard to European law that was favoured in Parliament.[141] At the same time, towards the end of the 1970s, Parliament became increasingly critical of the actual compliance with the European law that the government valued so highly. In spite of its high principles, the Dutch administration ran into similar problems that plagued its counterparts in the other member states, as academics were increasingly eager to point out.

Obviously, from the very ratification of the Treaties of Rome, the consequences of European primary and secondary law had, on some occasions, been deliberately contained as the example of the competition clauses discussed above demonstrated. Similarly, during the challenging times of the economic crisis of the 1970s, domestic interests were allowed to prevail over warnings by European law specialists for example when the politically sensitive state aid law, Wet investeringsrekening, was prepared.[142] At the time, critical legal commentary pointed out the clear conflicts of

1975–1984, inv. no. 19035. Internal memo Borchardt November 1979; also see the many documents in MinBuZa 1975–1984 inv. no. 19036.

138 Rasmussen 2017.

139 NA-NL, PV Brussel, inv. no. 4. Report in telex 14 May 1979; MinBuZa 1975–1984 inv. no. 18575. In instructions DIE to minister 10 May 1979: 'Duidelijk zou moeten blijken dat het Hof, zijnde een in het Verdrag voorziene instelling, volstrekt onafhankelijk is. Slechts Verdragswijziging – waar Nederland niet aan zou meewerken indien deze beperking van de bevoegdheden van het Hof zou beogen – zou daar wijziging in kunnen brengen. Ook al zijn, voor zover bekend, de bevoegdheden van het Hof op zichzelf niet in het geding, toch zou Nederland als zijn mening te kennen moeten geven dat het ontoelaatbaar is dat de Raad zich uitspreekt over het functioneren van het Hof.'

140 MinBuZa 1975–1984 inv. no. 19035. Internal memo Borchardt Nov 1979 and memo Borchardt to M 16 November 1979.

141 See documents in MinBuZa 1975–1984, inv. no. 14935.

142 This 'Wet investeringsrekening' in 1979 would become subject of a Commission procedure against Philip Morris: European Court of Justice (1979) 730/79, *Philip Morris Holland BV v Commission of the European Communities*, 1980, ECLI:EU:C:1980:209.

this law with European law and argued that it probably was caused by a certain disinterest and lack of knowledge by the responsible ministries.[143] In other cases, however, the containment of European law was clearly intentional as in the politically very sensitive field of television broadcasting. Here, in order to secure a difficult political compromise, the Dutch government relentlessly introduced new legislation prohibiting the entrance of foreign commercial television to domestic cable networks even after the ECJ started to develop a jurisprudence based on the freedom to provide services.[144]

The problematic implementation of these and other rules initially had merely been noticed by specialists in the separate policy fields. A more systematic analysis was launched however after the Dutch European law association, NVER, dedicated its 1968 conference to the theme.[145] Subsequently, the state of the implementation of European law became the key research subject of the interuniversity Asser Institute which had just been was just established in 1965 to enhance cooperation between Dutch law faculties in the fields of international and European law. Apart from providing Dutch European law scholars and practitioners with an additional meeting ground by organising conferences and colloquia on topics varying from particular aspects of European law to the status of European law in the law curricula at Dutch universities, the Asser Institute served as the main documentation centre on European law in the Netherlands.[146] Its research on the implementation of European law, however, conducted by teams of academic researchers and public officials, arguably made for most of the institute's impact in the 1970s. Its thematic reports exposed how the Dutch administration in many regards struggled to meet the terms and time limits set in the increasing number of regulations and directives that made up European law.[147]

As one of founders of the academic project and later State Secretary of European Affairs (1973–1977) and member of parliament (1978–1982), it fell upon Laurens Jan Brinkhorst to confront the government with the findings of the reports by asking

143 VerLoren van Themaat 1977, 743; interviews of the author with P. J. G. Kapteyn 15 October 2013, The Hague and B. H. ter Kuile 23 Septmber 2013, The Hague.

144 Van Leeuwen 2017, 65. The key cases were 352/85, *Bond van Adverteerders and others v The Netherlands State*, 1988, ECLI:EU:C:1988:196 and 288/89 *Stichting Collectieve Antennevoorziening Gouda and others v Commissariaat voor de Media*, 1991, ECLI:EU:C:1991:323.

145 1968. *Tenuitvoerlegging van gemeenschapsrecht door de Nederlandse overheid: pre-adviezen*, edited by L. J. Brinkhorst. Haarlem: Tjeenk Willink. The conference was jointly organised by the Vereniging voor Administratief Recht and the NVER.

146 See the overview of colloquia published on the institute's website: www.asser.nl/media/1231/lijst-van-colloquiumverslagen.pdf. The Asser institute had moreover started to develop a documentation system that for a short period was even promoted by the Dutch government as superior to the CELEX-system developed by the European Commission: MinBuZa 1975–1984 inv. no. 1493. Conseil, Note sur le rapport du Comité de direction de l'Office des Publications sur la création d'un répertoire des actes de droit communautaire (R/1952/1/78) 26 September 1978; interview of the author with A. Kellerman 28 September 2015. On the transformative impact of the CELEX system on the EC 'acquis', see Vauchez 2015, 172–197.

147 Audretsch et al., 1972–1976.

critical questions regarding the delay in implementation of European legislation in parliament.[148] Related questions followed in subsequent years, even though the matter drew relatively little attention compared to some of the other issues challenging European integration at the time, such as the budgetary question and the plans for reforming agricultural policy.[149] The immediate results were minimal. In 1981, the government still could not present an overview of which directives had been implemented and which had not, even though the interdepartmental Coordination Committee for European affairs already established an ad hoc group to deal with the matter in 1979.[150] At the same time, and in quite some contrast to the domestic situation, the Dutch Permanent Representative in Brussels enthusiastically welcomed the initiative from the Legal Service of the Commission in 1978 to monitor member state compliance more diligently and bring infringement charges when necessary.[151] The progressive self-understanding with regard to European law in general evidently had not been affected by the many examples of problematic compliance.

TREATIES AND A CONSTITUTIONAL TRADITION

An even more clear illustration of this progressive self-image can be found in the debates marking the 1983 general revision of the constitution – which also reassessed the 1953/1956 constitutional clauses that had guided the Dutch position towards the European legal order. Not only did Parliament decide to leave these clauses unaltered, thanks to the intervention of Brinkhorst, it explicitly confirmed its understanding of the constitution as favouring integration in a resolution stating that 'in case of doubt, provisions of the Constitution should be explained in such a way that the European integration process is not hindered by it'.[152] When, in the immediate aftermath of this constitutional revision, consecutive waves of deepening European integration indeed appeared on the horizon in the shape of the Single European Act in 1986 and the Maastricht Treaty in 1992 respectively, the Brinkhorst Resolution strongly resonated in the ratification debates; if any critical observations were raised regarding the transfer of national competencies demanded by these new far-reaching Treaties, the criticism focused on the improvement of democratic guarantees at the supranational level rather than taking the shape of constitutional reservations.

The first of the new Treaties, the Single European Act, passed Parliament without any explicit consideration of its constitutionality. Presented by the government as

148 *HTK* 1978–1979, no. 624. Brinkhorst's question referred to Maas and Bentvelsen 1978, 443.

149 See for example HTK 1980–1981 UCV 25, p. 7; *HTK* 1983–1984, Aanhangsel no. 252.

150 *HTK* 1981–1982, B 17100 V no. 2. On the establishment of the ad hoc group, see the memorandum dated 19 December 1979 in MinBuZa inv. no. 18586.

151 MinBuZa 1975–1984, inv. no. 14931. Letter J. H. Lubbers to Minister 10 March 1978 quoting Audland, adj. secretary of the Commission.

152 *HTK* 1979–1980, B 15049 no. 16. Translation from Hollander 2013, 144.

merely a continuation of the integration process set in motion in 1957, there hardly seemed any ground to invoke the special ratification procedure for Treaties affecting constitutional powers. Instead, the large pro-integration parliamentary majority urged for a further strengthening of the European Parliament, now that 'Europe' was rapidly expanding its powers.[153] This concern for democratic control became more eminent during the ratification of the follow-up to the Schengen Treaty of 1985 on the removal of border controls, the 'Schengen II' agreement in 1990.[154] Presented as introducing merely 'administrative' changes, the original Schengen treaty had been approved with tacit consent.[155] During the implementation of the new treaty, however, Parliament gradually came to realise how this so-called administrative treaty hit upon crucial policy areas such as immigration and soft drugs. Thus, when Schengen II was presented for ratification, Parliament for the first time seriously threatened to block this further step towards integration, helped by a very critical evaluation of the convention by the Raad van State (Council of State), the long standing (since 1531) advisory body to the Dutch government which reviews the legal quality of the proposed legislation.[156] In particular, the loss of democratic control to an intergovernmental 'Executive Committee' with legislative authority was deemed to go against the same Dutch Constitution that had been interpreted with so much flexibility on other occasions. Although the agreement eventually found sufficient support, the Schengen debates had stirred a more critical voice within Dutch politics, especially where democratic control was concerned.[157]

In this respect, the Maastricht Treaty establishing the European Union was warmly welcomed in the Dutch Parliament, although most political parties had wished for it to include an even stronger role for the European Parliament in return for the competencies this new treaty demanded the member states to give up. The tone was already set in Spring 1991 with the overwhelming acceptance of the resolution Van der Linden c.s., which, among its demands for the new European treaty, prominently listed 'improvement of the democratic functioning of the Community by strengthening the European Parliament' and 'reinforcement of the European legal order' by introducing sanctions for non-compliance to legislation and ECJ rulings.[158] This inspired the Dutch government during its presidency of the Council to design a new proposal for the European Union, replacing the pillar structure designed by the Luxembourg presidency by a single

153 Hollander 2013, 168–170; Harryvan and van der Harst 2013, 147–154.

154 Officially the Convention on the Implementation of the Schengen Agreement. The central role of the Schengen agreements in Dutch political debate on integration has been analysed in depth by Hollander 2013, 180–197.

155 *HTK* 1985–1986, B 19326 no. 3.

156 *HTK* 1990–1991, B 22140 B.

157 Hollander 2013, 189–196.

158 *HTK* 1990–1991, 21952 en 22052, no. 22 'Motie van het lid Van der Linden c.s.'. The resolution was passed with the support of all but a few very small parties. Indeed, did the EU treaty, parallel to the ECJ's 1991 Francovich ruling on financial liability, introduce a such sanction for non-compliance to legal obligations.

supranational structure; the Dutch proposal was firmly rejected however by most member states.[159] Although the eventual treaty concluded several months later in Maastricht did not live up to the lofty aspirations of the Dutch Parliament, important improvements made with regard to the new powers of the European Parliament, as well as the new references to fundamental human rights, and the subsidiarity principle contributed to a generally very favourable reception of the treaty in the Netherlands.[160]

In spite of its obvious undermining of national competencies, for example on monetary policy, the question of constitutional conformity of the Maastricht Treaty met with less concern than the Schengen II convention did. Probably, this resulted from the fact that the matter was explicitly addressed in the government memorandum accompanying the treaty. Referring to the dominant tradition of constitutional openness, the government, with the consent of the Raad van State, here argued that the transfer of powers could be reconciled with the Dutch constitution. Hence, it suggested that ratification of this treaty did not even require the special ratification procedure for treaties going against the constitution.[161] This suggestion almost went uncontested in Parliament, even though a small minority in Parliament brought up the possibility of a ratification referendum following the examples set by Denmark and France.[162] Public debate also showed a broad consensus supporting the line of thought developed in the government memorandum. In newspapers, articles regarding the 'constitutionality' of the Maastricht Treaty were generally reserved for foreign news pages, for example regarding the French constitutional reform or the Maastricht Judgment of the German Constitutional Court in 1993.[163] The Maastricht Treaty in these reports was mostly approached as an accomplished fact, which could at worst be delayed by a possible negative outcome of the more complicated ratification procedures in neighbouring states.[164]

That the Maastricht Treaty did not raise any more fundamental discussions on the constitutionality of European integration in the 1990s seems to have been due to the strong political majority favouring deeper integration and democratisation of the EC. The perceived tradition of constitutional openness, which guided the constitutional reforms of 1953/1956, well fit this political agenda. Only in 2000 did the Dutch Senate halt this development. Discussing a special legal procedure to speed up the still faltering implementation of European law by passing the usual legislative

159 A major Dutch newspaper described the defeat as a 'total humiliation': Schaling, Frits. 1991. 'Vernedering voor Den Haag totaal', *NRC Handelsblad*, 1 Oct. In Dutch literature, the day of the defeat – 30 September 1991 – is generally known as 'Black Monday'.

160 Hollander 2013, 200–220.

161 *HTK* 1991–1992, B 22647, nos. 1–2.

162 The suggestion to organise a referendum came from the green party (GroenLinks): *HTK* 1992–1993, B 22647 no. 7. Some constitutional lawyers did raise the issue of unconstitutionality, though: Heringa 1992, 749–752 and Besselink 1992, 864–865.

163 BVerfGE 89, 155, 12.10.1993, *Maastricht*, 2 BvR 2134, 2159/92.

164 Based on an analysis of all national Dutch newspaper articles mentioning both 'grondwet' and 'Maastricht' in the period 1992–1994 via 'Krantenbank' (lexisnexis.nl).

safeguards, it held that the progress made in developing democratic safeguards at the European level did not sufficiently compensate for the loss of national safeguards anymore.[165] This is highly reminiscent of the position taken by the German Constitutional Court with its demands for 'structural congruence' between national and European legal system. This position is detailed in Chapter 6 of this volume. Therefore, it urged for an evaluation of the constitutional clauses on EU-membership and of the legislative procedures regarding the implementation of EU law.[166] Even though the impact of the evaluation remained limited, it clearly demonstrated a new, more critical position vis-à-vis the consequences of European integration for legal security, a position that had already influenced parliamentary discussions on the Treaty of Amsterdam in 1997.[167] Together with the rise of Euroscepticism from which Dutch political debate could not remain aloof, this more critical assessment of the legal aspects of integration eventually softened the ground for a referendum on the ratification of the Constitutional treaty in 2005.[168] While the surprisingly negative outcome of this referendum has deeply upset and ultimately changed the public and political debate on European integration in the Netherlands, the constitutional settlement was not significantly affected, nor the favourable attitude of many Dutch lawyers, companies and courts towards EU law.[169]

CONCLUSION

If the European legal system is to be regarded as a 'negotiated compromise' that took its shape only gradually, and not the least in conversation with national courts and actors, what then did the Netherlands contribute to this conversation?[170] Reduced to its cliché image of champion of European law, this question used to possess a rather straightforward answer. After 'delivering' the ECJ its first preliminary rulings, not much was to be expected from the Netherlands, happily taking in all that came from either Brussels or Luxembourg. By adding some important nuances to the story of the 'unproblematic' Dutch interaction with the European legal order, however, this chapter also complicates the assessment of the Dutch contribution to the development of this legal system.

165 See for similar concerns in the Second Chamber *HTK* 1998–1999, B 26200 VI, no. 65, p. 2.

166 Gewijzigde motie-Jurgens (PvdA) c.s. inzake implementatie van EG-regelgeving, *HEK* 1999–2000, 26200 VI no. 65/37b, resulting in a report by Besselink et al. 2002. The new legal procedure in part was a response to the failing implementation uncovered in the so-called 'Securitel affair' that followed from the 1996 ECJ judgement against Belgium with that name (194/94, *CIA Security International SA v Signalson SA and Securitel SPRL*, 1996, ECLI:EU:C:1996:172).

167 Hollander 2013, 230–231.

168 Harryvan and van der Harst 2013, 146–148; Vollaard and Boer 2005.

169 Van der Harten 2015, 242.

170 Davies 2012b, 211; Claes et al. 2012.

As this chapter has recapped with new historical evidence, Dutch courts, but more importantly also companies and their legal representatives, most famously contributed to the development of the European legal order through the preliminary references they sent to the ECJ in the early 1960s. In the years in which Gaullist plans for an intergovernmental political union caused heated discussions over the future of the EC, these references enabled the Luxembourg court to develop its 'constitutional' doctrines by acknowledging the direct effect of some clauses of the EEC Treaty. As this chapter has demonstrated, explanations for the prominent role of the Netherlands in these trailblazing court cases cannot exclusively be found in the special constitutional system, which explicitly required courts to distinguish between treaty provisions with and without 'any binding character'. Nor can the sole responsibility of the Dutch breakthrough be placed with the federalist notions or the presumed 'pioneering' tradition of the Netherlands in international law that could be found in Parliament and amongst legal scholars – even though both were pivotal in first realising the special constitutional system in 1953–1956, and then in pushing Dutch courts beyond their initial hesitation to use the preliminary reference procedure in the early 1960s. Instead, as this chapter has argued, the famous court rulings were ironically as much a result of the resistance by the Dutch government to the constitutional interpretation of European law promoted by these scholars, as well as by its containment of the effects of specific treaty clauses in the fields of competition and tariffs.

The questions that reached the court from the Netherlands were raised elsewhere as other chapters in this volume highlight. Nevertheless, it was the Dutch constitutional settlement that, in the wording of the Tariefcommissie, provoked the ECJ's focus on direct effect – as well as the terminology in which the ECJ eventually chose to settle the matter. Moreover, Dutch European law specialists had raised the issue as a study topic for their FIDE associates – even when the latter eventually addressed the matter in a much more abstract manner than their Dutch counterparts. In its positioning in Luxembourg as well as in parliament, the Dutch government generally demonstrated a similar practice-oriented approach, following from the fact that the Ministry of Foreign Affairs often left the initiative in matters of implementation and intervention in pending ECJ cases to the technical departments.

In striking contrast with this pragmatic positioning at home, the Dutch government developed into an ardent advocate of the European legal order when it came under attack from member states such as France and the United Kingdom. The ECJ's *Costa v ENEL* ruling marked an important breakthrough in this regard, as it promised to realise what Dutch parliament already aimed for when accepting the 1953 constitutional revision: supremacy of European law meant that the other member states would be bound by treaty obligations to the same extent that the Netherlands had already voluntarily accepted to do in 1953. As a consequence, the Netherlands not only pushed for the acceptance of this doctrine across its borders but also stepped in for the ECJ when its position was threatened by the larger member states within the Council.

Stepping in its role of defender of the European legal order, the Dutch government thereby built upon a self-image which had its roots in early twentieth-century debates on international law and which from the 1950s onwards had often been brought up both in scholarly publications as well as in Parliament. One of the striking findings of this chapter in this regard must be the prominent role of Leiden-based scholars: where Van Eysinga, inspired by predecessors such as Krabbe and van Vollenhoven, crucially contributed to (the framing of) the 1953 constitutional reform, Polak, Samkalden and Brinkhorst, moving from academia to politics and back, continued his work by promulgating both practical knowledge and a missionary narrative with regard to the developing European legal order amongst their peers as well as amongst a broad audience of the legal practitioners. Hence, before it was embraced as official government policy, the narrative of the pioneering member state with its special relation to international law had already impacted Dutch interaction with European law in many ways.

A final note on the narrative itself: After tracing its emergence, development and impact in the historical period under assessment here, this chapter cannot conclude without signalling that it has been partly due to this narrative that, in assessing the Dutch interaction with European law, scholarship until this day has generally disregarded moments of conflicts and contestation in favour of an overall 'favourable' image. By demonstrating that, in fact, the Netherlands behaved more like the other member states than these previous studies suggested, this chapter not only nuances current interpretations of the Dutch positioning but also urges for a reconsideration of their underlying narrative. By understanding this narrative not as a structural feature but rather as the product of specific historical actors and circumstances, this chapter hopefully will open the field for new more instrumental and contextual analyses of Dutch interactions with European law.

9

A Job for the Civil Servants: Denmark and European Law

Jonas Langeland Pedersen

Just like Britain, Denmark has traditionally been considered a reluctant member of the European Community (EC).[1] As a member state, Denmark strongly supported free trade and had great economic interest in participating in the Common Agricultural Policy (CAP) but generally opposed moves towards a more supranational or even federal Europe. In 1972, Denmark had entered the EC on the basis of a domestic consensus forged by the Social Democratic government that highlighted the economic advantages of membership and made quite explicit the opposition to any institutional deepening of the EC.[2] Danish EC membership was based on this consensus until the Single European Act in 1986, which was initially rejected by the Danish parliament, but subsequently endorsed by a referendum pushed through by a right-wing minority government keen on Danish participation in the Single European Market. In the aftermath of the referendum, under the impression of the new dynamics of European integration and the détente between East and West, a major political shift in Danish European policy occurred and eventually brought all the major Danish parties behind the Maastricht Treaty in 1992. This shift was not fully reflected in the attitudes of the electorate, however, which in a referendum in June 1992 rejected what was generally perceived in the Danish public as a huge step towards a more integrated Europe. It was only after Denmark received several 'opt outs' at the Edinburgh Summit in December 1992 that the Danish voters accepted the treaty in a second referendum.[3]

Considering this record of scepticism towards the European project one might expect a dramatic and eventful history of popular Danish resistance to the constitutional practice of European law. Surprisingly, the issue was, for almost the entire period under consideration here, ignored by the broader public and did not play any significant part in the broader political battle over Danish European policy either. Instead, the story told in this chapter is essentially an administrative one. The Danish

[1] This chapter is based on Pedersen 2016. I would like to thank Magnus Esmark for his comments to the chapter. They were very useful in improving the text.

[2] Rasmussen 2004.

[3] Petersen 2004, 504–520.

government and state administration actively contained the effects of European law by the means of administrative techniques, and by exercising a subtle control over how national courts interpreted European law. At the same time, despite limited political support for supranational governance, Danish governments apparently defended the ECJ and its constitutional interpretation in the EC, because it was believed that a strong European legal system would benefit a small member state like Denmark.[4]

DENMARK'S ROAD TO EC MEMBERSHIP

Denmark had attempted to become a member of the EC since Britain applied for membership in 1961. An EC enlarged with Britain would receive almost 70 per cent of Danish exports and clearly made alternatives economically unsustainable. Given the overwhelmingly strong commercial interests in EC membership, a broad majority of the Danish parliament backed it from 1961 onward on the condition that Britain joined as well. Unfortunately, for Danish commercial interests,[5] the repeated French rejections of British membership in 1963 and 1967 made Danish accession politically impossible. Despite the economic incentives to join the EC even without Britain, Danish national identity and socialist ideology made the centre-left of Danish politics fear the consequences of Danish EC membership. The conservative and capitalist governments of Continental Europe, combined with the dominance of Catholicism, created deep apprehension in a protestant country where Nordic cooperation attracted popular backing as a bastion of democracy, social democracy and the universalist welfare state. Danish EC membership thus could only attract the necessary parliamentary majority if it happened as part of a broader enlargement involving at a minimum Britain, but preferably also Norway.[6]

In 1970, enlargement negotiations finally began between the EC and Britain, Norway, Ireland and a Danish state led by a centre-right majority government led by a Prime Minister, Hilmar Baunsgaard, from the Social Liberal Party (Det Radikale Venstre). However, to the main parliamentary opposition, Social Democratic Party (Socialdemokratiet) the question of EC membership was far from simple politically. Despite the strong support to EC membership by the party leadership, an important opposition existed in the party particularly from the new young 1968 generation. The question was therefore how the party could win the forthcoming 1971 election and support EC membership without jeopardising the support of young socialist voters. The key step towards solving the first part of this dilemma was to remove the question of Danish EC membership from the agenda of the upcoming election by the means

4 For a general treatment of this topic in twentieth-century Danish history please consult Gram-Skjoldager 2012.

5 Rasmussen 2011a.

6 The Danish European movement completely failed to get popular backing in contrast to most countries in Continental Europe. Rasmussen 2005, 47–74.

of a popular referendum. The Social Democratic Party succeeded setting up a referendum with the help of Baunsgaard's Social Liberal Party that also had a minority opposed to Danish EC membership, even if his coalition partners the conservatives and liberals protested loudly. In the end this tactical manoeuvre made it possible for the Social Democratic Party to win the election of 21 September 1971. Now the challenge was of course how to win the referendum. Here the tactics of the new Social Democratic Government led by Jens Otto Krag was to emphasise the economic incentives of membership and to make it clear that Denmark would have a veto right over any political and institutional deepening of European integration. The future of the Danish model of democracy and the welfare state would therefore not be endangered by EC accession. In order to cement this position in Danish public opinion, the new Minister for the European Market and Nordic Affairs, Ivar Nørgaard, controversially stated this position before the EC Council during the enlargement negotiations. Here, he explained to the other member states that Denmark would not surrender any sovereignty over social, fiscal and economic policy in the context of the future economic and monetary union, which at the time was planned by the EC, but later abandoned. This was not well received by the EC, which made clear that the Community built on collective solutions, but it gave a clear indication of what kind of member state Denmark would become in the following decades.[7]

The tactical approach to winning the referendum worked, and the Social Democratic Government managed to create a consensus that brought Denmark into the EC with a significant majority of 63.3 per cent of the votes. The victory would come at a high price, however, as the nature of the consensus would shape and restrict Danish European policy in decades to come. Denmark joined the EC for commercial and economic gains. The Danish perception of the EC was that it was largely an intergovernmental organisation dominated by national governments. The veto right would ensure that Denmark, and thus the Danish electorate, could control the future development of the integration process.

THE LEGAL FOUNDATIONS OF DANISH EC MEMBERSHIP

The legal foundations of Danish EC membership did not help to mitigate the widespread political scepticism vis-à-vis European integration in part of the political elite and the broader public. The Danish Constitution, which dated back to 1849, received a revision in 1953, including a new Article 20 that defined the conditions for the transfer of powers to international organisations. Until then, any transfer of sovereignty had not been possible from a constitutional point of view. The inclusion of the article was initiated by the famous Danish professor of international law, Max Sørensen, who served as an advisor to the Danish Ministry of Foreign Affairs from

7 Rasmussen 2004, 337–340, 402.

the end of the Second World War until 1973. His academic authority made him one of the most important actors shaping how European law was understood in Denmark in the 1950s and 1960s. Thus, it was no coincidence that Max Sørensen became the first Danish judge at the ECJ from 1973 to 1979.[8]

The inclusion of Article 20 in the new Danish Constitution was a response to the legal problems caused by Denmark's accession to NATO, and the wave of new international organisations that were established in the immediate post war era. It was believed that the decision to join NATO involved a transfer of sovereignty. However, Article 19 – that traditionally formed the basis for Danish participation in international organisations – did not include any stipulations about such a transfer. The paramount political importance of joining NATO, due to the threat from the Soviet Union, forced the government to produce a legal argument that would allow Danish membership.[9] The responsibility for forming the legal argument fell to Sørensen. He concluded that according to the Danish Constitution the Danish armed forces could only be subordinated to a foreign authority in peacetime if the latter were controlled by an organ in which Denmark had a veto right. The official Danish interpretation was that a unified NATO command did not in principle impede the rights of the individual member states to decide whether they would use armed forces in the case of an attack on another member country. Furthermore, it was argued that it was crucial that the administrative control with the Danish contribution to the united forces remained in Danish hands.[10]

The constitutional difficulties of joining NATO demonstrated the need for an amendment to the Danish Constitution.[11] The new Article 20 of the 1953 constitutional revision allowed a transfer of powers to international organisations to take place by means of a statute if it was backed by a five-sixths majority of the Parliament, or alternatively through a referendum if the government proceeded with the proposal. Overall, these relatively strict conditions would contribute to a trend where decisions on possible transfers of sovereignty were removed from Parliament to popular referenda. However, when the clause was first formulated, a five-sixths majority in Parliament could easily be achieved if the four largest political parties agreed.[12] It was only from 1971 onwards, during the enlargement negotiations, that

8 Nørgaard, Carl Aage, 1988, *Max Sørensen – 19. februar 1913 – 11. oktober 1981*. Obituary https://auhist.au.dk/fileadmin/user_upload/Person_-_Max_Soerensen-nekrolog-binder__1_.pdf.

9 Olesen and Villaume 2006, 157–158.

10 Olesen and Villaume 2006, 157–158.

11 The debate over the basic challenges related to the nature of the conferral of competences to the EU have continued in recent years and was the subject of a now famous case before the Danish Supreme Court. (Højesteret, 6 December 2016, *Dansk Industri (DI) acting on behalf of Ajos A/S v Estate of A*, Case no. 15/2014.) For an analysis of the judgment in a broad political perspective see: Madsen et al. 2017, 140–150.

12 The Danish party system had since the beginning of the twentieth century been dominated by the Social Democratic Party, the Social Liberal Party (Det radikale venstre), the Liberal Party (Venstre) and the Conservative Party. Their dominance of the parliament only disappeared with the protest election of 1973, which completely crushed the four-party system.

the political parties on the extreme left and right gained sufficient political strength to hinder a five-sixths majority.[13] In addition to the relatively strict conditions for a transfer of sovereignty, Article 20 also included a somewhat peculiar formulation that would haunt the constitutional debate over Danish EC membership until the *Maastricht* judgment of the Danish Supreme Court (Højesteret) in 1998:[14] a transfer of sovereignty could only happen 'to a clearly defined extent as shall be provided by the Statute'.[15] This begged the question of course if the Danish sovereignty transfer to a EC that was supposed to develop into an 'ever closer union' be described as 'a clearly defined extent'? It is not surprising that the Danish EC opponents found a basis for their claim that Danish EC membership was inherently unconstitutional. The question whether Danish EC membership was constitutional was politically important. In a situation where a five-sixths majority existed in Parliament in favour of EC membership (if Britain also joined), which was the case from 1961 to 1971, the only way to stop Danish accession was to declare it unconstitutional. If Danish membership required a new constitutional change, this could only be achieved by a complex procedure involving two majority votes in Parliament with an election in between, then followed by a popular referendum in favour of the change representing at least 40 per cent of the electorate. Although, this was perhaps not much more difficult than a five-sixths majority in Parliament, it would turn the question of Danish membership into a prolonged political battle.[16]

Apart from the peculiarities of the constitutional basis of Danish EC membership, the Danish Constitution combined two factors that made the acceptance of a constitutional practice of European law difficult. First, Denmark's reception of international law was based on a dualist theory, requiring incorporation of international law by a Statute of Parliament or by an administrative act in pursuance of a Statute of the Parliament. Moreover, Danish courts would interpret international law based on the so-called rules of interpretation and presumption. According to the rule of interpretation, a Statute or act that could be interpreted in several ways should be interpreted in conformity with Denmark's international obligations. At the same time, the rule of presumption meant that Danish law was assumed to be in accordance with international law, and that under no circumstance could courts act against national law.[17] Second, Denmark had a longstanding tradition of parliamentary sovereignty. As a result, Danish courts rejected playing any political role and there has been virtually no tradition of judicial review. Until 1999, Højesteret had

13 Rasmussen 2004, 411.

14 Højesteret, 6 April 1998, *Treaty of Maastricht*, Case 361/1997.

15 The relevant part of Article 20 reads: 'Powers vested in the authorities of the Realm under this Constitution Act may, to a clearly defined extent as shall be provided by Statute, be delegated to international authorities set up by mutual agreement with other states for the promotion of international rules of law and cooperation.' See also Spiermann 2008, 41, 43.

16 The Danish Constitution Article 88.

17 Spiermann 2008, 47.

never ruled that a law was unconstitutional.[18] A further aspect which over time would complicate the Danish reception of European law was the high level of loyalty felt by Danish judges towards the Ministry of Justice and the State Prosecutor which together were seen to represent the highest expertise on European law in Denmark. The high degree of loyalty came from the way judges were recruited in Denmark. More than half of the Danish judges were recruited from within the ranks of the Ministry of Justice.[19]

In 1962, the constitutionality of a future Danish accession to the EC was brought into question for the first time by the newly formed Danish Socialist People's Party (Socialist Folkeparti). The party was established in 1959 after a split in the Communist Party and turned into a viable political force to the left of the Social Democratic Party. It played a leading role as opponents of EC membership until 1993. The party chairman, Aksel Larsen, claimed that Article 235 of the EEC Treaty meant that the powers transferred through Article 20 did not fulfil the criteria of being clearly defined. To counter the claim, the Social Democratic government asked Max Sørensen to write a legal response. Sørensen rejected Larsen's claim by pointing out that Article 235 was merely intended to fill in unintended gaps in the EEC treaty, and did not widen its jurisdiction. Larsen replied that the legal opinion was coloured by the intimacy of Sørensen with the government. He therefore insisted on an independent legal opinion from both Danish university professors as well as from the European institutions.[20] His demands were rejected by the government.[21]

In late 1970, the question of constitutionality reappeared. In December of that year, Sørensen delivered a memorandum that maintained his 1962 analysis of the implications of Article 235 of the EEC Treaty.[22] This did not close the debate this time. In a fierce attack on the government in 1971, Professor Erik Siesby from University of Copenhagen, who was also a member of the grassroots organisation, The People's Movement against the EC (Folkebevægelsen mod EF), claimed that the doctrine of primacy of European law was at odds with the Danish constitution. According to Siesby, Article 20 did not allow Denmark to comply with the primacy of European law because the present Danish parliament was unable to commit a future parliament except by a constitutional amendment. Since an act of Article 20 can be repealed by an ordinary Statute, Siesby argued that any later Danish Statutes which were contrary to an earlier Community rule implicitly revoked the delegation of powers under Article 20. To Siesby, the principle of primacy constituted such a radical step because it involved a transfer of loyalty from the Danish courts to the

18 Wind and Rytter 2011, 475.

19 Wind 2010, 1050–1051.

20 Primary sources fully document Larsen's suspicion. In private Sørensen wrote to his colleague Korsbæk in the Ministry of Foreign Affairs that his view obviously was shaped by his ardent support of European integration in general and Danish membership in particular.

21 Rasmussen 2004, 412.

22 Rasmussen 2004, 413.

ECJ which, in his view, required at the very least an explicit statement of acceptance by the government.[23]

Max Sørensen and Professor Alf Ross, two of the most dominant figures in Danish legal academia, quickly and publicly countered Siesby in a response that clearly did not fully embrace the nature of the primacy doctrine.[24] According to Sørensen, the transfer of powers under Article 20 implied an acceptance of the direct effect and primacy of European law. The primacy of European law could be adhered to by Danish institutions simply by Parliament not passing statutes that were in contradiction with European law. Sørensen and Ross also concurred that Danish courts, in any case under the principle of presumption, would presume that it had not been the intention of the Parliament to pass legislation contrary to European law, and therefore, would be able to grant the latter primacy. Ross pointed out that in the extreme case in which the Parliament did not want to fulfil its European obligations Danish courts would have to follow the former.[25] There was, of course, no real chance that the government would allow a dispute over the interpretation of the constitution to block the Danish accession to the EC. The official response from the Ministry of Justice published in July 1972, as supplement to the Act of Danish EC membership, followed Sørensen and Ross. It was argued that the Danish state fulfilled its treaty obligations as long as Danish authorities acted in accordance with the intentions of the Treaties of Rome. However, it was also underlined that Denmark by a simple statute could end its EC membership.[26]

The fact that the Danish Administration did not deviate from this largely intergovernmental approach to the EC can also be seen in a legal analysis of the key claim that Nørgaard presented in Brussels about the presumed veto right of the member states. Although the reaction from the Council of Ministers clearly suggested that the Danish view was somewhat amiss, the internal legal analysis by Per Lachman, who was on track to become the Head of the Office of European Law in the Ministry of Foreign Affairs,[27] followed Nørgaard's claim. Lachman argued that the political consequences of the Luxembourg Compromise were of such a fundamental nature that they redefined the legal playing field of the EC. The analysis followed what seems to have been the general view in both the government and the Ministry of Foreign Affairs.

> Thus, the Luxembourg declaration must be seen as the solemn expression of the political wish to safeguard the main purpose of the cooperation and the treaties of the EC: the most extensive solidarity among the member states. During the

23 Siesby 1971, 414–427 and 1972, 129–132 and 220–221.

24 Sørensen 1971, 434–440 and 1972, 117–129; Ross 1972, 161–165.

25 For a broad treatment of the debate see: Due and Gulmann 1972, 265–267.

26 Review of July 1972 by the Ministry of Justice of a number of legal problems relating to the Danish accession to the European Communities.

27 The biographical information about Per Lachmann is based on a personal e-mail correspondence of 26 November 2015.

> cooperation of the EC this solidarity, based on mutual trust, have only been possible to achieve when the member state (great or small) has been able to feel absolutely sure that, no matter the treaty provisions, in cases of vital importance they will not be overruled. Everybody within the EC: the old member states, the candidate countries and the Commission recognizes this principle. The Luxembourg declaration is a political agreement between the member states which does not formally change the treaties, but which makes a political decision about the use of certain treaty provisions in view of the aim of the treaties. This political agreement, which at the same time is an integral part of the EC's foundation, should not and cannot be changed within the foreseeable future.[28]

According to Lachman, the Luxembourg Compromise meant that whenever Danish sovereignty or vital interests were under threat, Denmark would be able to block new initiatives in the Council of Ministers. The future development of the EC could thus be controlled. The analysis did not take note that the Luxembourg Compromise in fact was an agreement to disagree. Five member states disagreed with the French view that a veto right existed when vital interests were at stake. Moreover, the compromise was informal, had no clear legal status, and was consequently not part of the legal foundations of the EC. It is hard to imagine a legal analysis further removed from the constitutional interpretation of the ECJ, which was based on a teleological interpretation of the objectives of the Treaties of Rome and would give no weight for the informal Luxembourg Compromise.

CONTAINING THE EFFECTS OF EUROPEAN LAW IN DENMARK, 1973–1979

Danish European policy in the 1970s was constrained by the general lack of popular support of the EC with figures below 50 per cent in favour of Danish membership in the opinion polls. There was a broad majority in the Parliament, including the Social Democratic Party and the Social Liberal Party, that still favoured the original consensus about Danish EC membership that developed in 1971–1972. As a result,

[28] Authors translation from original: 'Luxembourg-deklarationen må således ses som det højtidelige udtryk for det politiske ønske om at sikre EF-samarbejdets og traktatens hovedmål: den størst mulige solidaritet mellem medlemslandene. Det har under samarbejdet vist sig, at denne solidaritet mellem medlemslandene, baseret på gensidig tillid, kun har kunnet realiseres i det omfang hver stat, stor som lille – kunne føle sig overbevist om, at den – uanset traktatens bestemmelser – ikke kan risikere at blive overstemt i sager af væsentlig betydning for den pågældende stat. Alle inden for EF såvel nuværende medlemslande som kandidatlande, og Kommissionen anerkender dette princip. Luxembourg-deklarationen er en politisk aftale mellem alle medlemsregeringerne som ikke formelt ændrer traktaten, men som træffer en politisk afgørelse om anvendelsen af visse traktatbestemmelser af hensyn til opfyldelsen af traktatens målsætning. Denne politiske aftale, der samtidig er en integrerende del af EF's grundlag, bør ikke og kan ikke ændres inden for en overskuelig fremtid.' Archive of the Danish Ministry of Foreign Affairs (UM).400.A.3. Note concerning the Luxembourg settlement. By Per Lachmann, 23 July 1973.

Denmark focused narrowly on the economic interests and was wary of possible consequences of membership to the welfare system and the labour market. In addition, Danish governments generally opposed institutional reform and supported the continued existence of the veto right. Nonetheless, the Danish attitude to the ECJ and its constitutional interpretation of European law was somewhat more complex.

During the 1970s, the EC was split regarding how to address the challenges of the world economic crisis that broke out in 1973. Denmark adopted Keynesian economic policies, which proved less than successful, and – like most other member states – adopted various protectionist measures to protect the home market and Danish jobs in a situation of high unemployment.[29] During the 1970s where the functioning of the Common Market was hampered by the rise of protectionism in the member states, the ECJ delivered several important judgments to consolidate trade liberalisation.[30] When implementing European legislation, or adapting Danish law to new ECJ case law, the priority of the Danish administration was to avoid any detrimental effects on the protection of the home market, as well as the Danish welfare state and labour market model.

Despite the constitutional case law of the ECJ, which defined member state courts as guardians of European law in the member states,[31] Danish courts at first tended to ignore European law, and did not avail themselves of the preliminary reference mechanism to the same extent as most other member states, even if a certain run-in period could be expected.[32] We can mostly speculate what were the precise reasons for this timid start. One factor that seems quite evident was the general lack of knowledge about European law in a court system that regarded the EC as part of foreign policy. Second, the Danish courts had no tradition for exercising judicial review on national legislation and may therefore have found the preliminary reference mechanism somewhat daring. Finally, Danish judges were nominated by the Ministry of Justice and had typically served as rank-and-file civil servants in that same Ministry. This gave the Ministry of Justice an indirect influence over the attitudes of national courts towards European law in that it had shaped the outlook of Danish judges more generally.[33] As a result the story that emerges from the archival documentation is one where the Danish Administration developed a strong influence over how Danish courts would interact with the ECJ. The objective seems to have been to maintain freedom to delay, adjust and even

[29] For a general treatment of this period of European integration see Warlouzet 2018; Olesen 2018.

[30] 8/74, *Procureur du Roi v Benoît and Gustave Dassonville*, 1974, ECLI:EU:C:1974:82 and 120/78, *Rewe-Zentral AG v Bundesmonopolverwaltung für Branntwein*, 1979, ECLI:EU:C:1979:42. See also Leucht 2017.

[31] 106/77 *Amministrazione delle finanze dello Stato v Simmenthal*, 1978, ECLI:EU:C:1978:49.

[32] Grønning-Nielsen 1992, 337–340 argues that Danish courts sent too few preliminary references. See also Broberg and Fenger 2021, who argue that the number of cases was what could be expected by a new member state.

[33] Wind 2010, 1051.

sidestep what was perceived as possible negative effects of European legislation, and minimise the role of the ECJ and its case law in a Danish context. This approach could to some extent be justified with a reference to how the Danish Constitution defined the reception of international law, and it meant that the constitutional case law developed by the ECJ was not always followed. Considering the negative Danish attitude to institutional reform of the EC until 1986, this administrative behaviour fell well within the general approach by shifting Danish governments to European integration.[34]

Administratively, the tasks of managing the Danish response to European law fell into the hands of a small group of civil servants who would come to dominate this policy area in the 1970s and 1980s. The key civil servants who took on this job operated within the strong committee structure which was put in place before the Danish accession to the EC.[35] At the very top of the administrative machinery was the at the time unique Parliamentary Committee of Market Affairs[36] which reflected a need for parliamentary coordination with regard to the Danish input to the legislative process of the EC due to the tradition for minority governments. To help coordinate the government's position, a similar Governmental Market Committee[37] was comprised of key ministers. Supporting this committee was the Administrative EC Committee,[38] in which the ten most important ministries were represented, and yet beneath that was a string of subcommittees dealing with specific areas of European policy.[39]

Despite this complex administrative set up, it was only after the accession that a committee to deal with the questions arising from European law was established. This committee was named the EC Special Committee for Legal Questions,[40] and it included experts on European law from the Ministry of Foreign Affairs, the Ministry of Justice and the Ministry of Commerce. The Chairman of the Committee was Ole Due, Head of Office in the Ministry of Justice, the three other permanent members were Hans Duborg (Ministry of Commerce), Per Lachmann (Ministry of Foreign Affairs) and Karsten Hagel-Sørensen (Ministry of Justice).[41] The Special Committee was placed in the administrative hierarchy between the EC Committee and the numerous sub-committees. This reflected the intermediate role of the Special Committee which was given a strong mandate

34 For a different analysis based on interviews consult: Esmark 2022, 115–123 and Esmark 2020, 23–42.

35 Christensen 1990, 13–17.

36 Danish name: Folketingets markedsudvalg. After 1994: Europaudvalg.

37 Danish name: Regeringens markedsudvalg.

38 Danish name: EF-udvalget.

39 Christensen 1990, 14–15.

40 Danish name: EF-specialudvalget for juridiske spørgsmål.

41 UM.108.C.13. Terms of reference for the EC Special Committee for Legal Questions and M.J. nr. 400.C.4–0. 18. September 1973; Department of Foreign. Minutes of EC Committee meeting 19/1973. 12 June 1973.

by the EC Committee to coordinate how the ministries would deal with questions regarding European law.[42]

The first years after the accession were relatively calm. The Danish courts, unlike the Irish and the British, did not send any preliminary references to the ECJ, but the case law of the latter soon proved increasingly difficult to contain.[43] A first hint of the challenges ahead concerned the right to establishment in agriculture. The Danish government had secured a five-year transitional period for fully implementing Community legislation which only partially liberalised the right to establishment in the sector. However, in the *Reyners* judgment,[44] the ECJ undermined the Danish transitional arrangement. By declaring that Articles 52 and 55 of the EEC Treaty had direct effect, the judgment immediately swept away all European legislation already adopted, and it fully liberalised the right to establishment.[45]

Another important case that directly interfered with the Danish Social Model started to unfold in the mid-1970s. Article 119 of EEC Treaty stipulated equal pay between the genders. However, there according to the Danish labour market model, salary was negotiated between the parties of the labour market and not by the means of legislation from Parliament. This also included the question of equal pay. As a consequence, the trade unions and employer organisations had a very strong influence on the question and they had deliberately not addressed the persistent inequalities. In the EC, progress in the field of equal pay between the genders had also been embarrassingly slow. The *Defrenne* judgment[46] of the ECJ broke the first barrier by giving Article 119 of the EEC Treaty direct effect, after which the Council on 10 February 1975 passed a new directive to clarify the main definition in Article 119 of the EEC Treaty as equal pay for work of equal value. Denmark was now under serious pressure. The implementation of the directive in Denmark could potentially undermine the treasured collective agreements.[47] Initially Danish lawmakers considered whether the principle of equal pay was covered by the compromise in 1973 produced by the Conciliation Officers of the labour market which established the principle of equal pay in collective agreements. However, the Danish government decided that legislation was still necessary to implement the directive. The law passed by the Danish Parliament on 4 February 1976[48] did not embrace the directive in full. It simply stipulated that equal pay already should be meted out for equal work. The law was an attempt by Parliament to protect the compromise on equal pay

42 Archive of the Danish Ministry of Justice (JM).A.I. 7/73. JMT. EC Special Committee for Legal Questions. Guide on the member states access to intervene or give statements in cases at the ECJ and to Council declarations. 8 November 1973.

43 Grønning-Nielsen 1992, 337–340.

44 2/74, *Jean Reyners v Belgian State*, 1974, ECLI:EU:C:1974:68.

45 Rasmussen 2004, 277.

46 43/75, *Gabrielle Defrenne v Société anonyme belge de navigation aérienne Sabena*, 1976, ECLI:EU:C:1976:56.

47 Martinsen 2007, 549–553.

48 Danish Law no. 32. 4 February 1976.

always adopted by the Danish labour market model.[49] It was only in 1979 that the Commission caught on to the discrepancy, and in the following years initiated an infringement procedure against Denmark. The position of the Danish government was, as late as 1983, that the substance of the Danish law complied with the directive.[50] Finally, on 30 January 1985 the ECJ delivered its ruling and found that Denmark failed to fulfil its obligations by not implementing the directive.[51] Through these tactics of stalling and delaying, the Danish government was able to maintain the Danish system for ten more years.

Another case that forced the Danish Administration to engage with the ECJ concerned Danish duties applicable to spirits. Denmark had, like France, Italy and the United Kingdom, been found by the Commission to be distorting the Common Market by protecting national products through special tax arrangements. On 22 December 1975, the Commission initiated an infringement case against Denmark. In response, the Market Secretariat of the Ministry of Foreign Affairs and the experts in the Ministry of Taxation and Levies deployed a tactic of delaying the process by producing increasingly imaginative arguments as to why the Danish taxation scheme was lawful. This included arguments about the process of distillation, and the reference to public health objectives of lowering the level of consumption of alcohol in Denmark.[52] It quickly became clear that the case could not be won, but for political reasons it was decided to see the case through. By not changing the Danish rules already when the infringement was identified, the Danish state was again able to maintain its own rules until the final ruling of the ECJ on 27 February 1980.[53]

The Danish courts were slow to engage with the European legal system. However, in November 1977, the 13th Department of the City Court of Copenhagen submitted the first preliminary reference to the ECJ.[54] The case concerned two goldsmiths who had come into conflict with the national rules monitored by the agency, State Control of Precious Metals. The relevant law prescribed that companies which manufactured, imported or resold works of precious metals, and which had a registered name stamp, were subject to supervision from the agency. The supervision was funded by a small duty paid by the companies working with precious metals, and it was this duty that the two goldsmiths involved, Preben Larsen and

49 Martinsen 2007, 551–552.

50 Historical Archives of the Commission (HAC).BAC 32/1992 no. 177. C-143/83. 143/83–15. Received by the ECJ on 12 October 1983. Letter from Laurids Mikaelsen from the Ministry of Foreign Affairs in response to the note from the Court no. 17609 of 18 July 1983 and no. 181066 of 26 August 1983.

51 143/83, *Commission of the European Communities v Kingdom of Denmark*, 1985, ECLI:EU:C:1985:34. See also Miller 2019.

52 UM.400.A-5–3–4–0. 10 February 1976. Draft of answer to the Commissions letter of 22 December 1975 written by the EC Special Committee for Taxation.

53 171/78 *Commission of the European Communities v Kingdom of Denmark. Tax arrangements applicable to spirits*, 1980, ECLI:EU:C:1980:54.

54 UM.400.A.5–3–3. Notat: EF-udvalgets møde den 7. februar 1978. A-punkt. Dansk indlæg i sag 142/77 for EF-domstolen. 3 February 1978.

Flemming Kjerulf, refused to pay.[55] Both goldsmiths claimed that their manufactured goods (which were directly exported without the name stamp) should not be subject to the duty. On 4 March 1975, the City Court of Copenhagen ruled in favour of the two goldsmiths. The case was then appealed to the Eastern High Court which reversed the ruling. However, the ruling was not final. In the City Court of Copenhagen, Peter Dyhr, who represented the goldsmiths, made a subsidiary claim that the duty was in conflict with European law. Since this had not been a part of the ruling in the first instance, the question was resubmitted to the City Court of Copenhagen. This resulted in a decision to submit a preliminary reference to the ECJ.[56] On 16 November 1977, the Court sent four questions to the ECJ. The first three questions related to Article 16 of the EEC Treaty. These three were concerned with whether the duty was to be considered a customs duty on exports. The fourth question would only be relevant if the duty were not found to be equal to a customs duty on exports. In this case the question was whether the duty had the same effect as an internal tax that protected national products violating Article 95 of the EEC Treaty.[57]

The action by the City Court of Copenhagen is a classic example of how the system of preliminary references was supposed to work. This system where a national court asked the ECJ for the authoritative interpretation of European law was designed by the ECJ through case law as a means to circumvent the interference of the national administrations which perhaps had not implemented European law properly.[58] From the perspective of the Danish Administration, the situation looked very different. If Danish courts began sending preliminary reference cases to the ECJ the result would become rather chaotic.[59] The ruling by the ECJ in 1978 was ultimately in favour of the Danish state.[60] Despite the victory, the civil servants of the EC Special Committee for Legal Questions were rattled by the experience.

55 HAC.BAC 371/1991.0134.JUR/137/78. The Commission's recommendation to the President of the ECJ and the members of the Court by the agent of the Commission Rolf Wägenbaur and Bjarne Hoff-Nielsen (assistant). 20 January 1978.

56 HAC.BAC 371/1991.0134.JUR/137/78. The Commission's recommendation to the President of the ECJ and the members of the Court by the agent of the Commission Rolf Wägenbaur and Bjarne Hoff-Nielsen (assistant). 20 January 1978.

57 HAC.BAC 371/1991.0134.JUR/137/78. The Commission's recommendation to the President of the ECJ and the members of the Court by the agent of the Commission Rolf Wägenbaur and Bjarne Hoff-Nielsen (assistant). 20 January 1978.

58 Three key judgments that helped define the preliminary reference system in this manner were: 13/61, *Kledingverkoopbedrijf de Geus en Uitdenbogerd v Robert Bosch GmbH et al.*, 1962, ECLI:EU:C:1962:11; 26/62, *Van Gend en Loos v Nederlandse Administratie der Belastingen*, 1963, ECLI:EU:C:1963:1 and 6/64, *Costa v ENEL*, 1964, ECLI:EU:C:1964:66. The original Treaties of Rome did not envisage that the preliminary reference system focused directly on the correct application of European law (this was in principle within the competence of national courts), but rather introduced the system to ensure that European law was interpreted in a uniform way across member states (through the published judgments of the ECJ). See Rasmussen 2023, 23–29.

59 UM.400.C.4-1-19. MS. Note: Procedures in Denmark for treating court cases at the ECJ where the Danish state is a party. 27 April 1978.

60 142/77, *Statens Kontrol med ædle Metaller v Preben Larsen et al.*, 1978, ECLI:EU:C:1978:144.

Karsten Hagel-Sørensen from the Committee believed the victory was 'somewhat a Pyrrhic victory in that the European Court of Justice has seized the opportunity to perform the most far-reaching lawmaking'.[61] In the judgment, the ECJ argued that Article 95, when read together with the other fiscal stipulations of the EEC treaty, should be interpreted to mean that any fiscal discrimination of products which were to be exported to other member states were banned. This of course had quite far-reaching consequences if the Danish Administration chose to apply the new principle beyond the case.[62] In the eyes of the EC Special Committee for Legal Questions, the ECJ used the case to significantly broaden the understanding of Article 95 of the EEC Treaty, and many felt that the views presented by the Danish state had been ignored. The case highlighted the importance of getting involved in potential cases as early as possible. If the Committee were involved from the start, it would probably have been able to prevent the preliminary reference from being sent, or at the very least would have been able to influence the questions formulated by the Danish Court.[63]

The administrative response came quickly. In June 1978, the EC Special Committee for Legal Questions drafted a memorandum entitled 'Procedures in Denmark for treating court cases at the ECJ where the Danish state is a party'.[64] The following memorandum was distributed to all civil servants working with European law in the ministries:

> The experiences tell us that it is vital to the course of such preliminary references how the Danish court has formulated its questions to the ECJ. It is therefore important that the EC Special Committee for Legal Questions and potentially the EC Committee is given the opportunity to estimate whether a given case, wherein the Danish state is a party, should be brought to the ECJ, and if so, how the questions to the ECJ in this case should be formulated.[65]

The EC Special Committee for Legal Questions thus established itself as a clearinghouse for evaluating which cases Danish courts should send to the ECJ. The effectiveness of the system is clear by the numbers. By 1985, only eleven preliminary reference cases from Danish courts were decided by the ECJ, and

61 Author's translation from original: 'Sejren er dog noget af en Pyhrrus-sejr, idet EF-domstolen har benyttet lejligheden til at foretage den mest vidtgående lovgivning, der er set i mange år.' JM.60112/21g. 7 July 1978. Note on the ruling of case 142/77 by Karsten Hagel-Sørensen.

62 Hagel-Sørensen 1994, 134.

63 JM.60112/21g. Note on the ruling of case 142/77 by Karsten Hagel-Sørensen. 7 July 1978.

64 UM.400.C.4–1–19. MS. Note: Procedures in Denmark for treating court cases at the ECJ where the Danish state is a party. 27 April 1978.

65 Author's translation from original: 'Erfaringerne viser, at det er afgørende for sådanne præjudicielle sagers forløb, hvorledes den danske domstol udformer spørgsmålene til EF-domstolen. Det er derfor vigtigt, at juridisk specialudvalg og eventuelt EF-udvalget får lejlighed til at tage stilling til, hvorvidt en given sag, hvori staten er part, bør indbringes for EF-domstolen, og hvorledes spørgsmålene til EF-domstolen i givet fald bør formuleres.' UM.400.C.4–1–19. MS. Note: Procedures in Denmark for treating court cases at the ECJ where the Danish state is a party. 27 April 1978.

only once did the Luxembourg-based Court rule against the opinion of the Danish government representative.[66] The statistics show that Denmark submitted relatively few preliminary references. In the period from 1974 to 1980 an average of only 1.1 cases were submitted per year. The number increased over time to 2.4 cases for the period from 1981 to 1987 and 3.6 cases for the period from 1988 to 1994.[67]

By the end of the 1970s, the administrative practice of delaying implementation of problematic Community legislation and containing the effects of ECJ case law by controlling the participation of Danish courts in the preliminary reference mechanism was well established. However, at this point the attitude of the Commission to the continuing problems of the enforcement of European law of the member states changed. The Commission originally was reluctant to use the infringement procedure and hoped that the preliminary reference mechanism could provide an alternative road to enforcement of European law in the member states through the means of private litigation. However, since the latter did not yield satisfactory results (as the number of preliminary reference cases were still relatively low and their indirect effect on the enforcement of European legislation unclear) the new Director of the Legal Service, Claus-Dieter Ehlermann, launched a policy which used the infringement procedure systematically based on a comprehensive monitoring of how member states implemented European legislation. On this basis more than one hundred cases were submitted between 1977 and 1983.[68] This shift in tactics by the Legal Service of the Commission was also felt in Denmark. In 1979 and 1980 alone, more than twenty treaty infringement procedures were initiated against Denmark, compared to only fourteen cases from 1973 to 1977.[69]

In the Danish administration, this was translated into a need for more control with potential Danish infringement cases. Consequently in 1981, the EC Special Committee for Legal Questions was given a more powerful mandate. The Committee had a negative view of the Commission, which it found to be rather arbitrary and formalistic. It did not sufficiently take into consideration whether the violation in the application of European law actually had a serious material impact or not. However, despite this critique, the administration also felt that since Denmark was generally interested in a strong European legal system that would be followed by the other member states, there was no reason to complain. Therefore, the only way Denmark could get some level of control over future infringement cases was by strengthening the national system of monitoring and validating cases.[70] This became the task of the EC Special Committee for Legal Questions. The Committee would gather and review all the possible treaty infringement cases,

66 Hagel-Sørensen and Rasmussen 1985.

67 Sweet and Brunell 1998.

68 Vauchez 2015, 188–191.

69 UM.MS.400.A.3. Treaty infringement cases against Denmark. Note by Laurids Mikaelsen. 7 January 1981.

70 UM.MS.400.A.3. Treaty infringement cases against Denmark. Note by Laurids Mikaelsen. 7 January 1981.

even candidate cases not yet raised by the Commission, and submit its recommendations to the government. Despite these efforts, it became increasingly clear by the mid-1980s that the system did not manage to limit the number of infringement procedures raised against the Danish state.[71]

EUROPEAN LAW IN DANISH EUROPEAN POLICY

The Danish government was forced to declare its position in the late 1970s as the resistance to the ECJ in key member states culminated. The advances of ECJ case law in the field of human rights, implied powers to the European institutions, direct effect of directives and primacy, created some levels of animosity in the member states, particularly in France. As a result, in May 1979, the French government asked if the ECJ reform should be discussed at the annual informal 'Gymnich' meeting of the ministers of foreign affairs of the Member States held at the Chateau Mercuès near Cahors.[72] What would be the Danish response?

On the one hand, the Danish state administration held many of the same grievances as the French government.[73] Like the French government, the Danish Ministry of Foreign Affairs also perceived the ECJ as activist and promoting integration beyond what had originally been set out in the Treaties of Rome: 'The Court has in reality assumed a role which is akin to the American Supreme Court. The Court's interpretation of the Treaties is in this way remarkably free and only subscribes little importance to the wording of the provisions and the preparatory works.'[74]

The Market Secretariat of the Ministry of Foreign Affairs would have preferred it if the ECJ had adopted an interpretation of European law that followed the letter of the Treaties more closely. Instead in the 1970s, the ECJ pursued a constitutional interpretation of European law, which the Danish diplomats believed had a bias towards deepening the integration process. However, at the same time, the Market Secretariat maintained that the traditional Danish position in support of the strengthening of international law was still valid with regard to the EC. To a small state, it was moreover an 'absolute advantage'[75] that the ECJ had acquired the authority to pass rulings against the large member states. It was the latter view that became the official Danish position for the meeting at Chateau Mercuès. The speaking notes to the liberal Minister of Foreign Affairs, Henning Christophersen,

71 UM.MS.400.A.3. Note – Treatment and expedition of treaty infringement cases against Denmark. 12 April 1985.

72 See Chapter 7.

73 UM.MS.400.A.5–3. Note – Gymnich meeting 12–13 May 1979 on the praxis of the ECJ. 9 May 1979.

74 Author's translation from original: 'Domstolen har i realiteten tiltaget sig en rolle, som minder om den Amerikanske højesterets. Domstolens fortolkning af traktaterne er således særdeles fri, og der lægges kun lidt vægt på ordlyden af bestemmelserne og forarbejderne.' UM.MS.400.A.5–3. Note – Gymnich meeting 12–13 May 1979 on the praxis of the ECJ. 9 May 1979.

75 Authors translation from original: 'Det må for et lille land være en klar fordel, at Domstolen har den fornødne autoritet til at afsige domme, som går imod et eller flere store lande.' UM.MS.400.A.5–3. Note – Gymnich meeting 12–13 May 1979 on the praxis of the ECJ. 9 May 1979.

even sharpened the point. Here it said that the ECJ was in fact 'probably the best functioning institution in the EC'.[76] It is clear that there was no appetite in the Danish government for reforming the ECJ. In this way, the Danish attitude and position towards the ECJ and the Commission was developed in ambivalence between two sets of interests. On the one hand, there was real concern and annoyance with the integrationist practices of both institutions. On the other hand, there was an understanding that strong and independent institutions were necessary to control the larger member states. In this sense, Denmark resembled another small member states, namely the Netherlands which also supported the ECJ and its constitutional case law, while trying to contain some of the effects of European legislation and ECJ case law. (See Chapter 8.)

THE POLITICAL CONSENSUS OF DANISH EC MEMBERSHIP UNDER PRESSURE

By the late 1970s, two major questions were gradually endangering the underlying political consensus on which the Danish EC membership rested: namely the way the EC used Article 235 of the EEC Treaty, and the increasing pressure on the veto right in the Council.

As the EC in the 1970s was unable to contemplate treaty reform because it would involve solving the intractable problems related to the CAP and Community financing, Article 235 of the EEC Treaty was increasingly used by the Council to expand the powers of the EC into new policy fields that all member states agreed needed European solutions. During the Danish accession negotiations, public debate had focused on Article 235 of the EEC Treaty, which by EC opponents was considered to constitute an unlimited carte blanche for the EC to pass legal acts in new policy fields if the Council by unanimity could agree to do this. If this interpretation was true, the Danish accession could be construed as unconstitutional. However, the Danish government and most legal experts agreed that Article 235 of the EEC Treaty could only be used to implement legislation that would support the fulfilment of the Common Market. It was vital for Denmark that Article 235 was only applied with this purpose. Otherwise, the extent of the powers which Denmark transferred to the Community could not be said to be specifically defined as it was required in the Danish Constitution.

By the late 1970s, Article 235 of the EEC Treaty had developed into a significant problem for the Danish government. Unable to carry through comprehensive treaty reform, the EC now began to use the Article in order to legislate in new policy fields which did not strictly relate to the Common Market. This was seen as unproblematic to most Member States because of the practice of consensus decision-making in the Council. Also, the Danish government had initially endorsed the use of the

[76] UM.MS.400.A.5-3. Note – Gymnich meeting 12–13 May 1979 on the praxis of the ECJ. 9 May 1979.

Article in fields like agriculture, customs, energy, research, environment and social questions.[77] However, at the same time the Danish government believed that no member state could be coerced to accept the Article as legislative basis, but in practice this had been difficult to maintain because the Commission had the right of legislative initiative.[78]

In a note from August 1979, Per Lachmann from the Ministry of Foreign Affairs anticipated the further use of the Article in relation to policy areas such as education, medical research and rights of residence for non-workers. The problem from a Danish point of view was that these three policy areas were considered to fall outside the scope of the Treaties of Rome. This meant that the Danish government could not accept the legislative agenda. This placed the Danish government in an uncomfortable position vis-à-vis the other member state governments who cared little for Danish constitutional oddities.[79] However, at a Council meeting in March 1980, Danish State Secretary, Niels Ersbøll, pointed out to the member states that unless the use of Article 235 lived up to the requirements mentioned in the treaty text, this would lead to a serious constitutional crisis in Denmark.[80] The dilemmas posed by Article 235 did not only haunt the Danish governments and administration, but it also provided ammunition to the agitation of the Danish grassroot organisation, the People's Movement Against the EC, in the public debate during the early 1980s.

The problems concerning Article 235 of the EEC Treaty were followed by an increasing pressure on the national veto right in the Council. An example of the changing attitude to the veto right in a number of member state governments came in late April 1980, when British objections to the composition of the Community budget were overruled by a majority of the Council.[81] This led to a difficult debate in the Danish Parliament in May 1982, where Social Democratic Minister of Foreign Affairs, Kjeld Olesen, explained how it was possible for the Council to overrule a British veto. The Socialist People's Party saw the Council's decision to ignore the British veto as the culmination of a tendency to undermine the veto right. The Danish Minister of Foreign Affairs agreed that the Luxembourg Compromise was undermined by the episode with Britain.[82] According to Olesen there was, however, no need for alarm since the reactions to the negotiations confirmed that the

77 UM.MS.400.A.3. Note. Vedr.: anvendelsen af bestemmelserne i artikel 235 i EØF-traktaten. Danmarks holdning til anvendelsen af artikel 235. Rådets møde (udenrigsministrene) den 18. marts 1980. Talepunkter fra statssekretær Niels Ersbølls redegørelse. 25 March 1980.

78 UM.MS.400.A.3. Note from the Market Secretariat. Rom-Traktatens artikel 235. 6 March 1980.

79 UM.MS.400.A.3. Note by Per Lachmann: Samarbejde 'på kanten af Romtraktaten' – art. 235. 22 August 1979.

80 UM.MS.400.A.3. Note. Vedr.: anvendelsen af bestemmelserne i artikel 235 i EØF-traktaten. Danmarks holdning til anvendelsen af artikel 235. Rådets møde (udenrigsministrene) den 18. marts 1980. Talepunkter fra statssekretær Niels Ersbølls redegørelse. 25 March 1980.

81 Gilbert 2012, 123.

82 UM.MS.400.A.3. Folketingstidende 26.5.1982 question to the minister in Case 767.

principles of the Luxembourg Compromise were still in effect.[83] The Danish government was satisfied with the reassurances it had received from the other member states.

What the problems relating to Article 235 of the EEC Treaty, and the diminishing status of the veto right demonstrated was that the dynamics of the integration process could not easily be contained by a single member state. The domestic Danish consensus about the nature of EC membership was under increasing pressure from the political and institutional dynamics of the EC. The belief that the veto right could block the deepening of integration seemed increasingly unfounded.

By 1983, ideas and initiatives to modernise the EC were debated across the European institutions. Nonetheless, the gravity of the situation was extremely slow to dawn on the Danish politicians. Before the Milan Summit in July 1985, the new right-wing minority government under the leadership of Conservative Prime Minister, Poul Schlüter, boldly stated that it would be able to block future institutional reforms and maintain the right to veto.[84] To the surprise of the Danish government, however, the Italian Presidency of the Council called a majority vote under Article 236 of the EEC Treaty to decide whether to launch an intergovernmental conference on treaty reform. The vote was seven in favour and three against; with Denmark, Greece and Britain opposed. The British decision to respect the vote furthermore isolated Denmark in opposition to the intergovernmental conference. This was a completely new situation for the Danish government; they could no longer rely on Britain to bloc institutional reforms. This forced the Danish government to play a new and more active role in the upcoming intergovernmental conference.[85]

In October 1985, the Danish negotiators were still uncertain whether the intergovernmental conference would lead to a revision of the Treaties of Rome. When the prospects of an agreement were discussed in the Parliamentary Market Committee in November 1985, the Social Democratic Party, which now used European policy to sharpen its role in opposition, wanted a Danish veto to treaty revision because it represented a breach with the original consensus on which Danish EC membership rested. With a similar view from the Social Liberal Party, a majority of Parliament opposed the reform, and consequently the Danish government was unable to sign the Single European Act (SEA) at the meeting of the Ministers of Foreign Affairs on 16 and 17 December 1985. Back in Denmark the Liberal Minister of Foreign Affairs, Uffe Ellemann-Jensen, declared that the real issue at stake now was whether or not Denmark wanted to stay in the future EC. After a negative vote in the parliament on the SEA, the government called an indicative referendum, which the Social Democratic Party and the Social Liberal Party

83 UM.MS.400.A.3. Folketingstidende 26.5.1982 question to the minister in Case 767.

84 UM.MS.400.A.3. Question number 1331 of 19 June 1985 to the Prime Minister from Steen Gade (the Socialist Party). 21 June 1985.

85 Petersen 2004, 381–383.

promised to respect. Here the Danish electorate approved the SEA on 27 February 1986 with a clear majority of 56.2 per cent against 43.8 per cent. To a jubilant Minister of Foreign Affairs, the victory served as a proof that the reluctant Danish European policy had to end. Now Denmark could finally play a more active role in the EC.[86]

EUROPEAN LAW NOW MATTERS: THE CONSEQUENCES OF THE SINGLE EUROPEAN ACT

With Denmark accepting the SEA, and the new economic and political dynamics of the Single Market Program, the Social Democratic Party and the Social Liberal Party went through a thorough reappraisal of their views on European integration. This was reinforced by the end of the Cold War in 1989. By the early 1990s both parties fully backed Danish EC membership.[87] In addition, Danish economic policy had moved decisively in a neoliberal direction since the centre-right government took over in 1982 with systematic liberalisation and privatisation of the Danish economy.[88] Thus, Denmark was ready to adapt to the new challenges ahead and take advantage of the opportunities offered by the Single Market project.

The ambitious Single Market Program involved the removal of non-tariff barriers to trade and the harmonisation of product standards.[89] From the perspective of the right-wing minority government, the SEA constituted a positive compromise. The establishment of the Single Market was a major opportunity to improve the sluggish Danish economy, and the protection of the natural and working environments included in the treaty reform were satisfactory from a Danish point of view.[90] What was more difficult seen from a Danish point of view was the institutional reform included in the SEA. This implied an introduction of majority voting in the field of the Single Market and thus an abandonment of both the consensus culture and the veto right. This created a new challenge to the Danish legislators and administration. When Denmark could no longer rely on the ability to veto new proposals, the Danish negotiators needed a more flexible mandate from the Parliamentary Market Committee when voting in the Council. The decision-making process in Denmark needed to be streamlined.[91] The Single Market project represented a significant shift away from the more protectionist approach taken by the Danish Administration before 1986. Finally, the SEA meant that the Commission more actively focused on the implementation of European law, but also that the case law of the ECJ took on a new importance, because the legal order

86 Petersen 2004, 384–395.
87 Petersen 2004, 496–499.
88 Olesen 2019.
89 Togeby et al. 2004, 307.
90 Gulmann 1987b, 32–34.
91 Hagel-Sørensen 1994, 128.

that would underpin the new Single Market not only consisted of Council legislation but also ECJ case law and doctrines. It still took several hard lessons for the Danish governments and administrative system to find out that the traditional containment of European law was now less effective.

'BUY DANISH CLAUSE'

The first ECJ case which illustrated the new political situation for Denmark concerned a 'buy Danish clause' which was applied to the public procurement in connection with the construction of the western bridge over the Great Belt. Trouble began in October 1987 when the procurement related to the bridge was announced. The procurement conditions included a clause that obliged contractors 'to as much as possible use Danish materials, commodities, Danish workers and goods'.[92] This condition became known as the 'buy Danish clause'. During the preparations of the procurement requirements, the political coalition that supported the building of the bridge, the centre-right government and the Social Democratic Party, decided to move around the established administrative practices and sideline the legal experts in the ministries. They did this by establishing a 100 per cent state-owned limited liability company, the A/S Storebæltsforbindelsen, and hiring executives from the private sector. This solution was preferred at the expense of letting the Ministry of Traffic and the central administration manage the project. The composition of the board of A/S Storebæltsforbindelsen was decided by the government and the social democrats. Prominent Social Democrats like Georg Poulsen, Knud Heinesen and Jens Kampmann were appointed to the board. An additional committee of politicians was also established to monitor the project, but without any official authority to directly influence any decisions.[93] This organisation of the project, however, allowed the politicians to exert a certain control with A/S Storebæltsforbindelsen, and make sure that creating Danish jobs and contracts for Danish companies was a priority. The protectionist approach chosen meant that when a note highlighting the problems related to European law began to circulate, it was ignored at the board level in June 1987.[94] The available knowledge about EC law in the Ministry of Foreign Affairs and the Ministry of Justice was simply discarded.

In the end, what brought the case to light was a complaint by the French firm, Bouygues, which was part of an alliance of firms forming the Western Bridge Joint Venture consortium and lost the bid to build the western bridge over the Great Belt.

92 Authors translation from original: 'Entreprenøren er forpligtet til i størst muligt omfang at anvende danske materialer og forbrugsgods, dansk arbejdskraft og materiel'. 243/89, *Commission of the European Communities v Kingdom of Denmark*, 1993, ECLI:EU:C:1993:257.

93 Report by the Danish Commission Court regarding the 'buy Danish clause'. Delivered by the Commission Court on 1 May 1990. Published July 1991. 17–21.

94 Report by the Danish Commission Court regarding the 'buy Danish clause'. Delivered by the Commission Court on 1 May 1990. Published July 1991. 37, 40 and Note by Henrik Brøndum, 'Forholdet til de Europæiske Fællesskaber' on 16 June 1987.

The contract instead went to European Storebælt Group (ESG). After contacting the French government with little result, Francis Bouygues, who knew Jacques Delors personally, involved the Commission to stop the Danish state from signing the contract with ESG.[95] The Commission's interest in the case meant that the Danish administration needed to get involved. Just like in the aforementioned ECJ cases regarding gender equality and spirits taxation, the Danish civil servants tried to prolong the proceedings. By June 1989, two competing strategies developed. The Ministry of Foreign Affairs recommended to the Danish government to admit the infringement of European law, while A/S Storebæltsforbindelsen emphasised the economic costs involved and how it would prolong the construction work if this were done. It was therefore recommended to sign the contract so that the construction work could begin. Despite the personal involvement of the Minister of Foreign Affairs, Uffe Ellemann-Jensen, the government decided to support the position of the A/S Storebæltsforbindelsen as this would disrupt the construction process the least.[96]

The challenge remained, however, that if the Danish state signed the contract, which it did on 26 June, the Commission might respond with an injunction. The strategy of the government was to explain to the Commission that the 'buy Danish clause' would be removed from the contract but also to insist less convincingly that it had had no practical effect on the decision. Unsurprisingly, the Commission did not buy this argument and instigated infringement procedures on 1 August 1989 and also filed an injunction to stop the work on the western bridge. In September, a Danish delegation including State Solicitor Michael Gregers Larsen, Jørgen Molde agent from the Ministry of Foreign Affairs and Karsten Hagel Sørensen from the Ministry of Justice went to deal with the injunction case in Luxembourg. According to the analysis of Magnus Esmark, both the Danish government and the Commission were interested in a settlement. The costs and political backlash of stopping the work on the western bridge would be serious to the Danish government, while Commission officials did not feel confident that the ECJ would accept an injunction even if the infringement case would be a slam dunk. In the office of the Danish President of the ECJ, Ole Due (who was not present), the Danish legal experts and Martin Bangemann and Robert Coleman from the Commission found a compromise that allowed Bouygues and other members of the Western Bridge Joint Venture consortium to sue for damages from A/S Storebæltsforbindelsen if they could demonstrate a justified claim according to the general principles of Danish law. After a phone call from Bangemann to Delors, this solution satisfied all parties. The politically disastrous and financially expensive injunction was thus avoided, and the substantial meaning of the case had disappeared.[97] The Danish government could consequently readily admit its infringement and accept the ruling of ECJ that was

95 Esmark 2022, 135–152.
96 For an in-depth analysis of the case concerning 'the buy Danish clause' see Pedersen 2016, 180–203.
97 Esmark 2022, 143–146.

delivered on 22 June 1993. Here the Court found that Denmark violated Articles 30, 48 and 59 of the Treaty.[98]

The Danish government managed to sidestep the worst consequences of infamous 'buy Danish clause' of A/S Storebæltsforbindelsen with the avoidance of a costly injunction that would have cast into disarray the whole construction of the western bridge. While Bouygues and couple of other firms sought to have their losses covered, the judgment of the Danish Eastern High Court only awarded the plaintiffs some damages for the bidding costs after a reduction of the latter based on a discretionary basis since they 'to a non-significant degree are subject to uncertainty'.[99] Generally, however, the whole affair did not reflect well on the willingness of the Danish government to respect European law. In a reaction to the ruling, Peter Vesterdorf, from the Danish Federation of Small and Medium-sized Enterprises who had previously worked in the Market Secretariat of the Ministry of Foreign Affairs, said: 'The ECJ ruling in the western bridge case is not suited to enhance Denmark's reputation in the EC – we always talk about us being the good pupil in the EC, but there are many cases which show that we have double standards to an extreme degree.'[100]

To Vesterdorf the case could not be seen in isolation, and he also referred to the AMBI (Arbejdsmarkedsbidrag) case as another example of how European law was not respected in Denmark.[101]

AMBI

The AMBI (Arbejdsmarkedsbidrag) was a special labour market levy which all employers were forced to pay. On 1 January 1988, it replaced the existing system of employer contribution and was designed in a way which meant that importing companies would carry the highest costs while exporting companies would receive a refund on export.[102]

In the mid-1980s, Denmark suffered from a serious balance of payments deficit, and accumulated state debt that seriously threatened economic stability. This led to a series of initiatives by the centre-right government which intended to dampen

98 243/89, *Commission of the European Communities v Kingdom of Denmark*, 1993, ECLI:EU:C:1993:257.

99 Esmark 2022, 146. The citation is from the same page.

100 Authors translation from original: 'EF-dommen i vestbrosagen er ikke egnet til at øge Danmarks omdømme i EF – vi taler altid om, at vi er "klassens flinke dreng" i EF-sammenhæng, men der er mange sager, der viser at vi er enormt dobbeltmoralske.' News Agency Ritzau 22.06.1993: EF-ekspert: Dommen øger ikke vores omdømme.

101 News Agency Ritzau 22.06.1993: EF-ekspert: Dommen øger ikke vores omdømme.

102 Markedsudvalg. Samlingen 1991–92 alm.del bilag 567. Collected material relating to the AMBI case and Archive of Peter Wiese, The Prime Minister's Office, no. 415819.(APW).M.S., j.nr. 400 Q/JUR. Note by Peter Vesterdorf, Omlægning af arbejdsgiverafgifterne. Spørgsmålet om forenelighed med EF-retten. 14 September 1987.

domestic consumption.[103] In addition to this, it was important to strengthen the competitiveness of Danish firms in international markets. In July 1987, the Ministry of Labor invented the AMBI tax scheme which brought in the much-needed income to the state yet were designed to not undermine the competitiveness of Danish firms in international markets.[104] The Danish administration was well aware that such a scheme did not live up to the European law on the Common Market. Laurids Mikaelsen from the Market Secretariat of the Ministry of Foreign Affairs, and Karsten Hagel-Sørensen from the Ministry of Justice, were asked to find technical and legal solutions that would give the tax the appearance of legality in order to buy time. The solution was to divide the system into smaller elements, which individually looked legal. It was then hoped that the Commission would not realise what the Danish government was doing.[105]

Despite the Commission's initial concern expressed in March 1988, it looked like the Danish administration had successfully postponed any interference from the EC. However, when the two Danish firms, Denkavit and P. Poulsen Trading, filed a case against the Danish Ministry of Taxation in Danish courts, the case quickly became difficult to handle. The case ended up in Luxembourg in the docket of the ECJ in 1991 by the means of a preliminary reference.[106] It was evident to the Danish Ministry of Taxation that the case could not be won. In this light and to pre-empt the severe financial consequences of an ECJ ruling, the Danish government quickly replaced the AMBI with a general VAT increase that came into force on 1 January 1992.[107] By this time the AMBI scheme had been successfully maintained for four years, and the Danish Treasury had collected up to 55 billion Danish Kroner from it.[108] Therefore, when the ruling of the ECJ was presented on 31 March 1992, it came as no surprise to the Minister of Taxation, Anders Fogh Rasmussen, and the rest of the government.[109] The ECJ established that the AMBI was in violation with Article 33 of the Sixth VAT Directive on the Harmonization of the Laws of the Member States Relating to Turnover Taxes.[110] The ruling also contained a very unwelcome surprise. Anders Fogh Rasmussen, and the civil servants in his Ministry,

103 Busck and Poulsen 2002, 412–413.

104 Markedsudvalg. Samlingen 1991–92 alm.del bilag 567. Collected material relating to the AMBI case and APW. Note from the Ministry of Finance July 2 1987 – Initiatives to better the competitiveness. 6 April 1992.

105 Markedsudvalg. Samlingen 1991–92 alm.del bilag 567. Collected material relating to the AMBI case. M.S., j.nr. 400 Q/JUR. Letter from Laurids Mikaelsen to Karsten Hagel-Sørensen on 17 September 1987 and M.S., j. nr. 400. Q/jur. 6 October 1987. Note – proposal to rearrange the employer levy. EC legal considerations of the main elements.

106 200/90, *Dansk Denkavit ApS and P. Poulsen Trading ApS v Skatteministeriet*, 1992, ECLI:EU:C:1992:152.

107 Newspaper Articles: 29.11.1991. BT. Grit Bendixen: 'Her er Momsens Bagmand' and 13.7.1993. News Agency Ritzaus Bureau: 'Ambiens sidestykke for EF-domstolen'.

108 Tynell 2014, 254–255.

109 200/90, *Dansk Denkavit ApS and P. Poulsen Trading ApS v Skatteministeriet*, 1992, ECLI:EU:C:1992:152.

110 Directive 77/388/EC, art. 33.

assumed that the ECJ ruling would stipulate that the AMBI was illegal, and as of the ruling could not legally be collected. To their surprise, the ECJ opened the question of the reimbursement of the AMBI. This resulted in frantic meeting activities in the government. Anders Fogh Rasmussen promised to give a full statement on the day of the ruling, but as the implications of the ruling created uncertainty in the administration, Fogh Rasmussen was unable to present a reply. Fifty-five billion Danish Kroner were at stake.[111] In the days following the ECJ ruling, the media were rife with stories characterising the AMBI case as a scandal similar in scale to the ongoing *Tamil* case, which eventually brought down the centre-right government in 1993.[112]

In order to handle the repayment, the Danish Parliament enacted a special procedure – the Repayment Act – whereby claimants were to file and document their claim to the regional Tax Office. This would avoid an unmanageable influx of cases before national courts. The substantiable requirements for repayment or compensation would be based on general principles of Danish law – a reference very similar to the handling of damages in the Great Belt case – and emphasised that the claimants had to document an economic loss.[113] This requirement was crucial because a levy typically was added to the ultimate price of a product and thus did not necessarily incur an economic loss on a firm. In 1995, enough private parties had contacted the Commission criticising this special requirement to prompt the latter to send a letter to the Danish government suggesting an infringement procedure could be raised. Since the Danish state successfully avoided this by changing the language of the Repayment Act, the effect of this turned out to be limited eventually. Clearly the Danish parliament did not intend to repay the AMBI but only cover losses with the burden of proof for loss laid on the claimants. In the decades that followed, Danish firms attempted to obtain a repayment of the illegal levy. However, as in the case of the damages paid after the Great Belt case, Danish courts based their handling of the cases on the Repayment Act and ended up minimising the amounts paid.[114] In 2012 the Danish Supreme Court finally decided that the remaining claims for reimbursement of the AMBI should not be allowed to continue.[115]

The two cases illustrate the increasing pressure on Denmark to adhere to European law due to the new dynamic of European integration caused by the

111 Newspaper Articles: 1.4.1992. BT. Grit Bendixen. 'Rystet over EF-dom -Regeringen kæmper desperat mod Ambi-katastrofen' and 1.4.1992. Berlingske Tidende. Per Lyngby: 'AMBI-dommen ryster christiansborg'.

112 The Tamil scandal led to the resignation of the centre-right government in 1993. In 1987, the Minister of Justice Erik Ninn-Hansen ordered a stop to granting asylum to Tamil refugees. The order was imposed despite the bureaucrats in the Ministry of Justice informing the minister that it was illegal. See Busck and Poulsen 2002, 422–423. With regard to the newspaper coverage on AMBI see for example newspaper Articles: BT. 02.04.1992. Grit Bendixen. 'AMBI'en en ny Tamilsag' and BT. 03.04.1992. Karsten Madsen. 'Ambi-tamil'. and Weekendavisen. 02.10.1992. Michael Kristiansen. 'Regeringen vidste ambi var ulovlig'.

113 Esmark 2022, 163.

114 For a detailed sociological analysis of how this legal battled played out see Esmark 2022, 173–188.

115 Højesteret, 10 September 2012, Case 33/2012.

Single Market project. However, the analysis also showed that in the last resort the Danish state did manage to defend its core economic interests. In the *Great Belt* case the contract with the ESG was kept and the costs of the payment of damages to Bouygues and a couple of other firms were kept at an acceptable level. In the AMBI case, the state tax base was expanded while boosting the competitiveness of Danish firms and again the repayment to Danish firms in court cases were minimised. The main reasons for this were the fact that the legal afterplay dealing with damages or the repayment of levies took place in the Danish legal arena where national courts could apply Danish law in the best interest of the Danish state.[116] Nevertheless, the two cases did signal that old practices in a bid to protect Danish economic and political interests could not be continued. The two cases turned into two very public scandals imposing serious political costs on the Danish government. Any defence of Danish economic and political interests now had to take European law much more seriously.

EUROPEAN LAW IN PUBLIC AND ACADEMIC DEBATE, 1970S–1980S

Since European law was primarily overseen by the Danish administration, it only seldomly required the involvement of the governments or the parliament. The general public debate only rarely touched upon the question of how Denmark should respond to the development of European law. In a way, this is an odd omission considering the relatively strong role of anti-European sentiment in Danish public and political life in the 1970s and 1980s. However, from the early 1990s, European law entered the scene of public debate as a consequence of the *Maastricht* case at the Danish courts – a case that challenged the constitutionality of the Danish EU membership.

Even though the Danish EC membership was supported by a significant majority of the electorate at the referendum in 1972, opinion polls suggested already in 1974 that the majority had gone. By now, the majority of the electorate wanted to exit the EC. The People's Movement Against the EC, had been established during the debate on Danish EC membership between 1970 and 1972.[117] As a consequence of the increasing scepticism it became the biggest Danish group in the European Parliament in the first direct election in 1979. The movement won four of the fifteen Danish seats.[118] Throughout the period from 1980 to 1985, all opinion polls showed a majority against Danish membership of the EC. But when the Danish electorate finally voted on the Single European Act in a referendum in February 1986, the economic incentives still swayed a clear majority to support continued Danish EC membership.[119]

116 Esmark 2022, 186–188.
117 Rasmussen 2004, 511.
118 Petersen 2004, 89.
119 Petersen 2004, 367–369.

European law hardly figured in the public debates in the 1970s, but it appeared briefly in the early 1980s, when the People's Movement Against EC membership demanded a stricter constitutional control with Denmark's participation in the integration process. The prominent member of the movement, Jens Peter Bonde, argued that the EC used Article 235 to expand the powers of the EC beyond what the Danish electorate had mandated in 1972.[120] The government dismissed the argument as groundless, even though internally the constitutional dangers of a flexible interpretation of Article 235 were taken very seriously, as aforementioned. The question would return with a vengeance in the 1990s due to Danish legal academia.

In the 1970s, questions of European law found little space in Danish law journals.[121] The most active authors were civil servants like Karsten Hagel-Sørensen and Claus Gulmann. The prominence of civil servants in the debate was logical since they were the first to experience and work with European law in Denmark. Their knowledge of European law was also used at Danish universities where Hagel-Sørensen and Gulmann taught the subject at Aarhus University and University of Copenhagen, respectively. After the accession, practical issues concerning how Denmark ought to adapt to European law characterised the academic debate. Broader discussions on the nature of European law were almost non-existent. *Nordisk Tidsskrift for International Ret* was a standout journal on the new topic, but the Danish experts also began publishing in international journals such as the *Common Market Law Review*.[122]

The European law association in Denmark, the Danish Society for European Law (DSE), did not play as important a role in the Danish reception of EC law as the sister associations in West Germany, France or the Netherlands. The DSE was first established by the Danish academic Ole Lando, who in 1967, launched an Institute for European Law at the Copenhagen Business School. The institute was recognised in international legal circles, and Lando participated as one of the few Danish scholars at the various Fédération Internationale pour le Droit Européen (FIDE) Congresses in the 1960s.[123] Thus, it was natural that in 1971, the President of FIDE, Pierre Pescatore, asked Lando to set up the Danish branch of the association. Lando enthusiastically accepted the idea, and the Danish association was established in May 1973.[124]

The first board of the DSE was chaired by Ole Lando. Ole Due, from the Ministry of Justice, and Jens Christensen, from the Ministry of Foreign Affairs, secured a high-ranking presence of the Danish administration on the board. Max

[120] UM.MS.400.A.3. Newspaper Article. Jyllandsposten. Jens Peter Bonde. 'EF på kant med Grundloven'. 29 June 1981.

[121] For an analysis see Esmark 2020, 23–42.

[122] See for example: Gulmann 1983; Lachmann 1981.

[123] See for example FIDE 1963 2nd Congress – list of participants. 449.

[124] Archive Ole Lando (AOL). 500 523 III. Statement from FIDE and correspondence between Pierre Pescatore and Ole Lando. September – November 1971 and AOL. Protokol fra ordinær generalforsamling i Dansk Forening for Europaret. 5 December 1973.

Sørensen, the Danish judge at the ECJ, was also a member, but he did not participate very actively and was more of a symbolic figurehead of the DSE. Finally, a young legal scholar named Hjalte Rasmussen performed the duty of Secretary of the DSE. In comparison to the French and German associations, the positions of the DSE members in the central administration meant that the DSE was less active when it came to lobbying the Danish government and administration. Instead, the focus was to disseminate knowledge of the relevance of European law in Denmark. To do this, the organisation arranged public meetings and conferences on subjects relating to European law as well as broader economic and political questions connected to the EC.[125] During the 1970s and well into the 1980s, the focus of the activities of the DSE was on disseminating knowledge about the importance of European law. This emphasis was only minimally revised in the late 1980s. One of the first activities of the DSE was to arrange a colloquium in Copenhagen in December 1974 entitled: 'The investigation and trail of cases concerning restrictive trade practices and monopolies by the Commission and the Court of the European Communities.' This very much set the tone for the work of the DSE; the activities generally avoided politics.[126] Whether the DSE just wanted to avoid potential political controversy, or whether the approach disguised fundamental political differences among the members, we can only speculate, but the presence of high-profile civil servants in the DSE made it difficult for the organisation to publicly engage in political activities and for example launch a critique of the practices of the Danish state in the field of European law.

Nonetheless, one of the core members of the DSE, Hjalte Rasmussen, shook the academic world when he published his DPhil thesis 'On Law and Policy in the European Court of Justice' in 1986. By the early 1980s, Rasmussen had grown increasingly frustrated with the practices of the ECJ. He was especially critical of the expansive interpretation of Article 235 of the EEC Treaty, which he perceived to be out of control. Rasmussen criticised the Danish administrative and political system for allowing the use of the Article.[127] In his book, he launched a general attack on the way the ECJ judges interpreted their mandate, and in particular the Court's constitutional interpretation of the Treaties of Rome. In the book, Rasmussen discussed where the limit of the judicial policy making by the ECJ should be drawn. He argued in favour of a wholesale reform of the ECJ that restricted its tasks. The policy-making role of judges should be limited to the absolute minimum.[128] The arguments presented were not very controversial in a Danish context where the ECJ was viewed with much scepticism. In 1987, Claus

[125] AOL.500 524 I. Notat fra 2002 med titlen *Hvad er Dansk Forening for Europaret?*

[126] AOL. Letters between Ole Lando and H. Daig, M. Waelbroek, J. Temple Lang, G. Bernini and A. Donner during September 1974 confirming their participation. Invitationer til oplægsholdere sendt fra Ole Lando.

[127] Rasmussen 1982, 602–603; Hagel-Sørensen and Rasmussen 1985.

[128] Rasmussen 1986.

Gulmann, who was also in the academic committee that evaluated Hjalte Rasmussen's thesis favourably, wrote a review of the book. Gulmann contended that while some of Rasmussen's arguments were perhaps provocatively phrased, they were not unreasonable and formed a good basis for a discussion of the activities of the ECJ.[129] Rasmussen's arguments were considerably more controversial internationally. It was the first academic book to really challenge the legitimacy of the ECJ. Joseph Weiler criticised both the methodology and the use of evidence of the book and consequently seriously questions its results.[130] Because of this, the book was initially not very influential. European law academia generally discarded it, and Hjalte Rasmussen was treated like an outcast.[131]

THE MAASTRICHT TREATY

In 1991, the member states of the EC launched an intergovernmental conference to negotiate what would become the Maastricht Treaty. By now after good progress with the establishment of the Single Market, the end of the Cold War and German reunification, the broad majority in the Danish Parliament was now in support of Danish EC membership. During the negotiations of the Maastricht Treaty in 1991, the centre-right government, supported by the Social Democratic Party and the Social Liberal Party, actively engaged in the European negotiations, and the government was pleased with the final outcome. The Danish government supported the pillar structure of the Maastricht Treaty and the intergovernmental dimension of the new European Union. As a result, Parliament ratified the Maastricht Treaty by an overwhelming majority in May 1992. The political consensus in Parliament was, however, not enough to persuade the Danish electorate in the referendum on the treaty. A narrow majority of 50.7 per cent voted 'no' on 2 June 1992. A significant part of the Danish electorate remained sceptical about European integration and did not like the idea of turning the EC into a Union with common citizenship, money and defence policy. Since the Danish government and Parliament knew very well that the other member states would establish the EU without Denmark, a national compromise was negotiated that could be brought back to the EC to allow some sort of Danish membership. The pro-European parties met with the most important party that rejected ratification, the Socialist People's Party. After difficult negotiations, four Danish opt outs were negotiated that would allow for a second referendum. At a meeting of the European Council at Edinburgh, the Danish government managed to secure the acceptance of the Danish opt-outs on citizenship, home and justice affairs, the third stage of economic and monetary union and defence policy. The Danish opt-outs were included in the Edinburgh Agreement, which the Danish

129 Gulmann 1987a, 189–192.
130 Weiler 1987.
131 Alter 2010, 5–6.

electorate subsequently approved by referendum in December 1992. Denmark could thus accede to the EU on 1 January 1993.[132]

The ECJ and European law only played a limited role in the Danish referendum debate on the Maastricht Treaty perhaps because questions like EU citizenship, economic and monetary union and defence cooperation seemed more important. Nevertheless, a circle of EU opponents decided to challenge whether the Danish accession to the Maastricht Treaty through the Edinburgh Agreement was constitutional. Just like the discussion leading up to the Danish accession to the EC in 1972, their arguments focused on whether the transfer of powers to the EU followed the requirement in Article 20 of the Danish Constitution and in particular whether the use of Article 235 transgressed this barrier. After a hard battle, the plaintiffs registered a success when the Højesteret accepted to hear the case in 1996. Scholars like Erik Siesby, Ole Krarup and Hjalte Rasmussen were never persuaded by the legal arguments developed in the Danish ministries in the early 1970s and early 1980s. As a result, Hjalte Rasmussen especially provided the EU opponents with legal expertise and ammunition.

Would a ruling by Højesteret be enough to close the debate? When the ruling was delivered on 6 April 1998, it confirmed that the ratification of the Maastricht Treaty did not infringe the Danish Constitution. Regarding Article 20, the court said that the requirement that the transfer of sovereignty could only happen 'to a clearly defined extent as shall be provided by the Statute'[133] should not be read to define the limits of the powers transferred but to exclude that an international organisation could independently take on new powers. With regard to Article 235 of the EEC Treaty, Højesteret further argued that it could only be used in order to obtain the objectives of the Community with regard to the operation of the Common Market, but only if the intended action was within the scope of the operation of the Common Market. In this sense, the Supreme Court found that Article 235 was covered by Article 20. The question of the activism of the ECJ was also commented upon in the ruling, and again Højesteret insisted that this could not be considered a violation of the Danish Statute of Accession nor was it contrary to Article 20.[134] Højesteret's ruling also made the principled point that the Danish courts were bound by the interpretations of the ECJ when it came to interpreting the scope of the application of the Treaties. Højesteret raised an important caveat to this, however. Danish courts had the authority to answer cases concerning whether an EU law exceeded the transferred sovereignty. In this way the ruling of the Supreme Court can be compared with the ruling of the German Bundesverfassungsgericht from 1993,[135] in that

[132] Petersen 2004, 504–520.

[133] The relevant part of § 20 reads: 'Powers vested in the authorities of the Realm under this Constitution Act may, to a clearly defined extent as shall be provided by Statute, be delegated to international authorities set up by mutual agreement with other states for the promotion of international rules of law and cooperation.' See also Spiermann 2008, 41, 43.

[134] Højesteret, 6 April 1998, *Treaty of Maastricht*, Case 361/1997 and Lachman 1998.

[135] BVerfGE 89, 155, 12.10.1993, *Maastricht*, 2 BvR 2134, 2159/92.

it established that the Danish constitution could not be transgressed. The decision of Højesteret to even hear the case demonstrated the willingness of the court to play a more active role than it had done traditionally.[136] Even though the decision of the Højesteret was clear, the EU opponents would continue to criticise the ECJ for its activism in the coming years. Hjalte Rasmussen did not back off, and he continued his criticism of the ECJ; he even engaged as a consultant to the right-wing Danish Peoples Party (Dansk Folkeparti), which during 2000s, became the most significant Eurosceptic force in Denmark. In the end, the constitutional practice in European law came to play a significant role in Danish Euroscepticism in the new millennium.

CONCLUSION

In July 1972, when the Ministry of Justice argued that Denmark could accede to the EC without a constitutional amendment, the interpretation of the relationship between European law and Danish law was set and finally in 1998 reaffirmed with the Maastricht Judgement. The unique Danish way of adapting to European law was full of contradictions – just like the Danish relationship to the EC was in general. Parliamentary sovereignty, the courts' approach to international law, and an administrative practice of dealing with law all made it difficult for Denmark to adapt to the constitutional practice established by the ECJ – at the same time Denmark supported the ECJ politically due to its long-standing view on the importance of strong international law for smaller European states. This ambivalence materialised in concerted efforts to limit the effects of European law in Denmark without confronting the European legal system. Both the implementation of European law and the academic debate about European law were dominated by the central administration. This, coupled with a lack of public interest, allowed the Danish governments to conduct a broad economic policy that would shield the Danish market from strong European competition. The effects of European legislation, or ECJ case law on the regulation of the Danish market, or for example, the unique Danish labour market model was minimised through the coordinated efforts of the Danish administration. The picture that emerges from the archival sources is of an attitude to European law where the crucial objective was to maintain the full freedom to implement European directives to suit Danish interests and to minimise the role of the ECJ and its case law in a Danish context. This approach could easily be justified with reference to the constitutional framework defining the reception of international law, but it obviously meant deliberately ignoring the emerging constitutional practices developed by the ECJ. However, considering the generally negative Danish attitude to institutional reform that would strengthen the supranational institutions of the EC until 1986, this administrative behaviour fell well within the

[136] Højesteret, 6 April 1998, *Treaty of Maastricht*, Case 361/1997 and Lachman 1998.

general Danish approach to European integration. The Single European Act signified a change in the Danish attitude to the EC by the politicians culminating with the Maastricht Treaty. The Danish electorate were not swayed by the new winds blowing, and they rejected the Treaty. The decision to ratify the treaty, based on the opt outs received at the Edinburgh Summit, brought the question of the constitutionality of the Danish EC membership to a head. In 1998, the Højesteret ruled that the Danish commitments to the EC were constitutional.

Archives Consulted

EUROPEAN ARCHIVES

Archive of Fédération Internationale de Droit Européen, held by the association (AFIDE)

Archive of the Common Market Law Review, held by the journal (ACMLREV)

Archive of the Legal Service of the European Commission, Brussels (ALSC)

Historical Archive of the Commission, Brussels (HAC)

Historical Archive of the Council of Ministers, Brussels (HACM)

Historical Archives of the European Parliament, Luxembourg (HAEP)

Historical Archives of the European Union, Florence (HAEU)

BELGIUM

Archives of the Belgian Ministry of Foreign Affairs, Brussels (ABMFA)

Archives of the Université libre de Bruxelles (AUB)

National Archives of Belgium, Brussels (NAB)

DENMARK

Archive of Dansk Forening for Europaret, held by the association, Copenhagen (ADFE)

Archive of the Danish Ministry of Justice, held at the Danish National Archives (JM)

Danish National Archives, Copenhagen (DaNA)

FRANCE

Archive of the National Assembly, Paris (ANA)

Archive of the French Ministry of Foreign Affairs, held at the Diplomatic Archives of La Courneuve, Paris (MAE)

Conseil d'État Archives, Paris (CEA)

French National Archives, Paris (FNA)

GERMANY

Archives of the German Federal Parliament (ADBT)

Archives of the German Ministry of Foreign Affairs, Berlin (PAAA)

German Federal Archives, Koblenz (BArch)

ITALY

Archive of the Associazione Italiana dei Giuristi Europei, held by the association, Rome (AAIGE)

Italian Presidential Archives, Rome (IPA)

NETHERLANDS

Archives Ministry of Foreign Affairs, The Hague (MinBuZa)

Archives of the Europa Instituut, Leiden (AEI)

Dutch National Archives, The Hague (NA-NL)

Noord-Hollands Archief, Haarlem (NHA)

Philips Company Archives (PCA)

PRIVATE ARCHIVES

Archive of Emile Noël, held at the Historical Archive of the European Union, Florence (AEM)

Archive of Eric Stein, held at Bentley Historical Library, Ann Arbor, Michigan (AES)

Archive of Fernand Dehousse, held at the Historical Archive of the European Union, Florence (AFD)

Archive of François Lamoureux, held at the Historical Archive of the European Union, Florence (AFL)

Archive of Ganshof van der Meersch, held at the Archive of Université libre de Bruxelles (AGVM)

Archive of Ivo Samkalden, held at the International Institute of Social History, Amsterdam (AIS)

Archive of Jean Rey, held at the Archive of Université libre de Bruxelles (AJR)

Archive of Klaus Meyer (AKM)

Archive of Louis Delvaux, held by the Archief Katholiek Verbond België (ALD)

Archive of Marinus van der Goes van Naters, held at the Dutch National Archive, The Hague (AMGN)

Archives of Mauro Cappelletti, held at the Historical Archive of the European Union, Florence (AMC)

Archive of Michel Debré, held at the Centre d'histoire de Sciences Po, Paris (AMD)

Archive of Michel Gaudet, held at the Foundation Jean Monnet pour l'Europe, Lausanne (AMG)

Archive of Michel Waelbroeck, held at the Historical Archive of the European Union, Florence (AMW)

Archive Ole Lando, held by Dansk forening for europaret (AOL)

Archive of Peter Wiese, held at the Danish Prime Minister's Office, Copenhagen (APW)

Archive of Robert Krawielicki, held with the family (ARK)

Archives of Walter Hallstein, held at the German Federal Archives, Koblenz (AWH)

Archive of Walter Much, held at the Historical Archive of the European Union, Florence (AWM)

Archive of Walter Strauss, held at the Institut für Zeitgeschichte, München (AWS)

Bibliography

'Hommage à Paul Leleux'. 1980. *Journal of European Integration* 3 (3): 261. https://doi.org/10.1080/07036338008428764.

Abbenhuis, Maartje. 2019. *The Hague Conference and International Politics, 1898–1915*. London: Bloomsbury.

Albors-Llorens, Albertina, Catherine Barnard, and Brigitte Leucht, eds. 2021. *Cassis de Dijon: 40 Years On*. Oxford: Hart Publishing.

Alter, Karen. 1998a. 'National Courts: Explaining National Court Acceptance of European Court Jurisprudence: A Critical Evaluation of Theories of Legal Integration'. In *The European Court and National Courts – Doctrine and Jurisprudence: Legal Change in Its Social Context*, edited by Joseph H. H. Weiler, Anne-Marie Slaughter, and Alec Stone Sweet, 227–252. Oxford: Hart Publishing.

Alter, Karen. 1998b. 'Who Are the "Masters of the Treaty"? European Governments and the European Court of Justice'. *International Organization* 52 (1): 121–174.

Alter, Karen. 2001. *Establishing the Supremacy of European Law*. Oxford: Oxford University Press.

Alter, Karen. 2009a. *The European Court's Political Power*. Oxford: Oxford University Press.

Alter, Karen. 2009b. 'Jurist Advocacy Movements in Europe: The Role of Euro-law Associations in European Integration (1953–1975)'. In *The European Court's Political Power: Selected Essays*, edited by Karen Alter, 63–91. Oxford: Oxford University Press.

Alter, Karen. 2010. 'On Law and Policy in the European Court of Justice: An American Perspective'. In *Europe: The New Legal Realism: Essays in Honour of Hjalte Rasmussen*, edited by Henning Koch, Karsten Hagel-Sørensen, Ulrich Haltern, and Joseph H. H. Weiler, 1–10. Aarhus: DJØF Publishing.

Andeweg, Rudy B., and Galen A. Irwin. 2014. *Governance and Politics of the Netherlands*. Basingstoke: Palgrave Macmillan.

Andry, Aurélie. 2022. *Social Europe, the Road Not Taken: The Left and European Integration in the Long 1970s*. Oxford: Oxford University Press.

Anghie, Anthony. 2007. *Imperialism, Sovereignty and the Making of International Law*. Cambridge: Cambridge University Press.

Arena, Amedeo. 2018. 'How European Law Became Supreme: The Making of Costa v. ENEL'. *Jean Monnet Working Paper* no. 05/18.

Arena, Amedeo. 2019. 'From an Unpaid Electricity Bill to the Primacy of EU Law: Gian Galeazzo Stendardi and the Making of Costa v. E.N.E.L'. *European Journal of International Law* 30 (3): 1017–1037.

Audretsch, H.A.H., Petrus van Dijk, J. P. G. W. Purnot, et al., 1972–1976. *De uitvoering van het gemeenschapsrecht in de Nederlandse rechtsorde*. Haarlem: Tjeenk Willink.

Baardman, B. 1960. 'Enkele gevolgen van het E.E.G.-kartelrecht voor het Nederlands privaatrecht'. In *De kartelbepalingen in het E.E.G.-verdrag: praeadviezen*, edited by M. Bos and B. Baardman, 51–112. Zwolle: Tjeenk Willink.

Bail, Christoph, and Hagen Lichtenberg. 1975. 'German Case Law (The Application of Community Law in Germany: Bundesverfassungsgericht)'. *Common Market Law Review* 12: 275–307.

Bailleux, Julie. 2010. 'Comment l'Europe vint au droit: Le premier congrès international d'études de la CECA (Milan-Stresa 1957)'. *Revue française de science politique* 60 (2): 295–318.

Bailleux, Julie. 2013. 'Michel Gaudet as a Law Entrepreneur: The Role of the Legal Service of the European Executives and the Invention of EC Law and of the *Common Market Law Review*'. *Common Market Law Review* 50 (2): 359–367.

Bailleux, Julie. 2014. *Penser l'Europe par le droit: L'Invention du droit communautaire en France*. Paris: Dalloz.

Bailleux, Julie, and Simon Jackson. 2010. 'How Europe Became Law: The First International Academic Congress on the ECSC (Milan-Stresa 1957)'. *Revue française de science politique (English Edition)* 60 (2): 67–90.

Bajon, Philip. 2011. 'De Gaulle Finds His "Master": Gerhard Schröder's "Fairly Audacious Politics" in the European Crisis of 1965–66'. *Journal of European Integration History* 17 (2): 253–269.

Bajon, Philip. 2012. *Europapolitik 'am Abgrund': Die Krise des 'leeren Stuhls' 1965–66*. Stuttgart: Steiner.

Bajon, Philip. 2018a. 'Autobiographische Zeugnisse und historische Mythen im Prozess der europäischen Einigung: Charles de Gaulle und Walter Hallstein'. In *Das eigene Leben als ästhetische Fiktion: Autobiographie und Professionsgeschichte*, edited by Dietrich Erben and Tobias Zervosen, 155–174. Bielefeld: Transcript.

Bajon, Philip. 2018b. 'The Human Factor: French–German Bilateralism and the "Logic of Appropriateness" in the European Crisis of the Mid-1960s'. *Diplomacy & Statecraft* 29 (3): 455–476.

Bajon, Philip. 2025. *Informal Decision Making in the European Community under the Luxembourg Compromise: The Law That Never Was*. Oxford: Hart Publishing.

Bebr, Gerhard. 1962. *Judicial Control of the European Communities*. London: Stevens.

Bebr, Gerhard. 1974. 'A Critical Review of Recent Case Law of National Courts'. *Common Market Law Review* 11: 408–431.

Bebr, Gerhard. 1983. 'The Rambling Ghost of "Cohn-Bendit": Acte Clair and the Court of Justice'. *Common Market Law Review* 20: 439–472.

Bebr, Gerhard. 1988. 'The Reinforcement of the Constitutional Review of Community Acts Under Article 177 EEC Treaty'. *Common Market Law Review* 25: 667–691.

Beetham, David, and Christopher Lord. 1998. *Legitimacy and the EU*. London: Longman.

Bernier, Alexandre. 2012. 'Constructing and Legitimating: Transnational Jurist Networks and the Making of a Constitutional Practice of European Law, 1950–1970'. *Contemporary European History* 21 (3): 399–415.

Bernier, Alexandre. 2014. Between Luxembourg and De Gaulle. French Reception of European Law 1958–1975 (unpublished conference paper 2014).

Bernier, Alexandre. 2017. *La France et le Droit Communautaire, 1958–1981: Histoire d'une Réception et d'une Coproduction*. PhD diss., University of Copenhagen.

Bernier, Alexandre. Forthcoming. 'Michel Debré: A Biography Against the Backdrop of French National Sovereignty.' In *Key Biographies in the Legal History of the European Union, 1950–1993*, edited by Stefan Vogenauer and Philip Bajon.

Berstein, Serge, and Pierre Milza. 1991. *Histoire de la France au XXe Siècle: 1945–1958*. Brussels: Editions Complexe.

Besselink, Leonard F. M. 1992. 'Het Verdrag van Maastricht wijkt ook op andere punten af van de Grondwet en eveneens van het Statuut'. *Nederlands Juristenblad* 67 (27): 864–865.

Besselink, Leonard F. M., H. R. B. M. Kummeling, R. de Lange, and P. Mendelts. 2002. *De Nederlandse Grondwet en de Europese Unie*. Groningen: Europa Law Publishing.

Bickerton, Christopher J., Dermot Hodson, and Uwe Puetter. 2015. *The New Intergovernmentalism: States and Supranational Actors in the Post-Maastricht Era*. Oxford: Oxford University Press.

Bieber, Roland. 1984. 'The Settlement of Institutional Conflict on the Basis of Article 4 of the EEC Treaty'. *Common Market Law Review* 21: 505–523.

Bieber, Roland, and Dietmar Nickel, eds. 1981. *Das Europa der Zweiten Generation: Gedächtnisschrift für Christoph Sasse*. Kehl am Rhein: N. P. Engel Verlag.

Bignami, Francesca. 2011. 'Comparative Law and the Rise of the European Court of Justice'. European Union Studies Association 2011 Annual Conference, 3–6.

Bjøl, Erling. 1966. *La France devant l'Europe: La Politique Européenne de la IVe République*. Copenhagen: Munksgaard.

Bobek, Michal, ed. 2015. *Selecting Europe's Judges: A Critical Review of the Appointment Procedures to the European Courts*. Oxford: Oxford University Press.

Boerger, Anne. 2012. 'Negotiating the Foundations of European Law, 1950–1957: The Legal History of the Treaties of Paris and Rome'. *Contemporary European History* 21 (3): 339–356.

Boerger, Anne. 2014. 'At the Cradle of Legal Scholarship on the European Union: The Life and Early Work of Eric Stein'. *American Journal of Comparative Law* 62 (4): 859–892.

Boerger, Anne, and Bill Davies. 2017. 'Imagining the Course of European Law? Parti Ecologiste "Les Verts" v. Parliament as a Constitutional Milestone'. In *EU Law Stories: Contextual and Critical Histories in European Jurisprudence*, edited by Bill Davies and Fernanda Nicola, 83–102. Cambridge: Cambridge University Press.

Boerger, Anne, and Morten Rasmussen. 2014. 'Transforming European Law: The Establishment of the Constitutional Discourse from 1950 to 1993'. *European Constitutional Law Review* 10 (2): 199–225.

Boerger, Anne, and Morten Rasmussen. 2017. 'The Making of European Law: Exploring the Life and Work of Michel Gaudet'. *American Journal of Legal History* 57 (1): 51–82.

Bogdandy, Armin von. 2000. 'A Bird's Eye View on the Science of European Law: Structures, Debates, and Development Prospects of Basic Research on the Law of the European Union in a German Perspective'. *European Law Journal* 6 (3): 208–238.

Bougrab, Jeannette. 2002. *Aux Origines de la IVe République*. Paris: Dalloz.

Bouwens, Bram, and Joost Dankers. 2011. 'The Invisible Handshake: Cartelization in the Netherlands, 1930–2000'. *Business History Review* 84: 751–771.

Brijnen, P. W. L., and H. W. Wertheimer. 1957. 'De Interpretatie van de Kartelbepalingen in het Europese Economische Gemeenschap-verdrag'. *Sociaal-Economische Wetgeving* 5 (9): 253–257.

Brinkhorst, L. J. 1963. *De Jurist en de Europese Economische Gemeenschap: Elementen van een Europese Rechtsorde*. Den Haag: Europese Beweging.

Brinkhorst, L. J. 1966. 'De Nederlandse Rechter en het Gemeenschapsrecht'. *Sociaal-Economische Wetgeving* 14: 65.

Broberg, Morten, and Niels Fenger. 2021. *Broberg and Fenger on Preliminary References to the European Court of Justice*. Oxford: Oxford University Press.

Bruin, Robin de. 2014. *Elastisch Europa: De Integratie van Europa en de Nederlandse Politiek, 1947–1968*. Amsterdam: Wereldbibliotheek.

Buffet-Tchakaloff, Marie-France. 1985. *La France devant la Cour de Justice des Communautés Européennes*. Paris: Economica.

Bulmer, Simon. 1985. 'The European Council's First Decade: Between Interdependence and Domestic Politics'. *Journal of Common Market Studies* 24 (2): 89–104.

Burley, Anne-Marie, and Walter Mattli. 1993. 'Europe Before the Court: A Political Theory of Legal Integration'. *International Organization* 47 (1): 41–76.

Busck, Steen, and Henning Poulsen, eds. 2002. *Danmarks Historie – I Grundtræk*. Aarhus: Aarhus Universitetsforlag.

Byberg, Rebekka. 2017a. 'A Miscellaneous Network: The History of FIDE 1961–1994'. *American Journal of Legal History* 57 (2): 142–165.

Byberg, Rebekka. 2017b. 'The History of *Common Market Law Review* 1963–1993: Carving Out an Academic Space for European Law'. *European Law Journal* 23 (1–2): 45–65.

Byberg, Rebekka. 2017c. 'The History of the Integration Through Law Project: Creating the Academic Expression of a Constitutional Legal Vision for Europe'. *German Law Journal* 18 (6): 1531–1556.

Byberg, Rebekka. 2017d. *Academic Allies: The Key Transnational Institutions of the Academic Discipline of European Law and Their Role in the Development of the Constitutional Practice, 1961–1993*. PhD diss., University of Copenhagen.

Calabresi, Guido. 1985. 'Introductory Remarks to Mauro Cappelletti: Repudiating Montesquieu? The Expansion and Legitimacy of "Constitutional Justice"'. *Catholic University Law Review* 35 (1): 1–32.

Camps, Miriam. 1966. *European Unification in the Sixties: From the Veto to the Crisis*. New York: McGraw-Hill.

Capotorti, Francesco. 1960. 'Sulla Interpretazione Uniforme dei Trattati Europei'. *Rivista di Diritto Internazionale* 43 (1): 3–25.

Cappelletti, Mauro, Monica Seccombe, and Joseph H. H. Weiler, eds. 1985–1988. *Integration Through Law: Europe and the American Federal Experience*. Vols. 1–5. Berlin: Walter de Gruyter.

Carbonell, Mauve. 2014. *De la guerre à l'union de l'Europe: Itinéraires luxembourgeois*. Brussels: PIE-Peter Lang.

Cartabia, M and Lupo, N. 2023. *The Constitution of Italy. A Contextual Analysis*. London: Bloomsbury Press.

Catalano, Nicola. 1957. *La Comunità economica europea e l'Euratom*. Milan: Giuffrè.

Catalano, Nicola. 1965. *Droit communautaire et droit national: Community Law and National Law*. Bruges: De Tempel.

Chivvis, Christopher S. 2010. *The Monetary Conservative: Jacques Rueff and Twentieth-Century Free Market Thought*. DeKalb: Northern Illinois University Press.

Christensen, Søren. 1990. 'Det indre marked og den offentlige sektors administrative struktur'. *Ledelse & Erhvervsøkonomi* 54: 13–19.

Claes, Monica, and Bruno De Witte. 1998. 'Report on the Netherlands'. In *The European Court and National Courts: Doctrine and Jurisprudence – Legal Change in Its Social Context*, edited by Anne Marie Slaughter, Alec Stone Sweet, and Joseph H. H. Weiler, 171–194. Oxford: Hart Publishing.

Claes, Monica, Maartje C. B. F. Visser, P. de Popelier, and Catherine van de Heyning. 2012. *Constitutional Conversations in Europe: Actors, Topics, and Procedures*. Cambridge: Intersentia.

Cohen, Antonin. 2007. 'Constitutionalism Without Constitution: Transnational Elites Between Political Mobilization and Legal Expertise in the Making of a Constitution for Europe (1940s–1960s)'. *Law & Social Inquiry* 32 (1): 109–135.

Cohen, Antonin. 2013a. 'Juge et expert: L'Affaire Rueff ou la codification des règles de la circulation internationale'. *Critique Internationale* 59 (2): 69–88.

Cohen, Antonin. 2013b. 'Ten Majestic Figures in Long Amaranth Robes: The Formation of the Court of Justice of the European Communities'. In *Lawyering Europe: European Law as a Transnational Social Field*, edited by Bruno De Witte and Antoine Vauchez, 21–24. London: Hart Publishing.

College of Europe. 1964. *Semaine de Bruges: European Integration and Economic Reality*. Tempelhof: Bruges.

College of Europe. 1965. *Semaine de Bruges: Community Law and National Law*. Tempelhof: Bruges.

Collings, Justin. 2015. *Democracy's Guardian. A History of the Federal Constitutional Court, 1951–2001*. Oxford: Oxford University Press.

Combrexelle, Jean-Denis. 2004. 'Fernand Grévisse, une certaine idée de l'État au service de l'Europe.' In *Hommage à Fernand Grévisse*, edited by Louise Cadoux and Roger Errera, 102–107. Paris: La Documentation Française.

Conant, Lisa J. 2002. *Justice Contained: Law and Politics in the European Union*. Cornell University Press.

Conant, Lisa J. 2007. 'Review Article: The Politics of Legal Integration'. *Journal of Common Market Studies* 45 (1): 45–66.

Condorelli-Braun, Nicole. 1972. *Commissaires et juges dans les Communautés européennes*. Paris: Librairie Générale de Droit et de Jurisprudence.

Coppolaro, Lucia. 2013. *The Making of a World Trading Power: The European Economic Community (EEC) in the GATT Kennedy Round Negotiations (1963–1967)*. Aldershot: Ashgate.

Corduwener, P. 2012. 'Risee van de wereld of land van Grotius? De synthese tussen nationalisme en internationalisme in het Nederlandse fin de siècle'. *Tijdschrift voor Geschiedenis* 125: 202–215.

Coutard, Jean. 1946. 'Les libertés en régime démocratique'. In *Refaites une constitution: Treize études*, edited by Jean De Soto, Jean Coutard, Raymond Malezieu et al., 35–58. Paris: La Jeune Parque.

Curtin, Deirdre. 1993. 'The Constitutional Structure of the Union: A Europe of Bits and Pieces'. *Common Market Law Review* 30: 17–69.

Dallen Jr., Russel M. 1990. 'An Overview of European Community Protection of Human Rights, with Some Special References to the UK'. *Common Market Law Review* 27: 761–790.

Dankers, J. J., and J. Verheul. 1996. *Twee eeuwen op weg: Van Gend & Loos 1796–1996*. Den Haag: SDU Uitgevers.

Dard, Olivier. 2004. 'Les réseaux technocratiques français face au processus de construction européenne des années 1930 aux années 1950'. In *Réseaux économiques et construction européenne*, edited by Michel Dumoulin, 41–53. Brussels: Peter Lang.

Davies, Bill. 2008. 'Meek Acceptance? The West German Ministries' Reaction to the Van Gend En Loos and Costa Decisions'. *Journal of European Integration History* 14 (2): 57–76.

Davies, Bill. 2012a. 'Pushing Back: What Happens When Member States Resist the European Court of Justice? A Multi-Modal Approach to the History of European Law'. *Contemporary European History* 21 (3): 434–459.

Davies, Bill. 2012b. *Resisting the ECJ: West Germany's Confrontation with European Law, 1949–1979*. Cambridge: Cambridge University Press.

Davies, Bill. 2015. 'Resistance to European Law and Constitutional Identity: Germany'. *European Law Journal* 21 (4): 442–443.

Davies, Bill. 2016. 'Integrity or Openness? Reassessing the History of the CJEU's Human Rights Jurisprudence'. *American Journal of Comparative Law* 64 (4): 801–805.

Davies, Bill. 2017. 'Internationale and the Miscalculation at the Inception of the CJEU's Human Rights Jurisprudence'. In *EU Law Stories: Contextual and Critical Histories in European Jurisprudence*, edited by Bill Davies and Fernanda Nicola, 157–177. Cambridge: Cambridge University Press.

Davies, Bill. Forthcoming. 'EU Law's Quiet Man: The Formative Years of Walter Much'. In *Key Biographies of Legal History of the European Union, 1950–1993*, edited by Stefan Vogenauer and Philip Bajon.

Davies, Bill, and Morten Rasmussen. 2012. 'Introduction: Towards a New History of European Law'. *Contemporary European History* 21 (3): 305–318.

Davies, Bill, and Morten Rasmussen. 2014. 'From International Law to a European Rechtsgemeinschaft, 1950–1979'. In *The Institutions and Dynamics of the European Community, 1973–83*, edited by Johnny Laursen, 97–130. Baden-Baden: Nomos.

Davies, Gareth. 2016. 'The European Legislature as an Agent of the European Court of Justice'. *Journal of Common Market Studies*, 54 (4): 1–16.

De Gaulle, Charles. 1970. *Pour l'Effort 1962–1965*. Paris: Plon.

Debré, Michel. 1994. *Trois Républiques pour une France tome 5: Combatre toujours*. Paris: Albin Michel.

Dehousse, Renaud. 1998. *The European Court of Justice: The Politics of Judicial Integration*. London: Macmillan.

Delfs, Hauke. 2015. *Komplementäre Integration. Grundlegung und Konstitutionalisierung des Europarechts im Kontext*. Tübingen: Mohr Siebeck.

Di Fabio, Udo. 1993. 'Der Neue Art. 23 des Grundgesetzes. Positivierung Vollzogenen Verfassungswandels oder Verfassungsneuschöpfung'. *Der Staat* 32 (2): 191–218.

Di Nolfo, Ennio. 2012. *Power in Europe 2, Great Britain, France, Germany and Italy and the Origins of the EEC 1952–1957*. Berlin: De Gruyter.

Dijk, P. van. 1969. 'The Implementation and Application of the Law of the European Communities Within the Legal Order of the Netherlands'. *Common Market Law Review* 6: 283–308.

Dinan, Desmond. 2010. *Ever Closer Union. An Introduction to European Integration*. Basingstoke: Lynne Rienner Publishers.

Dinan, Desmond. 2018. 'Historiography of the European Parliament: Changing Perceptions of the Institution from the 1950s to Today'. *European Parliament History Series. PE* 630 (270): 1–72.

Dinan, Desmond. 2021. 'The European Parliament: Moving to the Centre of Historical Interest in the European Union'. *Journal of European Integration History* 27 (1): 137–153.

Donner, André M. 1963. 'National Law and the Case Law of the Court of Justice of the European Communities'. *Common Market Law Review* 1: 8–16.

Donner, Andreas M. 1974. 'The Constitutional Powers of the Court of Justice of the European Communities'. *Common Market Law Review* 11: 127–140.

Donner, Andreas M., et al. 1966. *Le juge national et le droit communautaire*. Brussels: F. Larcier.

Dûchene, François. 1994. *Jean Monnet: The First Statesman of Interdependence*. New York: W.W. Norton & Company.

Due, Ole, and Claus Gulmann. 1972. 'Constitutional Implications of the Danish Accession to the European Communities'. *Common Market Law Review* 9 (3): 256–270.

Dumbrovsky, Tomas, Bilyana Petkova, and Marijn Van der Sluis. 2014. 'Judicial Appointments: The Article 255 TFEU Advisory Panel and Selection Procedures in the Member States'. *Common Market Law Review* 51 (2): 445–482.

Duynstee, F. J. F. M. 1954. *Grondwetsherziening 1953: De nieuwe bepalingen omtrent de buitenlandse betrekkingen in de grondwet*. Deventer: Kluwer.

Eckel, Jan. 2017. 'Vieldeutige Signatur: Menschenrechte in der Politik des 20. Jahrhunderts'. In *Das 20. Jahrhundert vermessen: Signaturen eines vergangenen Zeitalters*, edited by Martin Sabrow and Peter Ulrich Weiß, 284–304. Göttingen: Wallstein.

Egan, Michelle. 2015. *Single Markets: Economic Integration in Europe and the United States*. Oxford: Oxford University Press.

Ehlermann, Claus-Dieter. 1983. 'The Role of Lawyers in the European Communities'. *International Business Lawyer*, 172–173.

Ehlermann, Claus-Dieter. 1984. 'Talk About Community Decision Making'. *Conference of the British-German Jurists' Association*, 15 March 1984.

Ehlermann, Claus-Dieter. 1992. 'The European Community: Its Law and Lawyers – The Second Wilberforce Lecture'. *Common Market Law Review* 29: 213–227.

Emde Boas, M. J. van. 1963. 'Europees Babel in de Rolzaal'. *Sociaal-Economische Wetgeving* 11: 603–604.

Erades, L. 1950. 'De verhouding tussen volkenrecht en nationaal recht in Nederland'. *Nederlands Juristenblad* 25 (11): 217–222.

Erades, L. 1952. 'De voorstellen tot herziening der Grondwetsbepalingen betreffende het buitenlands beleid'. *RM Themis* 113: 170–188.

Erades, Lambertus and P. S. R. F. Mat Mathijsen. 1964. *De verhouding van de rechtspraak van het Hof der Europese Gemeenschappen tot die van de nationale rechters in de lid-staten: Preadvies*. Baarn: Hollandia.

Erler, Georg, and Werner Thieme. 1959. 'Das Grundgesetz und die öffentliche Gewalt internationaler Staatengemeinschaften'. *Veröffentlichungen der Vereinigung der Deutschen Staatsrechtslehrer* 18: 7–112.

Esmark, Magnus. 2020. 'Le droit communautaire – c'est moi!' Statsmonolpol, national ret og euro-integrationisme i tiden efter Danmarks indtræden i EF", *Praktiske Grunde: Nordisk tidsskrift for kultur- og samfundsvidenskab* 1–2: 23–42.

Esmark, Magnus. 2022. *Without Verona Walls: The Production of Danish European Union Law*, 1973–2020. PhD diss., University of Copenhagen.

European Commission. 2014. *The European Commission 1973–86: History and Memories of an Institution*. Luxembourg: Publications Office of the European Union.

European Commission. 2019. *The European Commission 1986–2000: History and Memories of an Institution*. Luxembourg: Publications Office of the European Union.

European Commission. 2007. *The European Commission 1958–1972: History and Memories*. European Commission. Luxembourg: Publications Office of the European Union.

Eysinga, W. J. M. van. 1950. *Geschiedenis van de Nederlandsche Wetenschap van Het Volkenrecht*. Amsterdam: Noord-Hollandsche Uitgevers Mij, 34–35.

Eysinga, W. J. M. van. 1955. 'Eenige kantteekeningen op het rapport der Commissie-Kranenburg'. *Nederlands Juristenblad* 30: 615–620.

Feld, Werner. 1963. 'The Judges of the Court of Justice of the European Communities'. *Villanova Law Review* 9 (1): 37–58.

Finnemore, Martha, and Kathryn Sikkink. 1998. 'International Norm Dynamics and Political Change'. *International Organization* 52 (4): 887–917.

Fitzpatrick, Barry. 1992. 'Community Social Law After Maastricht'. *Industrial Law Journal* 21 (3): 199–213.

Fleuren, J. W. A. 2004. *Een ieder verbindende bepalingen van verdragen*. Den Haag: Boom, 98–109.

Forman, John, and Trevor Stevens. 1976. 'The Attitude of British Courts to Community Law, the First Three Years'. *Common Market Law Review* 13: 388–414.

Fossum, John Erik, and Augustín José Menéndez. 2011. *The Constitution's Gift: A Constitutional Theory for Democratic European Union*. London: Rowman & Littlefield Publishers.

Foyer, Jean. 2006a. 'Après l'arrêt Canal: le général de Gaulle et la non-réforme du Conseil d'État'. *La Revue administrative* 59 (349): 6–12.

Foyer, Jean. 2006b. *Sur les chemins du droit avec le Général*. Paris: Fayard.

Fritz, Vera. 2015. 'The First Member State Rebellion? The European Court of Justice and the Negotiations of the "Luxembourg Protocol" of 1971'. *European Law Journal* 21 (5): 680–699.

Fritz, Vera. 2017. 'Tessili vs. Dunlop 1976: The Political Background of Judicial Restraint'. In *EU Law Stories*, edited by Fernanda Nicola and Bill Davies, 357–368. Cambridge: Cambridge University Press.

Fritz, Vera. 2018. *Juges et avocats généraux de la Cour de Justice de l'Union européenne (1952–1972)*. Frankfurt am Main: Kolstermann.

Fritz, Vera. 2019. 'La légitimité des "juges-experts" de la Cour européenne de Justice, 1952–1972.' In *L'échelle des régulations politiques, XVIIIe-XXIe siècles*, edited by Virginie Albe, Jacques Commaille and Florent le Bot, 143–154. Villeneuve-d'Ascq: Presses Universitaires Septentrion.

Fritz, Vera. 2020. 'Activism on and Off the Bench: Pierre Pescatore and the Law of Integration'. *Common Market Law Review* 57 (2): 475–502.

Frowein, Jochen Abr. 1973. 'Zur institutionellen Fortentwicklung der Gemeinschaft'. *Kölner Schriften zum Europarecht: Die institutionelle Entwicklung der Europäischen Gemeinschaften in den 70er Jahren* 22: 83–105.

Gallo, Daniele, Roberto Mastroianni, Fernanda Nicola and Lorenzo Cecchetti, eds. 2024. *The Italian Influence on European Law. Judges and Advocates General*. Oxford: Hart Publishing.

Garavini, Giuliano. 2012. *After Empires: European Integration, Decolonization, and the Challenge from the Global South, 1957–1986*. Oxford: Oxford University Press.

Garrett, Geoffrey. 1995. 'The Politics of Legal Integration in the European Union'. *International Organization* 49 (1): 171–181.

Geertman, J. 1961. 'Vrije import'. *Economisch-Sociale Berichten* 46: 379–380.

Gfeller, Aurélie Élisa, Wilfried Loth, Matthias Schulz et al. 2011. 'Democratizing Europe: Reaching Out to the Citizens – The Transforming Powers of the European Parliament'. *Journal of European Integration History* 17 (1): 5–12.

Gilbert, Mark. 2012. *European Integration: A Concise History*. Maryland: Rowman & Littlefield.

Gillingham, John. 1991. *Coal, Steel, and the Rebirth of Europe, 1945–1955: The Germans and French from Ruhr Conflict to Economic Community*. Cambridge: Cambridge University Press.

Girault, René, and Robert Frank, eds. 1995. *La puissance en Europe, 1938–1940*. Paris: Publications de la Sorbonne.

Girault, René. 1994. *Identité et conscience européennes au XXe siècle*. Paris: Hachette.

Golub, Jonathan. 2006. 'Did the Luxembourg Compromise Have Any Consequences?' In *Visions, Votes and Vetoes: The Empty Chair Crisis and the Luxembourg Compromise Forty Years On*, edited by Jean-Marie Palayret, Helen Wallace and Pascaline Winand, 279–299. Brussels: P.I.E.-Peter Lang.

Gram-Skjoldager, Karen. 2012. *Fred og folkeret: Dansk internationalistisk udenrigspolitik 1899–1939*. Copenhagen: Museum Tusculanums Forlag.

Grande, Elisabetta. 2006. 'Development of Comparative Law in Italy'. In *The Oxford Handbook of Comparative Law*, edited by M. Reimann and R. Zimmermann, 108–125. Oxford: Oxford University Press.

Greaves, Rosa. 2007. 'The First Advocate General, Maurice Lagrange'. In *The Advocate General and EC Law*, edited by Noreen Burrows and Rosa Greaves, 59–88. Oxford: Oxford University Press.

Grewe, Wilhelm G. 2013. *The Epochs of International Law*. Berlin: De Gruyter.

Griffiths, Richard T. 2000. *Europe's First Constitution: The European Political Community, 1952–1954*. London: Federal Trust.

Griffiths, Richard T. 2020. 'The European Defence Community'. In *Oxford Research Encyclopedia of Politics*, edited by William R. Thompson, 1–18. Oxford: Oxford University Press.

Grimm, Dieter. 2015. 'The Democratic Costs of Constitutionalisation: The European Case'. *European Law Journal* 21 (4): 460–473.

Grønning-Nielsen, Leif. 1992. 'Præjudicielle forelæggelser for EF-domstolen'. *Ugeskrift for Retsvæsen* 126 (39): 337–340.

Groux, Jean, and Philip Manin. 1984. *Les Communautés européennes dans l'ordre international*. Luxembourg: OPOCE.

Grünsteudel, Günther. 1998. 'Otto Weinkamm'. In *Stadtlexikon Augsburg*, 2nd ed., edited by Günther Grünsteudel, Günter Hägele and Rudolf Frankenberger et al. Augsburg: Wißner-Verlag.

Guieu, Jean-Michel, and Dzovinar Kévonian. 2012. 'Introduction: Juristes et relations internationales'. *Relations Internationales* 1 (149): 3–11.

Gulmann, Claus. 1983. 'The Position of International Law Within the Danish Legal Order'. *Nordisk Tidsskrift for International Ret* 52 (3–4): 45–52.

Gulmann, Claus. 1987a. 'Anmeldelse af On Law and Politics in the European Court of Justice'. *Ugeskrift for retsvæsen* 24: 189–192.

Gulmann, Claus. 1987b. 'The Single European Act: Some Remarks from a Danish Perspective'. *Common Market Law Review* 24: 31–40.

Haas, Ernst B. 1958. *The Uniting of Europe: Political, Social, and Economic Forces, 1950–1957*. Stanford: Stanford University Press.

Hagel-Sørensen, Karsten, and Hjalte Rasmussen. 1985. 'The Danish Administration and Its Interaction with the Community Administration'. *Common Market Law Review* 22: 273–300.

Hagel-Sørensen, Karsten. 1994. 'Fællesskabsretten som en del af dansk ret'. In *Festskrift til Ole Due*, edited by Jens Rosenløv and Kirsten Thorup, 113–137. København: Gads Forlag.

Hallstein, Walter, Hans Herbert Götz, and Karl-Heinz Narjes 1969. *Der unvollendete Bundesstaat: Europäische Erfahrungen und Erkenntnisse*. Düsseldorf: Econ Verlag.

Hammes, Charles-Léon. 1966. 'Les caractères essentiels de la nature de la Cour de Justice des Communautés européennes'. *Bulletin du Cercle François Laurent* 3 (1): 3–14.

Harryvan, A. G. 2009. *In Pursuit of Influence: The Netherlands' European Policy During the Formative Years of the European Union, 1952–1973*. Brussels: Peter Lang.

Harryvan, A. G., and Jan van der Harst. 2013. *Verloren consensus: Europa in het Nederlandse parlementair-politieke debat 1945–2013*. Amsterdam: Boom.

Harst, Jan van der, ed. 2003. *Journal of European Integration History*, 9 (2). Special Issue on the Hague Summit.

Harst, Jan van der, ed. 2007. *Beyond the Customs Union: The European Community's Quest for Deepening, Widening and Completion, 1969–1975*. Brussels: Bruylant.

Harten, H. van. 2015. 'Over de Europese attitude van de Nederlandse rechter'. In *Van aanvallen! Naar verdedigen: De opstelling van Nederland ten aanzien van de Europese integratie, 1945–2015*, edited by H. Vollaard, J. van der Harst and G. Voerman, 242. Den Haag: Boom Bestuurskunde, 223–248.

Hayes-Renshaw, Fiona, and Helen Wallace. 2006. *The Council of Ministers*. Basingstoke: Palgrave Macmillan.

Heerikhuizen, A. van. 1998. *Pioniers van een Verenigd Europa: Bovennationaal denken in het Nederlandse parlement (1946–1951)*. Amsterdam: Aksant.

Heisenberg, Dorothee. 2007. 'Informal Decision-Making in the Council: The Secret of the EU's Success?' In *Making History: European Integration and Institutional Change at Fifty*, edited by Sophie Meunier and Kathleen R. McNamara, 67–87. Oxford: Oxford University Press.

Heringa, A. W., 1992. 'De verdragen van Maastricht in strijd met de Grondwet'. *Nederlands Juristenblad* 67: 749–752.

Herman, Valentine, and Juliet Lodge. 1978. 'The Dual Mandate'. In *The European Parliament and the European Community*, 141–156. London: MacMillan Press.

Hollander, Jieskje. 2013. *Constitutionalising Europe: Dutch Reactions to an Incoming Tide (1948–2005)*. Groningen: Europa Law Publishers.

Hommelhoff, Peter, and Paul Kirchhof, eds. 1994. *Der Staatenverbund der Europäischen Union*. Heidelberg: C. F. Müller.

Hommes, W. 2023. *Co-creating European Human Rights: How the Netherlands Received and Shaped the European Convention on Human Rights, 1945–2022*. PhD diss., Universiteit van Amsterdam.

Houben, Piet-Hein. 1964. *Les Conseils des Ministres des Communautés européennes*. Leiden: A. W. Sythoff.

Itzcovich, Giulio. 2006. *Teorie e ideologie del diritto comunitario*. Torino: G. Giappichelli Editore.

Jacqué, Jean-Paul, and Joseph H. H. Weiler. 1990. 'On the Road to European Union: A New Judicial Architecture – An Agenda for the Intergovernmental Conference'. *Common Market Law Review* 27: 185–207.

Jacqué, Jean-Paul, ed. 2012. *A Man for All Treaties: Liber Amicorum en honneur de Jean-Claude Piris*. Brussels: Bruylant.

Jans, J. H. 2010. 'VNO.' In *Het recht van de Europese Unie in 50 klassieke arresten*, edited by T. W. B. Beukers, H. J. van Harten and S. Prechal, 136–142. The Hague: BJU.

Jensen, Steven. 2016. *The Making of International Human Rights: The 1960s, Decolonization, and the Reconstruction of Global Values*. Cambridge: Cambridge University Press.

Joëlle, Pierre. 2020. *George Pompidou, Willy Brandt, l'axe franco-allemand et la construction europénne: 1969–1974*. Brussels: P.I.E. Peter Lang.

Kaijser, Arne, Markku Lehtonen, Jan-Henrik Meyer and Mar Rubio-Varas. 2021. *Engaging the Atom: The History of Nuclear Energy and Society in Europe from the 1950s to the Present*. Morgantown: West Virginia University Press.

Kaiser, Wolfram, and Antonio Varsori, eds. 2010. *European Union History: Themes and Debates*. London: Palgrave.

Kaiser, Wolfram, and Jan-Henrik Meyer, eds. 2013. *Societal Actors in European Integration: Polity-Building and Policy-Making 1958–1992*. Basingstoke: Palgrave.

Kaiser, Wolfram, and Kiran K. Patel. 2017. 'Multiple Connections in European Co-Operation: International Organizations, Policy Ideas, Practices and Transfers, 1967–1992'. *European Review of History: Revue européenne d'histoire* 24 (3): 337–357.

Kaiser, Wolfram, and Kiran K. Patel. 2018. 'Special Issue: Continuity and Change in European Cooperation During the Twentieth Century'. *Contemporary European History* 27 (2): 165–182.

Kaiser, Wolfram, Brigitte Leucht, and Morten Rasmussen, eds. 2008. *The History of the European Union: Origins of a Trans- and Supranational Polity 1950–1972*. London: Routledge.

Kaiser, Wolfram, Michael Gehler and Brigitte Leucht, eds. 2010. *Transnational Networks in Regional Integration: Governing Europe 1945–1983*. Basingstoke: Palgrave.

Kaiser, Wolfram. 2007. *Christian Democracy and the Origins of European Union*. Cambridge: Cambridge University Press.

Kaiser, Wolfram. 2018. *Shaping European Union: The European Parliament and Institutional Reform (1979–1989)*. European Parliament History Series. PE 630.271.

Kapteyn, Jos. 1975. 'Conseil d'État (Assemblée), Decision of 22 December 1978, Cohn-Bendit'. *Common Market Law Review* 16: 701–707.

Kelemen, R. Daniel, and Alec Stone Sweet. 2017. 'Assessing the Transformation of Europe: A View from Political Science'. In *The Transformation of Europe: Twenty-Five Years On*, edited by Miguel Poiares Maduro and Marlene Wind, 193–205. Cambridge: Cambridge University Press.

Kenney, Sally J. 1998. 'The Members of the Court of Justice of the European Communities'. *Columbia Journal of European Law* 5 (1): 101–133.

Kersten, Albert E. 1988. 'A Welcome Surprise? The Netherlands and the Schuman Plan Negotiations'. In *Die Anfänge Des Schuman-Plans 1950/51*, edited by Klaus Schwabe, 285–304. Baden-Baden: Nomos.

Klerk, Y. S., and L. van Poelgeest. 1991. 'Ratificatie a contre coeur: de reserves van de Nederlandse regering jegens het Europees Verdrag voor de Rechten van de Mens en het individueel'. *RM Themis* 220: 225.

Knudsen, Ann-Christina L. 2009. *Farmers on Welfare: The Making of Europe's Common Agricultural Policy – A Historical Study*. Ithaca: Cornell University Press.

Knudsen, Ann-Christina L. 2012. 'Modes de recrutement et de circulation des premiers membres britanniques et danois du Parlement européen'. *Cultures et Conflits* 85 (86): 61–79.

Knudsen, Ann-Christina L. 2014. 'The European Parliament and Political Careers at the Nexus of European Integration and Transnational History'. In *The Institutions and Dynamics of the European Community, 1973–1983*, edited by Johnny Laursen, 76–96. Baden-Baden: Nomos.

Knudsen, Ann-Christina L., and Morten Rasmussen. 2008. 'A European Political System in the Making, 1958–1970: The Relevance of Emerging Committee Structures'. *Journal of European Integration History* 14 (1): 51–68.

Korte, Joest, and Alfred E. Kellermann. 1991. *Primus Inter Pares: The European Court and National Courts: The Follow-up by National Courts of Preliminary Rulings Ex Art. 177 of the Treaty of Rome*. Baden-Baden: Nomos.

Koskenniemi, Martti. 2001. *The Gentler Civilizer of Nations: The Rise and Fall of International Law, 1870–1960*. Vol. 14. Cambridge: Cambridge University Press.

Krabbe, Hugo. 1906. *Die Lehre der Rechtssouveränität: Beitrag zur Staatslehre*. Groningen: Wolters.

Kraus, Herbert. 1952. 'Das Erfordernis struktureller Kongruenz zwischen der Verfassung der Europäischen Verteidigungsgemeinschaft und dem Grundgesetz'. In *Der Kampf um den Wehrbeitrag*, Vol. 2, 545. Munich: Isar Verlag.

Krawielicki, Robert. 1952. *Das Monopolverbot im Schumanplan*. Tübingen: Mohr.

Kreyssig, Gerhard. 1957. 'Probleme und Problematik des Europaparlaments'. *Die Neue Gesellschaft* 4 (4): 337–346.

Kruizinga, Samuël. 2016. 'A Small State? The Size of the Netherlands as a Focal Point in Foreign Policy Debates, 1900–1940'. *Diplomacy & Statecraft* 27: 420–436.

Krumrey, Jacob. 2018. *The Symbolic Politics of European Integration: Staging Europe*. London: Macmillan.

Kutscher, Hans. 1976. 'Methods of Interpretation as Seen by a Judge at the Court of Justice'. *Court of Justice of the European Communities, Judicial and Academic Conference*, 27–28 September 1976.

Lachman, Per. 1998. 'The Treaty of Maastricht vs. the Danish Constitution'. *Nordic Journal of International Law* 67: 365–368.

Lachmann, Per. 1981. 'Some Danish Reflections on the Use of Article 235 of the Rome Treaty'. *Common Market Law Review* 18: 447–461.

Laderchi, P. Ruggeri. 1998. 'Report on Italy'. In *The European Court and National Courts – Doctrine and Jurisprudence*, edited by Anne-Marie Slaughter, Alec Stone Sweet and Joseph H. H. Weiler, 147–202. Oxford: Hart Publishing.

Lahr, Rolf. 1983. 'Die Legende vom Luxemburger Kompromiß'. *Europa-Archiv*: 223–239.

Larqué, Lionel, and Julien Lusson. 2006. 'Réflexions sur l'Europe puissance'. *Mouvements* 47–48 (5–6): 209–218.

Larsen, Signe Rehling. 2021. *The Constitutional Theory of the Federation and the European Union*. Oxford: Oxford University Press.

Larsen, Signe Rehling. 2022. 'European Public Law After Empires'. *European Law Open* 1: 6–25.

Lauwaars, R. H., M. G. Lyklema, and M. J. Kuiper. 1973. 'Jurisprudence sur les problèmes généraux de l'intégration: rapport national néerlandais'. In *FIDE – Congrès international pour le droit européen* 6. Luxembourg.

Lecourt, Robert. 1963. 'L'unification du droit européen est aussi un moyen de construire l'Europe'. *France-Forum*, 27–31.

Leeuwen, Karin van. 2012. 'On Democratic Concerns and Legal Traditions: The Dutch 1953 and 1956 Constitutional Reforms "Towards" Europe'. *Contemporary European History* 21 (3): 357–374.

Leeuwen, Karin van. 2013. *Uit het spoor van Thorbecke: Grondwetsherziening en staatsvernieuwing in naoorlogs Nederland*. Amsterdam: Boom.

Leeuwen, Karin van. 2014. *The Perspective of a Pioneer: The Early Dutch Reception of Costa/ENEL*. Unpublished paper presented at the Costa/ENEL symposium, University of Amsterdam, June 2014.

Leeuwen, Karin van, 2017. 'Inbraak in "sprookjesland". Het Europees recht en de politieke strijd rondom de commercialisering van de Nederlandse televisie'. *Tijdschrift voor Geschiedenis* 130.

Leeuwen, Karin van. 2018. 'Paving the Road to "Legal Revolution": The Dutch Origins of the First Preliminary References in European Law (1957–1963)'. *European Law Journal* 24 (6): 408–421.

Leeuwen, Karin van. 2019. 'The Legal Service'. In *The European Commission 1986–2000: History and Memories of an Institution*, 129–134. Luxembourg: Publications Office of the European Union.

Leeuwen, Karin van. 2024. 'Ordering Through Competition Law? Pieter VerLoren van Themaat and Social Democratic Thinking About Competition in the Early Postwar Netherlands'. In *Social Democracy and Cartels, Concentrations, and Competition in Europe*, edited by Brian Shaev and Sigfrido Ramirez Perez. London: Routledge.

Lequesne, Christian. 2015. 'France and the European Union: A Story of Reason Rather Than Love'. *NUPI Policy Brief* 5. Oslo: Norwegian Institute of International Affairs.

Leucht, Brigitte. 2008. *Transatlantic Policy Networks and the Formation of Core Europe*. Unpublished PhD dissertation, University of Portsmouth.

Leucht, Brigitte. 2013. 'American Influences on EEC Competition Law: A Belated Europeanization Through Convergence?' In *The Historical Foundations of EU Competition Law*, edited by Kiran K. Patel and Heike Schweitzer, 125–162. Oxford: Oxford University Press.

Leucht, Brigitte. 2017. 'The Policy Origins of the European Economic Constitution'. *European Law Journal* 24: 191–205.

Leucht, Brigitte, and Mel Marquis. 2013. 'American Influences on EEC Competition Law: A Belated Europeanization Through Convergence?' In *The Historical Foundations of EU Competition Law*, edited by Kiran K. Patel and Heike Schweitzer, 125–162. Oxford: Oxford University Press.

Liber Amicorum en l'honneur de Gregorio Garzón Clariana, le Jurisconsulte du Parlement Européen: au service du droit Communautaire. 2006. Luxembourg: OPOCE.

Lindseth, Peter L. 2010. *Power and Legitimacy: Reconciling Europe and the Nation-State*. New York: Oxford University Press.

Lindseth, Peter L. 2016. 'The Perils of "As If" European Constitutionalism'. *European Law Journal* 22 (5): 696–718.

Lipgens, Walter, ed. 1985. *Documents on European Integration*, Vol. 1. Berlin and New York: De Gruyter.

Lipgens, Walter, ed. 1986. *Documents on European Integration*, Vol. 2. Berlin and New York: De Gruyter.

Lipgens, Walter, and Wilfred Loth, eds. 1988. *Documents on European Integration*, Vol. 3. Berlin: De Gruyter.

Lipgens, Walter, and Wilfred Loth, eds. 1991. *Documents on European Integration*, Vol. 4. Berlin: De Gruyter.

Loth, Wilfried. 1991. 'De Gaulle und Europa: Eine Revision'. *Historische Zeitschrift* 253: 629–660.

Loth, Wilfried. 1995. 'Hallstein und de Gaulle: Die verhängnisvolle Konfrontation'. In *Walter Hallstein – Der vergessene Europäer?*, edited by Wilfried Loth, William Wallace and Wolfgang Wessels, 171–188. Bonn: Europa-Union-Verlag.

Loth, Wilfried. 2013. 'Negotiating the Maastricht Treaty'. *Journal of European Integration History* 19 (1): 67–85.

Loth, Wilfried. 2015. *Building Europe: A History of European Unification*. Berlin: De Gruyter Oldenbourg, 36–52.

Loth, Wilfried, William Wallace and Wolfgang Wessels, eds. 1995. *Walter Hallstein – Der vergessene Europäer?* Bonn: Europa-Union-Verlag.

Lucas, Hans-Dieter. 1992. *Europa vom Atlantik bis zum Ural? Europapolitik und Europadenken im Frankreich der Ära de Gaulle (1958–1969)*. Bonn: Bouvier.

Ludlow, N. Piers. 1999. 'Challenging French Leadership in Europe: Germany, Italy, the Netherlands and the Outbreak of the Empty Chair Crisis of 1965–1966'. *Contemporary European History* 8 (2): 231–248.

Ludlow, N. Piers. 2001. 'The Eclipse of the Extremes: Demythologising the Luxembourg Compromise'. In *Crises and Compromises: The European Project 1963–1969*, edited by Wilfried Loth, 247–264. Baden-Baden: Nomos.

Ludlow, N. Piers. 2005. 'A Controlled Experiment'. In *Les administrations nationales et la construction européenne: Une approche historique (1919–1975)*, edited by Laurence Badel, Stanislas Jeannesson and Piers N. Ludlow, 337–356. Brussels: Euroclio.

Ludlow, N. Piers. 2006a. *The European Community and the Crises of the 1960s: Negotiating the Gaullist Challenge*. London: Routledge.

Ludlow, N. Piers. 2006b. 'Crises of the 1960s'. In *Visions, Votes and Vetoes: The Empty Chair Crisis and the Luxembourg Compromise Forty Years On*, edited by Jean-Marie Palayret, Helen Wallace and Pascaline Winand. Brussels: P.I.E.-Peter Lang.

Ludlow, N. Piers. 2008. 'The European Commission and the Rise of COREPER: A Controlled Experiment'. In *The History of the European Union: Origins of a Trans- and Supranational Polity 1950–1972*, edited by Wolfram Kaiser, Brigitte Leucht and Morten Rasmussen, 189–205. New York: Routledge.

Ludlow, N. Piers. 2010. 'Governing Europe: Charting the Development of a Supranational Political System'. In *European Union History: Themes and Debates*, edited by Wolfram Kaiser and Antonio Varsori, 109–127. London: Palgrave Macmillan.

Ludlow, N. Piers. 2013. 'European Integration in the 1980s: On the Way to Maastricht?' *Journal of European Integration History* 19 (1): 11–23.

Ludlow, N. Piers. 2015. 'Jacques Delors (1985–1995): Navigating the European Stream at Full Flood'. In *An Impossible Job? The Presidents of the European Commission 1958–2014*, edited by Jan van der Harst and Gerrit Voerman. 173–196. London: John Harper Publishing.

Ludlow, N. Piers. 2016. *Roy Jenkins and the European Commission Presidency, 1976–1980: At the Heart of Europe*. London: Palgrave Macmillan.

Lynch, Frances. 1997. *A History of the French Economy: From Vichy to Rome, 1944–1958*. London: Routledge.

Maas, H.H., and Bentvelsen, C. W. J., 1978. 'De tijdige uitvoering van EEG-richtlijnen in Nederland'. *Bestuurswetenschappen* 32: 443–453.

Madsen, Mikael Rask, Henrik Palmer Olsen and Urska Sadl. 2017. 'Competing Supremacies and Clashing Institutional Rationalities: The Danish Supreme Court's Decision in the Ajos Case and the National Limits of Judicial Cooperation'. *European Law Journal* 23 (1–2): 140–150.

Maestripieri, Cesare. 1975. 'National Case Law'. *Common Market Law Review* 12: 431–442.

Maidani, Damien. 2004. 'Le juge et l'ami.' In *Hommage à Fernand Grévisse*, edited by Louise Cadoux and Roger Errera, 108–113. Paris: La Documentation Française.

Mancini, G. Frederico. 1989. 'The Making of a Constitution for Europe'. *Common Market Law Review* 26: 595–614.

Mangenot, Michel. 2000. *Une Europe improbable: Les hauts fonctionnaires français dans la construction européenne, 1948–1992*. Unpublished doctoral dissertation, University of Strasbourg.

Mangenot, Michel. 2004. 'Le Conseil d'État et l'institutionnalisation du système juridique communautaire'. Intervention au colloque CRPS-CURAPP/Groupe Polilexes, *Les juristes et la construction d'un ordre politique européen*.

Mangenot, Michel, ed. 2023. 'Un légiste de Vichy à la Communauté européenne Maurice Lagrange: une biographie professionnelle'. *Civitas Europa* 1 (50) (Special issue).

Mangold, Anna Katharina. 2011. *Gemeinschaftsrecht und deutsches Recht: Die Europäisierung der deutschen Rechtsordnung in historisch-empirischer Sicht*. Tübingen: Mohr Siebeck.

Mann, Clarence. 1972. *The Function of Judicial Decision in European Economic Integration*. The Hague: Martinus Nijhoff Publishers.

Martinsen, Dorte S. 2007. 'The Europeanisation of Gender Equality: Who Controls the Scope of Non-Discrimination?' *Journal of European Public Policy* 14 (4): 544–553.

Martinsen, Dorte S. 2015. *An Ever More Powerful Court? The Political Constraints of Legal Integration in the European Union*. Oxford: Oxford University Press.

Marzocchi, Ottavio. 2018. *The Protection of Fundamental Rights in the EU*. Brussels: European Parliament. www.europarl.europa.eu/factsheets/en/sheet/146/the-protection-of-fundamental-rights-in-the-eu.

McNaughton, Anne. 2017. 'Acts of Creation: The ERTA Decision as a Foundation Stone of the EU Legal System'. In *EU Law Stories: Constitutional and Critical Histories of European Jurisprudence*, edited by Fernanda Nicola and Bill Davies, 134–154. Cambridge: Cambridge University Press.

Meij, A. W. H. 1999. 'Europese rechtspraak in de Nederlandse rechtspleging: Impressies uit Den Haag en Luxemburg'. In *Internationale rechtspraak in de Nederlandse rechtsorde*, 135–221. Deventer: W. E. J. Tjeenk Willink.

Melchionni, Maria Grazia. 2007. *Roberto Ducci: La genèse des Traites de Rome*. Lausanne: Jean Monnet Foundation.

Meuwissen, D. H. M. 1965. 'Enige opmerkingen over de plaats van het internationale recht in de nationale rechtsorde'. *Nederlands Juristenblad* (1965) 3, 57–66.

Meyer, Jan-Henrik. 2011. 'Green Activism: The European Parliament's Environmental Committee Promoting a European Environmental Policy in the 1970s.' *Journal of European Integration History* 17 (1): 73–85.

Meyer, Jan-Henrik. 2014. 'Getting Started: Agenda-Setting in European Environmental Policy in the 1970s'. In *The Institutions and Dynamics of the European Community, 1973–1983*, edited by Johnny Laursen, 221–242. Baden-Baden: Nomos.

Meyer, Jan-Henrik. 2017. 'Making the Polluter Pay: How the European Communities Established Environmental Protection'. In *International Organizations and Environmental Protection: Conservation and Globalization in the Twentieth Century*, edited by Wolfram Kaiser and Jan-Henrik Meyer, 182–210. New York: Berghahn Books.

Meyer, Jan-Henrik. 2020. 'Responding to the European Public? Public Debates, Societal Actors and the Emergence of a European Environmental Policy'. In *The Environment and European Public Sphere: Perception, Actors, Policies*, edited by Christian Wenkel, Eric Bussière, Anahita Grisono, and Hélène Miard-Delacroix, 221–240. Winwick: White Horse Press.

Meyer, Jan-Henrik. 2021. 'Pushing for a Greener Europe: The European Parliament and Environmental Policy in the 1970s and 1980s'. *Journal of European Integration History* 27 (1): 57–77.

Meyer, Jan-Henrik, and Wolfram Kaiser, eds. 2016. *International Organizations and Environmental Protection: Conservation and Globalization in the Twentieth Century*. London: Berghahn Books.

Middlelaar, Luuk van. 2013. *The Passage of Europe*. New Haven: Yale University Press.

Miller, Jeffrey. 2019. 'Explaining Paradigm Shifts in Danish Anti-Discrimination Law'. *Maastricht Journal of European and Comparative Law* 26 (4): 540–557.

Milward, Alan S. 1984. *The Reconstruction of Western Europe, 1945–1951*. London: Routledge.

Milward, Alan S. 1992. *The European Rescue of the Nation State*. London: Routledge.

Milward, Alan S., ed. 1993. *The Frontier of National Sovereignty*. London: Routledge.

Mok, M. R. 1961. 'Van Kolynos tot KIM-Sieverding'. *Sociaal-Economische Wetgeving* 9: 98–100.

Monaco, Riccardo. 1963. 'I principi di interpretazione seguiti dalla corte di giustizia delle comunità europee'. *Rivista di diritto europeo* 3 (1): 3–13.

Mosler, Hermann. 1968. 'Begriff und Gegenstand des Europarechts'. *Zeitschrift für ausländisches öffentliches Recht und Völkerrecht* 28: 481–502.

Mourlon-Druol, Emmanuel. 2010. 'The Victory of the Intergovernmental Method? The Emergence of the European Council in the EEC's Institutional Set-up, 1974–1977'. In *The Road Europe Travelled Along: The Evolution of EEC/EU Institutions and Policies*, edited by Daniela Preda and Daniele Pasquinucci, 27–40. Brussels: Peter Lang.

Mourlon-Druol, Emmanuel. 2012a. *A Europe Made of Money: The Emergence of the European Monetary System*. Ithaca: Cornell University Press.

Mourlon-Druol, Emmanuel. 2012b. 'Regional Integration and Global Governance: The Example of the European Council 1974–1986'. *Les Cahiers IRICE* 1: 91–104.

Mourlon-Druol, Emmanuel. 2016. 'Steering Europe: Explaining the Rise of the European Council, 1975–1986'. *Contemporary European History* 25 (3): 409–437.

Mourlon-Druol, Emmanuel, and Federico Romero, eds. 2014. *International Summitry and Global Governance: The Rise of the G7 and the European Council, 1974–1991*. London: Routledge.

Moyn, Samuel. 2010. *The Last Utopia: Human Rights in History*. Cambridge: Cambridge University Press.

Mura, Alvatore. 2017. *Antonio Segni: La politica e le istituzioni*. Bologna: Il Mulino.

Nairn, Tom. 1977. *The Break-Up of Britain: Crisis and Neo-Nationalism*. London: NLB.

Narjes, Karl-Heinz. 1995. 'Walter Hallstein in der Frühphase der EWG'. In *Walter Hallstein: Der vergessene Europäer?*, edited by Wilfried Loth, William Wallace and Wolfgang Wessels, 139–163. Bonn: Europa-Union-Verlag.

Newhouse, John. 1967. *Collision in Brussels: The Common Market Crisis of 30 June 1965*. New York: Norton.

Nicola, Fernanda, and Bill Davies, eds. 2017. *EU Law Stories*. Cambridge: Cambridge University Press.

Nicoll, William. 1984. 'The Luxembourg Compromise'. *Journal of Common Market Studies* 23: 35–43.

Noel, Émile. 1995. 'Walter Hallstein: Ein persönliches Zeugnis'. In *Walter Hallstein: Der vergessene Europäer?*, edited by Wilfried Loth, William Wallace and Wolfgang Wessels, 165–169. Bonn: Europa-Union-Verlag.

Nussbaum, Arthur. 1947. *A Concise History of Law of Nations*. London: MacMillan.

Olesen, Niels Wium. 2019. *Poul Schlüters tid: De danske ministerier 1972–1993*. Copenhagen: Gad.

Olesen, Thorsten B. 2018. *Anker Jørgensens tid*, 1972–1982. Copenhagen: Gad.

Olesen, Thorsten B., and Poul Villaume. 2006. *I blokopdelingens tegn: 1945–1972*. Copenhagen: Danmarks Nationalleksikon.

Olmi, Giancarlo. 1983. 'Introduzione'. In *Trent'anni di diritto comunitario*, edited by Commissione delle Comunità Europee, 1–17. Luxembourg: OPOCE.

Ophüls, Carl-Friedrich. 1951. 'Juristische Grundgedanken des Schumanplans'. *Neue Juristische Wochenschrift* 4 (8): 289–291.

Palayret, Jean-Marie, Helen Wallace, and Pascaline Winand, eds. 2006. *Visions, Votes and Vetoes: The Empty Chair Crisis and the Luxembourg Compromise Forty Years On*. Brussels: P.I.E.-Peter Lang.

Palayret, Jean-Marie. 1996. 'A University For Europe: Prehistory of the European University Institute of Florence (1948–1976)'. Florence: Presidency of the Council of Ministers, Dept. of Information and Pub.

Panhuys, H. F. van. 1953. 'The Netherlands Constitution and International Law'. *American Journal of International Law* 47: 537–558.

Panhuys, H. F. van. 1955. 'Preadvies'. *Mededelingen van de Nederlandse Vereniging voor Internationaal Recht* 34: 1–56.

Panhuys, H. F. van. 1966. 'De verhouding tussen het volkenrecht, het Gemeenschapsrecht en het recht der lid-staten in het licht van het mandaat van rechters.' In *De rechtsorde der Europese gemeenschappen tussen het internationale en het nationale recht*, edited by H. F. van Panhuys, A. M. Donner, and P. J. G. Kapteyn, 13–36. Deventer: Kluwer.

Parson, Craig. 2003. *A Certain Idea of Europe*. Ithaca: Cornell University Press.

Patel, Kiran K. 2013b. 'Provincialising European Union: Co-operation and Integration in Europe in a Historical Perspective'. *Contemporary European History* 22 (4): 649–673.

Patel, Kiran K. 2020. *Project Europe: A History*. Cambridge: Cambridge University Press.

Patel, Kiran K., and Christian Salm. 2021. 'The European Parliament During the 1970s and 1980s: An Institution on the Rise?' *Journal of European Integration History* 27 (1): 5–19.

Patel, Kiran K., ed. 2009. *Fertile Ground for Europe? The History of European Integration and the Common Agricultural Policy Since 1945*. Baden-Baden: Nomos.

Patel, Kiran K., ed. 2013a. *The Cultural Politics of Europe: European Capitals of Culture and European Union Since the 1980s*. London: Routledge.

Patijn, S., 1967. 'De communautaire rechtsorde en het beleid van de minister van Buitenlandse Zaken II'. *Nederlands Juristenblad* 42: 926–929.

Pavone, Tommaso. 2018. 'Revisiting Judicial Empowerment in the European Union: Limits of Empowerment, Logics of Resistance'. *Journal of Law and Courts* 6 (2): 303–331.

Pavone, Tommaso. 2022. *The Ghostwriters. Lawyers and the Politics behind the Judicial Construction of Europe*. Cambridge: Cambridge University Press.

Payk, Marcus. 2018. *Frieden durch Recht? Der Austieg des modernen Völkerrechts und der Friedenschluss nac dem Ersten Weltkrieg*. Berlin: Walter De Gruyter.

Pedersen, Jonas Langeland. 2016. *Constructive Defiance? Denmark and the Effects of European Law, 1973–1993*. PhD diss., Aarhus University.

Pérez, Sigfrido M. Ramírez. 2014. 'Le Service Juridique'. In *La Commission Européenne: 1973-1986: Histoire et mémoires d'une institution*, edited by Vincent Dujardin, Eric Bussière, Piers Ludlow et al., 117–123. Luxembourg: OPOCE.

Perillo, Ezio and Alberto Trabucchi. 2024. 'The Defender of the European Citizens' Rights and the Van Gend & Loos Ruling of the Court of Justice'. In *The Italian Influence on European Law. Judges and Advocates General (1952–2000)*, edited by Danielle Gallo, Roberto Mastroianni, Fernanda G. Nicola and Lorenzo Cecchetti. Oxford: Hart Publishing.

Pernice, Ingolf. 2003. 'Begründung und Konsolidierung der Europäischen Gemeinschaft als Rechtsgemeinschaft'. In *Der Beitrag Walter Hallsteins zur Zukunft Europas. Referate zu Ehren Walter Hallsteins*, edited by Manfred Zuleeg, 56–70. Baden-Baden: Nomos.

Pescatore, Pierre. 1965. 'La Cour en tant que juridiction fédérale et constitutionnelle'. In *Zehn Jahre Rechtsprechung des Gerichtshofs der Europäischen Gemeinschaften, Kölner Kongress vom 24.–26. April 1963*, edited by Europäische Arbeitstagung, Universität zu Köln Institut für das Recht der Europäischen Gemeinschaften,520–553. Cologne: Heymann.

Pescatore, Pierre. 1982. 'Les Travaux du "Groupe Juridique" dans la Négociation des Traités de Rome'. *Hémecht* 34 (2): 145–161.

Petersen, Nikolaj. 2004. *Europæisk og Globalt Engagement, 1973–2003*. Copenhagen: Gyldendal.

Phelan, William. 2016. 'Supremacy, Direct Effect, and Dairy Products in the Early History of European Law'. *International Journal of Constitutional Law* 14: 6–25.

Phelan, William. 2017. 'The Revolutionary Doctrines of European Law and the Legal Philosophy of Robert Lecourt'. *European Journal of International Law* 28: 935–957.

Phelan, William. 2019. *Great Judgments of the European Court of Justice: Rethinking the Landmark Decisions of the Foundational Period*. Cambridge: Cambridge University Press.

Phelan William. 2024. 'The Promise of Judicial Biography for the Study of the European Court of Justice'. In *Interdisciplinary Research Methods in EU Law*, edited by Deplano Rossana, Gentile Giulia, Lonardo Luigi, and Nowak Tobias, 59–74. Cheltenham: Edward Elgar.

Plötner, Jens. 1998. 'Report on France'. In *The European Courts and National Courts – Doctrine and Jurisprudence*, edited by Anne-Marie Slaughter, Alec Stone Sweet, and J. H. H. Weiler, 41–75. Oxford: Hart Publishing.

Poehls, Kerstin. 2009. *Europa Backstage: Expertenwissen, Habitus und kulturelle Codes im Machtfeld der EU*. Bielefeld: Transcript.

Polak, C. H. F. 1960. 'Het recht der Europese Economische Gemeenschap'. *Advocatenblad* 40: 349–362.

Pollack, Mark A. 1997. 'Delegation, Agency, and Agenda Setting in the European Community'. *International Organization* 51 (1): 99–134.

Pollack, Mark A. 2013. 'The New EU Legal History: What's New, What's Missing?' *American University International Law Review* 28 (5): 1257–1310.

Pot, C. W. van der. 1952. 'De grondwetsherziening 1952 II'. *Nederlands Juristenblad* 27 (13): 29–39.

Pot, C. W. van der, and B.M. Telders. 1937. 'Verslag eerste zitting'. *Handelingen NJV* 67, 1: 1–97.

Prechal, Sacha. 2005. *Directives in EC Law*. Oxford: Oxford University Press.

Priemel, Kim Christian. 2016. *The Betrayal: The Nuremberg Trials and German Divergence*. Oxford: Oxford University Press.

Ramírez Pérez, Sigfrido M. 2016a. 'Entrevista a Gregorio Garzón Clariana, 14-09-2015'. *Studia Storica: Historia Contemporanea* 34: 191–211.

Ramírez Pérez, Sigfrido M. 2016b. 'Le principe fédéral à l'épreuve de l'histoire de l'intégration européenne. Un succès paradoxal'. *Politique Européenne* 3: 110–129.

Ramírez Pérez, Sigfrido M. and Sebastian van der Scheur. 2013. 'The Evolution of the Law on Articles 85 and 86 EEC: Ordoliberalism and Its Keynesian Challenge'. In *The Historical Foundations of EU Competition Law*, edited by Kiran K. Patel and Heike Schweitzer, 19–54. Oxford: Oxford University Press.

Rasmussen, Hjalte. 1982. 'Denmark in Face of Her Community Obligations'. *Common Market Law Review* 19 (4): 601–624.

Rasmussen, Hjalte. 1986. *On Law and Policy in the European Court of Justice: A Comparative Study in Judicial Policymaking*. Dordrecht: Martinus Nijhoff.

Rasmussen, Morten. 2004. *Joining the European Communities: Denmark's Road to EC-Membership, 1961–1973*. Unpublished PhD dissertation, European University Institute.

Rasmussen, Morten. 2005. 'The Hesitant European: History of Denmark's Accession to the European Communities 1970–1973'. *Journal of European Integration History* 11 (2): 47–74.

Rasmussen, Morten. 2007. 'State Power and the Acquis Communautaire in the European Community of the Early 1970s'. In *Beyond the Customs Union: The European Community's Quest for Deepening, Widening and Completion, 1969–1975*, edited by Jan van der Harst, 359–376. Brussels: Bruylant.

Rasmussen, Morten. 2008. 'Origins of a Legal Revolution: The Early History of the European Court of Justice'. *Journal of European Integration History* 14 (2): 77–98.

Rasmussen, Morten. 2010a. 'From Costa v. ENEL to the Treaties of Rome: A Brief History of a Legal Revolution'. In *The Past and Future of EU Law: The Classics of EU Law Revisited*

on the 50th Anniversary of the Rome Treaty, edited by Miguel Maduro and Loïc Azoulai, 69–85. London: Hart Publishing.
Rasmussen, Morten. 2010b. 'Constructing and Deconstructing "Constitutional" European Law: Some Reflections on How to Study the History of European Law'. In *Europe. The New Legal Realism*, edited by Henning Koch, Karsten Hagel-Sørensen, Ulrich Haltern and Joseph H. H. Weiler. 639–660. Copenhagen: DJØF Publishing.
Rasmussen, Morten. 2011a. 'How to Defend Danish Agricultural Exports: The Dark Side of European Regionalism in the 1960s'. In *Multilateralism and the Trente Glorieuses in Europe*, edited by Regine Peron and Guido Thiemeyer, 119–137. Paris: Editions Alphil-Presses Universitaires Suisses & Editions Delibreo.
Rasmussen, Morten. 2011b. 'Review of *Power and Legitimacy: Reconciling Europe and the Nation-State* by Peter Lindseth'. *Journal of European Integration History* 17 (1): 138–142.
Rasmussen, Morten. 2012. 'Establishing a Constitutional Practice of European Law: The History of the Legal Service of the European Executive, 1952–1965'. *Contemporary European History* 21 (3): 375–397.
Rasmussen, Morten. 2013a. 'Establishing a Constitutional Practice: The Role of the European Law Associations'. In *Societal Actors in European Integration: Polity-Building and Policy-Making, 1958–1992*, edited by Wolfram Kaiser and Jan-Henrik Meyer, 173–197. London: Palgrave Macmillan.
Rasmussen, Morten. 2013b. 'Rewriting the History of European Public Law: The New Contribution of Historians'. *American University International Law Review* 28 (5): 1187–1221.
Rasmussen, Morten. 2014. 'Revolutionizing European Law: A History of the Van Gend en Loos Judgment'. *International Journal of Constitutional Law* 12 (1): 136–163.
Rasmussen, Morten. 2017. 'How to Enforce European Law: A New History of the Battle over the Direct Effect of Directives, 1958–1987'. *European Law Journal* 23 (3–4): 290–308.
Rasmussen, Morten. 2019b. 'From International Law to a Constitutional Dream? The History of European Law and the European Court of Justice, 1950 to 1993'. In *The Dream of International Courts: A History*, edited by Ignacio de la Rasilla y del Moral and Jorge E. Vinuales, 287–312. Cambridge: Cambridge University Press.
Rasmussen, Morten. 2021a. 'Agents of Constitutionalism: The Quest for a Constitutional Breakthrough in European Law, 1945–1964'. In *Crafting the International Order: Practitioners and Practices of International Law Since c. 1800*, edited by Marcus Payk and Kim Christian Priemel, 249–276. Oxford: Oxford University Press.
Rasmussen, Morten. 2021b. 'Towards a Legal History of European Law'. *European Papers* 6 (2): 2–8.
Rasmussen, Morten. 2022. 'History and International Law: A Reappraisal of a Difficult Relationship'. *Temple Journal of International Law* 36 (2): 37–52.
Rasmussen, Morten. 2023. 'Between Constraints and Innovation: The Role of the Groupe de Rédaction and the Legal Shape of the EEC Treaty'. *Jean Monnet Working Paper*, Jean Monnet Center for International and Regional Economic Law & Justice, New York School of Law.
Rasmussen, Morten, and Dorte Sindbjerg Martinsen. 2019. 'EU Constitutionalisation Revisited: Redressing a Central Assumption in European Studies'. *European Law Journal* 25 (3): 251–272.
Reuter, Paul. 1968. *Droit international public*. Paris: PUF.
Riphagen, Willem. 1955. *De juridische structuur der Europese Gemeenschap voor Kolen en Staal*. Leiden: Universitaire Pers.
Risse, Thomas. 2009. 'Social Constructivism and European Integration'. In *European Integration Theory*, edited by Antje Wiener and Thomas Diez, 144–160. Oxford: Oxford University Press.

Rittberger, Berthold. 2007. *Building Europe's Parliament*. Oxford: Oxford University Press.
Rittberger, Berthold. 2009. 'The Historical Origins of the EU's System of Representation'. *Journal of European Public Policy* 16 (1): 43–61.
Roellecke, Gerd. 2003. 'Karlsruhe'. In *Deutsche Erinnerungsorte II*, edited by Etienne François and Hagen Schulze, 549–566. Munich: C. H. Beck.
Roos, Mechthild. 2020. 'Becoming Europe's Parliament: Europeanization Through MEPs' Supranational Activism, 1952–1979'. *Journal of Common Market Studies* 58 (6): 1413–1432.
Ross, Alf. 1972. *Juristen* 1972: 161–165.
Roussell, Eric. 2002. *Charles de Gaulle*. Paris: Gallimard.
Rupp, Hans Heinrich. 1970. 'Die Grundrechte und das Europäische Gemeinschaftsrecht'. *Neue Juristische Wochenschrift* 9: 953–959.
Sabatier, Paul A. 1998. 'The Advocacy Coalition Framework: Revisions and Relevance for Europe'. *Journal of European Public Policy* 5 (1): 98–130.
Sacriste, Guillaume. 2012. 'L'Europe est-elle un état comme les autres? Retour sur la distinction public/privée au sein de la commission juridique du Parlement européen des années 1960'. *Cultures et Conflits* 85/86: 35–60.
Salomonson, F. 1961. 'Het colloquium over Europees recht te Brussel'. *Sociaal-Economische Wetgeving* 9 (1): 228–230.
Salomonson, F. 1967. 'De communautaire rechtsorde en het beleid van de minister van Buitenlandse Zaken'. *Nederlands Juristenblad* 42: 431–433.
Samkalden, I. 1955. 'Over de juridische structuur van de Kolen- en Staalgemeenschap'. *Nederlands Juristenblad* 36: 813–820.
Samkalden, I. 1957. 'De Europese integratie als vraagstuk van nationale wetgeving'. *Netherlands International Law Review* 4 (2): 121–132.
Samkalden, I. 1960. 'Het recht van de Europese Gemeenschappen en zijn betekenis voor de balie'. *Advocatenblad* 40: 334–348.
Samkalden, I. 1964. 'Verslag van de Algemene Ledenvergadering d.d. 14 maart 1964'. *Mededelingen van de Nederlandse Vereniging voor Internationaal Recht* 50.
Samkalden, I. 1966. 'De uitlegging van het gemeenschapsrecht'. In *De rechtsorde der Europese gemeenschappen tussen het internationale en het nationale recht*, edited by H. F. van Panhuys, A. M. Donner, and P. J. G. Kapteyn, 161–174. Deventer: Kluwer.
Scheingold, Stuart A. 1965. *The Rule of Law in European Integration*. New Haven: Yale University Press.
Schemers, Henry. 1990. 'The Scales in Balance: National Constitutional Court v. Court of Justice'. *Common Market Law Review* 27: 97–105.
Schepel, Harm, and Rein Wesseling. 1997. 'The Legal Community: Judges, Lawyers, Officials and Clerks in the Writing of Europe'. *European Law Journal* 3 (2): 164–188.
Schmidt, Susanne K. 2018. *The European Court of Justice and the Policy Process: The Shadow of Case Law*. Oxford: Oxford University Press.
Schmutzer, A. K. M. 1966. 'Débats du Parlement européen de juin 1965: Primauté du droit communautaire et harmonisation des législations nationales'. *Revue internationale de droit comparé* 18 (1): 93–120.
Schorkopf, Frank. 2019. 'Robert Krawielicki (1905–1966): Arbeit am Schmelztiegel eines allgemeinen europäischen Rechts'. *Jahrbuch des öffentlichen Rechts* 67: 553–566.
Schorkopf, Frank. 2023. *Die unentschiedene Macht: Verfassungsgeschichte der Europäischen Union, 1948–2007*. Göttingen: Vandenhoeck & Ruprecht.
Schütze, Robert. 2018. 'Re-reading Dassonville: Meaning and Understanding in the History of European Law'. *European Law Journal* 24 (4): 376–407.

Schwartz, Joan M., and Terry Cook. 2002. 'Archives, Records, and Power: The Making of Modern Memory'. *Archival Science* 2: 1–19.

Segers, Mathieu. 2013. *Reis naar het continent: Nederland en Europese integratie, 1950 tot heden*. Amsterdam: Bert Bakker.

Segni, Antonio. 1961. 'Norme Communitarie'. *Rivista di diritto europeo* 1 (3): 363–366.

Seidel, Katja. 2010. *The Process of Politics in Europe: The Rise of European Elites and Supranational Institutions*. London: I.B. Tauris.

Shaev, Brian and Sigfrido M. Ramírez Pérez. 2024. *The Development of European Competition Policy: Social Democracy and Regulation*. Abingdon: Routledge.

Siesby, Erik. 1971. 'EF og Danmarks grundlov'. *Juristen* 53 (9): 414–427.

Siesby, Erik. 1972. 'EF's "Supremacy Clause" og grundlovens § 20'. *Juristen* 54: 129–132, 220–221.

Snyder, Sarah B. 2011. *Human Rights Activism and the End of the Cold War: A Transnational History of the Helsinki Network*. Cambridge: Cambridge University Press.

Spierenburg, Dirk, and Raymond Poidevin. 1994. *The History of the High Authority of the European Coal and Steel Community: Supranationality in Operation*. London: Weidenfeld and Nicolson.

Spiermann, Ole. 2008. 'Grundlovens §20 og det danske medlemskab'. In *Europæiseringen af dansk ret*, edited by Birgitte Egelund Olsen and Karsten Engsig Sørensen, 41. Copenhagen: Jurist- og Økonomforbundets Forlag.

Stein, Eric, and Peter Hay. 1960. 'New Legal Remedies of Enterprises'. *American Journal of Comparative Law* 9: 375–424.

Stein, Eric, and Terrance Sandelow. 1982. *Courts and Markets: Perspectives from the United States and Europe*, Vols. 1–2. Oxford: Oxford University Press.

Stein, Eric. 1959. 'The European Parliamentary Assembly: Techniques of Emerging "Political Control"'. *International Organization* 13 (2): 233–254.

Stein, Eric. 1965. 'Towards Supremacy of Treaty-Constitution by Judicial Fiat: On the Margin of the Costa Case'. *Michigan Law Review* 63 (3): 491–518.

Stein, Eric. 1978. 'The Emerging European Constitution'. *Proceedings of the Annual Meeting (American Society of International Law)*: 166.

Stein, Eric. 1981. 'Lawyers, Judges and the Making of a Transnational Constitution'. *American Journal of International Law* 75 (1): 1–27.

Steinberg, Rudolf. 2003. 'Grußwort des Präsidenten Professor Dr. Rudolf Steinberg anlässlich des Festaktes im Rahmen des Walter-Hallstein-Symposiums, am 16. November 2001 im Kaisersaal, Rathaus Römer'. In *Der Beitrag Walter Hallsteins zur Zukunft Europas: Referate zu Ehren Walter Hallsteins*, edited by Manfred Zuleeg, 104–109. Baden-Baden: Nomos.

Streinz, Rudolf. 1984. *Die Luxemburger Vereinbarung: Rechtliche und politische Aspekte der Abstimmungspraxis im Rat der Europäischen Gemeinschaften seit der Luxemburger Vereinbarung vom 29. Januar 1966*. Munich: Beck.

Sweet, Alec Stone, and Thomas L. Brunell. 1998. 'Constructing a Supranational Constitution: Dispute Resolution and Governance in the European Community'. *American Political Science Review* 92 (1): 63–81.

Sweet, Alec Stone, and Thomas L. Brunell. 2004. 'Constructing a Supranational Constitution'. In *The Judicial Construction of Europe*, edited by Alec Stone Sweet, 45–108. Oxford: Oxford University Press.

Sweet, Alec Stone. 2000. *Governing with Judges: Constitutional Politics in Europe*. Oxford: Oxford University Press.

Sweet, Alec Stone. 2004. *The Judicial Construction of Europe*. Oxford: Oxford University Press.

Sørensen, Max. 1971. 'Forfatningsretslige problemer i forbindelse med Danmarks indtræden i De Europæiske Fællesskaber'. *Juristen* 53 (9): 434–440.

Sørensen, Max. 1972. 'Danmarks tilslutning til de Europæiske Fællesskaber: Forfatningsretlige problemer'. *Juristen* 54 (3): 117–129.

Tallon, Denis, and Hélène Gaudemet-Tallon. 1971. 'Observations'. *Cahiers de droit européen* 7 (3): 363.

Tammes, A. J. P. 1966. 'De bronnen van het Gemeenschapsrecht'. In *De rechtsorde der Europese gemeenschappen tussen het internationale en het nationale recht*, edited by H. F. van Panhuys, A. M. Donner, and P. J. G. Kapteyn, 103–114. Deventer: Kluwer.

Teasdale, Anthony. 1993. 'The Life and Death of the Luxembourg Compromise'. *Journal of Common Market Studies* 31 (4): 567–579.

Thiele, Martin. 2019. *Motor der Integration*. Tübingen: Mohr Siebeck.

Togeby, Lise, Jørgen Goul Andersen, Peter Munk Christiansen, Torben Beck Jørgensen, and Signild Vallgårda, eds. 2004. *Magt og Demokrati i Danmark: Hovedresultater fra Magtudredningen*. Aarhus: Aarhus Universitetsforlag.

Tomuschat, Christian. 1990. 'Alle guten Dinge sind III? Zur Diskussion um die Solange-Rechtsprechung des BVerfG'. *Europarecht* 25 (4): 340–361.

Tromm, J. J. M. 1981. 'De Nederlandse jurisprudentie inzake het recht der Europese Gemeenschappen: Overzicht van de periode 1973–1977'. *Sociaal-Economische Wetgeving* 29: 461–482.

Tuori, Klaus. 2015. *European Constitutionalism*. Cambridge: Cambridge University Press.

Tynell, Jesper. 2014. *Mørkelygten*. Copenhagen: Samfundslitteratur.

Vaisse, Maurice. 1995. 'Changement et continuité dans la politique européenne de la France'. In *Georges Pompidou et l'Europe, Actes du colloque du 25 et 26 novembre 1993*, edited by Jean-René Bernard, François Caron, Maurice Vaïsse, and Michel Woimant, 29–43. Bruxelles: Editions Complexe.

Vaisse, Maurice. 1998. *La grandeur: Politique étrangère du général de Gaulle, 1958–1969*. Paris: Fayard.

Vauchez, Antoine. 2008a. 'The Force of a Weak Field: Law and Lawyers in the Government of the European Union (For a Renewed Research Agenda)'. *International Political Sociology* 2 (2): 128–144.

Vauchez, Antoine. 2008b. 'Integration-through-Law: Contribution to a Socio-History of EU Political Commonsense'. UI Working Paper No. RSCAS 2008/10, available at SSRN: https://ssrn.com/abstract=1260166 or http://dx.doi.org/10.2139/ssrn.1260166.

Vauchez, Antoine. 2010a. 'The Transnational Politics of Judicialization: Van Gend en Loos and the Making of EU Polity'. *European Law Journal* 16 (1): 1–28.

Vauchez, Antoine. 2010b. 'The Making of the European Union's Constitutional Foundations: The Brokering Role of Legal Entrepreneurs and Legal Networks'. In *Transnational Networks in Regional Integration: Governing Europe 1945–1983*, edited by Wolfram Kaiser, Brigitte Keucht, Michael Gehler et al., 108–128. Basingstoke: Palgrave.

Vauchez, Antoine. 2013. *L'Union par le droit: L'invention d'un programme institutionnel pour l'Europe*. Paris: Les Presses de Sciences Po.

Vauchez, Antoine. 2015. *Brokering Europe: Euro-lawyers and the Making of a Transnational Polity*. Cambridge: Cambridge University Press.

Vauchez, Antoine, and Stephanie Lee Mudge. 2012. 'Building Europe on a Weak Field: Law, Economics, and Scholarly Avatars in Transnational Politics'. *American Journal of Sociology* 118 (2): 449–492.

Veegens, D. J., et al. 1966. 'Rapport néerlandais'. In *Deuxième colloque international de droit européen, organisé par l'Association Néerlandaise pour le Droit Européen, La Haye, 24–26 oct. 1963*, 49–113. Zwolle: Tjeenk Willink.

I. W. VerLoren van Themaat, N. W. Adema, F. Rijnsbergen, J. F. Schutte and K. Sevinga. 1998. 'National Application of Community Competition Law'. *Sociaal Economische Wetgeving* 46 (1998) 4, 137–148.

VerLoren van Themaat, P. 1977. 'De Europese aspecten van de voorgestelde Wet investeringsregeling'. *Sociaal Economische Wetgeving* 25: 743–757.

Vollaard, H., and B. Boer. 2005. *Euroscepsis in Nederland*. Utrecht: Lemma.

Vollenhoven, C. van. 1932. *Scope and Content of International Law (1898)*. Leiden: E. J. Brill.

Waarden, F. van, and Y. Hildebrand. 2009. 'From Corporatism to Lawyocracy? On Liberalization and Juridification'. *Regulation & Governance* 3 (3): 259–286.

Warlouzet, Laurent. 2011a. *Le choix de la CEE par la France: L'Europe économique en débat de Mendès France à de Gaulle (1955–1969)*. Paris: CHEFF.

Warlouzet, Laurent. 2011b. 'De Gaulle as Father of Europe: The Unpredictability of the FTA's Failure and the EEC's Success (1956–1958)'. *Contemporary European History* 20 (4): 419–434.

Warlouzet, Laurent. 2017. 'The Difficult Quest to Implement Cartel Control: Grundig-Consten (1966) and Philip Morris (1987)'. In *EU Law Stories: Contextual and Critical Histories of European Jurisprudence*, edited by Fernanda Nicola and Bill Davies, 263–278. Cambridge: Cambridge University Press.

Warlouzet, Laurent. 2018. *Governing Europe in a Globalizing World: Neoliberalism and its Alternatives Following the 1973 Oil Crisis*. London: Routledge.

Warlouzet, Laurent, and Tobias Witschke. 2012. 'The Difficult Path to an Economic Rule of Law: European Competition Policy 1950–1991'. *Contemporary European History* 21 (3): 437–455.

Weiler, Joseph H. H. 1982a. *Supranational Law and the Supranational System: Legal Structure and Political Process in the European Community*. PhD diss., European University Institute.

Weiler, Joseph H. H. 1982b. 'The Community System: The Dual Character of Supranationalism'. *Yearbook of European Law* 1: 267–306.

Weiler, Joseph H. H. 1987. 'The Court of Justice on Trial: A Review of Hjalte Rasmussen's on Law and Policy in the European Court of Justice'. *Common Market Law Review* 24 (3): 555–589.

Weiler, Joseph H. H. 1991. 'The Transformation of Europe'. *Yale Law Journal* 100: 2403–2483.

Weiler, Joseph H. H. 1994. 'A Quiet Revolution: The European Court of Justice and Its Interlocutors'. *Comparative Political Studies* 26 (4): 510–534.

Weiler, Joseph H. H. 1995. 'Does Europe Need a Constitution? Demos, Telos and the German Maastricht Decision'. *European Law Journal* 1: 219–258.

Weinkamm, Otto. 'Supplementary Report Drawn Up on Behalf of the Legal Committee on the Paramountcy of Community Law over the Law of the Member States, 18 October 1965'. European Parliament Working Documents 1965–66, 95: 1–2, 2.

Wessels, Wolfgang. 1980. *Der Europäische Rat: Stabilisierung statt Integration? Geschichte, Entwicklung und Zukunft der EG-Gipfelkonferenzen*. Bonn: Europa Union Verlag.

Wessels, Wolfgang. 2000. *Die Öffnung des Staates: Modelle und Wirklichkeit grenzüberschreitender Verwaltungspraxis, 1960–1995*. Opladen: Eske & Budrich.

Westlake, Martin. 1995. *The Council of the European Union*. London: Gale.

Wind, Marlene, and Jens Elo Rytter. 2011. 'In Need of Juristocracy? The Silence of Denmark in the Development of European Legal Norms'. *International Journal of Constitutional Law* 9 (2): 470–504.

Wind, Marlene, Dorte S. Martinsen, and Gabriel Pons Rotger. 2009. 'The Uneven Legal Push for Europe: Questioning Variation When National Courts Go to Europe'. *European Union Politics* 10 (1): 63–88.

Wind, Marlene. 2010. 'The Nordics, the EU and the Reluctance Towards Supranational Judicial Review'. *Journal of Common Market Studies* 48 (4): 1039–1063.

Wit, Joke de. 2012. *Artikel 94 Grondwet toegepast*. Den Haag: BJU.

Witschke, Tobias. 2009. *Gefahr für den Wettbewerb? Die Fusionskontrolle der Europäischen Gemeinschaft für Kohle und Stahl und die 'Rekonzentration' der Ruhrstahlindustrie, 1950–1963*. Berlin: De Gruyter.

Witte, Bruno De. 1998. 'Sovereignty and European Integration: The Weight of Legal Tradition'. In *The European Court and National Courts: Doctrine and Jurisprudence*, edited by Anne-Marie Slaughter, Alec Stone Sweet, and Joseph H. H. Weiler, 277–304. Oxford: Hart Publishing.

Witte, Bruno De. 2013. 'European Union Law: A Unified Academic Discipline?' In *Lawyering Europe: European Law as a Transnational Social Field*, edited by Bruno de Witte and Antoine Vauchez, 101–116. Oxford: Hart Publishing.

Index

Printed by Integrated Books International,
United States of America